The Royal Path of Life

Compliments of.

Y. E. Hinshaw

Rock Creek

Ohi

THE

ROYAL PATH

OF LIFE;

—OR—

AIMS AND AIDS TO SUCCESS AND HAPPINESS.

BY

T. L. HAINES, A. M.

AND

L. W. YAGGY, M. S.

Author of "Our Home Counselor."

REVISED EDITION.

A. P. T. ELDER & CO.

CHICAGO, ILL.

1882

PREFACE

THE subject-matter of this book, Success and Happiness, has been the consideration of every eminent pen, from the days of Solomon to the present. To say any thing strictly new would be impossible; nor would we presume that our knowledge and experience would be as valuable as the maxims of the wise and the sublime truths which have become a part of the standard literature. The best, therefore, that any one can expect to do is to recombine the experience of the past, and compile such thoughts and extracts as have chimed in with the testimony of earnest and aspiring minds, and offer them in a novel and fascinating form. In the words of the poet:

"We have gathered posies from other men's flowers,
Nothing but the thread that binds them is ours."

In life there is a Royal Path. Alas! that so many not being urged to seek life's prizes, fail to find them. It is hoped that this book shall be a counselor to those who have become indifferent to life's purposes; a comfort to those who have long traveled on this Royal Path; and if it shall serve to awaken the slumbering genius within the youth, stimulate and impel them to noble thoughts and actions, and lead them on to honor, success and happiness, the authors will consider themselves amply repaid for their labor.

" Life is before you ! from the fated road
    You cannot turn ; then take ye up the load,
    Not yours to tread or leave the unknown way,
    Ye must go o'er it, meet ye what ye may.
    Gird up your souls within you to the deed,
    Angels and fellow-spirits bid you speed ! "

—Butler.

Contents.

THE

Royal Path of Life.

Life.

WE point to two ways in life, and if the young man and maiden, whose feet are lingering in soft green meadows and flowery paths, will consider these two ways soberly and earnestly, before moving onward, and choose the one that truth and reason tell them leads to honor, success and happiness, they have wisely chosen the "Royal Path of Life." The other way is too well known to need description. It is a sad thing, after the lapse of twenty years, to find ourselves amid ruined hopes;—to sit down with folded hands and say, "Thus far life has been a failure"! Yet, to how many is this the wretched summing up at the end of a single score of years from the time that reason takes the helm! Alas! that so few who start wrong, ever succeed in finding the "Royal Path"; life proving, even to its last burdened years a millstone about the neck.

Dear reader, life is a "Royal Path," and to you it
shall be a millstone about your neck, or a diadem on
your brow.   Decide at once upon a noble purpose,
then take it up bravely, bear it off joyfully, lay it down
triumphantly.   Your greatest inheritance is a purpose
in pursuit of which you will find employment and happiness, for

> "The busy world shoves angrily aside
> The man who stands with arms akimbo set
> Until occasion tells him what to do;
> And he who waits to have his task marked out
> Shall die and leave his errand unfulfilled."

Life is not mean—it is grand.   If it is mean to any,
he makes it so.   God made it glorious.   Its channel
He paved with diamonds.   Its banks He fringed with
flowers.   He overarched it with stars.   Around it He
spread the glory of the physical universe—suns, moons,
worlds, constellations, systems—all that is magnificent
in motion, sublime in magnitude, and grand in order
and obedience.   God would not have attended life with
this broad march of grandeur, if it did not mean something.   He would not have descended to the blade
of grass, the dew-drop, and the dust-atom, if every
moment of life were not a letter to spell out some word
that should bear the burden of a thought.   How much
life means, words refuse to tell, because they can not.
The very doorway of life is hung around with flowery
emblems, to indicate that it is for some purpose.   The
mystery of our being, the necessity of action, the relation of cause to effect, the dependence of one thing
upon another, the mutual influence and affinity of all

things, assure us that life is for a purpose to which every outward thing doth point.

The trees with leaves "like a shield or like a sword" wage vigorous warfare with the elements. They bend under the wind, make music of it, then stand up again and grow more stalwartly straight up toward the heart of the heavens. A man is to learn of the oak, and cling to his plans as it to its leaves till pushed off by new ones; and be as tenacious of life, when lopt, send-ing up branches straight as the old trunk, and when cut off, sending up a brood of young oaks, crowning the stump with vigorous defenders. He that floats lazily down the stream, in pursuit of something borne along by the same current, will find himself indeed moved forward; but unless he lays his hand to the oar, and increases his speed by his own labor, must be always at the same distance from that which he is fol-lowing. In our voyage of life we must not *drift* but *steer*.

Every youth should form, at the outset of his career, the solemn purpose to make the most and the best of the powers which God has given him, and to turn to the best possible account every outward advantage within his reach. This purpose must carry with it the assent of the reason, the approval of the conscience, the sober judgment of the intellect. It should then embody within itself whatever is vehement in desire, inspiring in hope, thrilling in enthusiasm and intense in desperate resolve. Such a plan of life will save him from many a damaging contest with temptation. It will regulate his sports and recreations. It will go

with him by day to trample under foot the allurements
of pleasure.   It will hold his eyes waking as he toils
by the evening lamp.   It will watch over his slumbers
to jog him at the appointed hour, and summon him to
the cheerful duties of his chosen pursuit.   Those who
labor and study under the inspiration of such a purpose, will soon soar out of sight of those who barely
allow themselves to be carried along by the momentum of the machinery to which they are attached.

Many pass through life without even a consciousness of where they are, and what they are doing.
They gaze on whatever lies directly before them, "in
fond amusement lost."   Human life is a watchtower.
It is the clear purpose of God that every one—the
young especially—should take their stand on this
tower.   Look, listen, learn, wherever you go, wherever
you tarry.   Something is always transpiring to reward
your attention.   Let your eyes and ears be always
open, and you will often observe in the slightest inci-
dents, materials of advantage and means of personal
improvement.

In nothing is childhood more strongly distinguished
from manhood than in this, that the child has no purpose, no plan of life, no will by which his energies are
directed.   He lives, in a great measure, to enjoy the
passing scene, and to find his happiness in those agreeable consciousnesses which from hour to hour come to
him by chance.   If his life is governed by a plan, a
purpose, it is the purpose of another—not his own.
The man has his own purpose, his own plan, his own
life and aim.   The sorrowful experience of multitudes

in this respect is that they are never men, but children all their days. Think out your work, then work out your thought. No one can pursue a worthy object, with all the powers of his mind, and yet make his life a failure. A man may work in the dark, yet one day light shall arise upon his labor; and though he may never, with his own lips, declare the victory complete, some day others will behold in his life-work the traces of a great and thinking mind.

Take life like a man. Take it just as though it was — as it is — an earnest, vital, essential affair. Take it just as though you personally were born to the task of performing a merry part in it — as though the world had waited for your coming. Take it as though it was a grand opportunity to do and to achieve, to carry forward great and good schemes; to help and cheer a suffering, weary, it may be a heart-broken, brother. The fact is, life is undervalued by a great majority of mankind. It is not made half as much of as should be the case. Now and then a man stands aside from the crowd, labors earnestly, steadfastly, confidently, and straightway becomes famous for wisdom, intellect, skill, greatness of some sort. The world wonders, admires, idolizes; and yet it only illustrates what each may do if he takes hold of life with a purpose. One way is right to go; the hero sees it and moves on that aim and has the world under him for foot and support. His approbation is honor, his dissent infamy. Man was sent into the world to be a growing and exhaustless force. The world was spread out around him to be seized and conquered. Realms of infinite truth burst open above him, inviting him to tread those shining coasts along which Newton dropped his plummet and Herschel sailed,—a Columbus of the skies. Some, because they have once or twice met with rebuffs, sink in discouragement. Such should know, that our own errors may often teach us more than the grave precepts of others. We counsel the young man never to despair. If he can make nothing by any work that presents itself now, he can at least make himself; or what is equivalent, he can save himself from the sure death of a pusillanimous, halting, irresolute spirit. Never be cast down by misfortunes. If a spider break his web, over and over he will mend it again. And do not you fall behind the very insect on your walls. If the sun is going down look up to the stars; if earth is dark, keep your eye on heaven. With the presence and promise of God, we can bear up under any thing; and should press on, and never falter or fear.

It is my firm conviction that man has only himself to blame if his life appears to him at any time void of interest and of pleasure. Man may make life what he pleases and give it as much worth, both for himself and others, as he has energy for. Over his moral and intellectual being his sway is complete.

The first great mistake that men fall into is that they do not use integrity and truth and good sense in judging of what they are fit for. They take the things that they want and not the things that they deserve. They aspire after things that are pleasing to their ambition, and not after things to which they are adapted by their capacity. And when a man is

brought into as sphere of his ambition for which he
has not the requisite powers, and where he is goaded
on every side in the discharge of his duties, his temptation is at once to make up by fraud and appearance
that which he lacks in reality. Men are seen going
across-lots to fortune; and a poor business many of
them make of it. Oftentimes they lose their way;
and when they do not, they find so many hills and
valleys, so many swells and depressions, so many ris-
ings and fallings, so many ups and downs, that though
by an air-line the distance might be shorter, in reality
the distance is greater than by the lawful route; and
when they come back they are ragged and poor and
mean. There is a great deal of going across-lots to
make a beggar of a man's self in this world. Whereas,
the old-fashioned homely law that the man who was to
establish himself in life must take time to lay the foundations of reality, and gradually and steadily build
thereon, holds good yet. Though you slur it over,
and cover it up with fantasies, and find it almost impossible to believe it, it is so.

Rely not upon others; but let there be in your own
bosom a calm, deep, decided, and all-pervading principle. Look first, midst, and last to God, to aid you
in the great task before you; and then plant your foot
on the right. Let others live as they please,—tainted
by low tastes, debasing passions, a moral putrefaction.
Be you the salt of the earth; incorrupt in your deeds,
in your inmost thoughts and feelings. Nay more,
incorruptible, like virtue herself; your manners blame-
less; your views of duty, not narrow, false and destruc-

tive, but a savor of life to all around you. Let your speech be always with grace, seasoned with the salt of truth, honor, manliness and benevolence. Wait not for the lash of guilt to scourge you to the path of God and heaven. Be of the prudent who forsee the evil and hide themselves from it; and not of the simple, who pass on and are punished. Life, to youth, is a fairy tale just opened; to old age, a tale read through, ending in death. Be wise in time, that you may be happy in eternity.

Man and Woman.

MAN is bold—woman is beautiful. Man is courageous—woman is timid. Man labors in the field— woman at home. Man talks to persuade—woman to please. Man has a daring heart—woman a tender, loving one. Man has power—woman taste. Man has justice—woman mercy. Man has strength— woman love; while man combats with the enemy, struggles with the world, woman is waiting to prepare his repast and sweeten his existence. He has crosses, and the partner of his couch is there to soften them; his days may be sad and troubled, but in the chaste arms of his wife he finds comfort and repose. Without woman, man would be rude, gross, solitary. Woman spreads around him the flowers of existence, as the creepers of the forests, which decorate the trunks of sturdy oaks with their perfumed garlands. Finally, the

Christian pair live and die united; together they rear the fruits of their union; in the dust they lie side by side; and they are reunited beyond the limits of the tomb.

Man has his strength and the exercise of his power; he is busy, goes about, thinks, looks forward to the future, and finds consolation in it; but woman stays at home, remains face to face with her sorrow, from which nothing distracts her; she descends to the very depths of the abyss it has opened, measures it, and often fills it with her vows and tears. To feel, to love, to suffer, to devote herself, will always be the text of the life of woman. Man has a precise and distinct language, the words being luminous speech. Woman possesses a peculiarly musical and magical language, interspersing the words with song. Woman is affectionate and suffers; (she is constantly in need of something to lean upon, like the honeysuckle upon the tree or fence.) Man is attached to the fireside by his affection for woman, and the happiness it gives him to protect and support her. Superior and inferior to man, humiliated by the heavy hand of nature, but at the same time inspired by intuitions of a higher order than man can ever experience, she has fascinated him, innocently bewitched him forever. And man has remained enchanted by the spell. Women are generally better creatures than men. Perhaps they have, taken universally, weaker appetites and weaker intellects, but they have much stronger affections. A man with a bad heart has been sometimes saved by a strong head; but a corrupt woman is lost forever.

One has well said: "We will say nothing of the
manner in which that sex usually conduct an argument;
but the *intuitive judgments of women* are often more to
be relied upon than the conclusions which we reach by
an elaborate process of reasoning.   No man that has
an intelligent wife, or who is accustomed to the society
of educated women, will dispute this.   Times without
number, you must have known them decide questions
on the instant, and with unerring accuracy, which you
had been poring over for hours, perhaps with no other
result than to find yourself getting deeper and deeper
into the tangled maze of doubts and difficulties.   It
were hardly generous to allege that they achieve these
feats less by reasoning than by a sort of sagacity which
approximates to the sure instinct of the animal races;
and yet, there seems to be some ground for the remark
of a witty French writer, that, when a man has toiled
step by step up a flight of stairs, he will be sure to find
a woman at the top; but she will not be able to *tell
how she got there.*   How she got there, however, is of
little moment."

   It is peculiar with what a degree of tact woman will
determine whether a man is honest or not.   She cannot
give you the reason for such an opinion, only that she
does not like the looks of the man, and feels that he is
dishonest.   A servant comes for employment, she looks
him in the face and says he is dishonest.   He gives
good references, and you employ him; he robs you,—
you may be quite sure he will do that.   Years after,
another man comes; the same lady looks him in the
face, and says he, too, is not honest; she says so, again,

fresh from her mere insight; but you, also, say he is not honest. You say, I remember I had a servant with just the same look about him, three years ago, and he robbed me. This is one great distinction of the female intellect; it walks directly and unconsciously, by more delicate insight and a more refined and a more trusted intuition, to an end to which men's minds grope carefully and ploddingly along. Women have exercised a most beneficial influence in softening the hard and untruthful outline which knowledge is apt to assume in the hands of direct scientific observers and experimenters; they have prevented the casting aside of a mass of most valuable truth, which is too fine to be caught in the material sieve, and eludes the closest questioning of the microscope and the test-glass; which is allied with our passions, our feelings; and especially holds the fine boundary-line where mind and matter, sense and spirit, wave their floating and undistinguishable boundaries, and exercise their complex action and reaction.

When a woman is possessed of a high degree of tact, she sees, as by a kind of second sight, when any little emergency is likely to occur, or when, to use a more familiar expression, things do not seem to go right. She is thus aware of any sudden turn in conversation, and prepared for what it may lead to, but above all, she can penetrate into the state of mind of those she is placed in contact with, so as to detect the gathering gloom upon another's brow, before the mental storm shall have reached any formidable height; to know when the tone of voice has altered; when any unwelcome thought shall have presented itself, and when the

pulse of feeling is beating higher or lower in consequence of some apparently trifling circumstance. In
such and innumerable other instances of much the
same character, woman, with her tact, will notice
clearly the fluctuations which constantly change the
feeling of social life, and she can change the current
of feeling suddenly and in such a way that no one
detects her; thus, by the power which her nature
gives her, she saves society the pain and annoyance
which arise very frequently from trifles, or the mis-
management of some one possessing less tact and
social adaptation.

Man is the creature of interest and ambition. His
nature leads him forth into the struggle and bustle of
the world. Love is but the embellishment of his early
life, or a song piped in the intervals of the acts. He
seeks for fame, for fortune, for space in the world's
thought, and dominion over his fellow-men. But a
woman's whole life is the history of the affections. The
heart is her world; it is there her ambition strives for
empire; it is there her avarice seeks for hidden treasures. She sends forth her sympathies on adventure;
she embarks her whole soul in the traffic of affection;
and if shipwrecked, her case is hopeless, for it is the
bankruptcy of the heart.

To a man, the disappointment of love may occasion
some bitter pangs; it wounds some feelings of tenderness; it blasts some prospects of felicity; but he
is an active being; he may dissipate his thoughts in
the whirl of varied occupation, or may plunge into
the tide of pleasure; or, if the scene of disappoint-

ment be too full of painful associations, he can shift his abode at will, and taking, as it were, the wings of the morning, can "fly to the uttermost parts of the earth, and be at rest."

We find man the cap-stone of the climax of paradoxes; a complex budget of contradictions; a heterogeneous compound of good and evil; the noblest work of God, bespattered by Lucifer; an immortal being, cleaving to things not eternal; a rational being, violating reason; an animal with discretion, glutting, instead of prudently feeding appetite; an original, harmonious compact, violating order and reveling in confusion. Man is immortal without realizing it; rational, but often deaf to reason; a combination of noble powers, waging civil war, robbing, instead of aiding each other; yet, like the Siamese twins, compelled to remain in the same apartment.

The following shows the love, tenderness, and fortitude of woman. The letter, which was bedimmed with tears, was written before the husband was aware that death was fixing its grasp upon the lovely companion, and laid in a book which he was wont to peruse:

"When this shall reach your eyes, dear G——, some day when you are turning over the relics of the past, I shall have passed away forever, and the cold white stone will be keeping its lonely watch over lips you have so often pressed, and the sod will be growing green that shall hide forever from your sight the dust of one who has so often nestled close to your warm heart. For many long and sleepless nights, when all my thoughts were at rest, I have wrestled with the consciousness of approaching death, until at last it has forced itself on my mind. Although to you and to others it might now seem but the nervous imagination of a girl, yet, dear G——, it is so! Many weary hours have I passed in the endeavor to reconcile myself to leaving you, whom I love so well, and this bright world of sunshine and beauty; and hard indeed is it to struggle on silently and alone, with the sure conviction that I am about to leave forever and go down alone into the dark valley. 'But I know in whom I have trusted,' and leaning upon His arm, 'I fear no evil.' Don't blame me for keeping even all this from you. How could I subject you, of all others, to such a sorrow as I feel at parting, when time will soon make it apparent to you? I could have wished to live, if only to be at your side when your time shall come, and pillowing your head upon my breast, wipe the death damps from your brow, and commend your departing spirit to its Maker's presence, embalmed in woman's holiest prayer. But it is not to be so; and I submit. Yours is the privilege of watching, through long and dreary nights, for the spirit's final flight, and of transferring my sinking head from your breast to my Savior's bosom! And you shall share my last thought, the last faint pressure of my hand, and the last feeble kiss shall be yours; and even when flesh and heart shall have failed me, my eye shall rest on yours until glazed by death; and our spirits shall hold one fast communion, until gently fading from my view, the last of earth, you shall mingle with the first bright glimpses of the unfading glories of that better world, where partings are unknown. Well do I know the spot, dear G——, where you will lay me; often have we stood by the place, as we watched the mellow sunset, as it glanced its quivering flashes through the leaves, and burnished the grassy mounds around us with stripes of gold. Each perhaps has thought that one of us would come alone; and whichever it might be, your name would be on the stone. We loved the spot, and I know you'll love it none the less when you see the same quiet sunlight and gentle breezes play among the grass that grows over your Mary's grave. I know you'll go often alone there, when I am laid there, and my spirit shall be with you then, and whisper among the waving branches, 'I am not lost, but gone before.'"

A woman has no natural gift more bewitching than a sweet laugh. It is like the sound of flutes upon the water. It leads from her in a clear sparkling rill; and the heart that hears it feels as if bathed in the cool, exhilarating spring. Have you ever pursued an unseen figure through the trees, led on by a fairy laugh, now here, now there, now lost, now found? We have. And we are pursuing that wandering voice to this day. Sometimes it comes to us in the midst of care and sorrow, or irksome business, and then we turn away and listen, and hear it ringing throughout the room like a silver bell, with power to scare away the evil spirits of the mind. How much we owe to that sweet laugh! It turns prose to poetry; it flings showers of sunshine over the darkness of the wood in which we are traveling.

Quincy being asked why there were more women

than men, replied, "It is in conformity with the arrangements of nature. We always see more of heaven than of earth." He cannot be an unhappy man who has the love and smile of woman to accompany him in every department of life. The world may look dark and cheerless without—enemies may gather in his path—but when he returns to his fireside, and feels the tender love of woman, he forgets his cares and troubles, and is comparatively a happy man. He is but half prepared for the journey of life, who takes not with him that friend who will forsake him in no emergency—who will' divide his sorrows—increase his joys—lift the veil from his heart—and throw sunshine amid the darkest scenes. No, that man cannot be miserable who has such a companion, be he ever so poor, despised, and trodden upon by the world.

No trait of character is more valuable in a female than the possession of a sweet temper. Home can never be made happy without it. It is like the flowers that spring up in our pathway, reviving and cheering us. Let a man go home at night, wearied and worn by the toils of the day, and how soothing is a word by a good disposition! It is sunshine falling on his heart. He is happy, and the cares of life are forgotten. Nothing can be more touching than to behold a woman who had been all tenderness and dependence, and alive to every trivial roughness while treading the prosperous path of life, suddenly rising in mental force to be the comforter and supporter of her husband under misfortune, and abiding with unshrinking firmness the bitterest winds of adversity. As the vine which has long twined its graceful foliage about the oak, and been lifted by it in sunshine, will, when the hardy tree is riven by the thunderbolt cling round it with its caressing tendrils and bind up its shattered boughs, so it is beautifully ordained that woman, who is the mere dependent and ornament of man in happiest hours, should be his stay and solace when smitten by sudden calamity.

A woman of true intelligence is a blessing at home, in her circle of friends, and in society. Wherever she goes, she carries with her a healthgiving influence. There is a beautiful harmony about her character that at once inspires a respect which soon warms into love. The influence of such a woman upon society is of the most salutary kind. She strengthens right principles in the virtuous, incites the selfish and indifferent to good actions, and gives to even the light and frivolous a taste for food more substantial than the frothy gossip with which they seek to recreate their minds.

Thackeray says: "It is better for you to pass an evening once or twice a week in a lady's drawing-room, even though the conversation is slow, and you know the girl's song by heart, than in a club, a tavern, or pit of a theatre. All amusements of youth to which virtuous women are not admitted, rely on it, are deleterious in their nature. All men who avoid female society have dull perceptions, and are stupid, or have gross tastes, and revolt against what is pure. Your club swaggerers, who are sucking the butts of billiard-cues all night, call female society insipid. Poetry is uninspiring to a jockey; beauty has no charms for a blind man; music does not please a poor beast who does not know one tune from another; but as a pure epicure is hardly tired of water, sauces, and brown bread and butter, I protest I can sit for a whole evening talking with a well regulated, kindly woman about her girl Fanny, or her boy Frank, and like the evening's entertainment. One of the great benefits a man may derive from a woman's society is that he is bound to be respectful to her. The habit is of great good to your moral men, depend upon it. Our education makes us the most eminently selfish men in the world."

Tom Hood, in writing to his wife, says: "I never was anything till I knew you; and I have been better, happier and a more prosperous man ever since. Lay that truth by in lavender, and remind me of it when I fail. I am writing fondly and warmly; but not without good cause. First, your own affectionate letter, lately received; next, the remembrance of our dear children, pledges of our old familiar love; then a delicious impulse to pour out the overflowings of my heart into yours; and last, not least, the knowledge that your dear eyes will read what my hands are now writing. Perhaps there is an after-thought that, whatever may befall me, the wife of my bosom will have this acknowledgment of her tenderness, worth and excellence, of all that is wifely or womanly, from my pen."

Among all nations the women ornament themselves more than the men; wherever found, they are the same kind, obliging, humane, tender beings; they are ever inclined to be gay and cheerful, timorous and modest. They do not hesitate like a man, to perform any hospitable or generous action; not haughty or arrogant, or supercilious, but full of courtesy, and fond of society, industrious, economical, ingenious, more liable, in general, to err than man, but, in general, also, more virtuous, and performing more good actions than he.

The gentle tendrils of woman's heart sometimes twine around a proud and sinful spirit, like roses and jessamines around a lightning-rod, clinging for support to what brings down upon them the blasting thunderbolt.

These are the national traits of woman's character: The English woman is respectful and proud; the French is gay and agreeable; the Italian is ardent and passionate; the American is sincere and affectionate. With an English woman love is a principle; with a French it is a caprice; with an Italian it is a passion; with an American it is a sentiment. A man is married to an English lady; united to a French; cohabits with an Italian; and is wedded to an American. An English woman is anxious to secure a lord; a French, a companion; an Italian, a lover; an American, a husband. The Englishman respects his lady; the Frenchman esteems his companion; the Italian adores his mistress; the American loves his wife. At night the Englishman returns to his house; the Frenchman to his establishment; the Italian to his retreat; the American to his home. When an Englishman is sick his lady visits him; when a Frenchman is sick, his companion pities him; when an Italian is sick, his

mistress sighs over him; when an American is sick,
his wife nurses him. When an Englishman dies, his
lady is bereaved; when a Frenchman dies, his companion grieves; when an Italian dies, his mistress
laments; when an American dies, his wife mourns.
An English woman instructs her offspring; a French
woman teaches her progeny; an Italian rears her
young; an American educates her child.

The true lady is known wherever you meet her.
Ten women shall get into the street car or omnibus,
and, though we never saw them, we shall point out
the true lady. She does not giggle constantly at
every little thing that transpires, or does some one
appear with a peculiar dress, it does not throw her
into confusion. She wears no flowered brocade to
be trodden under foot, nor ball-room jewelry, nor
rose-tinted gloves; but the lace frill round her face is
scrupulously fresh, and the strings under her chin
have evidently been handled only by dainty fingers.
She makes no parade of a watch, if she wears one;
nor does she draw off her dark, neatly-fitting glove
to display ostentatious rings. Still we notice, nestling in the straw beneath us, a trim little boot, not
paper soled, but of an anti-consumption thickness.
The bonnet upon her head is of plain straw, simply
trimmed, for your true lady never wears a "dress
hat" in an omnibus. She is quite as civil to the
poorest as to the *richest* person who sits beside her,
and equally regardful of their rights. If she attracts
attention, it is by the unconscious grace of her person and manner, not by the ostentation of her dress.

We are quite sorry when she pulls the strap and disappears; if we were a bachelor we should go home to our solitary den with a resolution to become a better and a—married man.

The strongest man feels the influence of woman's gentlest thoughts, as the mightiest oak quivers in the softest breeze. We confess to a great distrust of that man who persistently underrates woman. Never did language better apply to an adjective than when it called the wife the "better half." We admire the ladies because of their beauty, respect them because of their virtues, adore them because of their intelligence, and love them because *we can't help it.*

Man was made to protect, love and cherish, not to undervalue, neglect or abuse women. Treated, educated and esteemed, as she merits, she rises in dignity, becomes the refiner, and imparts a milder, softer tone to man. No community has ever exhibited the refinements of civilization and social order where women were held in contempt and their rights not properly respected and preserved. Degrade woman and you degrade man more. She is the fluid of the thermometer of society, placed there by the hand of the great Creator. Man may injure the instrument, but can neither destroy or provide a substitute for the mercury. Her rights are as sacred as those of the male sex. Her mental powers are underrated by those only who have either not seen, or were so blinded by prejudice, that they would not see their development. Educate girls as boys, put women in the business arena designed for men, and they will

acquit themselves far better than boys and men would
if they were placed in the departments designed for
females.

The perception of woman, especially in cases of
emergency, is more acute than that of man; unquestionably so designed by an all-wise Creator for the
preservation and perpetuity of our race. Her patience and fortitude, her integrity and constancy, her
piety and devotion, are naturally stronger than in the
other sex. If she was first in transgression, she was
first in prayer. Her seed has bruised the serpent's
head. She stood by the expiring Jesus, when boast-
ing Peter and the other disciples had forsaken their
Lord. She was the last at his tomb, embalmed his
sacred body, and the first to discover that he had
burst the bars of death, risen from the cleft rock, and
triumphed over death and the grave.

Under affliction, especially physical, the fortitude
of woman is proverbial. As a nurse, one female will
endure more than five men. That she is more honest
than man, our penitentiaries fully demonstrate. That
she is more religiously inclined, the records of our
churches will show. That she is more devotional,
our prayer meetings will prove.

Women have exercised a most remarkable judgment
in regard to great issues. They have prevented the
casting aside of plans which led to very remarkable
discoveries and inventions. When Columbus laid a
plan to discover the new world, he could not get a
hearing till he applied to a woman for help. Woman
equips man for the voyage of life. She is seldom a

leader in any project, but finds her peculiar and best attitude as helper. Though man executes a project, she fits him for it, beginning in his childhood. So everywhere; man performs, but woman trains the man. Every effectual person, leaving his mark on the world, is but another Columbus, for whose furnishing some Isabella, in the form of his mother, lays down her jewelry, her vanities, her comforts.

Mother.

IT is true to nature, although it be expressed in a figurative form, that a mother is both the morning and the evening star of life. The light of her eye is always the first to rise, and often the last to set upon man's day of trial. She wields a power more decisive far than syllogisms in arguments, or courts of last appeal in authority. Nay, in cases not a few, where there has been no fear of God before the eyes of the young—where His love has been unfelt and His law outraged, a mother's affection or her tremulous tenderness has held transgressors by the heart-strings, and been the means of leading them back to virtue and to God.

Woman's charms are certainly many and powerful. The expanding rose, just bursting into beauty, has an irresistible bewitchingness;—the blooming bride, led triumphantly to the hymeneal altar, awakens admiration and interest, and the blush of her cheek fills with delight;—but the charm of maternity is more sublime than all these.

Heaven has imprinted in the mother's face something beyond this world, something which claims kindred with the skies—the angelic smile, the tender look, the waking, watchful eye, which keeps its fond vigil over her slumbering babe.

Mother! ecstatic sound so twined round our hearts that they must cease to throb ere we forget it! 'tis our first love; 'tis part of religion. Nature has set the mother upon such a pinnacle that our infant eyes and arms are first uplifted to it; we cling to it in manhood; we almost worship it in old age. He who can enter an apartment and behold the tender babe feeding on its mother's beauty—nourished by the tide of life which flows through her generous veins, without a panting bosom and a grateful eye, is no man, but a monster.

"Can a mother's love be supplied? No! a thousand times no! By the deep, earnest yearning of our spirits for a mother's love; by the weary, aching void in our hearts; by the restless, unsatisfied wanderings of our affections, ever seeking an object on which to rest; by our instinctive discernment of the *true* maternal love from the *false*—as we would discern between a lifeless statue and a breathing man; by the hallowed emotions with which we cherish in the depths of our hearts the vision of a grass-grown mound in a quiet graveyard among the mountains; by the reverence, the holy love, the feeling akin to idolatry with which our thoughts hover about an angel form among the seraphs of Heaven—by all these, we answer, no!"

"Often do I sigh in my struggles with the hard, uncaring world, for the sweet, deep security I felt when, of an evening, nestling in her bosom, I listened to some quiet tale, suitable to my age, read in her tender and untiring voice. Never can I forget her sweet glance cast upon me when I appeared asleep; never her kiss of peace at night. Years have passed away since we laid her beside my father in the old church-yard; yet, still her voice whispers from the grave, and her eye watches over me, as I visit spots long since hallowed to the memory of my mother."

Oh! there is an enduring tenderness in the love of a mother to her son that transcends all other affections of the heart. It is neither to be chilled by selfishness, nor daunted by danger, nor weakened by worthlessness, nor stifled by ingratitude. She will sacrifice every comfort to his convenience; she will surrender every pleasure to his enjoyment; she will glory in his fame and exult in his prosperity; and if misfortune overtake him, he will be the dearer to her from misfortune; and if disgrace settle upon his name, she will still love and cherish him in spite of his disgrace; and if all the world beside cast him off, she will be all the world to him.

Alas! how little do we appreciate a mother's tenderness while living. How heedless are we in youth of all her anxieties and kindness? But when she is dead and gone, when the cares and coldness of the world come withering to our hearts, when we experi-

ence how hard it is to find true sympathy, how few to
love us for ourselves, how few will befriend us in misfortune, then it is that we think of the mother we have
lost.

Over the grave of a friend, of a brother, or a sister,
we would plant the primrose, emblematical of youth;
but over that of a mother, we would let the green
grass shoot up unmolested, for there is something in
the simple covering which nature spreads upon the
grave, that well becomes the abiding place of decaying age. O, a mother's grave! Earth has some
sacred spots where we feel like loosing shoes from
our feet, and treading with reverence; where common
words of social converse seem rude, and friendship's
hands have lingered in each other; where vows have
been plighted, prayers offered, and tears of parting
shed. Oh! how thoughts hover around such places,
and travel back through unmeasured space to visit
them! But of all spots on this green earth none is so
sacred as that where rests, waiting the resurrection,
those we have once loved and cherished—our brothers, or our children. Hence, in all ages, the better
part of mankind have chosen spots for the dead, and
on these spots they have loved to wander at eventide.
But of all places, even among the charnel-houses of
the dead, none is so sacred as a mother's grave.
There sleeps the nurse of infancy, the guide of our
youth, the counselor of our riper years—our friend
when others deserted us; she whose heart was a
stranger to every other feeling but love—there she
sleeps, and we love the very earth for her sake.

Engraved & Printed by Sinclair Brothers

In what Christian country can we deny the influence which a mother exerts over the whole life of her children. The roughest and hardest wanderer, while he is tossed on the ocean, or while he scorches his feet on the desert sands, recurs in his loneliness and suffering to the smiles which maternal affection shed over his infancy; the reckless sinner, even in his hardened career, occasionally hears the whisperings of those holy precepts instilled by a virtuous mother, and, although they may, in the fullness of guilt, be neglected, there are many instances of their having so stung the conscience that they have led to a deep and lasting repentence; the erring child of either sex will then, if a mother yet exists, turn to her for that consolation which the laws of society deny, and in the lasting purity of a mother's love will find the way to heaven. How cheerfully does a virtuous son labor for a poverty-stricken mother! How alive is he to her honor and high standing in the world! And should that mother be deserted—be left in "worse than widowhood," how proudly he stands forth her comforter and protector! Indeed, the more we reflect upon the subject, the more entirely are we convinced, that no influence is so lasting, or of such wide extent, and the more extensively we do feel the necessity of guiding this sacred affection, and perfecting that being from whom it emanates.

Science has sometimes tried to teach us that if a pebble be cast into the sea on any shore, the effects are felt though not perceived by man, over the whole area of the ocean. Or, more wonderful still, science

3

has tried to show that the effects of all the sounds ever uttered by man or beast, or caused by inanimate things, are still floating in the air: its present state is just the aggregate result of all these sounds; and if these things, be true, they furnish an emblem of the effects produced by a mother's power—effects which stretch into eternity, and operate there forever, in sorrow or in joy.

The mother can take man's whole nature under her control. She becomes what she has been called, "The divinity of infancy." Her smile is its sunshine, her word its mildest law, until sin and the world have steeled the heart. She can shower around her the most genial of all influences, and from the time when she first laps her little one in Elysium by clasping him to her bosom—"its first paradise"— to the moment when that child is independent of her aid, or perhaps, like Washington, directs the destinies of millions, her smile, her word, her wish, is an inspiring force. A sentence of encouragement or praise is a joy for a day. It spreads light upon all faces, and renders a mother's power more and more charm-like, as surely as ceaseless accusing, rebuking, and correcting, chafes, sours and disgusts. So intense is her power that the mere remembrance of a praying mother's hand, laid on the head in infancy, has held back a son from guilt when passion had waxed strong.

The mother is the angel-spirit of home. Her tender yearnings over the cradle of her infant babe, her guardian care of the child and youth, and her bosom companionship with the man of her love and choice, make her the personal centre of the interests, the hopes and the happiness of the family. Her love glows in her sympathies and reigns in all her thoughts and deeds. It never cools, it never tires, never dreads, never sleeps, but ever glows and burns with increasing ardor, and with sweet and holy incense upon the altar of home devotion. And even when she is gone to her last rest, the sainted mother in heaven sways a mightier influence over her wayward husband or child, than when she was present. Her departed spirit still hovers over his affections, over-shadows his path, and draws him by unseen cords to herself in heaven.

But in glancing at a mother's position in our homes, we should not overlook the sorrows to which she is often exposed. A mother mourning by the grave of her first-born is a spectacle of woe. A mother watching the palpitating frame of her child, as life ebbs slowly away, must evoke the sympathy of the sternest. A mother closing the dying eye of child after child, till it seems as if she were to be left alone in the world again, is one of the saddest sights of earth. When the cradle-song passes into a dirge, the heart is laden indeed.

Not long ago two friends were sitting together en-gaged in letter writing. One was a young man from India, the other a female friend, part of whose family resided in that far-off land. The former was writing to his mother in India. When the letter was finished his friend offered to enclose it in hers, to save postage. This he politely declined, saying: If it be sent sepa-

rately, it will reach her sooner than if sent through a
friend; and, perhaps, it may save her a tear." His
friend was touched at his tender regard for his mother's feelings, and felt with him, that it was worth paying the postage to save his mother a tear. Would
that every boy and girl, every young man and every
young woman were equally saving of a mother's tears.

The Christian mother especially can deeply plant
and genially cherish the seeds of truth. Is her child
sick? that is a text from which to speak of the Great
Physician. Is it the sober calm of evening, when
even children grow sedate? She can tell of the
Home where there is no night. Is it morning, when
all are buoyantly happy? The eternal day is sug-
gested, and its glories may be told. That is the wisdom which wins souls even more than the formal
lesson, the lecture, or the task.

There is one suggestion more. Perhaps the saddest
sentence that can fall upon the ear regarding any
child is—"He has no mother; she is dead!" It
comes like a voice from the sepulchre, and involves
the consummation of all the sorrows that can befall
the young. In that condition they are deprived of
their most tender comforter, and their wisest counselor. They are left a prey to a thousand temptations or a thousand ills, and freed from the restraint
of one who could curb without irritating, or guide
without affecting superiority. Now will mothers live
with their children as if they were thus to leave them
in a cold and inhospitable world? Will they guide
their little ones to Him who is pre-eminently the

God of the orphan, and who inspired his servant to
say—"Though father and mother forsake me, the
Lord will take me up."

Children.

WOE to him who smiles not over a cradle, and
weeps not over a tomb.   He who has never tried the
companionship of a little child, has carelessly passed
by one of the greatest pleasures of life, as one passes
a rare flower without plucking it or knowing its value.
The gleeful laugh of happy children is the best home
music, and the graceful figures of childhood are the
best statuary.   We are all kings and queens in the
cradle, and each babe is a new marvel, a new miracle.
The perfection of the providence for childhood is
willingly acknowledged.   The care which covers the
seed of the tree under tough husks, and stony cases
provides for the human plant, the mother's breast and
the father's house.   The size of the nestler is comic,
and its tiny, beseeching weakness is compensated
perfectly by the one happy, patronizing look of the
mother, who is a sort of high-reposing Providence
to it.   Welcome to the parents the puny struggler,
strong in his weakness, his little arms more irresistible than the soldier's, his lips touched with persuasion
which Chatham and Pericles in manhood had not.
His unaffected lamentations when he lifts up his voice
on high; the face all liquid grief, as he tries to swal-

low his vexation — soften all hearts to pity and to mirthful and clamorous compassion. The small despot asks so little that all reason and all nature are on his side. His ignorance is more charming than all knowledge, and his little sins more bewitching than any virtue. His flesh is angel's flesh, all alive. "Infancy," said Coleridge, "presents body and spirit in unity; the body is all animated." All day, between his three or four sleeps, he coos like a pigeon-house, sputters and purs, and puts on his faces of importance, and when he fasts, the little Pharisee fails not to sound his trumpet before him. By lamplight, he delights in shadows on the wall; by daylight, in yellow and scarlet. Carry him out of doors — he is overpowered by the light and by the extent of natural objects, and is silent. Then presently begins his use of his fingers, and he studies power — the lesson of his race.

Not without design has God implanted in the maternal breast that strong love of their children which is felt everywhere. This lays deep and broad the foundation for the child's future education from parental hands. Nor without designs has Christ commanded, "Feed my lambs,"—meaning to inculcate upon his church the duty of caring for the children of the church and the world at the earliest possible period. Nor can parents and all well-wishers to humanity be too earnest and careful to fulfill the promptings of their very nature and the command of Christ in this matter. Influence is as quiet and imperceptible on the child's mind as the falling of snowflakes on the meadow. One cannot tell the hour when the human mind is not in the condition of receiving impressions from exterior moral forces. In innumerable instances, the most secret and unnoticed influences have been in operation for months and even years to break down the strongest barriers of the human heart, and work out its moral ruin, while yet the fondest parents and and friends have been unaware of the working of such unseen agents of evil. Not all at once does any heart become utterly bad. The error is in this; that parents are not conscious how early the seeds of vice are sown and take root. It is as the Gospel declares, "While men slept, the enemy came and sowed tares, and went his way." If this then is the error, how shall it be corrected, and what is the antidote to be applied?

Never scold children, but soberly and quietly reprove. Do not employ shame, except in extreme cases. The suffering is acute; it hurts self-respect in the child to reprove a child before the family; to ridicule it, to tread down its feelings ruthlessly, is to wake in its bosom malignant feelings. A child is defenceless; he is not allowed to argue. He is often tried, condemned and executed in a second. He finds himself of little use. He is put at things he don't care for, and withheld from things which he does like. He is made the convenience of grown-up people; is hardly supposed to have any rights, except in a corner, as it were; is sent hither and thither; made to get up or sit down for everybody's convenience but his own; is snubbed and catechised until he learns to dodge government and elude authority, and then be whipped for being "such a liar that no one can believe him."

Children will not trouble you long. They grow up—nothing on earth grows so fast as children. It was but yesterday, and that lad was playing with tops, a buoyant boy. He is a man, and gone now! There is no more childhood for him or for us. Life has claimed him. When a beginning is made, it is like a raveling stocking; stitch by stitch gives way till all are gone. The house has not a child in it—there is no more noise in the hall—boys rush in pell-mell; it is very orderly now. There are no more skates or sleds, bats, balls or strings left scattered about. Things are neat enough now. There is no delay for sleepy folks; there is no longer any task, before you lie down, of looking after anybody, and tucking up the bedclothes. There are no disputes to settle, nobody to get off to school, no complaint, no opportunities for impossible things, no rips to mend, no fingers to tie up, no faces to be washed, or collars to be arranged. There never was such peace in the house! It would sound like music to have some feet to clatter down the front stairs! Oh for some children's noise! What used to ail us, that we were hushing their loud laugh, checking their noisy frolic, and reproving their slamming and banging the doors? We wish our neighbors would only lend us an urchin or two to make a little noise in these premises. A home without children. It is like a lantern and no candle; a garden and no flowers; a vine and no grapes; a brook and no water gurgling and gushing in its channel. We want to be tired, to be vexed, to be run over, to hear children at work with all its varieties

Bishop Earle says: "A child is man in a small letter, yet the best copy of Adam, before he tasted of Eve or the apple; and he is happy whose small practice in the world can only write his character. His soul is yet a white paper unscribbled with observations of the world, wherewith, at length, it becomes a blurred note-book. He is purely happy, because he knows no evil, nor hath made means by sin to be acquainted with misery. He arrives not at the mischief of being wise, nor endures evils to come, by forseeing them. He kisses and loves all, and when the smart of the rod is past, smiles on his beater. The older he grows, he is a stair lower from God. He is the Christian example, and the old man's relapse; the one imitates his pureness, and the other falls into his simplicity. Could he put off his body with his little coat, he had got eternity without a burden, and exchanged but one heaven for another."

Children are more easily led to be good by examples of loving kindness, and tales of well-doing in others, than threatened into obedience by records of sin, crime and punishment. Then, on the infant mind impress sincerity, truth, honesty, benevolence and their kindred virtues, and the welfare of your child will be insured not only during this life, but the life to come. Oh, what a responsibility, to form a creature, the frailest and feeblest that heaven has made,

into the intelligent and fearless sovereign of the whole
animated creation, the interpreter and adorer and
almost the representative of Divinity!

------◦◦◦------

Youth.

MEN glory in raising great and magnificent struc-
tures, and find a secret pleasure in seeing sets of their
own planting grow up and flourish; but it is a greater
and more glorious work to build up a man; to see a
youth of our own planting, from the small beginnings
and advantages we have given him, grow up into a
considerable fortune, to take root in the world, and to
shoot up to such a height, and spread his branches so
wide, that we who first planted him may ourselves
find comfort and shelter under his shadow.

Much of our early gladness vanishes utterly from
our memory; we can never recall the joy with which
we laid our heads on our mother's bosom, or rode
our father's back in childhood; doubtless that joy is
wrought up into our nature as the sunlight of long past
mornings is wrought up in the soft mellowness of the
apricot.

The time will soon come—if it has not already—
when you must part from those who have surrounded
the same paternal board, who mingled with you in
the gay-hearted joys of childhood, and the opening
promise of youth. New cares will attend you in new
situations; and the relations you form, or the busi-

ness you pursue, may call you far from the "play-place" of your "early days." In the unseen future, your brothers and sisters may be sundered from you; your lives may be spent apart; and in death you may be divided; and of you it may be said —

> "They grew in beauty, side by side,
> They filled one home with glee;
> Their graves are severed far and wide,
> By mount, and stream, and sea."

Let your own home be the cynosure of your affections, the spot where your highest desires are concentrated. Do this, and you will prove, not only the hope, but the stay of your kindred and home. Your personal character will elevate the whole family. Others may become degenerate sons, and bring the gray hairs of their parents with sorrow to the grave. But you will be the pride and staff of a mother, and an honor to your sire. You will establish their house, give peace to their pillow, and be a memorial to their praise.

Spend your evening hours, boys, at home. You may make them among the most agreeable and profitable of your lives, and when vicious companions would tempt you away, remember that God has said, "Cast not in thy lot with them; walk thou not in their way; refrain thy foot from their path. They lay in wait for their own blood; they lurk privily for their own lives. But walk thou in the way of good men, and keep the paths of the righteous."

Keep good company or none. Never be idle. If your hands cannot be usefully employed, attend to the cultivation of your mind. Always speak the truth.

Make few promises. Live up to your engagements. Keep your own secrets, if you have any. When you speak to a person, look him in the face. Good company and good conversation are the very sinews of virtue. Good character is above all things else. Your character cannot be essentially injured except by your own acts. If one speak evil of you, let life be such that none will believe him. Drink no kind of intoxicating liquors. Always live, misfortune excepted, within your income. When you retire to bed, think over what you have been doing during the day. Make no haste to be rich if you would prosper. Small and steady gains give competency with tranquillity of mind. Never play at any kind of game of chance. Avoid temptation through fear that you may not be able to withstand it. Never run into debt, unless you see a way to get out again. Never borrow if you can possibly avoid it. Never speak evil of any one. Be just before you are generous. Keep yourself innocent if you would be happy, Save when you are young to spend when you are old. Never think that which you do for religion is time or money misspent. Always go to meeting when you can. Read some portion of the Bible every day. Often think of death, and your accountability to God.

An honest, industrious boy is always *wanted*. He will be sought for; his services will be in demand; he will be respected and loved; he will be spoken of in words of high commendation; he will always have a home; he will grow up to be a man of known worth and established character.

He will be *wanted*. The merchant will want him for a salesman or a clerk; the master mechanic will want him for an apprentice or a journeyman; those with a job to let will want him for a contractor; clients will want him for a lawyer; patients for a physician; religious congregations for a pastor; parents for a teacher of their children; and the people for an an officer.

He will be *wanted*. Townsmen will want him as a citizen; acquaintances as a neighbor; neighbors as a friend; families as a visitor; the world as an acquaintance; nay, girls will want him for a beau and finally for a husband.

To both parents, when faithful, a child is indebted beyond estimation. If one begins to enumerate their claims, to set in order their labors, and recount their sacrifices and privations, he is soon compelled to desist from his task. He is constrained to acknowledge that their love for him is surpassed only by that of the great Spring of all good, whom—to represent in the strongest language our measureless indebtedness to Him—we call "Our Father in Heaven."

Parents do wrong in keeping their children hanging around home, sheltered and enervated by parental indulgence. The eagle does better. It stirs up its nest when the young eagles are able to fly. They are compelled to shift for themselves, for the old eagle literally turns them out, and at the same time tears all the down and feathers from the nest. 'Tis this rude and rough experience that makes the king of birds so fearless in his flight and so expert in the pursuit of prey. It is a misfortune to be born with a silver spoon in your mouth, for you have it to carry and plague you all your days. Riches often hang like a dead weight, yea like a millstone about the necks of ambitious young men. Had Benjamin Franklin or George Law been brought up in the lap of affluence and ease, they would probably never have been heard of by the world at large. It was the making of the one that he ran away, and of the other that he was turned out of doors. Early thrown upon their own resources, they acquired the energy and skill to overcome resistance, and to grapple with the difficulties that beset their pathway. And here I think they learned the most important lesson of their lives—a lesson that developed their manhood—forcing upon them Necessity, the most useful and inexorable of masters. There is nothing like being bound out, turned out, or even kicked out, to compel a man to do for himself. Rough handling of the last sort has often made drunken men sober. Poor boys, though at the foot of the hill, should remember that every step they take toward the goal of wealth and honor gives them increased energy and power. They have a *purchase* and, obtain a *momentum*, the rich man's son never knows. The poor man's son has *the heaviest weight to lift*, but without knowing it he is turning the *longest lever*, and that with the utmost *vim* and *vigor*. Boys, do not sigh for the capital or indulgence of the rich, but *use* the *capital* you have— I mean those God-given powers which every healthy youth of good habits has in and of himself. All a man wants in this life is a skillful hand, a well informed mind, and a good heart. In our happy land, and in these favored times of libraries, lyceums, liberty, religion and education, the humblest and poorest can aim at the greatest usefulness, and the highest excellence, with a prospect of success that calls forth all the endurance, perseverance and industry that is in man.

We live in an age marked by its lack of veneration. Old institutions, however sacred, are now fearlessly, and often wantonly, assailed; the aged are not treated with deference; and fathers and mothers are addressed with rudeness. The command now runs, one would think, not in the good old tenor of the Bible, "Children obey your parents in the Lord, for this is right," but thus: Parents obey your children. Some may go so far as to say this is right. "Why should I, who am so much superior to my father and my mother, bow down before them? Were they equal to me; did they appear so well in society; and, especially, were they not in destitute circumstances I could respect them. But"—my young friend, pause —God, nature, and humanity forbid you to pursue this strain. Because our parents are poor, are we absolved from all obligations to love and respect them? Nay, if our father was in narrow circumstances, and still did all that he could for us, we owe him, instead of less regard, an hundred fold the more. If our mother, with scanty means, could promote our comfort and train us up as she did, then, for the sake of reason, of right, of common compassion, let us not despise her in her need.

Let every child, having any pretence to heart, or manliness, or piety, and who is so fortunate as to have a father or mother living, consider it a sacred duty to consult at any reasonable, personal sacrifice, the known wishes of such a parent, until that parent is no more; and our word for it the recollection of the same through the after pilgrimage of life will sweeten every sorrow, will brighten every gladness, will sparkle every tear drop with a joy ineffable. But be selfish still, have your own way, consult your own inclinations, yield to the bent of your own desires, regardless of a parent's commands, and counsels, and beseechings, and tears, and as the Lord liveth your life will be a failure; because, "the eye that mocketh at his father, and despiseth to obey his mother, the ravens of the valley shall pick it out, and the young eagle shall eat it."

Consider, finally, that if you live on, the polluted joys of youth cannot be the joys of old age; though its guilt and the sting left behind, will endure. We know well that the path of strict virtue is steep and rugged. But, for the stern discipline of temperance, the hardship of self-denial, the crushing of appetite and passion, there will be the blessed recompense of cheerful, healthful manhood, and an honorable old age. Yes, higher and better than all temporal returns, live for purity of speech and thought, live for an incorruptible character; have the courage to begin the great race, and the energy to pursue the glorious prize; forsee your danger, arm against it, trust in God and you will have nothing to fear.

Home.

WHAT a hallowed name! How full of enchantment and how dear to the heart! Home is the magic
circle within which the weary spirit finds refuge; it is
the sacred asylum to which the care-worn heart
retreats to find rest from the toils and inquietudes of
life.

Ask the lone wanderer as he plods his tedious way,
bent with the weight of age, and white with the frost
of years, ask him what is home. He will tell you "it
is a green spot in memory; an oasis in the desert; a
centre about which the fondest recollections of his
grief-oppressed heart cling with all the tenacity of
youth's first love. It was once a glorious, a happy
reality, but now it rests only as an image of the
mind."

Home! That name touches every fiber of the soul,
and strikes every chord of the human heart with its
angelic fingers. Nothing but death can break its spell.
What tender associations are linked with home!
What pleasing images and deep emotions it awakens!
It calls up the fondest memories of life and opens in
our nature the purest deepest, richest gush of consecrated thought and feeling.

Some years ago some twenty thousand people gathered in the old Castle Garden, New York, to hear
Jennie Lind sing, as no other songstress ever had
sung, the sublime compositions of Beethoven, Handel,
etc. At length the Swedish Nightingale thought of

her home, paused, and seemed to fold ner wings for a higher flight. She began with deep emotion to pour forth "Home, Sweet Home." The audience could not stand it. An uproar of applause stopped the music. Tears gushed from those thousands like rain. Beethoven and Handel were forgotten. After a moment the song came again, seemingly as from heaven, almost angelic. *Home*, that was the word that bound as with a spell twenty thousand souls, and Howard Payne triumphed over the great masters of song. When we look at the brevity and simplicity of this home song, we are ready to ask, what is the charm that lies concealed in it? Why does the dramatist and poet find his reputation resting on so apparently narrow a basis? The answer is easy. Next to religion, the deepest and most ineradicable sentiment in the human soul is that of the home affections. Every heart vibrates to this theme.

Home has an influence which is stronger than death. It is law to our hearts, and binds us with a spell which neither time nor change can break; the darkest villainies which have disgraced humanity cannot neutralize it. Gray-haired and demon guilt will make his dismal cell the sacred urn of tears wept over the memories of home, and these will soften and melt into tears of penitence even the heart of adamant.

Ask the little child what is home? You will find that to him it is the world—he knows no other. The father's love, the mother's smile, the sister's embrace, the brother's welcome, throw about his home a heavenly halo, and make it as attractive to him as the

home of the angels. Home is the spot where the child
pours out all its complaints, and it is the grave of all
its sorrows. Childhood has its sorrows and its
grievances, but home is the place where these are
soothed and banished by the sweet lullaby of a fond
mother's voice.

Was paradise an abode of purity and peace? or
will the New Eden above be one of unmingled beati-
tude? Then "the Paradise of Childhood," "the
Eden of Home," are names applied to the family
abode. In that paradise, all may appear as smiling
and serene to childhood as the untainted garden did
to unfallen man; even the remembrance of it, amid
distant scenes of woe, has soothed some of the saddest hours of life, and crowds of mourners have
spoken of

> "A home, that paradise below
> Of sunshine, and of flowers,
> Where hallowed joys perennial flow
> By calm sequester'd bowers."

There childhood nestles like a bird which has built
its abode among roses; there the cares and the coldness of earth are, as long as possible, averted.
Flowers there bloom, or fruits invite on every side,
and there paradise would indeed be restored, could
mortal power ward off the consequences of sin. This
new garden of the Lord would then abound in
beauty unsullied, and trees of the Lord's planting,
bearing fruit to his glory, would be found in plenty
there—it would be reality, and not mere poetry, to
speak of

> " My own dear quiet home,
> The Eden of my heart."

Home of our childhood! What words fall upon
the ear with so much of music in their cadence as
those which recall the scenes of innocent and happy
childhood, now numbered with the memories of the
past! How fond recollection delights to dwell upon
the events which marked our early pathway, when
the unbroken home-circle presented a scene of loveliness vainly sought but in the bosom of a happy family! Intervening years have not dimmed the vivid
coloring with which memory has adorned those joyous
hours of youthful innocence. We are again borne on
the wings of imagination to the place made sacred
by the remembrance of a father's care, a mother's
love, and the cherished associations of brothers and
sisters.

Home! How often we hear persons speak of the
home of their childhood. Their minds seem to delight in dwelling upon the recollections of joyous
days spent beneath the parental roof, when their
young and happy hearts were as light and free
as the birds that made the woods resound with the
melody of their cheerful voices. What a blessing it
is, when weary with care and burdened with sorrow,
to have a home to which we can go, and there, in the
midst of friends we love, forget our troubles and dwell
in peace and quietness.

There is no happiness in life, there is no misery
like that growing out of the dispositions which con-
secrate or desecrate a home. Peace at home, that is
the boon. "He is happiest, be he king or peasant,
who finds peace in his home." Home should be

made so truly home that the weary tempted heart could turn toward it anywhere on the dusty highway of life and receive light and strength. It should be the sacred refuge of our lives, whether rich or poor. The affections and loves of home are graceful things, especially among the poor. The ties that bind the wealthy and the proud to home may be forged on earth, but those which link the poor man to his humble hearth are of the true metal and bear the stamp of heaven. These affections and loves constitute the poetry of human life, and, so far as our present existence is concerned with all the domestic relations, are worth more than all other social ties. They give the first throb to the heart and unseal the deep fountains of its love. Home is the chief school of human virtue. Its responsibilities, joys, sorrows, smiles, tears, hopes, and solicitudes form the chief interest of human life.

There is nothing in the world which is so venerable as the character of parents; nothing so intimate and endearing as the relation of husband and wife; nothing so tender as that of parents and children; nothing so lovely as those of brothers and sisters. The little circle is made one by a singular union of the affections. The only fountain in the wilderness of life, where man drinks of water totally unmixed with bitter ingredients, is that which gushes for him in the calm and shady recess of domestic life. Pleasure may heat the heart with artificial excitement, ambition may delude it with golden dreams, war may eradicate its fine fibres and diminish its sensitiveness, but it is only domestic love that can render it truly happy.

Even as the sunbeam is composed of millions of minute rays, the home life must be constituted of little tendernesses, kind looks, sweet laughter, gentle words, loving counsels; it must not be like the torch-blaze of natural excitement which is easily quenched, but like the serene, chastened light which burns as safely in the dry east wind as in the stillest atmosphere. Let each bear the other's burden the while— let each cultivate the mutual confidence which is a gift capable of increase and improvement—and soon it will be found that kindliness will spring up on every side, displacing constitutional unsuitability, want of mutual knowledge, even as we have seen sweet violets and primroses dispelling the gloom of the gray sea-rocks.

There is nothing on earth so beautiful as the household on which Christian love forever smiles, and where religion walks a counselor and a friend. No cloud can darken it, for its twin-stars are centered in the soul. No storms can make it tremble, for it has a heavenly support and a heavenly anchor.

Home is a place of refuge. Tossed day by day upon the rough and stormy ocean of life—harassed by worldly cares, and perplexed by worldly inquietudes, the weary spirit yearns after repose. It seeks and finds it in the refuge which home supplies. Here the mind is at rest; the heart's turmoil becomes quiet, and the spirit basks in the peaceful delights of domestic love.

Yes, home *is a place of rest*—we feel it so when we seek and enter it after the busy cares and trials of the day are over. We may find joy elsewhere, but it is not the joy, the satisfaction of home. Of the world the heart may soon tire; of the home, never. In the former there is much of cold formality, much heartlessness under the garb of friendship, but in the latter it is all heart—all friendship of the purest, truest character.

The road along which the man of business travels in pursuit of competence or wealth is not a Macadamized one, nor does it ordinarily lead through pleasant scenes and by well-springs of delight. On the contrary, it is a rough and rugged path, beset with "wait-a-bit" thorns and full of pit-falls, which can only be avoided by the watchful care of circumspection. After every day's journey over this worse than rough turnpike road, the wayfarer needs something more than rest; he requires solace, and he deserves it. He is weary of the dull prose of life, and athirst for the poetry. Happy is the business man who can find that solace and that poetry at home. Warm greetings from loving hearts, fond glances from bright eyes, the welcome shouts of children, the many thousand little arrangements for our comfort and enjoyment that silently tell of thoughtful and expectant love, the gentle ministrations that disencumber us and force us into an old and easy seat before we are aware of it; these and like tokens of affection and sympathy constitute the poetry which reconciles us to the prose of life. Think of this, ye wives and daugh-

ters of business men! Think of the toils, the anxieties, the mortification, and wear that fathers undergo
to secure for you comfortable homes, and compensate
them for their trials by making them happy by their
own firesides.

Is it not true, that much of a man's energy and
success, as well as happiness, depends upon the
character of his home? Secure *there*, he goes forth
bravely to encounter the trials of life. It encourages
him to think of his pleasant home. It is his point of
rest. The thought of a dear wife shortens the distance of a journey, and alleviates the harassings of
business. It is a reserved power to fall back upon.
Home and home friends! How dear they are to us
all! Well might we love to linger on the picture of
home friends! When all other friends prove false,
home friends, removed from every bias but love, are
the steadfast and sure stays of our peace of soul,—
are best and dearest when the hour is darkest and the
danger of evil the greatest. But if one have none to
care for him at home,—if there be neglect, or love of
absence, or coldness, in our home and on our hearth,
then, even if we prosper without, it is dark indeed
within! It is not seldom that we can trace alienation
and dissipation to this source. If no wife or sister care
for him who returns from his toil, well may he despair
of life's best blessings. Without home friends,
Home is nothing but a name.

The sweetest type of heaven is home—nay,
heaven itself is the home for whose acquisition we
are to strive the most strongly. Home, in one form

and another, is the great object of life. It stands at the end of every day's labor, and beckons us to its bosom; and life would be cheerless and meaningless did we not discern, across the river that divides it from the life beyond, glimpses of the pleasant mansions prepared for us.

Heaven! that land of quiet rest—toward which those, who, worn down and tired with the toils of earth, direct their frail barks over the troubled waters of life, and after a long and dangerous passage, find it—safe in the haven of eternal bliss. Heaven is the *home* that awaits us beyond the grave. There the friendships formed on earth, and which cruel death has severed, are never more to be broken; and parted friends shall meet again, never more to be separated.

It is an inspiring hope that, when we separate here on earth at the summons of death's angel, and when a few more years have rolled over the heads of those remaining, if "faithful unto death," we shall meet again in heaven, our eternal *home*, there to dwell in the presence of our Heavenly Father, and go no more out forever.

At the best estate, we are only pilgrims and strangers. Heaven is to be our eternal home. Death will never knock at the door of that mansion, and in all that land there will not be a single grave. Aged parents rejoice very much when on Christmas Day or Thanksgiving Day they have their children at home; but there is almost always a son or a daughter absent—absent from the country, perhaps absent from the world. But Oh, how our Heavenly Father will rejoice in the long thanksgiving day of heaven, when He has all His children with Him in glory! How glad brothers and sisters will be to meet after so long a separation! Perhaps a score of years ago they parted at the door of the tomb. Now they meet again at the door of immortality. Once they looked through a glass darkly. Now, face to face, corruption, incorruption—mortality, immortatlity. Where are now all their sorrows and temptations and trials? Overwhelmed in the Red Sea of death, while they, dry-shod, marched into glory. Gates of jasper cap-stone of amethyst! Thrones of dominion do not so much affect my soul as the thought of home. Once there, let earthly sorrows howl like storms and roll like seas. Home! Let thrones rot and empires wither. Home! Let the world die in earthquake struggles and be buried amid procession of planets and dirge of spheres. Home! Let everlasting ages roll in irresistible sweep. Home! No sorrow, no crying, no tears, no death; but home! sweet home! Beautiful home! Glorious home! Everlasting home! Home with each other! Home with angels! Home with God! Home, Home! Through the rich grace of Christ Jesus, may we all reach it.

Family Worship.

A PRAYERLESS family cannot be otherwise than irreligious. They who daily pray in their homes, do well; they that not only pray, but read the Bible, do better; but they do best of all, who not only pray and read the Bible, but sing the praises of God.

What scene can be more lovely on earth, more like the heavenly home, and more pleasing to God, than that of a pious family kneeling with one accord around the home-altar, and uniting their supplications to their Father in heaven! How sublime the act of those parents who thus pray for the blessing of God upon their household! How lovely the scene of a pious mother gathering her little ones around her at the bedside, and teaching them the privilege of prayer! And what a safeguard is this devotion, against all the machinations of Satan!

It is this which makes home a type of heaven, the dwelling place of God. The family altar is heaven's threshold. And happy are those children who at that altar have been consecrated by a father's blessing, baptised by a mother's tears, and borne up to heaven upon their joint petitions, as a voluntary thank-offering to God. The home that has honored God with an altar of devotion may well be called blessed.

The influence of family worship is great, silent, irresistible and permanent. Like the calm, deep stream, it moves on in silent, but overwhelming power. It strikes its roots deep into the human heart, and

spreads its branches wide over the whole being, like
the lily that braves the tempest, and the Alpine flower
that leans its cheek upon the bosom of eternal snows
—it is exerted amid the wildest storms of life, and
breathes a softening spell in our bosom, even when a
heartless world is drying up the fountains of sympathy and love.

It affords home security and happiness, removes
family friction, and causes all the complicated wheels
of the home-machinery to move on noiselessly and
smoothly.   It promotes union and harmony, expunges
all selfishness, allays petulant feelings and turbulent
passions, destroys peevishness of temper and makes
home intercourse holy and delightful.   It causes the
members to reciprocate each other's affections, hushes
the voice of recrimination, and exerts a softening and
harmonizing influence over each heart.   The dew of
Heaven falls upon the home where prayer is wont to
be made.   Its members enjoy the good and the pleas-
antness of dwelling together in unity.   It gives tone
and intensity to their affections and sympathies; it
throws a sunshine around their hopes and interests;
it increases their happiness, and takes away the poignancy of their grief and sorrow.   It availeth much,
therefore, both for time and eternity.   Its voice has
sent many a poor prodigal home to his father's house.
Its answer has often been, "This man was born
there!" The child, kneeling beside the pious mother,
and pouring forth its infant prayer to God, must
attract the notice of the heavenly host, and receive
into its soul the power of a new life.

But in order to do this, the worship must be regular and devout, and the whole family engage in it. Some families are not careful to have their children present when they worship. This is very wrong. The children, above all others, are benefited, and should always be present. Some do not teach the children to kneel during prayer, and hence, they awkwardly sit in their seats, while the parents kneel. This is a sad mistake. If they do not kneel, they naturally suppose they have no part or lot in the devotions, and soon feel that it is wrong for them to bow before the Lord. We have seen many cases where grown up sons and daughters have never bent the knee before the Lord, and thought it wrong to kneel till they were Christians. In this way they were made more shy and stubborn, and felt that there was an impassable barrier between them and Christ. This feeling is wrong, and unnecessary. If family worship had been rightly observed, they would have felt that they were very near the Savior, and would easily be inclined to give their hearts to him. Indeed, children thus trained, seldom grow to maturity without becoming practical Christians.

Family worship in itself embodies a hallowing influence that pleads for its observance. It must needs be that trials will enter a household. The conflict of wishes, the clashing of views, and a thousand other causes, will ruffle the temper, and produce jar and friction in the machinery of the family. There is needed, then, some daily agency that shall softly enfold the homestead with its hallowed and soothing power, and restore the fine, harmonious play of its various parts. The father needs that which shall gently lift away from his thoughts the disquieting burden of his daily business. The mother that which shall smooth down the fretting irritation of her unceasing toil and trial; and the child and domestic that which shall neutralize the countless agencies of evil that ever beset them. And what so well adapted to do this, as for all to gather, when the day is done, around the holy page, and pour a united supplication and acknowledgment to that sleepless Power, whose protection and scrutiny are ever around their path, and who will bring all things at last into judgment? And when darker and sadder days begin to shadow the home, what can cheer and brighten the sinking heart so much as resort to that fatherly One who can make the tears of the loneliest sorrow to be the seed-pearls of the brightest crown? See what home becomes with religion as its life and rule! Human nature is there checked and molded by the amiable spirit and lovely character of Jesus. The mind is expanded, the heart softened, sentiments refined, passions subdued, hopes elevated, pursuits ennobled, the world cast into the shade, and heaven realized as the first prize. The great want of our intellectual and moral nature is here met, and home education becomes impregnated with the spirit and elements of our preparation for eternity.

Compare an irreligious home with this, and see the vast importance of family worship. It is a moral waste; its members move in the putrid atmosphere

of vitiated feeling and misdirected power. Brutal
passions become dominant; we hear the stern voice
of parental despotism; we behold a scene of filial strife
and insubordination; there is throughout a heart-
blank. Domestic life becomes clouded by a thousand
crosses and disappointments; the solemn realities of
the eternal world are cast into the shade; the home-
conscience and feeling become stultified; the sense of
moral duty distorted, and all the true interests of
home appear in a haze. Natural affection is debased,
and love is prostituted to the base designs of self, and
the entire family, with all its tender chords, ardent
hopes, and promised interests, becomes engulfed in
the vortex of criminal worldliness! .

Family worship is included in the necessities of our
children, and in the covenant promises of God. The
penalties of its neglect, and the rewards of our faithful-
ness to it, should prompt us to its establishment in
our homes. Its absence is a curse; its presence a
blessing. It is a foretaste of heaven. Like manna,
it will feed our souls, quench our thirst, sweeten
the cup of life, and shed a halo of glory and of gladness around our firesides. Let yours, therefore, be
the religious home; and then be sure that God will
delight to dwell therein, and His blessing will
descend upon it. Your children shall "not be found
begging bread," but shall be like "olive plants around
your table,"—the "heritage of the Lord." Yours will
be the home of love and harmony; it shall have the
charter of family rights and privileges, the ward of
family interests, the palladium of family hopes and

happiness. Your household piety will be the crowning attribute of your peaceful home,—the living stars that shall adorn the night of its tribulation, and the pillar of cloud and of fire in its pilgrimage to a "better country." It shall strew the family threshold with the flowers of promise, and enshrine the memory of loved ones gone before, in all the fragrance of that "blessed hope" of reunion in heaven which looms up from a dying hour. It shall give to the infant soul its "perfect flowering," and expand it in all the fullness of a generous love and conscious blessedness, making it "lustrous in the livery of divine knowledge." And then in the dark hour of home separation and bereavement, when the question is put to you, mourning parents, "Is it well with the child? is it well with thee?" you can answer with joy, "It is well!"

Home Influence.

OUR nature demands home. It is the first essential element of our social being. This cannot be complete without the home relations; there would be no proper equilibrium of life and character without the home influence. The heart, when bereaved and disappointed, naturally turns for refuge to home-life and sympathy. No spot is so attractive to the weary one; it is the heart's moral oasis. There is a mother's watchful love and a father's sustaining influence;

there is a husband's protection and a wife's tender sympathy; there is the circle of loving brothers and sisters—happy in each other's love. Oh, what is life without these! A desolation, a painful, gloomy pilgrimage through "desert heaths and barren sands."

Home influence may be estimated from the immense force of its impressions. It is the prerogative of home to make the first impression upon our nature, and to give that nature its first direction onward and upward. It uncovers the moral fountain, chooses its channel, and gives the stream its first impulse. It makes the "first stamp and sets the first seal" upon the plastic nature of the child. It gives the first tone to our desires and furnishes ingredients that will either sweeten or embitter the whole cup of life. These impressions are indelible and durable as life. Compared with them, other impressions are like those made upon sand or wax. These are like "the deep borings into the flinty rock." To erase them we must remove every stratum of our being. Even the infidel lives under the holy influence of a pious mother's impressions. John Randolph could never shake off the restraining influence of a little prayer his mother taught him when a child. It preserved him from the clutches of avowed infidelity.

The home influence is either a blessing or a curse, either for good or for evil. It cannot be neutral. In either case it is mighty, commencing with our birth, going with us through life, clinging to us in death, and reaching into the eternal world. It is that unitive power which arises out of the manifold

5

relations and associations of domestic life.   The specific influences of husband and wife, of parent and
child, of brother and sister, of teacher and pupil,
united and harmoniously blended, constitute the home
influence.

From this we may infer the character of home
influence.   It is great, silent, irresistible and permanent.   Like the calm, deep stream, it moves on in
silent, but overwhelming power.   It strikes its roots
deep into the human heart, and spreads its branches
wide over our whole being.   It is exerted amid the
wildest storms of life and breathes a softening spell
in our bosom even when a heartless world is freezing
up the fountains of sympathy and love.   It is governing, restraining, attracting and traditional.   It holds
the empire of the heart and rules the life.   It restrains
the wayward passions of the child and checks him in
his mad career of ruin.

Our habits, too, are formed under the molding
power of home.   The "tender twig" is there bent,
the spirit shaped, principles implanted, and the whole
character is formed until it becomes a habit.   Goodness or evil are there "resolved into necessity."
Who does not feel this influence of home upon all
his habits of life?   The gray-haired father who wails
in his second infancy feels the traces of his childhood
home in his spirit, desires and habits.   Ask the
strong man in the prime of life whether the most firm
and reliable principles of his character were not the
inheritance of a parental home.

The most illustrious statesmen, the most distinguished warriors, the most eloquent ministers, and the greatest benefactors of human kind, owe their greatness to the fostering influence of home. Napoleon knew and felt this when he said, "What France wants is good mothers, and you may be sure then that France will have good sons." The homes of the American revolution made the men of the revolution. Their influence reaches yet far into the inmost frame and constitution of our glorious republic. It controls the fountains of her power, forms the character of her citizens and statesmen, and shapes our destiny as a people. Did not the Spartan mother and her home give character to the Spartan nation? Her lessons to her child infused the iron nerve into the heart of that nation, and caused her sons, in the wild tumult of battle, "either to live behind their shields, or to die upon them!" Her influence fired them with a patriotism which was stronger than death. Had it been hallowed by the pure spirit and principles of Christianity what a power of good it would have been!

But alas! the home of an Aspasia had not the heart and ornaments of the Christian family. Though "the monuments of Cornelia's virtues were the character of her children," yet these were not "the ornaments of a quiet spirit." Had the central heart of the Spartan home been that of the Christian mother, the Spartan nation would now perhaps adorn the brightest page of history.

Home, in all well constituted minds, is always associated with moral and social excellence. The higher men rise in the scale of being, the more important and interesting is home. The Arab or forest man may care little for his home, but the Christian man of cultured heart and developed mind will love his home, and generally love it in proportion to his moral worth. He knows it is the planting-ground of every seed of morality—the garden of virtue, and the nursery of religion. He knows that souls immortal are here trained for the skies; that private worth and public character are made in its sacred retreat. To love home with a deep and abiding interest, with a view to its elevating influence, is to love truth and right, heaven and God.

Our life abroad is but a reflex of what it is at home. We make ourselves in a great measure at home. This is especially true of woman. The woman who is rude, coarse and vulgar at home, cannot be expected to be amiable, chaste and refined in the world. Her home habits will stick to her. She cannot shake them off. They are woven into the web of her life. Her home language will be first on her tongue. Her home by-words will come out to mortify her just when she wants most to hide them in her heart. Her home vulgarities will show their hideous forms to shock her most when she wants to appear her best. Her home coarseness will appear most when she is in the most refined circles, and appearing there will abash her more than elsewhere. All her home habits will follow her. They have become a sort of second nature to her. It is much the same with men. It is indeed there that every man must

be known by those who would make a just estimate
either of his virtue or felicity; for smiles and embroid-
ery are alike occasional, and the mind is often dressed
for show in painted honor and fictitious benevolence.
Every young woman should feel that just what she is
at home she will appear abroad. If she attempts to
appear otherwise, everybody will soon see through
the attempt. We cannot cheat the world long about
our real characters. The thickest and most opaque
mask we can put on will soon become transparent.
This fact we should believe without a doubt. Deception most often deceives itself. The deceiver is the
most deceived. The liar is often the only one cheated.
The young woman who pretends to what she is not,
believes her pretense is not understood. Other people laugh in their sleeves at her foolish pretensions.
Every young woman should early form in her mind
an ideal of a *true home*. It should not be the ideal of
a *place*, but of the *character of home*. Place does
not constitute home. Many a gilded palace and scene
of luxury is not a home. Many a flower-girt dwelling and splendid mansion lacks all the essentials of
home. A hovel is often more a home than a palace.
If the spirit of the congenial friendship link not the
hearts of the inmates of a dwelling it is not a home.
If love reign not there; if charity spread not her
downy mantle over all; if peace prevail not; if contentment be not a meek and merry dweller therein;
if virtue rear not her beautiful children, and religion
come not in her white robe of gentleness to lay her
hand in benediction on every head, the home is not

complete. We are all in the habit of building for ourselves ideal homes. But they are generally made up
of outward things—a house, a garden, a carriage,
and the ornaments and appendages of luxury. And
if, in our lives, we do not realize our ideas, we make
ourselves miserable and our friends miserable. Half
the women in our country are unhappy because their
homes are not so luxurious as they wish.

The grand idea of home is a quiet, secluded spot,
where loving hearts dwell, set apart and dedicated to
improvement—to intellectual and moral improvement.
It is not a formal school of staid solemnity and rigid
discipline, where virtue is made a task and progress a
sharp necessity, but a free and easy exercise of all
our spiritual limbs, in which obedience is a pleasure,
discipline a joy, improvement a self-wrought delight.
All the duties and labors of home, when rightly
understood, are so many means of improvement.
Even the trials of home are so many rounds in the
ladder of spiritual progress, if we but make them so.
It is not merely by speaking to children about spiritual things that you win them over. If that be all you
do, it will accomplish nothing, less than nothing. It
is the sentiments which they hear at home, it is the
maxims which rule your daily conduct—the likings
and dislikings which you express—the whole regula-
tions of the household, in dress, and food, and furniture—the recreations you indulge—the company you
keep—the style of your reading—the whole complexion of daily life—this creates the element in
which your children are either growing in grace, and

preparing for an eternity of glory — or they are learning to live without God, and to die without hope.

Home Amusements.

"I HAVE been told by men, who had passed unharmed through the temptations of youth, that they
owed their escape from many dangers to the intimate
companionship of affectionate and pure-minded sisters. They have been saved from a hazardous meeting with idle company by some home engagement, of
which their sisters were the charm; they have
refrained from mixing with the impure, because they
would not bring home thoughts and feelings which
they could not share with those trusting and loving
friends; they have put aside the wine-cup, and
abstained from stronger potations, because they would
not profane with their fumes the holy kiss, with which
they were accustomed to bid their sisters good-night."

A proper amount of labor, well-spiced with sunny
sports, is almost absolutely necessary to the formation
of a firm, hardy, physical constitution, and a cheerful
and happy mind. Let all youth not only learn to
choose and enjoy proper amusements, but let them
learn to invent them at home, and use them there,
and thus form ideas of such homes as they shall wish
to have their own children enjoy. Not half the
people know how to make a home. It is one of the
greatest and most useful studies of life to learn how

to make a home—such a home as men, and women,
and children should dwell in. It is a study that
should be early introduced to the attention of youth.
It would be well if books were written upon this most
interesting subject, giving many practical rules and
hints, with a long chapter on *Amusements*.

That was a good remark of Seneca, when he said,
"Great is he who enjoys his earthen-ware as if it
were plate, and not less great is the man to whom
all his plate is no more than earthen-ware." Every
home should be cheerful. Innocent joy should reign
in every heart. There should be domestic amusements, fireside pleasures, quiet and simple it may be,
but such as shall make home happy, and not leave it
that irksome place which will oblige the youthful
spirit to look elsewhere for joy. There are a thous-
and unobtrusive ways in which we may add to the
cheerfulness of home. The very modulations of the
voice will often make a wonderful difference. How
many shades of feeling are expressed by the voice!
what a change comes over us at the change of its
tones! No delicately tuned harpstring can awaken
more pleasure; no grating discord can pierce with
more pain.

Let parents talk much and talk well at home. A
father who is habitually silent in his own house, may
be in many respects a wise man; but he is not wise
in his silence. We sometimes see parents, who are
the life of every company which they enter, dull,
silent and uninteresting at home among the children.
If they have not mental activity and mental stories

sufficient for both, let them first provide for their own household. Ireland exports beef and wheat, and lives on potatoes; and they fare as poorly who reserve their social charms for companions abroad, and keep their dullness for home consumption. It is better to instruct children and make them happy at home, than it is to charm strangers or amuse friends. A silent house is a dull place for young people, a place from which they will escape if they can. They will talk of being "shut up" there; and the youth who does not love home is in danger.

The true mother loves to see her son come home to her. He may be almost as big as her house; a whiskerando, with as much hair on his face as would stuff her arm chair, and she may be a mere shred of a woman; but he's "her boy;" and if he grew twice as big he'd be "her boy" still; aye, and if he take unto himself a wife, he's her boy still, for all that. She does not believe a word of the old rhyme—

"Your son is your son till he gets him a wife;
But your daughter's your daughter all the days of her life."

And what will bring our boys back to our home-steads, but our making those homesteads pleasant to them in their youth. Let us train a few roses on the humble wall, and their scent and beauty will be long remembered; and many a lad, instead of going to a spree, will turn to his old bed, and return to his work again, strengthened, invigorated, and refreshed, instead of battered, weakened, and, per-haps, disgraced.

Fathers, mothers, remember this: and if you would not have your children lost to you in after-life—if you would have your married daughters not forget their old home in the new one—if you would have your sons lend a hand to keep you in the old rose-covered cottage, instead of letting you go to the naked walls of a workhouse—make home happy to them when they are young. Send them out into the world in the full belief that there is "no place like home," aye, "be it ever so humble." And even if the old home should, in the course of time, be pulled down, or be lost to your children, it will still live in their memories. The kind looks, and kind words, and thoughtful love of those who once inhabited it, will not pass away. Your home will be like the poet's vase—

"You may break, you may ruin, the vase if you will,
But the scent of the roses will cling to it still."

Music is an accomplishment usually valuable as a home enjoyment, as rallying round the piano the various members of a family, and harmonizing their hearts, as well as their voices, particularly in devotional strains. We know no more agreeable and interesting spectacle than that of brothers and sisters playing and singing together those elevated compositions in music and poetry which gratify the taste and purify the heart, while their parents sit delighted by. We have seen and heard an elder sister thus leading the family choir, who was the soul of harmony to the whole household, and whose life was a perfect example. Parents should not fail to consider the great value of home music. Buy a good instrument and teach your family to sing and play, then they can produce sufficient amusement at home themselves so that the sons will not think of looking elsewhere for it, and thus often be led into dens of vice and immorality. The reason that so many become dissipated and run to every place of amusement, no matter what its character, making every effort possible to get away from home at night, is the lack of entertainment at home.

To Young Men.

YOUNG MEN! you are wanted. From the street corners, from the saloons and playhouses, from the loafers' rendezvous, from the idlers' promenade, turn your steps into the highway of noble aim and earnest work. There are prizes enough for every successful worker, crowns enough for every honorable head that goes through the smoke of conflict to victory.

There is within the young man an upspringing of lofty sentiment which contributes to his elevation, and though there are obstacles to be surmounted and difficulties to be vanquished, yet with truth for his watch-word, and leaning on his own noble purposes and indefatigable exertions, he may crown his brow with imperishable honors. He may never wear the warrior's crimson wreath, the poet's chaplet of bays, or the stateman's laurels; though no grand universal truth may at his bidding stand confessed to the world, —though it may never be his to bring to a successful issue a great political revolution—to be the founder of a republic, whose name shall be a "distinguished star in the constellation of nations,"—yea, more, though his name may never be heard beyond the narrow limits of his own neighborhood, yet is his mission none the less a high and holy one.

In the moral and physical world, not only the field of battle, but also the consecrated cause of truth and virtue calls for champions, and the field for doing good is "white unto the harvest;" and if he enlists in the ranks, and his spirit faints not, he may write his name among the stars of heaven. Beautiful lives have blossomed in the darkest places, as pure white lilies full of fragrance on the slimy, stagnant waters. No possession is so productive of real influence as a highly cultivated intellect. Wealth, birth, and official station may and do secure to their possessors an external, superficial courtesy; but they never did, and they never can, command the reverence of the heart. It is only to the man of large and noble soul, to him who blends a cultivated mind with an upright heart, that men yield the tribute of deep and genuine respect.

But why do so few young men of early promise, whose hopes, purposes, and resolves were as radiant as the colors of the rainbow, fail to distinguish themselves? The answer is obvious; they are not willing to devote themselves to that toilsome culture which is the price of great success. Whatever aptitude for particular pursuits nature may donate to her favorite children, she conducts none but the laborious and the studious to distinction.

God puts the oak in the forest, and the pine on its sand and rocks, and says to men, "There are your houses; go hew, saw, frame, build, make. God makes the trees; men must build the house. God supplies the timber; men must construct the ship. God buries iron in the heart of the earth; men must dig it, and smelt it, and fashion it. What is useful for the body, and, still more, what is useful for the mind, is to be had only by exertion — exertion that will work men more than iron is wrought — that will shape men more than timber is shaped.

Great men have ever been men of thought as well as men of action. As the magnificent river, rolling in the pride of its mighty waters, owes its greatness to the hidden springs of the mountain nook, so does the wide-sweeping influence of distinguished men date its origin from hours of privacy, resolutely employed in efforts after self-development. The invisible spring of self-culture is the source of every great achievement.

Away, then, young man, with all dreams of superiority, unless you are determined to dig after knowledge, as men search for concealed gold! Remember, that every man has in himself the seminal principle of great excellence, and he may develop it by cultivation if he will TRY. Perhaps you are what the world calls *poor*. What of that? Most of the men whose names are as household words were also the children of poverty. Captain Cook, the circumnavigator of the globe, was born in a mud hut, and started in life as a cabin boy. Lord Eldon, who sat on the woolsack in the British parliament for nearly half a century, was the son of a coal merchant. Franklin, the philosopher, diplomatist, and statesman, was but a poor printer's boy, whose highest luxury at one time, was only a penny roll, eaten in the streets of Philadelphia. Ferguson, the profound philosopher, was son of a half-starved weaver. Johnson, Goldsmith, Coleridge, and multitudes of others of high distinction, knew the pressure of limited circumstances, and have demonstrated that poverty even is no insuperable obstacle to success.

Up, then, young man, and gird yourself for the work of self-cultivation! Set a high price on your leisure moments. They are sands of precious gold. Properly expended, they will procure for you a stock of great thoughts—thoughts that will fill, stir and invigorate, and expand the soul. Seize also on the unparalleled aids furnished by steam and type in this unequaled age.

The great thoughts of great men are now to be procured at prices almost nominal. You can, therefore, easily collect a library of choice standard works. But above all, learn to reflect even more than you read. Without thought, books are the sepulchre of the soul,—they only immure it. Let thought and reading go hand in hand, and the intellect will rapidly increase in strength and gifts. Its possessor will rise in character, in power, and in positive influence. A

great deal of talent is lost in the world for the want
of a little courage. Every day sends to the grave a
number of obscure men, who have only remained in
obscurity because their timidity has prevented them
from making a first effort; and who, if they could
have been induced to begin, would, in all probability,
have gone great lengths in the career of fame. The
fact is, that to do anything in this world worth doing,
we must not stand back, shivering, and thinking of the
cold and the danger, but jump in and scramble through
as well as we can. It will not do to be perpetually
calculating tasks, and adjusting nice chances; it did
very well before the flood, where a man could consult
his friends upon an intended publication for a hundred and fifty years, and then live to see its success
afterward; but at present a man waits and doubts,
and hesitates, and consults his brother, and his uncle,
and particular friends, till, one fine day, he finds that
he is sixty years of age; that he has lost so much
time in consulting his first cousin and particular friends,
that he has no more time to follow their advice.

Man is born to dominion, but he must enter it by
conquest, and continue to do battle for every inch of
ground added to his sway. His first exertions are
put forth for the acquisition of the control and the
establishment of the authority of his own will. With
his first efforts to reduce his own physical powers to
subjection, he must simultaneously begin to subject
his mental faculties to control. Through the combined exertion of his mental and physical powers, he
labors to spread his dominion over the widest possible
extent of the world without.

Thus self-control and control over outward circumstances are alike the duty and the birthright of man.
But self-control is the highest and noblest form of
dominion.   "He that ruleth his own spirit is greater
than he that taketh a city."

If you intend to marry, if you think your happiness
will be increased and your interests advanced by
matrimony, be sure and "look where you're going."
Join yourself in union with no woman who is selfish,
for she will sacrifice you; with no one who is fickle,
for she will become estranged; have naught to do
with a proud one, for she will ruin you.   Leave a
coquette to the fools who flutter around her; let her
own fireside accommodate a scold; and flee from a
woman who loves scandal, as you would flee from the
evil one.   "Look where your going" will sum it all up.

Gaze not on beauty too much, lest it blast thee;
nor too long, lest it blind thee; nor too near, lest it
burn thee: if thou like it, it deceives thee; if thou
love it, it disturbs thee; if thou lust after it, it destroys
thee; if virtue accompany it, it is the heart's paradise;
if vice associate it, it is the soul's purgatory; it is the
wise man's bonfire, and the fool's furnace.   The Godless youth is infatuated by a fair face, and is lured to
his fate by a siren's smile.   He takes no counsel of
the Lord and is left to follow his own shallow fancies
or the instigations of his passions.   The time will
surely come in his life when he will not so much want
a pet as a heroine.   In dark and trying days, when
the waves of misfortune are breaking over him, and
one home comfort, and another, and another is swept

away, the piano—the grand instrument—gone to
the creditors, the family turned out on the sidewalk
by the heartless landlord, then what is the wife good
for if her lips that accompanied the piano in song,
cannot lift alone the notes, "Jesus, lover of my
soul?" The strongest arm in this world is not the
arm of a blacksmith, nor the arm of a giant; it is the
arm of a woman, when God has put into it, through
faith and submission to his will, his own moral omnipotence. If there is one beautiful spot on earth, it is
the home of the young family consecrated by piety,
the abode of the Holy Spirit, above which the hovering angels touch their wings, forming a canopy of
protection and sanctity.

There is no moral object so beautiful as a conscientious young man. We watch him as we do a
star in the heavens; clouds may be before him, but
we know that his light is behind them and will beam
again; the blaze of other's popularity may outshine
him, but we know that, though unseen, he illuminates
his own true sphere. He resists temptation, not without a struggle, for that is not virtue, but he does
resist and conquer; he bears the sarcasm of the
profligate, and it stings him, for that is a trait of
virtue, but he heals the wound with his own pure
touch. He heeds not the watchword of fashion if it
leads to sin; the Atheist, who says not only in his
heart, but with his lips, "There is no God!" controls
him not; he sees the hand of a creating God, and
rejoices in it. Woman is sheltered by fond arms and
loving counsel; old age is protected by its experience,

and manhood by its strength; but the young man
stands amid the temptations of the world like a self-
balanced tower.   Happy he who seeks and gains the
prop and shelter of morality.   Onward, then, conscientious youth—raise thy standard and nerve thyself for goodness.   If God has given thee intellectual power, awaken in that cause; never let it be said
of thee, he helped to swell the tide of sin by pouring
his influence into its channels.   If thou art feeble in
mental strength, throw not that drop into a polluted
current.   Awake, arise, young man! assume that
beautiful garb of virtue!   It is difficult to be pure
and holy.   Put on thy strength, then.   Let truth be
the lady of thy love—defend her.

A young man came to an aged professor of a distinguished continental university, with a smiling face,
and informed him that the long and fondly cherished
desire of his heart was at length fulfilled—his parents
had given their consent to his studying the profession
of the law.   For some time he continued explaining
how he would spare no labor or expense in perfecting
his education.   When he paused, the old man, who
had been listening to him with great patience and
kindness, gently said, "Well! and when you have
finished your studies, what do you mean to do then?"
"Then I shall take my degree," answered the young
man.   "And then?" asked the venerable friend.   "And
then," continued the youth, "I shall have a number of
difficult cases, and shall attract notice, and win a great
reputation."   "And then?" repeated the holy man.
"Why, then," replied the youth, "I shall doubtless

be promoted to some high office in the State." "And then?" "And then," pursued the young lawyer, "I shall live in honor and wealth, and look forward to a happy old age." "And then?" repeated the old man. "And then," said the youth, "and then—and then—and then I shall die." Here the venerable listener lifted up his voice, and again asked, with solemnity and emphasis, "And then?" Whereupon the aspiring student made no answer, and cast down his head, and in silence and thoughtfulness retired. The last "And then?" had pierced his heart like a sword, had made an impression which he could not dislodge.

To Young Women.

WHAT is womanhood? Is there any more important question for young women to consider than this? It should be the highest ambition of every young woman to possess a true womanhood. Earth presents no higher object of attainment. To be a woman, in the truest and highest sense of the word, is to be the best thing beneath the skies. To be a woman is something more than to live eighteen or twenty years; something more than to grow to the physical stature of women; something more than to wear flounces, exhibit dry-goods, sport jewelry, catch the gaze of lewd-eyed men; something more than to be a belle, a wife, or a mother. Put all these qualifications together and they do but little toward making a true woman.

Beauty and style are not the surest passports to womanhood—some of the noblest specimens of womanhood that the world has ever seen, have presented the plainest and most unprepossessing appearance. A woman's worth is to be estimated by the real goodness of her heart, the greatness of her soul, and the purity and sweetness of her character; and a woman with a kindly disposition and well-balanced temper, is both lovely and attractive, be her face ever so plain, and her figure ever so homely; she makes the best of wives and the truest of mothers. She has a higher purpose in living than the beautiful, yet vain and supercilious woman, who has no higher ambition than to flaunt her finery on the street, or to gratify her inordinate vanity by extracting flattery and praise from society, whose compliments are as hollow as they are insincere.

Beauty is a dangerous gift. It is even so. Like wealth it has ruined its thousands. Thousands of the most beautiful women are destitute of common sense and common humanity. No gift from heaven is so general and so widely abused by woman as the gift of beauty. In about nine cases in ten it makes her silly, senseless, thoughtless, giddy, vain, proud, frivolous, selfish, low and mean. "She is beautiful, and she knows it," is as much as to say she is spoiled. A beautiful girl is very likely to believe she was made to be looked at; and so she sets herself up for a show at every window, in every door, on every corner of the street, in every company at which opportunity offers for an exhibition of herself. And believing and acting thus, she soon becomes good for nothing else, and when she comes to be a middle-aged woman she is that weakest, most sickening of all human things—a faded beauty.

These facts have long since taught sensible men to beware of beautiful women—to sound them carefully before they give them their confidence. Beauty is shallow—only skin-deep; fleeting—only for a few years' reign; dangerous—tempting to vanity and lightness of mind; deceitful—dazzling often to bewilder; weak—reigning only to ruin; gross—leading often to sensual pleasure. And yet we say it need not be so. Beauty is lovely and ought to be innocently possessed. It has charms which ought to be used for good purposes. It is a delightful gift, which ought to be received with gratitude and worn with grace and meekness. It should always minister to inward beauty. Every woman of beautiful form and features should cultivate a beautiful mind and heart.

Young women ought to hold a steady moral sway over their male associates, so strong as to prevent them from becoming such lawless rowdies. Why do they not? Because they do not possess sufficient *force* of character. They have not sufficient resolution and energy of purpose. Their virtue is not vigorous. Their moral wills are not resolute. Their influence is not armed with executive power. Their goodness is not felt as an earnest force of benevolent purpose. Their moral convictions are not regarded as solemn resolves to be true to God and duty, come what may. This is the virtue of too many women. They would not have a drunkard for a husband, but they would drink a glass of wine with a fast young man. They would not use profane language, but they are not shocked by its incipient language, and love the society of men whom they know are as profane as Lucifer out of their presence. They would not be dishonest, but they will use a thousand deceitful words and ways, and countenance the society of men known as hawkers, sharpers and deceivers. They would not be irreligious, but they smile upon the most irreligious men, and even show that they love to be wooed by them. They would not be licentious, but they have no stunning rebuke for licentious men, and will even admit them on parol into their society. (This is the virtue of too many women)—a virtue scarcely worthy the name—really no virtue at all—a milk-and-water substitute—a hypocritical, hollow pretension to virtue as unwomanly as it is disgraceful. We believe that a young lady, by her constant, consistent Christian example, may exert an untold power. You do not know the respect and almost worship which young men, no matter how wicked they may be themselves, pay to a consistent Christian lady, be she young or old. If a young man sees that the religion which, in youth, he was taught to venerate, is lightly thought of, and perhaps sneered at, by the young ladies with whom he associates, we can hardly expect him to think that it is the thing for him.

Men love to trust their fortunes in their hands. The good love to gather around them for the blessing of their smiles; they strew their pathway with moral light. They bless without effort; they teach sentiments of duty and honesty in every act of their lives.

Such is the rectitude of character which every young woman should cultivate. Nothing will more surely secure confidence and esteem. There is especial need of such cultivation, for young women are doubted in many respects more generally than any other class of people. Most people seldom think of believing many things they hear from the lips of young women, so little is genuine integrity cultivated among them. We are sorry to make such a remark. We wish truth did not compel it. We would that young women would cultivate the strictest regard for truth in all things; in small as well as in important matters. Exaggeration or false coloring is as much a violation of integrity as a direct falsehood. Equivocation is often falsehood. Deception in all forms is opposed to integrity. Mock manners, pretended emotions, affectation, policy plans to secure attention and respect are all sheer falsehoods, and in the end injure her who is guilty of them. Respect and affection are the outgrowth of confidence. She who secures the firmest confidence will secure the most respect and love. Confidence can only be secured by integrity. The young woman with a high sense of duty will always secure confidence, and having this, she will secure respect, affection, and influence.

You have great influence. You cannot live without

having some sort of influence, any more then you can without breathing. One thing is just as unavoidable as the other. Beware, then, what kind of influence it is that you are constantly exerting. An invitation to take a glass of wine, or to play a game of cards, may kindle the fires of intemperance or gambling, which will burn forever. A jest given at the expense of religion, a light, trifling manner in the house of God, or any of the numerous ways in which you may show your disregard for the souls of others, may be the means of ruining many for time and eternity.

We want the girls to rival the boys in all that is good, and refined, and ennobling. We want them to rival the boys, as they well can, in learning, in understanding, in virtues; in all noble qualities of mind and heart, but not in any of those things that have caused them justly or unjustly, to be described as savages. We want the girls to be gentle—not weak, but gentle, and kind, and affectionate. We want, to be sure, that wherever a girl is, there should be a sweet, subduing and harmonizing influence of purity, and truth, and love, pervading and hallowing, from centre to circumference, the entire circle in which she moves. If the boys are savages, we want her to be their civilizer. We want her to tame them, to subdue their ferocity, to soften their manners, and to teach them all needful lessons of order, and sobriety, and meekness, and patience, and goodness. The little world of self is not the limit that is to confine all her actions. Her love was not destined to waste its fires in the narrow chamber of a single human heart;

no, a broader sphere of action is hers—a more expansive benevolence. The light and heat of her love are to be seen and felt far and wide. Who would not rather thus live a true life, than sit shivering over the smoldering embers of self-love? Happy is that maiden who seeks to live this true life! As time passes on, her own character will be elevated and purified. Gradually will she return toward that order of her being, which was lost in the declension of mankind from that original state of excellence in which they were created. She will become, more and more, a true woman; will grow wiser, and better, and happier. Her path through the world will be as a shining light, and all who know her will call her blessed.

A right view of life, then, which all should take at the outset, is the one we have presented. Let every young lady seriously reflect upon this subject. Let her remember that she is not designed by her Creator to live for herself alone, but has a higher and nobler destiny—that of doing good to others—of making others happy. As the quiet streamlet which runs along the valley nourishes a luxuriant vegetation, causing flowers to bloom and birds to sing along its banks, so do a kind look and happy countenance spread peace and joy around.

Kindness is the ornament of man—it is the chief glory of woman—it is, indeed, woman's true prerogative—her sceptre and her crown. It is the sword with which she conquers, and the charm with which she captivates. Young lady, would you be admired and beloved? would you be an ornament to your sex, and a blessing to your race? Cultivate this heavenly virtue. Wealth may surround you with its blandishments, and beauty, learning, or talents, may give you admirers, but love and kindness alone can captivate the heart. Whether you live in a cottage or a palace, these graces can surround you with perpetual sunshine, making you, and all around you, happy.

Seek ye, then, fair daughters, the possession of that inward grace, whose essence shall permeate and vitalize the affections,—adorn the countenance,—make mellifluous the voice,—and impart a hallowed beauty even to your motions! Not merely that you may be loved, would we urge this, but that you may, in truth, be lovely,—that loveliness which fades not with time, nor is marred or aliented by disease, but which neither chance nor change can in any way despoil. We urge you, gentle maiden, to beware of the silken enticements of the stranger, until your love is confirmed by protracted acquaintance. Shun the idler, though his coffers overflow with pelf. Avoid the irreverent,—the scoffer of hallowed things; and him "who looks upon the wine while it is red;"—him, too, "who hath a high look and a proud heart," and who "privily slandereth his neighbor." Do not heed the specious prattle about "first love," and so place, irrevocably, the seal upon your future destiny, before you have sounded, in silence and secresy, the deep fountains of your own heart. Wait, rather, until your own character and that of him who would woo you, is more fully developed Surely, if this "first love" cannot endure a short probation, fortified by "the pleasures of hope," how can it be expected to survive years of intimacy, scenes of trial, distracting cares, wasting sickness, and all the homely routine of practical life. Yet it is these that constitute life, and the love that cannot abide them is false and must die.

———————

Daughter and Sister.

THERE are few things of which men are more proud than of their daughters. The young father follows the sportive girl with his eye, as he cherishes an emotion of complacency, not so tender, but quite as active as the mother's. The aged father leans on his daughter as the crutch of his declining years. An old proverb says that the son is son till he is married, but the daughter is daughter forever. This is something like the truth. Though the daughter leaves the parental roof, she is still followed by kindly regards. The gray-haired father drops in every day to greet the beloved face; and when he pats the cheeks of the little grandchildren, it is chiefly because the bond which unites him to them passes through the heart of his darling Mary; she is his daughter still. There are other ministries of love more conspicuous than hers, but none in which a gentler, lovelier spirit dwells, and none to which the heart's warm requitals more joyfully respond. There is no such thing as a

comparative estimate of a parent's affection for one
or another child. There is little which he needs to
covet, to whom the treasure of a good child has been
given. A good daughter is the steady light of her
parent's house. His idea of her is indissolubly connected with that of his happy fireside. She is the
morning sunlight, and his evening star. The grace,
and vivacity, and tenderness of her sex, have their
place in the mighty sway which she holds over his
spirit. The lessons of recorded wisdom which he
reads with her eyes come to his mind with a new
charm, as they blend with the beloved melody of her
voice. He scarcely knows weariness which her song
does not make him forget, or gloom which is proof
against the brightness of her young smile. She is the
pride and ornament of his hospitality, and the gentle
nurse of his sickness, and the constant agent in those
nameless, numberless acts of kindness which one
chiefly cares to have rendered because they are unpre-
tending but all-expressive proofs of love.

But now, turning to the daughters themselves, one
of their first duties at home is to make their mother
happy—to shun all that would pain or even perplex
her. "Always seeking the pleasure of others, always
careless of her own," is one of the finest encomiums
ever pronounced upon a daugther. True: at that
period of life when dreams are realities, and realities
seem dreams, this may be forgotten. Mothers may
find only labor and sorrow where they had a right
to expect repose; but the daughter who would make
her home and her mother happy, should learn

betimes that, next to duty to God our Savior, comes duty to her who is always the first to rejoice in our joy, and to weep when we weep. Of all the proofs of heartlessness which youth can give, the strongest is indifference to a mother's happiness or sorrow.

How large and cherished a place does a good sister's love always hold in the grateful memory of one who has been blessed with the benefits of this relation as he looks back to the home of his childhood! How many are there who, in the changes of maturer years, have found a sister's love, for themselves, and others dearer than themselves, their ready and adequate resource. With what a sense of security is confidence reposed in a good sister, and with what assurance that it will be uprightly and considerately given, is her counsel sought! How initmate is the friendship of such sisters, not widely separated in age from one another! What a reliance for warning, excitement, and sympathy has each secured in each! How many are the brothers to whom, when thrown into circumstances of temptation, the thought of a sister's love has been a constant, holy presence, rebuking every wayward thought!

The intercourse of brothers and sisters forms another important element in the happy influences of home. A boisterous or a selfish boy may try to domineer over the weaker or more dependent girl, but generally the latter exerts a softening, sweetening charm. The brother animates and heartens, the sister mollifies, tames, refines. The vine and its sustaining elm are the emblems of such a relation—and by such agencies our "sons may become like plants grown up in their youth, and our daughters like corner-stones polished after the similitude of a temple." Among Lord Byron's early miseries, the terms on which he lived with his mother helped to sour the majestic moral ruin — he was chafed and distempered thereby. The outbreaks of her passion, and the unbridled impetuosity of his, made their companionship uncongenial, and at length drove them far apart. But Byron found a compensating power in the friendship of his sister, and to her he often turned amid his wanderings, or his misantrophy and guilt, as an exile turns to his home. "A world to roam in and a home with thee," were words which embodied the feelings of his void and aching heart, when all else that is lovely appeared to have faded away. He had plunged into the pleasures of sin till he was sated, wretched, and self-consumed — the very Sardanapalus of vice. But "his sister, his sweet sister," still shone like the morning star of memory upon his dark soul.

Sisters scarcely know the influence they have over their brothers. A young man testifies that the greatest proof of the truth of the Christian religion was his sister's life. Often the simple request of a lady will keep a young man from doing wrong. We have known this to be the case very frequently; and young men have been kept from breaking the Sabbath, from drinking, from chewing, just because a lady whom they respected, and for whom they had an affection, requested it. A tract given, an invitation to go to church, a request that your friend would read the Bible daily, will often be regarded, when a more powerful appeal from other sources would fall unheeded upon the heart. Many of the gentlemen whom you meet in society are away from the influence of parents and sisters, and they will respond to any interest taken in their welfare. We all speak of a young man's danger from evil associates, and the very bad influence which his dissipated gentlemen associates have upon him. We believe it is all true that a gentleman's character is formed to a greater extent by the ladies that he associates with before he becomes a complete man of the world. We think, in other words, that a young man is pretty much what his sisters and young lady friends choose to make him. We knew a family where the sisters encouraged their young brothers to smoke, thinking it was manly, and to mingle with gay, dissipated fellows because they thought it "smart;" and they did mingle with them, body and soul, and abused the same sisters shamefully. The influence began further back than with their gentleman companions. It began with their sisters, and was carried on through the forming years of their character. On the other hand, if sisters are watchful and affectionate they may in various ways — by entering into any little plan with interest, by introducing their younger brothers into good ladies' society — lead them along till their character is formed, and then a high respect for ladies, and a manly self-respect, will keep them from mingling in low society.

Associates.

Thou art noble; yet, I see,
Thy honorable Metal may be wrought
From that it is disposed. Therefore 'tis meet
That noble Minds keep ever with their Likes:
For who so firm, that cannot be seduced?

—SHAKSPEARE.

An author is known by his writings, a mother by her daughter, a fool by his words, and all men by their companions.

Intercourse with persons of decided virtue and excellence is of great importance in the formation of a good character. The force of example is powerful; we are creatures of imitation, and, by a necessary influence, our tempers and habits are formed on the model of those with whom we familiarly associate. Better be alone than in bad company. Evil communications corrupt good manners. Ill qualities are catching as well as diseases; and the mind is at least as much, if not a great deal more, liable to infection, than the body. Go with mean people, and you think life is mean.

The human race requires to be educated, and it is doubtless true that the greater part of that education is obtained through example rather than precept. This is especially true respecting character and habits. How natural is it for a child to look up to those around him for an example of imitation, and how readily does he copy all that he sees done, good or bad. The importance of a good example on which the young may exercise this powerful and active element of their nature, is a matter of the utmost moment. To the phrenologist every faculty assumes an importance almost infinite, and perhaps none more so than that of imitation. It is a trite, but true maxim, that "a man is known by the company he keeps." He naturally assimilates, by the force of imitation, to the habits and manners of those by whom he is surrounded. We know persons, who walk much with the lame, who have learned to walk with a hitch or limp like their lame friends. Vice stalks in the streets unabashed, and children copy it. Witness the urchin seven years old trying to ape his seniors in folly, by smoking the cigar-stumps which they have cast aside. In time, when his funds improve, he will wield the long nine, and be a full-fledged "loafer." This faculty is usually more active in the young than in adult life, and serves to lead them to imitate that which their seniors do, before their reasoning powers are sufficiently developed and instructed to enable them to reason out a proper course of action. Thus by copying others, they do that which is appropriate, right or wrong, without knowing why, or the principles and consequences involved in their actions.

The awfully sad consequences of evil associations is exhibited in the history of almost all criminals. The case of a man named Brown, recently executed in Toronto, Canada, is an example. He was born in Cambridgeshire, England, of parents who were members of the Church of England; and in a sketch of

7

his life, written at his dictation, he attributes his downfall to early disobedience and to bad companions,
which led to dissipation and finally plunged him into
associations with the most dissolute and lawless characters. They led him on in transgression and sin,
which ended in his being brought to the scaffold.
On the gallows he made the following speech: "This
is a solemn day for me, boys! I hope this will be a
warning to you against bad company—I hope it will
be a lesson to all young people, and old as well as
young, rich and poor. It was that that brought me
here to-day to my last end, though I am innocent of
the murder I am about to suffer for. Before my God
I am innocent of the murder! I never committed this
or any other murder. I know nothing of it. I am
going to meet my Maker in a few minutes. May the
Lord have mercy on my soul! Amen, amen." What
a terrible warning his melancholy example affords to
young men never to deviate from the straight line of
duty. Live with the culpable and you will be very
likely to die with the criminal. Bad company is like
a nail driven into a post, which after the first or second blow, may be drawn out with little difficulty; but
being once driven in up to the head, the pinchers
cannot take hold to draw it out, which can only be
done by the destruction of the wood. You may be ever
so pure, you cannot associate with bad companions
without falling into bad odor. Evil company is like
tobacco smoke—you cannot be long in its presence
without carrying away taint of it. "Let no man
deceive himself," says Petrarch, "by thinking that the

contagions of the soul are less than those of the body. They are yet greater; they sink deeper, and come on more unsuspectedly." From impure air, we take diseases; from bad company, vice and imperfection. Avoid, as much as you can, the company of all vicious persons whatever; for no vice is alone, and all are infectious.

Men carry unconscious signs of their life about them, those that come from the forge and those from the lime and mortar, and those from dusty travel bear signs of being workmen and of their work. One needs not ask a merry face or a sad one whether it hath come from joy or from grief. Tears and laughter tell their own story. Should one come home with fruit, we say—"You have come from the orchard." If with hands full of wild flowers, "You have come from the field." If one's garments smell of mingled odors, we say, "You have walked in a garden." So with associations—those that walk with the just, the upright, have the sweetest incense that has ever anointed man. Let no man deceive himself.

Do you love the society of the vulgar? Then you are already debased in your sentiments. Do you seek to be with the profane? In your heart you are like them. Are jesters and buffoons your choice friends? He who loves to laugh at folly is himself a fool. Do you love and seek the society of the wise and good? Is this your habit? Had you rather take the lowest seat among these than the highest seat among others? Then you have already learned to be good. You may not make very much progress,

' but even a good beginning is not to be despised.
Hold on your way, and seek to be the companion of
those that fear God. So you shall be wise for yourself, and wise for eternity.

No man of position can allow himself to associate,
without prejudice, with the profane, the Sabbath-
breakers, the drunken and the licentious, for he
lowers himself, without elevating them. The sweep
is not made the less black by rubbing against the
well-dressed and the clean, while they are inevitably
defiled. Nothing elevates us so much as the presence of a spirit similar, yet superior, to our own.
What is companionship, where nothing that improves
the intellect is communicated, and where the larger
heart contracts itself to the model and dimension of
the smaller?

Washington was wont to say, "Be courteous to
all, but intimate with few, and let those few be well
tried before you give them your confidence." It
should be the aim of young men to go into good
society. We do not mean the rich, the proud and
fashionable, but the society of the wise, the intelligent
and good. Where you find men that know more
than you do, and from whose conversation one can
gain information, it is always safe to be found. It
has broken down many a man by associating with
the low and vulgar, where the ribald song and the
indecent story were introduced to excite laughter.
If you wish to be respected—if you desire happiness
and not misery, we advise you to associate with the
intelligent and good. Strive for mental excellence

and strict integrity, and you never will be found in
the sinks of pollution, and on the benches of retailers
and gamblers. Once habituate yourself to a virtuous
course — once secure a love of good society, and no
punishment would be greater than by accident to be
obliged for half a day to associate with the low and
vulgar. Try to frequent the company of your bet-
ters. In book and life it is the most wholesome
society; learn to admire rightly; that is the great
pleasure of life. Note what the great men admire —
they admire great things; narrow spirits admire
basely and worship meanly. Some persons choose
their associates as they do other useful animals, pre-
ferring those from whom they expect the most service. Procure no friends in haste, nor, if once secured,
in haste abandon them. Be slow in choosing an
associate and slower to change him; slight no man
for poverty, nor esteem any one for his wealth.
Good friends should not be easily forgotten, nor
used as suits of apparel, which, when we have worn
them threadbare, we cast off and call for new. When
once you profess yourself a friend, endeavor to be
always such. He can never have any true friends,
that will be often changing them. Whoever moves
you to part with a true and tried friend, has certainly
a design to make way for a treacherous enemy. To
part with a tried friend without very great provocation,
is unreasonable levity. Nothing but plain malevo-
lence can justify disunion. The loss of a friend is
like that of a limb; time may heal the anguish of the
wound, but the loss cannot be repaired.

When you have once found your proper associate, then stick to him—make him your friend—a close friend; do all you can to improve him and learn all you can of him; let his good qualities become yours; one is not bound to bear a part in the follies of a friend, but rather to dissuade him from them; even though he cannot consent to tell him plainly, as Phocion did Antipater, who said to him, "I cannot be both your friend and flatterer." It is a good rule always to back your friends and face your enemies. Whoever would reclaim his friend, and bring him to a true and perfect understanding of himself, may privately admonish, but never publicly reprehend him. An open admonition is an open disgrace.

Have the courage to cut the most agreeable acquaintance you have, when you are convinced he lacks principle; a friend should bear with a friend's infirmities, but not with his vices. He that does a base thing in zeal for his friend, burns the golden thread that ties their hearts together.

If you have once chosen the proper person as an associate and a friend, then you have a friend for life-time, and you will always cherish and honor him; but the neglected child, the reckless youth, the wrecked and wretched man will haunt you with memories of melancholy, with grief and despair. How we will curse those associates that dragged us down to ruin and destruction, and how love to repeat the names of old friends.

"Old friends!" What a multitude of deep and varied emotions are called forth from the soul by the utterance of these two words. What thronging memories of other days crowd the brain when they are spoken. Ah, there is a magic in the sound and the spell which it creates is both sad and pleasing. As we sit by our fireside, while the winds are making wild melody without the walls of our cottage, and review the scenes of by-gone years which flit before us in swift succession, dim and shadowy as the recollections of a dream — how those "old familiar faces" will rise up and haunt our vision with their well remembered features. But ah, where are they? those friends of our youth — those kindred spirits who shared our joy and sorrows when first we started in the pilgrimage of life. Companions of our early days, they are endeared to us by many a tie, and we now look back through the vista of years upon the hours of our communion, as upon green oases in a sandy waste. Years have passed over us with their buds and flowers, their fruits and snows; and where now are those "old familiar faces?" They are scattered, and over many of their last narrow homes the thistle waves its lonely head; "after life's fitful fever they sleep well." Some are buffeting the billows of time's stormy sea in distant lands; though they are absent our thoughts are often with them.

Influence.

Away up among the Alleghanies there is a spring so small that a single ox on a summer's day could

drain it dry. It steals its unobtrusive way among the
hills, till it spreads out into the beautiful Ohio.
Thence it stretches away a thousand miles, leaving
on its banks more than a hundred villages and cities
and many a cultivated farm; then joining the Missis-
sippi, it stretches away some twelve hundred miles
more, till it falls into the emblem of eternity. It is
one of the greatest tributaries to the ocean, which
obedient only to God, shall roar till the angel with one
foot on the sea and the other on the land, shall aver
that time shall be no longer. So with moral influence.
It is a rill—a rivulet—an ocean, and as boundless
and fathomless as eternity.

"The stone, flung from my careless hand into the
lake, splashed down into the depths of the flowing
water, and that was all. No, it was not all. Look at
those concentric rings, rolling their tiny ripples among
the sedgy reeds, dippling the overhanging boughs of
yonder willow, and producing an influence, slight but
conscious, to the very shores of the lake itself. That
stray word, that word of pride or scorn, flung from
my lips in casual company, produces a momentary
depression, and that is all. No, it is not all. It
deepened that man's disgust at godliness, and it sharpened the edge of that man's sarcasm, and it shamed
that half-converted one out of his penitent misgivings,
and it produced an influence, slight, but eternal, on
the destiny of a human life. Oh, it is a terrible power
that I have—this power of influence—and it clings
to me. I cannot shake it off. It is born with me; it
has grown with my growth, and is strengthened with

my strength. It speaks, it walks, it moves; it is powerful in every look of my eye, in every word of my lips, in every act of my life. I cannot live to myself. I must either be a light to illumine, or a tempest to destroy. I must either be an Abel, who, by his immortal righteousness, being dead yet speaketh, or an Achan, the sad continuance of whose otherwise forgotten name is the proof that man perishes not alone in his iniquity. Dear reader, this necessary element of power belongs to you. The sphere may be contracted, thine influence may be small, but a sphere and influence you surely have."

Every human being is a centre of influence for good or for ill. No man can live unto himself. The meshes of a net are not more surely knit together than man to man. We may forget this secret, silent influence. But we are exerting it by our deeds, we are exerting it by our words, we are exerting it by our very thoughts—and he is wise with a wisdom more than that of earth who seeks to put forth the highest power for good, be his home a hut or a hall, a cabin or a palace.

Habit.

HABIT in a child is at first like a spider's web; if neglected it becomes a thread of twine; next, a cord of rope; finally, a cable—then who can break it? There are habits contracted by bad example, or bad management, before we have judgment to discern their approaches, or because the eye of reason is laid asleep, or has not compass of view sufficient to look around on every quarter.

Oh, the tyranny, the despotism of a bad habit! Coleridge, one of the subtlest intellects and finest poets of his time, battled for twenty years before he could emancipate himself from his tyrant, opium. He went into voluntary imprisonment. He hired a man to watch him day and night, and keep him by force from tasting the pernicious drug. He formed resolution after resolution. Yet, during all the best years of his life, he wasted his substance and his health, neglected his family and lived degraded and accursed because he had not resolution to abstain. He would lay plans to cheat the very man whom he paid to keep the drug from him, and bribe the jailer to whom he had voluntarily surrendered himself.

Terrible, *terrible* is the despotism of a bad habit. The case of Coleridge is an extreme one, of course. But there are many, whose eyes these lines will meet, who are as truly the slaves of a perverted appetite as he. Their despot may be opium, tobacco, drink, or worse; but they are so completely under the *dominion* of their master, that nothing short of a moral war of independence, which should task all their own strength, and all they could borrow from others, would suffice to deliver them.

John B. Gough uses the following as a powerful illustration: I remember once riding from Buffalo to Niagara Falls. I said to a gentleman, "What river is that, sir?"

"That," he said, "is Niagara river."

"Well, it is a beautiful stream," said I; "bright and fair and glassy. How far off are the rapids?"

"Only a mile or two," was the reply.

"Is it possible that only a mile from us we shall find the water in the turbulence which it must show near to the falls?"

"You will find it so, sir." And so I found it; and the first sight of Niagara I shall never forget. Now, launch your bark on that Niagara river; it is bright, smooth, beautiful and glassy. There is a ripple at the bow; the silver wave you leave behind adds to the enjoyment. Down the stream you glide, oars, sails and helm in proper trim, and you set out on your pleasure excursion. Suddenly some one cries out from the bank, "Young men, ahoy!"

"What is it?"

"The rapids are below you!"

"Ha! ha! we have heard of the rapids, but we are not such fools as to get there. If we go too fast, then we shall up with the helm, and steer to the shore; we will set the mast in the socket, hoist the sail, and speed to the land. Then on, boys; don't be alarmed—there is no danger."

"Young men, ahoy there!"

"What is it?"

"The rapids are below you!"

"Ha! ha! we will laugh and quaff, all things delight us. What care we for the future! No man ever saw it. Sufficient for the day is the evil thereof. We will enjoy life while we may; will catch pleasure

as it flies. This is enjoyment; time enough to steer
out of danger when we are sailing swiftly with the
current."

"Young men, ahoy!"

"What is it?"

"Beware! Beware! The rapids are below you!"

Now you see the water foaming all around. See
how fast you pass that point! Up with the helm!
Now turn! Pull hard! quick! quick! quick! pull for
your lives! pull till the blood starts from the nostrils,
and the veins stand like whip-cords upon the brow!
Set the mast in the socket! hoist the sail!—ah! ah!
it is too late! Shrieking, cursing, howling, blasphem-
ing, over they go.

Thousands go over the rapids every year, through
the power of habit, crying all the while, "When
I find out that it is injuring me I will give it up!"

Few people form habits of wrong-doing deliberately or willfully; they glide into them by degrees
and almost unconsciously, and before they are aware
of danger, the habits are confirmed and require resolute and persistent effort to effect a change. "Resist
beginning," was the maxim of the ancients, and
should be preserved as a landmark in our day. Those
who are prodigal or passionate, or indolent, or visionary, soon make shipwreck of themselves, and drift
about the sea of life, the prey of every wind and
current, vainly shrieking for help, till at last they
drift away into darkness and death.

Take care that you are not drifting. See that you
have fast hold of the helm. The breakers of life

forever roar under the lee, and adverse gales continually blow on the shore. Are you watching how she heads? Do you keep a firm grip of the wheel? If you give way but for one moment you may drift hopelessly into the boiling vortex. Young men, take care! It rests with yourselves alone under God, whether you reach port triumphantly or drift to ruin.

Be not slow in the breaking of a sinful custom; a quick, courageous resolution is better than a gradual deliberation; in such a combat, he is the bravest soldier who lays about him without fear or wit. Wit pleads, fear disheartens; he that would kill hydra, had better strike off one neck than five heads; fell the tree, and the branches are soon cut off.

Whatever be the cause, says Lord Kames, it is an established fact, that we are much influenced by custom; it hath an effect upon our pleasures, upon our actions, and even upon our thoughts and sentiments. Habit makes no figure during the vivacity of youth; in middle age it gains ground; and in old age, governs without control. In that period of life, generally speaking, we eat at a certain hour, take exercise at a certain hour, go to rest at a certain hour, all by the direction of habit; nay, a particular seat, table, bed, comes to be essential; and a habit in any of these cannot be contradicted without uneasiness.

Man, it has been said, is a bundle of habits; and habit is second nature. Metastasio entertained so strong an opinion as to the power of repetition in act and thought, that he said, "All is habit in mankind, even virtue itself."

Evil habits must be conquered, or they will conquer us and destroy our peace and happiness.

Vicious habits are so great a stain upon human nature, said Cicero, and so odious in themselves, that every person actuated by right reason would avoid them, though he was sure they would always be concealed both from God and man, and had no future punishment entailed upon them.

Vicious habits, when opposed, offer the most vigorous resistance on the first attack. At each successive encounter this resistance grows fainter and fainter, until finally it ceases altogether and the victory is achieved.

Habit is man's best friend or worst enemy; it can exalt him to the highest pinnacle of virtue, honor and happiness, or sink him to the lowest depths of vice, shame and misery.

We may form habits of honesty, or knavery; truth, or falsehood; of industry, or idleness; frugality, or extravagance; of patience, or impatience; self-denial, or self-indulgence; of kindness, cruelty, politeness, rudeness, prudence, perseverance, circumspection. In short, there is not a virtue, nor a vice, not an act of body, nor of mind, to which we may not be chained down by this despotic power.

It is a great point for young men to begin well; for it is in the beginning of life that that system of conduct is adopted which soon assumes the force of habit. Begin well, and the habit of doing well will become quite as easy as the habit of doing badly. Pitch upon that course of life which is the most excellent, and habit will render it the most delightful. Well begun is half ended, says the proverb; and a good beginning is half the battle. Many promising young men have irretrievably injured themselves by a first false step at the commencement of life; while others, of much less promising talents, have succeeded simply by beginning well, and going onward. The good practical beginning is, to a certain extent, a pledge, a promise, and an assurance, of the ultimate prosperous issue. There is many a poor creature, now crawling through life, miserable himself and the cause of sorrow to others, who might have lifted up his head and prospered, if, instead of merely satisfying himself with resolutions of well-doing, he had actually gone to work and made a good practical beginning.

Company.

Congenial passions souls together bind,
And every calling mingles with its kind;
Soldier unites with soldier, swain with swain,
The mariner with him that roves the main.

·F. LEWIS.

THAT we may be known by the company we frequent, has become proverbial. For, when unrestrained, we are prone to choose and associate with those whose manners and dispositions are agreeable and congenial to ours. Hence, when we find persons frequenting any company whatsoever, we are disposed to believe that such company is congenial with their feelings, not only in regard to their intellectual capacities and accomplishments, but also their moral disposition and their particular manner in life.

Good company not only improves our manners, but also our minds; for intelligent associates will become a source of enjoyment, as well as of edification. If they be pious they will improve our morals; if they be polite they will tend to improve our manners; if they be learned they will add to our knowledge and correct our errors. On the other hand, if they be immoral, ignorant, vulgar, their impress will most surely be left upon us. It therefore becomes a matter of no trivial concern to select and associate with proper company, while avoiding that which is certainly prejudicial.

We should always seek the company of those who are known to possess superior merit and natural endowments; for then, by being assimilated in manners and disposition, we rise. Whereas, by associating with those who are our inferiors in every respect, we become assimilated with them, and by that assimilation become degraded. Upon the whole much care and judgment are necessary in selecting properly that company which will be profitable. Yet this is not a point of so great interest among women as men; because they are not necessarily thrown into associations of such diversity of character as the latter. Nevertheless, the greater care and prudence are requisite to women, should they happen in such circles, to avoid the pernicious influence of such associations, to which many are too prone to yield.

Good company is that which is composed of intelligent and well-bred persons; whose language is chaste and good; whose sentiments are pure and edifying; whose deportment is such as pure and well-regulated education and correct morals dictate; and whose conduct is directed and restrained by the pure precepts of religion.

When we have the advantage of such company, it should be the object of our zeal "to imitate their real perfections; copy their politeness, their carriage, their address, and the easy well-bred turn of their conversation; but we should remember that, let them shine ever so bright, their vices (if they have any) are so many blemishes, which we should no more endeavor to imitate than we should make artificial warts on our faces because some very handsome lady happened to have one by nature. We should, on the contrary, think how much handsomer she would have been without it."

What can be more pleasing and more angelic than a young lady, virtuous and adorned with the graces and elegances of finished politeness based upon a sound intellect, and well improved mind!

"For her inconstant man might cease to range,
And gratitude forbid desire to change."

The reflection is pleasing, that it is in the power of all to acquire an elegance of manner, although they may be deprived of the advantages to be derived from a liberal education. At least they may attain to that degree of elegance and manners, by judicious selection of company, that will render them pleasing in any social circle, whether at home or abroad. This will excite interest, which will grow into respect; from which always springs that pure, ardent, and affectionate attachment which alone forms the only generous and indissoluble connection between the sexes; that which the lapse of time serves only to confirm, and nought but death can destroy.

If so much importance be attached to the prudent selection of company and associates, and if this be of such vital interest to every young female, how careful should she be not to take to her bosom for life a companion of dissolute habits and morals. Such an act might destroy all the domestic felicity she might have hoped to enjoy, and be a source of constant sorrow to her through life.

> "Oh shun, my friend, avoid that dangerous coast
> Where peace expires, and fair affection's lost."

For no connection or friendship can be fond and lasting, where a conformity of inclination and disposition does not exist; but where this exists, all passions and finer feelings of the soul gently harmonize, and form one common and lasting interest.

Force of Character.

WHAT you can effect depends on what you are. You put your whole self into all that you do. If that self be small, and lean, and mean, your entire life-work is paltry, your words have no force, your influence has no weight. If that self be true and high, pure and kind, vigorous and forceful, your strokes are blows, your notes staccatos, your work massive, your influence cogent — you can do what you will. Whatever your position, you are a power, you are felt as a kingly spirit, you are as one having authority. Too many think of character chiefly in its relation to the life beyond the grave. We certainly would not have less thought of it with reference to that unknown future, on the margin of which some of us undoubtedly are at this moment standing; but we do wish that more consideration were bestowed upon its earthly uses. We would have young men, as they start in life, regard character as a capital, much surer to yield full returns than any other capital, unaffected by panics and failures, fruitful when all other investments lie dormant, having as certain promise in the present life as in that which is to come.

Franklin, also, attributed his success as a public man, not to his talents or his powers of speaking — for these were but moderate — but to his known integrity of character. "Hence, it was," he says, "that I had so much weight with my fellow-citizens. I was but a bad speaker, never eloquent, subject to much hesitation in my choice of words, hardly correct in language, and yet I generally carried my point." Character creates confidence in men in every station of life. It was said of the first Emperor Alexander of Russia that his personal character was equivalent to a constitution. During the wars of the Fronde,

Montaigne was the only man among the French gentry who kept his castle gates unbarred; and it was said of him, that his personal character was worth more to him than a regiment of horse.

There are trying and perilous circumstances in life, which show how valuable and important a good character is. It is a sure and strong staff of support, when everything else fails. It is the Acropolis which remains impregnable, imparting security and peace when all the other defenses have been surrendered to the enemy. The higher walks of life are treacherous and dangerous; the lower full of obstacles and impediments. We can only be secure in either, by maintaining those principles which are just, praiseworthy, and pure, and which inspire bravery in ourselves and confidence in others.

Truthfulness, integrity and goodness—qualities that hang not on any man's breath—from the essence of manly character, or, as one of our old writers has it, "that inbred loyalty unto virtue which can serve her without a livery." He who possesses these qualities, united with strength of purpose, carries with him a power which is irresistible. He is strong to do good, he is strong to resist evil, and strong to bear up under difficulty and misfortune. When Stephen of Coloma fell into the hands of his base assailants, and they asked him, in derision, "Where is now your fortress?" "Here," was his bold reply, placing his hand upon his heart. It is in misfortune that the character of the upright man shines forth with the greatest lustre; and, when all else fails, he takes stand upon his integrity and his courage. In the famous pass of Thermopylæ, the three hundred Spartans withstood the enemy with such vigor that they were obliged to retire wearied and conquered during three successive days, till, suddenly falling upon their rear, they crushed the brave defenders to pieces.

Strength of character consists of two things—power of will and power of self-restraint. It requires two things, therefore, for its existence—strong feelings and strong command 'over them. Now, it is here we make a great mistake; we mistake strong feelings for strong character. A man who bears all before him, before whose frown domestics tremble, and whose bursts of fury make the children of the household quake—because he has his will obeyed, and his own way in all things, we call him a strong man. The truth is, that is the weak man; it is his passions that are strong; he, mastered by them, is weak. You must measure the strength of a man by the power of the feelings he subdues, not by the power of those which subdue him. And hence composure is very often the highest result of strength.

Did we never see a man receive a flagrant insult and only grow a little pale, and then reply quietly? This is a man spiritually strong. Or did we never see a man in anguish, stand, as if carved out of solid rock, mastering himself? Or one bearing a hopeless daily trial remain silent and never tell the world what cankered his home peace? That is strength. He who, with strong passions, remains chaste; he who,

keenly sensitive, with manly powers of indignation
in him, can be provoked, and yet restrain himself
and forgive—these are the strong men, the spiritual
heroes.

The truest criterion of a man's character and conduct, is, invariably, to be found in the opinion of his
nearest relations, who having daily and hourly opportunities of forming a judgment of him, will not fail in
doing so. It is a far higher testimony in his favor,
for him to secure the esteem and love of a few individuals within the privacy of his own home, than the
good opinion of hundreds in his immediate neighborhood, or that of ten times the number residing at a
distance. The most trifling actions that affect a man's
credit are to be regarded. The sound of your hammer at five in the morning, or nine at night, heard
by a creditor, makes him easy six months longer; but
if he sees you at a billiard table, or hears your voice
at a tavern, when you should be at work, he sends
for his money the next day.

Deportment, honesty, caution, and a desire to do
right carried out in practice, are to human character
what truth, reverence, and love are to religion. They
are the unvaried elements of a good reputation. Such
virtues can never be reproached, although the vulgar
and despicable may scoff at them; but it is not so
much in their affected revulsion at them, as it is in the
wish to reduce them to the standard of their own degraded natures, and vitiated passions. Let such
scoff and sneer — let them laugh and ridicule as much
as they may — a strict, upright, onward course will

evince to the world and to them, that there is more manly independence in one forgiving smile, than in all the pretended exceptions to worthiness in the society of the mean and vulgar. Virtue must have its admirers, and firmness of principle, both moral and religious, will ever command the proudest encomium of the intelligent world, to the exclusion of every other thing connected with human existence.

That character is power is true in a much higher sense than that knowledge is power. Mind without heart, intelligence without conduct, cleverness without goodness, are powers in their way, but they may be powers only for mischief. We may be instructed or amused by them, but it is sometimes as difficult to admire them as it would be to admire the dexterity of a pickpocket or the horsemanship of a highwayman.

Integrity.

YOUNG men look about them and see a great measure of worldly success awarded to men without principle. They see the trickster crowned with public honors, they see the swindler rolling in wealth, they see the sharp man, the over-reaching man, the unprincipled man, the liar, the demagogue, the time-server, the trimmer, the scoundrel who cunningly manages, though constantly disobeying moral law and trampling upon social courtesy, to keep himself out of the clutches of the legal police, carrying off

the prizes of wealth and place. All this is a demoralizing puzzle and a fearful temptation; and multitudes
of young men are not strong enough to stand before
it. They ought to understand that in this wicked
world there is a great deal of room where there is
integrity. Great trusts may be sought by scoundrels,
but great trusts never seek them; and perfect integrity
is at a premium even among scoundrels. There are
some trusts that they will never confer on each other.
There are occasions where they need the services of
true men, and they do not find them in shoals and in
the mud, but alone and in pure water.

Integrity is the foundation of all that is high in
character among mankind; other qualities may add to
its splendor, but if this essential requisite be wanting
all their lustre fades. Our integrity is never worth
so much to us as when we have lost everything to
keep it. Integrity without knowledge is weak;
knowledge without integrity is dangerous and dreadful. Integrity, however rough, is better than smooth
dissimulation. Let a man have the reputation of
being fair and upright in his dealings, and he will
possess the confidence of all who know him. Without
these qualities every other merit will prove unavailing. Ask concerning a man, "Is he active and
capable?" Yes. "Industrious, temperate, and regular
in his habits?" O, yes, "Is he honest? is he
trustworthy?" Why, as to that, I am sorry to say that
he is not to be trusted; he wants watching; he is a
little tricky, and will take an undue advantage, if he
can. "Then I will have nothing to do with him,"

will be the invariable reply. Why, then, is honesty
the best policy? Because, without it you will get a
bad name, and everybody will shun you.

The world is always asking for men who are not for
sale; men who are honest, sound from centre to circumference, true to the heart's core; men who will condemn
wrong in friend or foe, in themselves as well as others;
men whose consciences are as steady as the needle to
the pole; men who will stand for the right if the
heavens totter and the earth reels; men who can tell
the truth, and look the world and the devil right in
the eye; men who neither brag nor run; men who
neither flag nor flinch; men who can have courage
without shouting to it; men in whom the courage of
everlasting life runs still, deep, and strong; men who
do not cry, nor cause their voices to be heard on the
streets, who will not fail nor be discouraged till judgment be set in the earth; men who know their message
and tell it; men who know their places and fill them;
men who know their own business; men who will not
lie; men who are not too lazy to work, not too proud
to be poor; men who are willing to eat what they
have earned, and wear what they have paid for. It is
always safe to trust those who can trust themselves,
but when a man suspects his own integrity, it is time
he was suspected by others. Moral degradation always
begins at home. Honesty is never gained or lost
suddenly, or by accident. Moral strength or moral
weakness takes possession of us by slow and imperceptible degrees.

Avoid—and young men especially—avoid all base,

servile, underhand, sneaking ways. Part with anything rather than your integrity and conscious rectitude; flee from injustice as you would from a viper's
fangs; avoid a lie as you would the gates of hell.
Some there are who are callous as to this. Some
there are who, in stooping to mercantile dishonor and
business—in driving the immoral bargain—think
they have done a clever action. Things are often
called by their wrong names; duplicity is called
shrewdness, and wrong-heartedness is called long-
headedness; evil is called good, and good evil, and
darkness is put for light, and light for darkness.
Well! be it so. You may be prosperous in your own
eyes; you may have realized an envied fortune; you
may have your carriage, and plate, and servants, and
pageantry; but rather the shielding and the crust of
bread with a good conscience, than the stately dwelling or palace without it. Rather than the marble
mausoleum, which gilds and smothers tales of heartless villainy and fraud—rather, far rather, that lowly
heap of grass we were wont often to gaze upon in an
old village churchyard, with the simple record of a
cotter's virtues: *"Here lies an honest man!"* There
is nothing more sad than to be carried like a vessel
away from the straight course of principle; to be left
a stranded outcast thing on the sands of dishonor:
a man bolstering himself up in a position he is not
entitled to. "That is a man of *capital*," says the
world, pointing to an unscrupulous and successful
swindler. Capital! What is capital? Is it what a
man *has?* Is it counted by pounds and pence, stocks

and shares, by houses and lands? No! capital is not what a man *has*, but what a man *is*. Character is capital; honor is capital. That is the most fearful of ruin when *character* is gone, when integrity is sold, when honor is bartered for a miserable mess of earthly pottage. God save us from ruin like this! Perish what may; perish gold, silver, houses, lands; let the winds of misfortune dash our vessel on the sunken rock, but let *integrity* be like the valued keepsake which the sailor boy lashed with the rope round his body, the only thing we care to save. Let one die; but let angels read, if friends cannot afford to erect the grave stone: "*Here lies an honest man.*"

Poor Boys and Great Eminence.

MANY men have been obscure in their origin and birth, but great and glorious in life and death. They have been born and nurtured in villages, but have reigned and triumphed in cities. They were first laid in the mangers of poverty and obscurity, but have afterwards become possessors of thrones and palaces. Their fame is like the pinnacle which ascends higher and higher, until at last it becomes a most conspicuous and towering object of attraction.

Columbus was the son of a weaver, and a weaver himself. Cervantes was a common soldier. Homer was the son of a small farmer. Moliere was the son of a tapestry maker. Demosthenes was the son of a cutler. Terrence was a slave. Oliver Cromwell was the son of a London brewer. Howard was an apprentice to a grocer. Franklin was the son of a tallow-chandler and soap boiler. Dr. Thomas, Bishop of Worcester, was the son of a linen-draper. Daniel Defoe, was a hostler and son of a butcher. Whitfield was the son of an inn-keeper. Virgil was the son of a porter. Horace was the son of a shop keeper. Shakspeare was the son of a wood stapler. Milton was the son of a money scrivener. Robert Burns was a plowman in Ayrshire. Mohammed, called the prophet, was a driver of asses. Madame Bernadotte was a washerwoman of Paris. Napoleon was of an obscure family of Corsica. John Jacob Astor once sold apples on the streets of New York. Catherine, Empress of Russia, was a camp-follower. Cincinnatus was plowing in his vineyard when the dictatorship of Rome was offered him. Elihu Burritt was a blacksmith. Daniel Webster, while young, worked on a farm. Henry Clay was "the mill-boy of the slashes."

The young man who thinks of taking a short cut to fortune, should deliberately write down the names of a dozen of our richest men, and he will find that the largest part of the wealth of the Astors and Browns and Stewarts and Vanderbilts was accumulated after they had passed their fiftieth year.

"Without fame or fortune at forty, without fame or fortune always" is the sentiment of many, oftener expressed by the saying, that if a man is not rich at forty, he never will be. It was after forty that Sir

Walter Scott became the great unknown; it was after forty that Palmerston was found to be England's greatest prime minister of the century. At that age, many who now appear prominently in our political history were obscure citizens. Howe, of the sewing-machine, was utterly destitute at thirty-five, a millionaire six years later.

A long time ago, a little boy, twelve years old, on his road to Vermont, stopped at a country tavern, and paid for his lodging and breakfast by sawing wood, instead of asking for food as a gift. Fifty years later, the same boy passed that same little inn as George Peabody, the banker, whose name is the synonym of magnificent charities—the honored of two hemispheres. He was born poor in Danvers, Mass., and by beginning right and pursuing a course of strict honesty, integrity, industry, activity and Christian benevolence, he has been able to amass great wealth. Some years since he made a generous gift to his native town; and also remembered the city of Baltimore, Maryland, where he long resided, by a liberal donation. For nearly twenty-five years, having done business in London, and being past sixty years old, he had given £150,000—nearly $750,000—to be devoted to the benefit of the poor of that city.

When Cornelius Vanderbilt was a young man, his mother gave him fifty dollars of her savings to buy a small sail-boat, and he engaged in the business of transporting market-gardening from Staten Island to New York city. When the wind was not favorable he would work his way over the shoals by pushing the boat along by poles, putting his own shoulder to the pole, and was very sure to get his freight to market in season. This energy gave him always a command of full freights, and he accumulated money. After awhile he began to build and run steamboats, and he died worth more than eighty-five millions of dollars.

Mr. Tobin, formerly President of the Hudson River Railroad Company, is a millionaire. He is not yet forty years of age. He began life as a steamboat clerk with Commodore Vanderbilt. When he took his position the Commodore gave him two orders: first, to collect fare of everybody and have no dead-heads on the boat; second, to start the boat on time, and wait for nobody. The Commodore then lived at Staten Island. Tobin obeyed his orders so literally that he collected fare of the Commodore the first evening, and left him on the wharf the next morning, as the boat could not wait. The Commodore was coming down the wharf leisurely, and supposed, of course, the boat would wait for him. He proved a man after Vanderbilt's own heart. He became his confidential clerk and broker, bought and sold Harlem and made for himself a fortune.

Stephen Girard left his native country at the age of ten or twelve years, as a cabin boy on a vessel. He came to New York in that capacity. His deportment was distinguished by such fidelity, industry and temperance, that he won the attachment and confidence of his master, who generally bestowed upon him the appellation of "my Stephen." When his master gave up business he promoted Girard to the command of a small vessel. Girard was a self-taught man, and the world was his school. It was a favorite theme with him, when he afterwards grew rich, to relate that he commenced life with a sixpence, and to insist that a man's best capital was his industry. All professions and all occupations, which afforded a just reward for labor, were alike honorable in his estimation. He was never too proud to work.

In the time of the yellow fever, in 1793, when consternation had seized the whole population of the city of Philadelphia, Stephen Girard, then a rich merchant, offered his services as a nurse in the hospital. His offers were accepted, and in the performance of the most loathsome duties, he walked unharmed in the midst of the pestilence. He used to say to his friends, "When you are sick, if anything ails you, do not go to a doctor, but come to me, I will cure you."

Far back in the teens of the present century, a young man asked for employment in the Springfield armory; but he was poor and modest, and had no friends, so he went away without it; but, feeling the man within him, he sought work until he found it. An age later, he visited that armory a second time, not as a common day-laborer, but as the ablest speaker of the House of Representatives, and for many years Governor of Massachusetts.

Of P. R. Spencer, the author of the Spencerian system of penmanship, it is said that, "the smooth sand beach of Lake Erie constituted the foolscap in and on which, for want of other material, he perfected essentially the system which meets such general favor in our common and commercial schools, and in our business and literary circles." When we reflect upon the immense popularity of his system, which, passing beyond the limits of our own country, has been re-engraved in England, is used in the model counting rooms of London, Liverpool and Manchester, and is also the adopted system of the English Department of the University of Zurich, in Switzerland, we must accord to its honored author chaste and elevated powers of conception, with bold and tireless grasp, of just apprehension, and agree that the barefooted boy of fifty years ago *must have been thinking,* and thinking *aright,* and thinking with *no ordinary* mind, when he gave to his coinings in the sands such vitality of science that the world has adopted and embalmed them as the most beautiful imagery of "the art."

Masons and bricklayers can boast of Ben Jonson, who worked at the building of Lincoln's Inn with a trowel in his hand and a book in his pocket; Edwards and Telford, the engineers; Hugh Miller, the geologist, and Allen Cunningham, the writer and sculptor. John Hunter, the physiologist, Ronevey and Opie, the painters, Professor Lee, the orientalist, and John Gibbons, the sculptor, were carpenters. Wilson, the ornithologist, Dr. Livingstone, the missonary traveler, and Tannahill, the poet, were weavers. Samuel Drew, the essayist, and Gifford, the editor of the "Quarterly Review," were shoemakers. Admiral Hobson, one of the gallantest of British seaman, was originally a tailor.

It is not good for human nature to have the road of life made too easy. Better to be under the necessity of working hard and faring meanly, than to have everything done ready to our hand, and a pillow of down to repose upon. Indeed, to start in life with comparatively small means seems so necessary as a stimulus to work, that it may almost be set down as one of the essential conditions to success in life. Hence, an eminent judge, when asked what contributed most to success at the bar, replied, "Some succeed by great talent, some by high connections, some by miracle, but the majority by commencing without a shilling." So it is a common saying that the men who are most successful in business are those who begin the world in their shirt sleeves; whereas, those who begin with fortunes generally lose them. Necessity is always the first stimulus to industry, and those who conduct it with prudence, perseverence and energy will rarely fail. Viewed in this light, the necessity of labor is not a chastisement, but a blessing — the very root and spring of all that we call progress in individuals, and civilization in nations. It may, indeed, be questioned whether a heavier curse could be imposed on man than the complete gratification of all his wishes without effort on his part, leaving nothing for his hopes, desires or struggles. The feeling that life is destitute of any motive or necessity for action, must be, of all others, the most distressing and the most insupportable to a rational being.

9

Occupation.

THE man who has no occupation is in a bad plight.
If he is poor, want is ever and anon pinching him;
if he is rich, enui is a more relentless tormentor than
want. An unoccupied man cannot be happy — nor
can one who is improperly occupied. We have
swarms of idlers among us, the worst of whom are
gentlemen idlers; that is, men who pursue no useful
occupation, and sponge their way, often enjoying
the luxuries of life, living upon the hard earnings
of others — the cancers of community — pseudo patterns of bipeds — leeches on the body politic.

In this widespread and expanding country, no one
need be without some useful occupation. All trades
and professions are open, from the honest hod-carrier, up to the highest place in the agricultural, commercial and mechanical departments, and from the
humblest, but not least useful teacher of A, B, C, up
to the pinnacle of professional fame. Those occupations that require manual labor are the surest, most
healthy, and most independent.

Men or women with no business, nothing to do, are
an absolute pest to society. They are thieves, stealing that which is not theirs; beggars, eating that
which they have not earned; drones, wasting the
fruits of others' industry; leeches, sucking the blood of
others; evil-doers, setting an example of idleness and
dishonest living; hypocrites, shining in stolen and

false colors; vampires, eating out the life of the community. Frown upon them, O youth, Learn in your heart to despise their course of life.

Many of our most interesting youth waste a great portion of their early life in fruitless endeavors at nothing. They have no trade, no profession, no object before them, nothing to do; and yet have a great desire to do something, and something worthy of themselves. They try this and that, and the other; offer themselves to do anything, and everything, and yet know how to do nothing. Educate themselves, they cannot, for they know not what they should do it for. They waste their time, energies, and little earnings in endless changes and wanderings. They have not the stimulus of a fixed object to fasten their attention and awaken their energies; not a known prize to win. They wish for good things, but have no way to attain them; desire to be useful, but little means for being so. They lay plans, invent schemes, form theories, build castles, but never stop to execute and realize them. Poor creatures! All that ails them is the want of an object — a *single object*. They look at a hundred things, and see nothing. If they should look steadily at one, they would see it distinctly. They grasp at random at a hundred things and catch nothing. It is like shooting among a scattered flock of pigeons. The chances are doubtful. This will never do — no, never. Success, respectability, and happiness are found in a permanent business. An early choice of some business, devotion to it, and preparation for it, should be made by every youth.

When the two objects, business and character, as
the great end of life, are fairly before a youth, what
then? Why, he must attain those objects. Will
wishes and prayers bring them into his hands? By
no means. He must work as well as wish, labor as
well as pray. His hand must be as stout as his
heart, his arm as strong as his head. Purpose must
be followed by action. The choosing of an occupation, however, is not a small thing; great mistakes
are made and often the most worthy pursuits are left.
The young man who leaves the farm-field for the merchant's desk, or the lawyer's or doctor's office, thinking to dignify or ennoble his toil, makes a sad mistake. He passes by that step from independence to
vassalage. He barters a natural for an artificial pursuit; and he must be the slave of the caprice of cus
tomers, and the chicane of trade, either to suppor:
himself or to acquire a fortune. The more artificial a
man's pursuit, the more debasing is it, morally and
physically. To test it, contrast the merchant's clerk
with the plow-boy. The former may have the most
exterior polish, but the latter, under his rough outside, possesses the true stamina. He is the freer,
franker, happier, and nobler man. Would that young
men might judge of the dignity of labor by its usefulness, rather than by the superficial glosses it wears.
Therefore, we never see a man's nobility in his kid
gloves and toilet adornments, but in that sinewy arm,
whose outlines, browned by the sun, betoken a hardy,
honest toil, under whose farmer's or mechanic's vest
the kingliest heart may beat.

Above all, the notion that the "three black graces,"
Law, Medicine and Ministry, must be worshiped by
the candidate for respectability and honor, has done
incalculable damage to society. It has spoiled many
a good carpenter, done injustice to the sledge and the
anvil, cheated the goose and the shears out of their
rights, and committed fraud on the corn and the
potato field. Thousands have died of broken hearts
in these professions — thousands who might have
been happy at the plow, or opulent behind the coun-
ter; thousands, dispirited and hopeless, look upon
the healthful and independent calling of the farmer
with envy and chagrin; and thousands more, by a
worse fate still, are reduced to necessities which
degrade them in their own estimation, rendering the
most brilliant success but a wretched compensation
for the humilation with which it is accompanied, and
compelling them to grind out of the miseries of their
fellow men the livelihood which is denied to their
legitimate exertions. The result of all this is, that
the world is full of men who, disgusted with their
vocations, getting their living by their weakness
instead of by their strength, are doomed to hopeless
inferiority. "If you choose to represent the various
parts in life," says Sydney Smith, "by holes in a table
of different shapes — some circular, some triangular,
some square, some oblong — and the persons acting
these parts by bits of wood of similar shapes, we
shall generally find that the triangular person has got
into the square hole, the oblong into the triangular,
while the square person has squeezed himself into the

round hole." A French writer on agriculture observes that it is impossible profitably to improve land
by trying forcibly to change its natural character — as
by bringing sand to clay, or clay to sand.   The only
true method is to adapt the cultivation to the nature
of the soil.   So with the moral or intellectual qualities.   Exhortation, self-determination may do much
to stimulate and prick a man on in a wrong career
against his natural bent; but, when the crisis comes,
this artificial character thus laboriously induced will
break down, failing at the very time when it is most
wanted.

No need of spurs to the little Handel or the boy
Bach to study music, when one steals midnight inter-
views with a smuggled clavichord in a secret attic, and
the other copies whole books of studies by moonlight, for want of a candle, churlishly denied.   No
need of whips to the boy-painter, West, when he
begins in a garret, and plunders the family cat for
bristles to make his brushes.   On the other hand to
spend years at college, at the work-bench, or in a
store, and then find that the calling is a wrong one, is
disheartening to all but men of the toughest fibre.
The discovery shipwrecks the feeble, and plunges
ordinary minds into despair.   Doubly trying is this
discovery when one feels that the mistake was made
in defiance of friendly advice, or to gratify a freak of
fancy or an idle whim.   The sorrows that come upon
us by the will of God, or through the mistakes of our
parents, we can submit to with comparative resigna-
tion; but the sorrows which we have wrought by our

own hand, the pitfalls into which we have fallen by obstinately going on our own way, these are the sore places of memory which no time and no patience can salve over.

Be what nature intended you for, and you will succeed; be anything else, and you will be ten thousand times worse than nothing.

It is an uncontroverted truth, that no man ever made an ill figure who understood his own talents, nor a good one who mistook them. Let no young man of industry and perfect honesty despair because his profession and calling is crowded. Let him always remember that there is room enough at the top, and that the question whether he is ever to reach the top, or rise above the crowd at the base of the pyramid, will be decided by the way in which he improves the first ten years of his active life in securing to himself a thorough knowledge of his profession, and a sound moral and intellectual culture.

Employment.

I TAKE it that men and women were made for business, for activity, for employment. Activity is the life of us all. To do and to bear is the duty of life. We know that employment makes the man in a very great measure. A man with no employment, nothing to do, is scarcely a man. The secret of making men is to put them to work, and keep them at it. It is not study, not in t·uction, not careful moral training, not good parents, not good society that makes men. These are means; but back of these lies the grand molding influence of men's life. It is employment. A man's business does more to make him than every thing else. It hardens his muscles, strengthens his body, quickens his blood, sharpens his mind, corrects his judgment, wakes up his inventive genius, puts his wits to work, starts him on the race of life, arouses ambition, makes him feel that he is a man and must fill a man's shoes, do a man's work, bear a man's part in life, and show himself a man in that part. No man feels himself a man who is not doing a man's business. A man without employment is not a man. He does not prove by his works that he is a man. He cannot act a man's part. A hundred and fifty pounds of bone and muscle is not a man. A good cranium full of brains is not a man. The bone and muscle and brain must know how to act a man's part, do a man's work, think a man's thoughts, mark out a man's path, and bear a man's weight of character and duty before they constitute a man. A man is body and soul in action. A statue, if well dressed, may *appear* to be a man; so may a human being. But to *be* a man, and *appear* to be, are two very different things. Human beings *grow*, men are *made*. The being that grows to the stature of a man is not a man till he is made one. The grand instrumentality of man-making is employment. The world has long since learned that men cannot be made without employment. Hence it sets its boys to work; gives them trades, callings, professions; puts the instruments of man-making into their hands and tells them to work out their manhood. And the most of them do it somehow, not always very well. The men who fail to make themselves a respectable manhood are the boys who are put to no business, the young men who have nothing to do; the male beings that have no employment. We have them about us; walking nuisances; pestilential gasbags; fetid air-bubbles, who burst and are gone. Our men of wealth and character, of worth and power, have been early bound to some useful employment. Many of them were unfortunate orphan boys, whom want compelled to work for bread — the children of penury and lowly birth. In their early boyhood they buckled on the armor of labor, took upon their little shoulders heavy burdens, assumed responsibilities, met fierce circumstances, contended with sharp opposition, chose the ruggedest paths of employment because they yielded the best remuneration, and braved the storms of toil till they won great victories for themselves and stood before the world in the beauty and majesty of noble manhood. This is the way men are made. There is no other way. Their powers are developed in the field of employment.

Men are not born; they are made. Genius, worth, power of mind are more made than born. Genius born may grovel in the dust; genius made will mount to the skies. Our great and good men who stand along the paths of history bright and shining lights are witnesses of these truths. They stand there as everlasting pleaders for employment.

True Greatness.

THE forbearing use of power is a sure attribute of true greatness. Indeed, we may say that power, physical, moral, purely social or political, is one of the touchstones of genuine greatness.

The power which the husband has over his wife, in which we must include the impunity with which he may be unkind to her; the father over his children; the old over the young, and the young over the aged; the strong over the weak; the officer over his men; the master over his hands; the magistrate over the citizens, the employer over the employed; the rich over the poor; the educated over the unlettered; the experienced over the confiding. The forbearing and inoffensive use of all this power or authority, or a total abstinence from it, where the case admits it, will show the true greatness in a plain light.

"You are a plebeian," said a patrician to Cicero. "I *am* a plebeian," said the eloquent Roman; "the nobility of my family begins with me; that of yours will end with you. I hold no man deserves to be crowned with honor whose life is a failure; and he who lives only to eat and drink and accumulate money, is a failure. The world is no better for his living in it. He never wiped a tear from a sad face —never kindled a fire upon a frozen hearth. I repeat with emphasis, he is a failure. There is no flesh in his heart; he worships no God but gold." These were the words of a heathen.

Man is to be rated, not by his hoards of gold, not by the simple or temporary influence he may for a time exert; but by his unexceptionable principles relative both to character and religion. Strike out these, and what is he? A brute without a virtue — a savage without a sympathy! Take them away and his *manship* is gone; he no longer lives in the image of his maker! A cloud of sin hangs darkly on his brow; there is ever a tempest on his countenance, the lightning in his glance, the thunder in words, and the rain and whirlwind in the breathing of his angry soul. No smile gladdens his lip to tell that love is playing there; no sympathizing glow illuminates his cheek. Every word burns with malice, and that voice — the mystic gift of heaven — grates as harshly on the timid ear as rushing thunders beating amid falling cliffs and tumbling cataracts.

That which especially distinguishes a high order of man from a low order of man — that which constitutes human goodness, human greatness, human nobleness — is surely not the degree of enlightenment with which men pursue their own advantage; but it is self-forgetfulness; it is self-sacrifice; it is the disregard of personal pleasure, personal indulgence, personal advantage, remote or present, because some other line of conduct is more right.

The truest greatness is that which is unseen, unknown. Public martyrdom of every shade has a certain *eclat* and popularity connected with it that will often bear men up to endure with courage its trials; but those who suffer alone, without sympathy, for truth or principle, those who, unnoticed by men, maintain, their post, and in obscurity, and amid discouragement, patiently fulfill their trust, these are the real heroes of the age, and the suffering they bear is true greatness.

Let man go abroad with just principles, and what is he? An exhaustless fountain in a vast desert; a glorious sun shining ever, dispelling every vestige of darkness. There is love animating his heart, sympathy breathing in every tone. Tears of pity — dew drops of the soul — gather in his eye and gush impetuously down his cheek. A good man is abroad, and the world knows and feels it. Beneath his smiles lurks no degrading passions. Within his heart there slumbers no guile. He is not exalted in moral pride, not elevated in his own views; but honest, moral and virtuous before the world. He stands throned on truth; his fortress is wisdom and his dominion is the vast and limitless world. Always upright, kind and sympathizing; always attached to just principles and actuated by the same, governed by the highest motives in doing good.

Idleness.

MANY moralists have remarked that pride has, of all human vices, the widest dominion, appears in the greatest multiplicity of forms, and lies hidden under the greatest variety of disguises — which disguises, like the moon's veils of brightness, are both its lustre and its shade, and betray it to others though they hide it from themselves.

It is not our intention to degrade pride from its pre-eminence, yet we know not whether idleness may not maintain a very doubtful and obstinate position. Idleness predominates in many lives where it is not suspected, for, being a vice which terminates in itself, it may be enjoyed without injury to others, and therefore is not watched like fraud, which endangers property, or like pride, which naturally seeks its gratification in other's inferiority.

Idleness is a silent and peaceful quality that neither raises envy by ostentation nor hatred by opposition. There are some who profess idleness in its full dignity; they boast because they do nothing, and thank their stars that they have nothing to do — who sleep every night until they cannot sleep any longer, and then rise only that exercise may enable them to sleep again; who prolong the reign of darkness by double curtains, and never see the sun but to tell him how they hate his beams; whose whole labor is to vary the posture of indulgence, and whose day differs from their night but as a couch or a chair differs from a bed. These are the true and open votaries of idleness, who exist in a state of unruffled stupefied laziness, forgetting and forgotten, who have long ceased to live, and at whose death the survivors can only say that they have ceased to breathe. Such a person is an annoyance — he is of no use to anybody — he is an intruder

in the busy thoroughfare of every-day life—he is of
no advantage; he annoys busy men — he makes them
unhappy , he may have an income to support his idleness, or he may sponge on his good-natured friends,
but in either case he is despised; he is a criminal
prodigal, and a prolific author of want and shame; he
is a confused work-shop for the devil to tinker in, and
no good can ever be expected from him; in short, he
is a nuisance in the world, and needs abatement for
the public good.   Idleness is the bane of body and
mind, the nurse of haughtiness, the chief author of all
mischief, one of seven deadly sins—the cushion upon
which the devil reposes, and a great cause not only
of melancholy but of many other diseases, for the
mind is naturally active, and if it be not occupied about
some honest business, it rushes into mischief or sinks
into melancholy.   Of all contemptible things, there is
nothing half so wretched as a *lazy man*.   The Turks
say the devil tempts everybody, but the idle man
tempts the devil.   When we notice that a man can be
a professional loafer, a successful idler, with less capital, less brains, than are required to succeed in any
other profession, we cannot blame him so much after
all, for those are things that the idler is generally
destitute of; and we can notice it as an actual fact,
that they succeed in their business, and it costs them
no energy, no brains, no character, "no nothing."
They are dead beats; they should not be classed
among the living—they are a sort of dead men that
cannot be buried.

Idleness is an ingredient in the upper current,

which was scarcely known, and never countenanced, in the good old linsey-woolsey, tow-and-linen, mush-and-milk, pork-and-potato times of the pilgrim fathers, and revolutionary patriots. We now have those among us, who would rather go hungry and be clad in rags, than to work. We also have a numerous train of gentleman idlers, who pass down the stream of life at the expense of their fellow passengers. They live well, and dress well, as long as possible, by borrowing and sponging, and then take to gambling, swindling, stealing, robbing; and often pass on for years, before justice overtakes them. So long as these persons can keep up fashionable appearances, and elude the police, they are received into the company of the upper ten thousand. Many an idle knave, by means of a fine coat, a lily hand, and a graceful bow, has been received into the *polite* circles of society with *eclat*, and walked, rough-shod, over a worthy young mechanic or farmer, who had too much good sense to make a dash, or imitate the monkey-shines of an itinerant dandy. A fine dress, in the eyes of some, covers more sins than charity.

If thus the young man wishes to be nobody, his way is easy. He need only go to the drinking saloon to spend his leisure time; he need not drink much at first, only a little beer, or some other drink; in the meantime play dominoes, checkers, or something else, to kill time, so that he is sure not to read any useful books. If he reads at all, let it be some of the dime novels of the day. Thus go on, keep his stomach full and his head empty, and he will soon graduate a nobody, unless (as it is quite likely) he should turn out a drunkard or a professional gambler, which is worse than a nobody.

Young man, if you do not wish to be a nobody, or somebody much worse than nobody, then guard your youth. A lazy youth will be a lazy man, just as sure as a crooked sapling makes a crooked tree. Who ever saw a youth grow up in idleness who did not make a lazy, shiftless vagabond when he was old enough to be a man, though he was not a man by character. The great mass of thieves, paupers and criminals have come to what they are by being brought up to do nothing useful. Laziness grows on people; it begins in cob-web and ends in iron chains. If you will be nothing, just wait to be somebody. That man that waits for an opportunity to do much at once, may breathe out his life in idle wishes, and finally regret his useless intentions and barren zeal—a young man idle, an old man needy. Idleness travels very leisurely along, and poverty soon overtakes her—to be idle is to be poor. It is said that pride and poverty are inconsistent companions, but when idleness unites them the depth of wretchedness is complete. Leisure is sweet to those who have earned it, but burdensome to those who get it for nothing.

Arouse yourself, young man! Shake off the wretched and disgraceful habits of the do-nothing, if you have been so unfortunate as to incur them, and go to work at once! "But what shall I do?" you perhaps ask. *Anything*, rather than continue in dependent, and enfeebling, and demoralizing idleness.

If you can get nothing else to do, sweep the streets. But you are "ashamed" to do that. If so, your shame has been very slow in manifesting itself, seeing how long you have been acting, on life's great stage, the despicable parts of drone and loafer, *without* shame!

Idler! Take the foregoing home to yourself. Don't try to persuade yourself that the cap dose n't fit you. Honestly acknowledge its fitness. It will be a great point gained, to become honest with yourself. It will be a step forward — a step toward that justice to others which your present conduct absolutely ignores!

Education.

MANUFACTURERS find intelligent, educated mechanics more profitable to employ, even at higher wages, than those who are uneducated. We have never met any one who had much experience in employing large numbers of men who did not hold this opinion, and, as a general rule, those manufacturers are most successful who are most careful to secure intelligent and skillful workmen.

It requires extensive observation to enable one even partially to appreciate the wonderful extent to which all the faculties are developed by mental cultivation. The nervous system grows more vigorous and active, the touch is more sensitive, and there is greater mobility in the hand.

We once knew a weaving room filled with girls above the average in character and intelligence, and there was one girl among them who had been highly educated. Though length of arms and strength of muscle are advantages in weaving, and though this girl was short and small, she always wove the greatest number of pieces in the room, and consequently drew the largest pay at the end of every month. We might fill many pages with similar cases which have come under our own observation, but there is no occasion. It has long since been settled by the general observation of manufacturers, that intelligent workmen will do more and better work than ignorant ones.

But the excess in the amount of work performed is not the most important respect in which an intelligent workman is superior to a stupid one. He is far more likely to be faithful to the interests of his employer, to save from waste and to turn to profit every thing that comes to his hand. There is also the exalted satisfaction of being surrounded by thinking, active and inquiring minds, instead of by ignorance.

Such are some of the advantages to the "Captains of Industry," which result from the employment of intelligent workmen; not in one article, nor any number of articles, could these advantages be fully set forth. And if it is impossible to state the advantages to the employer, how vain must be the effort to describe those which result to the workman himself!

The increase of wages is the least and lowest of the rich rewards of mental culture. The whole being is enlarged and exalted; the scope of view is widened; the objects of interest are increased; the subjects of thought are multiplied; life is more filled with emotion; and the man is raised in the scale of creation.

To intelligent English travelers, nothing in the United States has excited so much wonder and admiration as Lowell, Nashua, Manchester, Lawrence, and the other manufacturing towns of New England. That factory-girls should play on the piano, and sustain a creditable magazine by their own contributions; that their residences should be clean, commodious, and elegant; that factory-men should be intelligent gentlemen, well-read in literature, and totally unacquainted with beer and its inspirations, have been, for many years, the crowning marvels of America to all travelers of right feeling and good judgment.

Daniel Webster says: "Knowledge does not comprise all which is contained in the large term of education. The feelings are to be disciplined, the passions are to be restrained; true and worthy motives are to be inspired; a profound religious feeling is to be instilled, and pure morality inculcated under all circumstances. All this is comprised in education."

Too many have imbibed the idea that to obtain a sufficient education to enable a man to appear advantageously upon the theatre, especially of public life; his boyhood and youth must be spent within the walls of some classical seminary of learning, that he may commence his career under the high floating banner of a collegiate diploma—with them, the first round in the ladder of fame.

That a refined, classical education is desirable, and one of the *accomplishments* of a man, we admit—that it is indispensably necessary, and always makes a man more useful, we deny. He who has been incarcerated, from his childhood, up to his majority, within the limited circumference of his school and boarding room, although he may have mastered all the classics, is destitute of that knowledge of men and things, indispensably necessary to prepare him for action, either in private or public life. Classic lore and polite literature are very different from that vast amount of common intelligence, fit for every day use, that he *must* have, to render his intercourse with society pleasing to himself, or agreeable to others. He is liable to imposition at every turn he makes. He may have a large fund of *fine* sense, but if he lacks *common* sense, he is like a ship without a rudder. Let boys and girls be taught, first and last, all that is necessary to prepare them for the common duties of life—if the classics and polite literature can be worked between the coarser branches, they will be much safer—as silk goods are, enclosed in canvas, or a bale. We wish not to undervalue high seminaries of learning—but rather to stimulate those to persevere in the acquirement of science, who are deprived of the advantage of their dazzling lights. Franklin, Sherman, and others, emerged from the work shop, and illuminated the world as brightly as the most profound scholar from a college. In this enlightened age, and in our free country, all who will, may drink, deeply, at the pure fountain of science. Ignorance is a voluntary misfortune. By a proper improvement of time, the apprentice of the mechanic may lay in a stock of useful knowledge, that will enable him, when he arrives at manhood, to take a respectable stand by the side of those who have grown up in the full blaze of a collegiate education—and with a better prospect of success at the start, because he is much better stocked with *common* information, without which a man is a poor, helpless animal.

Education of every kind has two values—value as knowledge and value as discipline. Besides its use for guidance in conduct, the acquisition of each order of facts has also its use as mental exercise; and its effects as a preparative for complete living have to be considered under both these heads.

Education cannot be acquired without pains and application. It is troublesome and deep digging for pure water, but when once you come to the springs, they rise up and meet you. Every grain helps fill the bushel, so does the improvement of every moment increase knowledge.

Says Swedenborg: "It is of no advantage to man to know much, unless he lives according to what he knows, for knowledge has no other end than goodness; and he who is made good is in possession of a far richer treasure than he whose knowledge is the most extensive, and yet is destitute of goodness; for, what the latter is seeking by his great acquirements, the former already possesses."

One of the most agreeable consequences of knowledge is the respect and importance which it communicates to old age. Men rise in character often as they increase in years; they are venerable from what they have acquired and pleasing from what they can impart. Knowledge is the treasure, but judgment the treasurer of a wise man. Superficial knowledge, pleasure dearly purchased, and subsistence at the will of another, are the disgrace of mankind.

The chief properties of wisdom are to be mindful of things past, careful for things present, and provident of things to come.

He that thinks himself the happiest man is really so; but he that thinks himself the wisest is generally the greatest fool.

A wise man, says Seneca, is provided for occurrences of any kind: the good he manages, the bad he vanquishes; in prosperity he betrays no presumption, and in adversity he feels no despondency.

By gaining a good education you shall have your reward in the rich stores of knowledge you have thus collected, and which shall ever be at your command. More valuable than earthly treasure—while fleets may sink, and storehouses consume, and banks may totter, and riches flee, the intellectual investments you have thus made will be permanent and enduring, unfailing as the constant flow of Niagara or Amazon —a bank whose dividends are perpetual, whose wealth is undiminished however frequent the drafts upon it; which, though moth may impair, yet thieves cannot break through nor steal.

Nor will you be able to fill these storehouses to their full. Pour into a glass a stream of water, and at last it fills to the brim and will not hold another drop. But you may pour into your mind, through a whole lifetime, streams of knowledge from every conceivable quarter, and not only shall it never be full, but it will constantly thirst for more, and welcome each fresh supply with a greater joy.

Nay, more, to all around you may impart of these gladdening streams which have so fertilized your own mind, and yet, like the candle from which a thousand other candles may be lit without diminishing its flame, your supply shall not be impaired. On the contrary, your knowledge, as you add to it, will itself attract still more as it widens your realm of thought; and thus will you realize in your own life the parable of the ten talents, for "to him that hath shall be given."

The beginning of wisdom is to fear God, but the end of it is to love him. The highest learning is to be wise; and the greatest wisdom is to be good. The wise man looks forward into futurity, and considers what will be his condition millions of ages hence, as well as what it is at present.

Opportunity.

MANY do with opportunity as children do at the sea-shore; they fill their little hands with sand, then let the grains fall through one by one, till they are all gone.

Four things come not back; the spoken word; the sped arrow; the past life; and the neglected opportunity. Opportunity has hair in front, behind she is bald; if you seize her by the forelock you may hold her, but if suffered to escape, not Jupiter himself can catch her again. Opportunities are the offers of God, Heaven gives us enough when it gives us opportunity. Great opportunities are generally the result of the wise improvement of small ones. Wise men make more opportunities than they find. If you think your opportunities are not good enough, you had better improve them. Remember you are responsible for talents, for time and for opportunities; improve them as one that must give an account. Make hay while the sun shines. Gather roses while they bloom.

As a general rule, those who have no opportunities despise small ones; and those who despise small opportunities never get large ones.

Opportunity does not only do great work, but if not heeded is often most disastrous.

A shipmaster once said, "It was my lot to fall in with the ill-fated steamer, the 'Central America.' The night was closing in, the sea rolling high; but I hailed the crippled steamer, and asked if they needed help. 'I am in a sinking condition,' cried Captain Herndon. 'Had you not better send your passengers on board directly?' I said. 'Will you not lay by me till morning?' answered Captain Herndon. 'I will try,' I replied; 'but had you not better send your passengers on board now?' 'Lay by me till morning,' again said Captain Herndon. I tried to lay by him; but at night such was the heavy roll of the sea I could not keep my position, and I never saw the steamer again. In an hour and a half after the captain said 'Lay by me till morning,' the vessel, with its living freight, went down—the captain and crew, and a great majority of passengers, found a grave in the deep." There is so little time for over-squeamishness at present that the opportunity slips away; the very period of life at which a man chooses to venture, if ever, is so confined that it is no bad rule to preach up the neccessity, in such instances, of a little violence done to the feelings, and of efforts made in defiance of strict and sober calculation and not pass one opportunity after another.

What may be done at any time, will be done at no time. Take time while time is, for time will away, say the English. When the fool has made up his mind, the market has gone by; Spanish. A little too late, much too late; Dutch. Some refuse roast meat, and afterwards long for the smoke of it; Italian.

There is sometimes wanting only a stroke of fortune to discover numberless latent good or bad qualities, which would otherwise have been eternally concealed; as words written with a certain liquor appear only when brought near the fire.

Accident does very little toward the production of any great result in life. Though sometimes what is called a "happy hit" may be made by a bold venture, the old and common highway of steady industry and application is the only safe road to travel.

It is not accident that helps a man in the world, but purpose and persistent industry. These make a man sharp to discern opportunities, and turn them to account. To the feeble, the sluggish, and purpose-less, the happiest opportunities avail nothing—they are passed by and no meaning is seen in them.

Spare Moments.

IF we are prompt to seize and improve even the shortest intervals of possible action and effort, it is astonishing how much can be accomplished. Watt taught himself chemistry and mechanics while work-ing at his trade of a mathematical instrument maker; and he availed himself of every opportunity to extend his knowledge of language, literature, and the principles of science. Stephenson taught himself arithmetic and mensuration while working as an engineer during the night shifts, and he studied mechanics during his spare hours at home, thus preparing himself for the great work of his life—the invention of the railway locomotive.

With perseverance, the very odds and ends of time may be worked up into results of the greatest value. An hour in every day withdrawn from frivolous pur-suits, would, if profitably employed, enable any man of ordinary capacity, very shortly to master a com-plete science. It would make an ignorant man a well-informed man in ten years. We must not allow the time to pass without yielding fruits, in the form of something learned worthy of being known, some good principle cultivated, or some good habit strengthened. Dr. Mason Good translated Lucretius while riding in his carriage in the streets of London, going his rounds among his patients. Dr. Darwin composed nearly all his works in the same way, while riding about in his "sulky," from house to house in the country — writing down his thoughts on little scraps of paper, which he carried about with him for the purpose. Hale wrote his "contemplations" while traveling on a circuit. Dr. Burney learned French and Italian while traveling on horseback from one musical pupil to another in the course of his profession. Kirk White learned Greek while walking to and from a lawyer's office ; and we personally know a man of eminent position in a northern manufacturing town, who learned Latin and French while going messages as an errand boy in the streets of Manchester.

Elihu Burritt attributed his first success in self-improvement, not to genius, which he disclaimed, but simply to the careful employment of those invaluable fragments of time, called "odd moments." While working and earning his living as a blacksmith, he mastered some eighteen ancient and modern languages, and twenty-two European dialects. Withal, he was exceedingly modest, and thought his achievements nothing extraordinary. Like another learned and wise man, of whom it was said that he could be silent in ten languages, Elihu Burritt could do the

same in forty. "Those who have been acquainted
with my character from my youth up," said he, writing
to a friend, "will give me credit for sincerity when I
say, that it never entered into my head to blazon
forth any acquisition of my own. * * * All that
I have accomplished, or expect, or hope to accomplish, has been and will be by that plodding, patient,
persevering process of accretion which builds the ant-
heap—particle by particle, thought by thought, fact
by fact. And if ever I was actuated by ambition, its
highest and warmest aspirations reached no further
than the hope to set before the young men of my
country an example in employing those invaluable
fragments of time called 'odd moments.'"

Daguesseau, one of the great chancellors of France,
by carefully working up his odd bits of time, wrote a
bulky and able volume in the successive intervals of
waiting for dinner; and Madame de Gentis composed
several of her charming volumes while waiting for the
princess to whom she gave her daily lessons. Jeremy
Bentham in like manner disposed of his hours of labor
and repose, so that not a moment should be lost, the
arrangement being determined on the principle that it
is a calamity to lose the smallest portion of time. He
lived and worked habitually under the practical consciousness that man's days are numbered, and that
the night cometh when no man can work.

What a solemn and striking admonition to youth is
that inscribed on the dial at All Souls, Oxford, England, "*Periunt et imputantur*," the hours perish and
are laid to our charge. For time, like life, can never

be recalled. Melanchthon noted down the time lost by him, that he might thereby reanimate his industry, and not lose an hour. An Italian scholar put over his door an inscription intimating that whosoever remained there should join in his labors. "We are afraid," said some visitors to Baxter, "we break in upon your time." "To be sure you do," replied the disturbed and blunt divine. Time was the estate out of which these great workers, and all other workers, carved a rich inheritance of thoughts and deeds for their successors.

Sir Walter Scott found spare moments for self-improvement in every pursuit, and turned even accidents to account. Thus it was in the discharge of his functions as a writer's apprentice that he first penetrated into the Highlands, and formed those friendships among the surviving heroes of 1745 which served to lay the foundation for a large class of his works. Later in life, when employed as quartermaster of the Edinburgh Light Cavalry, he was accidentally disabled by the kick of a horse, and confined for some time to his house; but Scott was a sworn enemy to idleness, and he forthwith set his mind to work, and in three days composed the first canto of "The Lay of the Last Minstrel," his first great original work.

Let not, then, the young man sit with folded hands, calling on Hercules. Thine own arm is the demi-god. It was given thee to help thyself. Go forth into the world trustful, but fearless. Exalt thine adopted calling or profession. Look on labor as honorable, and d'gnify the task before thee, whether it be in the

study, office, counting-room, work-shop, or furrowed
field.   There is an equality in all, and the resolute
will and pure heart may ennoble either.

———⟨⟩⟨⟩———

Books.

No MAN has a right to bring up his children without surrounding them with books.   It is a wrong to
his family.   He cheats them.   Children learn to read
by being in the presence of books.   The love of
knowledge comes with reading, and grows upon it.
And the love of knowledge in a young mind is almost
a warrant against the inferior excitement of passions
and vices.

A little library, growing larger every year, is an
honorable part of a young man's history.   It is a
man's duty to have books.   A library is not a luxury,
but one of the necessaries of life.   It is not like a
dead city of stones, yearly crumbling, and needing
repair; but like a spiritual tree.   There it stands and
yields its precious fruit from year to year and from
age to age.

Carlyle saw the influence of books many years ago.
"I say, of all the priesthoods, aristocracies—
governing classes at present extant in the world—
there is no class comparable for importance to the
priesthood of the writers of books."

The art of writing, and of printing, which is a

sequence to it, is really the most wonderful thing in the world. Books are the soul of actions, the only audible, articulate voice of the accomplished facts of the past. The men of antiquity are dead; their fleets and armies have disappeared; their cities are ruins; their temples are dust; yet all these exist in magic preservation in the books they have bequeathed us, and their manners and their deeds are as familiar to us as the events of yesterday. And these papers and books, the mass of printed matter which we call literature, are really the teacher, guide and law-giver of the world to-day.

The influence of books upon man is remarkable; they make the man. You may judge a man more truly by the books and papers which he reads than by the company which he keeps, for his associates are often, in a manner, imposed upon him; but his reading is the result of choice, and the man who chooses a certain class of books and papers unconsciously becomes more colored in their views, more rooted in their opinions, and the *mind becomes fettered to their views.*

All the life and feeling of a young girl fascinated by some glowing love romance, is colored and shaped by the page she reads. If it be false, and weak, and foolish, she will be false, and weak, and foolish, too; but if it be true, and tender, and inspiring, then something of its truth, and tenderness, and inspiration will grow into her soul and become a part of her very self. The boy who reads deeds of manliness, of bravery and noble daring, feels the spirit of emulation grow within him, and the seed is planted which will bring forth fruit of heroic endeavor and exalted life.

A good book is the most appropriate gift that friendship can make. It never changes, it never grows unfashionable or old. It is soured by no neglect, is jealous of no rival; but always its clean, clear pages are ready to amuse, interest and instruct. The voice that speaks the thought may change or grow still forever, the heart that prompted the kindly and cheering word may grow cold and forgetful; but the page that mirrors it is changeless, faithful, immortal. The Book that records the incarnation of divine love, is God's best gift to man, and the books which are filled with kindly thought and generous sympathy, are the best gifts of friend to friend.

Every family ought to be well supplied with a choice supply of books for reading. This may be seen from the consequences of its neglect and abuse on the one hand, and from its value and importance on the other. Parents should furnish their children the necessary means, opportunities and direction of a Christian education. Give them proper books. "Without books," says the quaint Bartholin, "God is silent, justice dormant, science at a stand, philosophy lame, letters dumb, and all things involved in Cimmerian darkness." Bring them up to the habit of properly reading and studying these books. "A reading people will soon become a thinking people, and a thinking people must soon become a great people." Every book you furnish your child, and which it reads with reflection, is "like a cast of the weaver's shuttle, adding another thread to the indestructible web of existence." It will be worth more to him than all your hoarded gold and silver.

Dear reader, be independent and make up your mind what it is best for you to read, and read it. Master a few good books. Life is short and books are many. Instead of having your mind a garret crowded with rubbish, make it a parlor with rich furniture, beautifully arranged, in which you would not be ashamed to have the whole world enter. "Readers," says Addison, "who are in the flower of their youth should labor at those accomplishments which may set off their persons when their bloom is gone, and to lay in timely provisions for manhood and old age." Says Dr. Watts: "A line of the golden verses of the Pythagoreans recurring in the memory hath often tempted youth to frown on temptation to vice." No less worthy is the following: "There are many silver books, and a few golden books; but I have one book worth more than all, called the Bible, and that is a book of bank notes." The parent who lives for his children's souls will often consider what other books are most likely to prepare his little ones for prizing aright that Book of Books, and make that object the pole star of his endeavors.

Every book has a moral expression, though as in the human face, it may not be easy to say what it consists in. We may take up some exquisite poem or story, with no distinctly religious bearing, and feel that it is religious, because it strikes a chord so deep in human nature that we feel that it is only the divine

nature, "God who encompasses," that can respond to
what it calls forth. When we feel the inspiring influence of books, when we are lifted on the wings of
ancient genius, we should jealously avoid the perver-
sion of the gift. The children of this world have
their research and accomplishment, and enough is
done for pleasure and fame; but the Christian scholar
will rebuke himself, unless he find it in his heart to be
more alive in devotion to heavenly things, at the very
moment when he has breathed the aroma of poetry
and eloquence. Some books are to be tasted, others
to be swallowed, and some few to be chewed and
digested: that is, some books are to be read only in
parts; others to be read, but not curiously; and some
few to be read wholly, and with diligence and attention. Some books also may be read by deputy, and
extracts made of them by others; but that would be
only in the less important arguments, and the meaner
sort of books; else distilled books are, like common
distilled waters, flashy things.

"Not to know what was before you were," as has
been truly said, "is to be always a child." And it
is equally true that he never becomes a complete
man, who learns nothing of the former days, from
reading. "Books," says a good writer, "are the
crystalline founts, which hold in eternal ice the imperishable gems of the past."

Good books are invaluable as a moral guard to a
young man. The culture of a taste for such reading,
keeps one quietly at home, and prevents a thirst for
exciting recreations and debasing pleasure. It makes

him scorn whatever is low, coarse, and vulgar. It prevents that weary and restless temper which drives so many to the saloon, if not the gambling table, to while away their leisure hours. Once form the habit of domestic reading, and you will, at any time, prefer an interesting book, to frequenting the haunts of vice.

Chief among the educational influences of a household are its books. Therefore, good sir or madam, wherever you economize, do not cut off the supply of good literature. Have the best books, the best papers, and the best magazines, though you turn your old black silk once more, and make the old coat do duty another season. Nothing will compensate to your boys and girls for the absence of those quiet, kindly teachers, who keep such order in their schools, and whose invaluable friendship never cools or suffers change. You may go without pies and cake, or without butter on your bread, but, if you care for your family's best happiness and progress, you will not go without the best of books, such as Shakspeare and the best authors of the day.

In books we live continually in the decisive moments of history, and in the deepest experience of individual lives. The flowers which we cull painfully and at long intervals in our personal history, blossom in profusion here, and the air is full of a fragrance which touches our own life only in the infrequent springs. In our libraries we meet great men on a familiar footing, and are at ease with them. We come to know them better, perhaps, than those who bear their names and sit at their tables. The reserve that makes

so many fine natures difficult of access is entirely lost.
No crudeness of manner, no poverty of speech or
unfortunate personal peculiarity, mars the intercourse
of author and reader. It is a relation in which the
interchange of thought is undisturbed by outward
conditions. We lose our narrow selves in the broader
life that is opened to us. We forget the hindrances
and limitations of our own work in the full comprehension of that stronger life that cannot be bound
nor confined, but grows in all soils and climbs heav-
enward under every sky. It is the privilege of
greatness to understand life in its height and depth.
Hazlitt has told us of his first interview with Coleridge, and of the moonlight walk homeward, when
the eloquent lips of the great conversationalist awoke
the slumbering genius within him, and made the old
familiar world strange and wonderful under a sky that
seemed full of new stars. Such intercourse with
gifted men is the privilege of few; but in the seclusion of the library there often grows up an acquaintance more thorough and inspiring. Books are rich,
not only in thought and sentiment, but in character.
Where shall we find in any capitals such majesty as
"doth hedge about" the kings of Shakspeare, or
such brave and accomplished gentlemen as adorn his
courts and measure wit and courtesy with the fair and
graceful women of his fancy?

The best society in the world is that which lives in
books. No taint of vulgarity attaches to it, no petty
strife for place and power disturbs its harmony, no
falsehood stains its perfect truth; and those who move

habitually in these associations find a strength which is the more controlling because molded by genius into forms of grace and refinement.

There is a certain monotony in daily life, and those whose aims are high, but who lack the inherent strength to stand true to them amid adverse influences, gradually drop out of the ever-thinning ranks of the aspiring. They are conquered by routine, and disheartened by the discipline and labor that guard the prizes of life. Even to the strongest there are hours of weakness and weariness. To the weak, and to the strong in their times of weakness, books are inspiring friends and teachers. Against the feebleness of individual efforts they proclaim the victory of faith and patience, and out of the uncertainty and discouragement of one day's work they prophesy the fuller and richer life, that grows strong and deep through conflict, sets itself more and more in harmony with the noblest aims, and is at last crowned with honor and power.

Reading.

THERE are four classes of readers. The first is like the hour-glass; and its reading being on the sand, it runs in and runs out and leaves no vestige behind. A second is like a sponge, which imbibes everything, and returns it in the same state, only a little dirtier. A third is like a jelly bag, allowing all that is pure to pass away, and retaining only the refuse and dregs. The fourth is like the slaves in the diamond minds of Golconda, who, casting aside all that is worthless, obtain only pure gems.

One's reading is, usually, a fair index of his character. Observe in almost any house you visit, the books which lie customarily on the centre-table; or note what are taken by preference from the public or circulating library; and you may judge, in no small degree, not only the intellectual tastes and the general intelligence of the family, but also—and what is of far deeper moment—you may pronounce on the moral attainments and the spiritual advancement of most of the household. "A man is known," it is said, "by the company he keeps." It is equally true that a man's character may be, to a great extent, ascertained by knowing what books he reads.

The tempation to corrupt reading is usually strongest at the period when the education of the schoolroom is about closing. The test of the final utility, however, is the time when our youth leave these schools. If the mind be now awakened to a manly independence, and start on a course of vigorous self-culture, all will be well. But if, on the other hand, it sink into a state of inaction, indifferent to its own needs, and to all the highest ends and aims of life, then woe to the man. For few, very few, ever rouse themselves in mid-life to a new intellectual taste, and to an untried application of their time and powers to that culture for which the Creator formed and endowed them.

To read books which present false pictures of human life is decidedly dangerous, and we would say stand aloof! Life is neither a tragedy nor a farce. Men are not all either knaves or heroes. Women are neither angels nor furies. And yet, if you depended upon much of the literature of the day, you would get the idea that life, instead of being something earnest, something practical, is a fitful and fantastic and extravagant thing. How poorly prepared are that young man and that young woman for the duties of to-day who spent last night wading through brilliant passages descriptive of magnificent knavery and wickedness! The man will be looking all day long for his heroine in the tin shop, by the forge, in the factory, in the counting-room, and he will not find her, and he will be dissatisfied. A man who gives himself up to the indiscriminate reading of novels will be nerveless, inane, and a nuisance. He will be fit neither for the store, nor the shop, nor the field. A woman who gives herself up to the indiscriminate reading of novels will be unfitted for the duties of wife, mother, sister, daughter. There she is, hair disheveled, countenance vacant, cheeks pale, hands trembling, bursting into tears at midnight over the fate of some unfortunate lover; in the day-time, when she ought to be busy, staring by the half hour at nothing; biting her finger-nails to the quick. The carpet that was plain before, will be plainer, after having, through a romance all night long, wandered in tessellated halls of castles. And your industrious companion will be more unattractive than ever, now that you have walked in the romance through parks with plumed princesses, or lounged in the arbor with the polished desperado.

Abstain from all those books which, while they have some good things about them, have also *an admixture of evil.* You have read books that had the two elements in them — the good and the bad. Which stuck to you? The bad! The heart of most people is like a sieve, which lets the small particles of gold fall through, but keeps the great cinders. Once in a while there is a mind like a loadstone, which, plunged amid steel and brass filings, gathers up the steel and repels the brass. But it is generally just the opposite. If you attempt to plunge through a hedge of burrs to get one blackberry, you will get more burrs than blackberries. You cannot afford to read a bad book, however good you are. You say, "The influence is insignificant." I tell you that the scratch of a pin has sometimes produced the lockjaw. Alas, if through curiosity, as many do, you pry into an evil book, your curiosity is as dangerous as that of the man who should take a torch into a gunpowder mill merely to see whether it really would blow up or not.

Inferior books are to be rejected, in an age and time whem we are courted by whole libraries, and when no man's life is long enough to compass even those which are good and great and famous. Why should we bow down at puddles, when we can approach freely to the crystal spring-heads of science and letters? Half the reading of most people is snatched up at random. Many stupefy themselves over the dullness of authors who ought never to have escaped oblivion. The invention of paper and printing—especially the production of both by a new motive power—may be said to have overdone the matter, and made it too easy to be born into the world of authorship. The race would be benefited by some new invention for strangling nine out of ten who sue for publicity. No man can do his friend or child a more real service than to snatch from his hand the book that relaxes and effeminates him, lest he destroy the solids and make his fibre flaccid by the slops and hashes of a catch-penny press. But especially is he a benefactor who instills the principle that no composition should be deliberately sought which is not good, beneficial, and above mediocrity.

To those who plead the want of time to read, we would say, be as frugal of your hours as you are of your dollars, and you can create time in the busiest day. Horace Greeley, the editor of a newspaper which reached what was then an almost incredible circulation, tells us, that when a boy, he would "go reading, to the wood-pile; reading, to the garden; reading, to the neighbors." His father was poor, and needed his services through the day; and it was a mighty struggle with him to get Horace to bed. "I would take a pine knot," he says, "put it on the back-log, pile my books around me, and lie down and read all through the long winter evenings; silent, motionless, and dead to the world around me, alive only to the world to which I was transported by my book."

In this country talent has a fair field to rise by culture from the humblest walks of life, and to attain the highest distinction of which it is capable. "Why," inquired a bystander of a certain carpenter, who was bestowing great labor in planing and smoothing a seat for the bench in a court-room, "why do you spend so much time on that seat?" "I do it," was the reply, "to make it easy for myself." And he kept his word; for, by industry, perseverance, and self-education, he rose, step by step, until he actually *did* afterwards sit as judge on that very bench he had planed as a carpenter.

Consider that what we carry *to* a book is always quite as important as what we receive *from* it. We may strike the keys of the best instrument, from earliest morn till latest night, but unless there be music in our soul, it can produce no harmony for us. While, to an earnest, inquiring, self-poised mind, "a good book is the plectrum by which our else silent lyres are struck." Master your reading, and let it never master you. Then it will serve you with an ever-increasing fidelity. Only read books aright, and they will charge your mind with the true electric fire. Take them up as among your best friends; and every volume you peruse will join the great company of joyous servitors who will wait around your immortal intellect. Then, too, your daily character will bear the signatures of the great minds you commune with in secret. And, as the years pass on, you will walk in the light of an ever-enlarging multitude of well-chosen, silent, but never-erring guides.

To read with profit, the books must be of a kind calculated to inform the mind, correct the head, and better the heart. These books should be read with attention, understood, remembered, and their precepts put in practice. It depends less on number than quality. One good book, well understood and remembered, is of more use than to have a superficial knowledge of fifty, equally sound. Books of the right character produce reflection, and induce investigation. They are a mirror of mind, for mind to look in. Of all the books ever written, no one contains so instructive, so sublime, and so great a variety as the Bible. Resolve to read three chapters each day, for one year, and you will find realities there, more wonderful than any pictures of fiction that have been drawn by the pencilings of the most practiced novel writer in the dazzling galaxy of ancient or modern literature.

The advice in regard to reading only the best selected works leads us to say, read slowly. We sometimes rush over pages of valuable matter, because, at a glance, they seem to be dull; and we leap along to see how the story, if it be a story, is to end. We do every thing in this age in a hurry; we demand not only fast horses, but fast writers, fast preachers, and fast lecturers. Said a noted seaman's preacher in one of our large cities, "I work in a hurry, I sleep in a hurry, and, if I ever die, I expect to die in a hurry." This is the history of much of the present reading.

No one can too highly appreciate the magic power

of the press, or too deeply deprecate its abuses. Newspapers have become the great highway of that intelligence which exerts a controlling power over our nation, catering the every-day food of the mind. Show us an intelligent family of boys and girls, and we will show you a family where newspapers and periodicals are plenty. Nobody who has been without these private tutors can know their educating power for good or evil. Have you ever thought of the innumerable topics of discussion which they suggest at the breakfast table; the important public measures with which thus early our children become acquainted; the great philanthropic questions of the day, to which, unconsciously, their attention is awakened, and the general spirit of intelligence which is evoked by these quiet visitors? Anything that makes home pleasant, cheerful and chatty, thins the haunts of vice and the thousand and one avenues of temptation, should certainly be regarded, when we consider its influence on the minds of the young, as a great social and moral light.

A child beginning to read becomes delighted with a newspaper, because he reads of names and things which are familiar, and he will progress accordingly. A newspaper, in one year is worth a quarter's schooling to a child. Every father must consider that information is connected with advancement. The mother of a family, being one of its heads, and having a more immediate charge of children, should herself be instructed. A mind occupied becomes fortified against the ills of life, and is braced for emergency. Children amused by reading or study are of course more considerate and easily governed.

How many thoughtless young men have spent their earnings in a tavern or grog shop who ought to have been reading! How many parents who have not spent twenty dollars for books for their families, would have given thousands to reclaim a son or daughter who had ignorantly or thoughtlessly fallen into temptation!

Take away the press, and the vast educating power of the school and the college would soon come to an end. Or, look one moment at the immense influence a single writer has had upon an age, or upon the world—Shakspeare in creating the drama, or Bacon and Descartes in founding different systems of philosophy. Who may estimate the influence of Charles Dickens upon society, when by the magic of his pen he touched the under world of poverty and want and sin, over which the rich and the gay glided on, not knowing or thinking what was beneath their feet, and marched all this ghastly array of ragged and hungry children and sorrowful women and discouraged men, and the famished forms from the poor-house, and the ugly visage of the criminal, into the parlors of wealth and culture, and there had them tell the story of their woes and their suffering? Or who can tell the influence of a MacDonald, or a Beecher, or an Eggleston in entering the wide realm of romance and compelling it to serve truth, humanity and religion? Or who knows the influence of Thomas Paine and Jefferson in strengthening the cause of liberty in our struggle for national independence? Take one single writer of our own land — Mrs. Harriet Beecher Stowe. The single tale of "Uncle Tom's Cabin," stirred the heart of this vast nation to its profoundest depths. At the simple moving of her pen millions of swords and bayonets gleamed and flashed in the air, and vast armies met in deadly array and fought face to face, till liberty, re-baptized in blood, was given to man as man. This vast world moves along lines of thought and sentiment and principle, made eloquent by the clangor of the printing-press

Perseverance.

"CONTINUAL dropping wears a stone." So persevering labor gains our objects. Perseverance is the virtue wanted, a lion-hearted purpose of victory. It is this that builds, constructs, accomplishes whatever is great, good, and valuable.

Perseverance built the pyramids on Egypt's plains, erected the gorgeous temple at Jerusalem, reared the seven-hilled city, inclosed in adamant the Chinese empire, scaled the stormy, cloud-capped Alps, opened a highway through the watery wilderness of the Atlantic, leveled the the forests of a new world, and reared in its stead a community of states and nations. It has wrought from the marble block the exquisite creations of genius, painted on the canvas the gorgeous mimicry of nature, and engraved on the metallic surface the viewless substance of the shadow. It has put in motion millions of spindles, winged as many flying shuttles, harnessed a thousand iron steeds to as many freighted cars, and set them flying from town to town and nation to nation, tunneled mountains of granite, and annihilated space with the lightning's speed. It has whitened the waters of the world with the sails of a hundred nations, navigated every sea and explored every land. It has reduced nature in her thousand forms to as many sciences, taught her laws, prophesied her future movements, measured her untrodden spaces, counted her myriad hosts of worlds, and computed their distances, dimensions, and velocities.

But greater still are the works of perseverance in the world of mind. What are the productions of science and art compared with the splendid achievements won in the human soul? What is a monument of constructive genius, compared with the living domes of thought, the sparkling temples of virtue, and the rich, glory-wreathed sanctuaries of religion, which perseverance has wrought out and reared in the souls of the good? What are the toil-sweated productions of wealth piled in vast profusion around a Girard, or a Rothschild, when weighed against the stores of wisdom, the treasures of knowledge, and the strength, beauty and glory with which this victorious virtue, has enriched and adorned a great multitude of minds during the march of a hundred generations? How little can we tell, how little know, the brain-sweat, the heart-labor, the conscience-struggles which it cost to make a Newton, a Howard, or a Channing; how many days of toil, how many nights of weariness, how many months and years of vigilant, powerful effort, was spent to perfect in them what the world has bowed to in reverence! Their words have a power, their names a charm, and their deeds a glory. How came this wealth of soul to be theirs? Why are their names watchwords of power set high on the temple of fame? Why does childhood lisp them in reverence, and age feel a thrill of pleasure when they are mentioned?

They were the sons of perseverance—of unremitting industry and toil. They were once as weak and helpless as any of us—once as destitute of wisdom, virtue and power as any infant. Once, the very alphabet of that language which they have wielded with such magic effect, was unknown to them. They toiled long to learn it, to get its sounds, understand its dependencies, and longer still to obtain the secret of its highest charm and mightiest power, and yet even longer for those living, glorious thoughts which they bade it bear to an astonished and admiring world. Their characters, which are now given to the world, and will be to millions yet unborn as patterns of greatness and goodness, were made by that untiring perseverance which marked their whole lives. From childhood to age they knew no such word as fail. Defeat only gave them power; difficulty only taught them the necessity of redoubled exertions; dangers gave them courage; the sight of great labors inspired in them corresponding exertions. So it has been with all men and all women who have been eminently successful in any profession or calling in life. Their success has been wrought out by persevering industry. Successful men owe more to their perseverance than to their natural powers, their friends, or the favorable circumstances around them. Genius will falter by the side of labor, great powers will yield to great industry. Talent is desirable, but perseverance is more so. It will make mental powers, or, at least, it will strengthen those already made. Yes, it will make mental power. The most available and successful kind of mental power is that made by the hand of cultivation.

It will also make friends. Who will not befriend the persevering, energetic youth, the fearless man of industry? Who is not a friend to him who is a friend to himself? He who perseveres in business, and hardships, and discouragements, will always find ready and generous friends in every time of need. He who perseveres in a course of wisdom, rectitude, and benevolence, is sure to gather around him friends who will be true and faithful. Honest industry will procure friends in any community and any part of the civilized world. Go to the men of business, of worth, of influence, and ask them who shall have their confidence and support. They will tell you, the men who falter not by the wayside, who toil on in their callings against every barrier, whose eye is bent upward, and whose motto is "Excelsior." These are the men to whom they give their confidence. But they shun the lazy, the indolent, the fearful, and faltering. They would as soon trust the wind as such men. If you would win friends, be steady and true to yourself; be the unfailing friend of your own purposes, stand by your own character, and others will come to your aid. Though the earth quake and the heavens gather blackness, be true to your course and yourself. Quail not, nor doubt of the result; victory will be yours.   Friends will come.   A thousand arms of strength will be bared to sustain you.

First, be sure that your trade, your profession, your calling in life is a good one — one that God and goodness sanctions; then be true as steel to it.   Think for it, plan for it, work for it, live for it; throw in your mind, might, strength, heart, and soul into your actions for it, and success will crown you her favored child. No matter whether your object be great or small, whether it be the planting of a nation or a patch of potatoes, the same perseverance is necessary.   Every body admires an iron determination, and comes to the aid of him who directs it to good.

But perseverance will not only make friends, but it will make favorable circumstances.   It will change the face of all things around us;   It is silly and cowardly to complain of the circumstances that are against us.   Clouds of darkness, evil forebodings, opposition, enemies, barriers of every kind, will vanish before a stout heart and resolute energy of soul.   The Alps stood between Napoleon and Italy, which he desired to conquer.   He scaled the mountain and descended upon his prey.   His startling descent more than half conquered the country. He forced every circumstance into his favor. His greatest barrier proved a sure means of victory. A conquered enemy is often the readiest slave. So a barrier once scaled affords a vantage-ground for our future efforts. Opposing circumstances often create strength, both mental and physical. Labor makes us strong. Opposition gives us greater power of resistance. To overcome one barrier gives greater ability to overcome the next. It is cowardice to grumble about circumstances. Some men always talk as though fate had woven a web of circumstances against them, and it were useless for them to try to break through it. Out upon such dastardly whining! It is their business to dash on in pursuit of their object against everything. Then circumstances will gradually turn in their favor, and they will deem themselves the favored children of destiny.

Look at nature. She has a voice, which is the voice of God, teaching a thousand lessons of perseverance. The lofty mountains are wearing down by slow degrees. The ocean is gradually, but slowly, filling up, by deposits from its thousand rivers. The Niagara Falls have worn back several miles through the hard limestone over which they pour their thundering columns of water, and will by-and-by drain the great lake which feeds their boiling chasm. The Red Sea and whole regions of the Pacific ocean are gradually filling up by the labors of a little insect, so small as to be almost invisible to the naked eye. These stupendous works are going on before our eyes, by a slow but sure process. They teach a great lesson of perseverance. Nature has but one voice on this subject, that is "Persevere!" God has but one voice, that is "Persevere!" and duty proclaims the same lesson. More depends upon an active perseverance than upon genius. Says a common-sense author upon this subject, "Genius, unexerted, is no more genius than a bushel of acorns is a forest of oaks." There may be epics in men's brains, just as there are oaks in acorns, but the tree must come out before we can measure it. We very naturally recall here that large class of grumblers and wishers, who spend their time in longing to be higher than they are, while it should have been employed to advance themselves. They bitterly moralize on the injustice of society. Do they want a change? Let them then change! Who prevents them? If you are as high as your faculties will permit you to rise in the scale of society, why should you complain of men?

It is God who arranged the law of precedence. Implead Him or be silent! If you have capacity for a higher station, take it. What hinders you? How many men would love to go to sleep beggars and wake up Rothschilds or Astors? How many would fain go to bed dunces, to be waked up Solomons? You reap what you have sown. Those who have sown dunce-seed, vice-seed, laziness-seed, usually get a crop. They who sow the wind reap a whirlwind. A man of mere "capacity undeveloped" is only an organized degradation with a shine on it.

A flint and a genius that will not strike fire are no better than wet junk-wood. We have Scripture for it, that "a living dog is better than a dead lion!" If you would go up, go—if you would be seen, shine. At the present day eminent position, in any profession, is the result of hard, unwearied labor. Men can no longer fly at one dash into eminent position. They have got to hammer it out by steady and rugged blows. The world is no longer clay, but rather iron, in the hands of its workers.

Work is the order of this day. The slow penny is surer than the quick dollar. The slow trotter will out-travel the fleet racer. Genius darts, flutters, and tires; but perseverance wears and wins. The all-day horse wins the race. The afternoon-man wears off the laurels. The last blow finishes the nail.

Men must learn to labor and to wait, if they would succeed. Brains grow by use as well as hands. The greatest man is the one who uses his brains the most, who has added most to his natural stock of power. Would you have fleeter feet? Try them in the race. Would you have stronger minds? Put them at rational thinking. They will grow strong by action. Would you have greater success? Use greater and more rational and constant efforts? Does competition trouble you? Work away; what is your competitor but a man? Are you a coward, that you shrink from the contest? Then you ought to be beaten. Is the end of your labors a long way off? Every step takes you nearer to it. Is it a weary distance to look at? Ah, you are faint-hearted! That is the trouble

with the multitude of youth. Youth are not so lazy
as they are cowardly. They may bluster at first, but
they won't "stick it out." Young farmer, do you
covet a homestead, nice and comfortable, for yourself
and that sweet one of your day-dreams? What
hinders that you should not have it? Persevering
industry with proper economy, will give you the farm.
A man can get what he wants if he be not faint-hearted. Toil is the price of success. Learn it, young
farmer, mechanic, student, minister, physician, Christian. Learn it, ye formers of character, ye followers
of Christ, ye would-be men and women. Ye must
have something to do, and do it with all your might.
Ye must harden your hands and sweat your brains.
Ye must work your nerves and strain your sinews.
Ye must be at it, and always at it. No trembling,
doubting, hesitating, flying the track. Like the boy
on the rock, ye cannot go back. Onward ye must
go. There is a great work for ye all to do, a deep
and earnest life-work, solemn, real and useful. Life
is no idle game, no farce to amuse and be forgotten.
It is a fixed and stern reality, fuller of duties than the
sky is of stars.

———— ◦•◦•❧•❁•❧•◦•◦ ————

Pluck.

THERE is seldom a line of glory written upon the
earth's face but a line of suffering runs parallel with
it; and they who read the lustrous syllables of the

one, and stop not to decipher the spotted and worn inscription of the other, get the lesser half of the lesson earth has to give.

The hopelessness of any one's accomplishing anything without pluck is illustrated by an old East Indian fable. A mouse that dwelt near the abode of a great magician was kept in such constant distress by its fear of a cat, that the magician, taking pity on it, turned it into a cat itself. Immediately it began to suffer from its fear of a dog, so the magician turned it into a dog. Then it began to suffer from fear of a tiger, and the magician turned it into a tiger. Then it began to suffer from its fear of huntsmen, and the magician, in disgust, said, "Be a mouse again. As you have only the heart of a mouse, it is impossible to help you by giving you the body of a nobler animal." And the poor creature again became a mouse.

It is the same with a mouse-hearted man. He may be clothed with the powers, and placed in the position of a brave man, but he will always act like a mouse; and public opinion is usually the great magician that finally says to such a person, "Go back to your obscurity again. You have only the heart of a mouse, and it is useless to try to make a lion of you."

Many depend on luck instead of pluck. The P left off that word makes all the difference. The English say luck is all; "it is better to be born lucky than wise." The Spanish, "The worst pig gets the best acorn." The French, "A good bone never falls to a good dog." The German, "Pitch the lucky man into the Nile, and he will come up with a fish in his mouth."

Fortune, success, fame, position are never gained, but by piously, determinedly, bravely sticking, living to a thing till it is fairly accomplished. In short, you must carry a thing through if you want to be anybody or anything. No matter if it do cost you the pleasure, the society, the thousand pearly gratifications of life. No matter for these. Stick to the thing and carry it through. Believe you were made for the matter, and that no one else can do it. Put forth your whole energies. Be awake, electrify yourself; go forth to the task. Only once learn to carry a thing through in all its completeness and proportion, and you will become a hero. You will think better of yourself; others will think better of you. The world in its very heart admires the stern, determined doer. It sees in him its best sight, its brightest object, its richest treasure. Drive right along, then, in whatever you undertake. Consider yourself amply sufficient for the deed, and you will succeed.

Self-Reliance.

God never intended that strong, independent beings should be reared by clinging to others, like the ivy to the oak, for support. The difficulties, hardships, and trials of life—the obstacles one encounters on the road to fortune—are positive blessings. They knit his muscles more firmly, and teach him self-reliance, just as by wrestling with an athlete, who is superior to us, we increase our own strength, and learn the secret of his skill. All difficulties come to us, as Bunyan says of temptation, like the lion which met Samson; the first time we encounter them they roar and gnash their teeth, but, once subdued, we find a nest of honey in them. Peril is the very element in which power is developed. "Ability and necessity dwell near each other," said Pythagoras.

The greatest curse that can befall a young man is to lean, while his character is forming, on others for support. He who begins with crutches will generally end with crutches. Help from within always strengthens, but help from without invariably enfeebles its recipient. It is not in the sheltered garden or the hot-house, but on the rugged Alpine cliffs, where the storms beat most violently, that the toughest plants are reared. The oak that stands alone to contend with the tempest's blasts, only takes deeper root and stands the firmer for ensuing conflicts; while the forest tree, when the woodman's ax has spoiled its surroundings, sways and bends and trembles, and perchance is uprooted. So it is with men. Those who are trained to self-reliance are ready to go out and contend in the sternest conflicts of life; while men who have always leaned for support on those around them, are never prepared to breast the storms of adversity that arise.

Many a young man—and for that matter, many a one who is older—halts at his outset upon life's battle-field, and falters and faints for what he conceives to be a necessary capital for a start. A few thousand dollars, or hundreds, or "something handsome" in the way of money in his purse, he *fancies* to be about the only thing needful to secure his fortune.

The best capital, in nine cases out of ten, a young man can start in the world with, is robust health, sound morals, a fair intelligence, a will to work his way honestly and bravely, and if it be possible, a trade—whether he follows it for a livelihood or not. He can always fall back upon a trade when other paths are closed. Any one who will study the lives of memorable men—apart from the titled, or hereditarily great—will find that a large majority of them rose from the ranks, with no capital for a start, save intelligence, energy, industry, and a will to rise and conquer. In the mechanic and artizan pursuits, in commerce, in agriculture, and in the paths of literature, science and art, many of the greatest names have sprung from poverty and obscurity. Dr. Johnson made himself illustrious by his intellect and industry—so did Franklin, and so have multitudes whose memories are renowned.

The greatest heroes of the battle-field—as Napoleon, Hannibal, Cromwell—some of the greatest statesmen and orators, ancient and modern—as Demosthenes, Chatham, Burke, and our own Webster and Clay—could boast no patrician advantages, no capital in gold, to start with. The grandest fortunes ever accumulated or possessed on earth were and are, the fruit of endeavor that had no capital to begin with save energy, intellect, and the will. From Crœsus down to Astor, the story is the same—not only in the getting of wealth, but also in the acquire-ment of various eminence—those men have won most, who relied most upon themselves.

The path of success in business is invariably the path of common sense. Notwithstanding all that is said about "lucky hits," the best kind of success in every man's life is not that which comes by accident. The only "good time coming" we are justified in hoping for, is that which we are capable of making for ourselves. The fable of the labors of Hercules is indeed the type of all human doing and success. Every youth should be made to feel that if he would get through the world usefully and happily, he must rely mainly upon himself and his own independent energies. Making a small provision for young men is hardly justifiable; and it is of all things the most prejudicial to themselves. They think what they have that which is much larger than it really is; and they make no exertion. The young should never hear any language but this: "You have your own way to make, and it depends upon your own exertions whether you starve or not." Outside help is your greatest curse. It handcuffs effort, stifles aspiration, shuts the prison door upon emulation, turns the key on energy.

The wisest charity is to help a man to help himself. To put a man in the way of supporting himself gives him a new lease of life, makes him feel young again, for it is very many times all the sick man needs to restore him to perfect health.

People who have been bolstered up and levered all their lives, are seldom good for anything in a crisis. When misfortune comes, they look around for somebody to cling to, or lean upon. If the prop is not there, down they go. Once down, they are as helpless as capsized turtles, or unhorsed men in armor, and they can not find their feet again without assistance.

There are multitudes of such men. They are like summer vines, which never grow even ligneous, but stretch out a thousand little hands to grasp the stronger shrubs; and if they can not reach them, they lie disheveled in the grass, hoof-trodden, and beaten of every storm. It will be found that the first real movement upward will not take place until, in a spirit of resolute self-denial, indolence, so natural to almost every one, is mastered. Necessity is, usually, the spur that sets the sluggish energies in motion. Poverty, therefore, is oftener a blessing to a young man than prosperity; for, while the one tends to stimulate his powers, the other inclines them to languor and disuse. But, is it not very discreditable for the young man, who is favored with education, friends, and all the outside advantages which could be desired as means to worldly success, to let those who stand, in these respects, at the beginning, far below him, gradually approach as the steady years move on, and finally outstrip him in the race? It is not only discreditable, but disgraceful. A man's true position in society is that which he achieves for himself—he is worth to the world no more, no less. As he builds for society in useful work, so he builds for himself. He is a man for what he does, not for what his father or his friends have done. If they have done well, and given him a position, the deeper the shame, if he sink down to a meaner level through self-indulgence and indolence.

If the boy be not trained to endure and to bear trouble, he will grow up a girl; and a boy that is a girl has all a girl's weakness without any of her regal qualities. A woman made out of a woman is God's noblest work; a woman made out of a man is his meanest. A child rightly brought up will be like a willow branch, which, broken off and touching the ground, at once takes root. Bring up your children so that they will root easily in their own soil, and not forever be grafted into your old trunk and boughs.

Labor.

THERE is dignity in toil—in toil of the hand as well as toil of the head—in toil to provide for the bodily wants of an individual life, as well as in toil to promote some enterprise of world-wide fame. All labor that tends to supply man's wants, to increase man's happiness, to elevate man's nature—in a word, all labor that is honest—is honorable too. Labor clears the forest, and drains the morass, and makes "the wilderness rejoice and blossom as the rose."

Labor drives the plow, and scatters the seeds, and
reaps the harvest, and grinds the corn, and converts
it into bread, the staff of life. Labor, tending the
pastures and sweeping the waters as well as cultivating the soil, provides with daily sustenance the thous-
and millions of the family of man. Labor gathers the
gossamer web of the caterpillar, the cotton from the
field, and the fleece from the flock, and weaves it into
raiment soft and warm and beautiful, the purple robe
of the prince and the gray gown of the peasant being
alike its handiwork. Labor molds the brick, and
splits the slate, and quarries the stone, and shapes
the column, and rears not only the humble cottage,
but the gorgeous palace, and the tapering spire, and
the stately dome. Labor, diving deep into the solid
earth, brings up its long-hidden stores of coal to
feed ten thousand furnaces, and in millions of homes
to defy the winter's cold.

Labor explores the rich veins of deeply-buried
rocks, extracting the gold and silver, the copper and
tin. Labor smelts the iron, and molds it into a
thousand shapes for use and ornament, from the massive pillar to the tiniest needle, from the ponderous
anchor to the wire gauze, from the mighty fly-wheel
of the steam-engine to the polished purse-ring or the
glittering bead. Labor hews down the gnarled oak,
and shapes the timber, and builds the ship, and
guides it over the deep, plunging through the billows,
and wrestling with the tempest, to bear to our shores
the produce of every clime. Labor, laughing at difficulties, spans majestic rivers, carries viaducts over

marshy swamps, suspends bridges over deep ravines, pierces the solid mountain with the dark tunnel, blasting rocks and filling hollows, and while linking together with its iron but loving grasp all nations of the earth, verifies, in a literal sense, the ancient prophecy, "Every valley shall be exalted, and every mountain and hill shall be brought low." Labor draws forth its delicate iron thread, and stretching it from city to city, from province to province, through mountains and beneath the sea, realizes more than fancy ever fabled, while it constructs a chariot on which speech may outstrip the wind, and compete with lightning, for the telegraph flies as rapidly as thought itself.

Labor, the mighty magician, walks forth into a region uninhabited and waste; he looks earnestly at the scene, so quiet in its desolation, then waving his wonder-working wand, those dreary valleys smile with golden harvests; those barren mountain-slopes are clothed with foliage; the furnace blazes; the anvil rings; the busy wheel whirls round; the town appears, the mart of commerce, the hall of science, the temple of religion, rear high their lofty fronts; a forest of masts, gay with varied pennons, rises from the harbor, representatives of far-off regions make it their resort; science enlists the elements of earth and heaven in its service; art, awakening, clothes its strength with beauty; civilization smiles; liberty is glad; humanity rejoices; piety exults, for the voice of industry and gladness is heard on every side. Working men walk worthy of your vocation! You

have one able scutcheon; disgrace it not. There is
nothing really mean and low but sin. Stoop not
from your lofty throne to defile yourselves by contamination with intemperance, licentiousness, or any
form of evil. Labor, allied with virtue, may look up
to heaven and not blush, while all worldly dignities,
prostituted to vice, will leave their owner without a
corner of the universe in which to hide his shame.
You will most successfully prove the honor of toil by
illustrating in your own persons its alliance with a
sober, righteous and godly life. Be ye sure of this,
that the man of toil who works in a spirit of obedient,
loving homage to God, does no less than cherubim
and seraphim in their loftiest flights and holiest songs.

Labor achieves grander victories, it weaves more
durable trophies, it holds wider sway, than the conqueror. His name becomes tainted and his monuments crumble; but labor converts his red battle-fields
into gardens, and erects monuments significant of
better things. Labor rides in a chariot driven by the
wind. It writes with the lightning. It sits crowned
as a king in a thousand cities, and sends up its roar
of triumph from a million wheels. It glistens in the
fabric of the loom, it rings and sparkles from the
steely hammer, it glories in shapes of beauty, it
speaks in words of power, it makes the sinewy arm
strong with liberty, the poor man's heart rich with
content, crowns the swarthy and sweaty brow with
honor, and dignity, and peace.

Don't live in hope with your arms folded; fortune
smiles on those who roll up their sleeves, and put

their shoulders to the wheel. You cannot dream yourself into a character; you must hammer and forge yourself one. To love and to labor is the sum of living, and yet how many think they live who neither love nor labor.

The man and woman who are above labor, and despise the laborer, show a want of common sense, and forget that every article that is used is the product of more or less labor, and that the air they breathe, and the circulation of the blood in the veins, is the result of the labor of the God of nature. The time was when kings and queens stimulated their subjects to labor by example. Queen Mary had her regular hours of work, and had one of her maids of honor read to her while she plied the needle. Sir Walter Raleigh relates a cutting reply made to him by the wife of a noble duke, at whose house he lodged over night. In the morning he heard her give directions to a servant relative to feeding the pigs. On going into the breakfast room he jocosely asked her if the pigs had all breakfasted. "All, sir, but the strange pig I am about to feed," was the witty reply. Sir Walter was mute, and walked up to the trough.

The noblest thing in the world is honest labor. It is the very preservative principle of the universe. Wise labor brings order out of chaos; it turns deadly bogs and swamps into grain-bearing fields; it rears cities; it adorns the earth with architectural monuments, and beautifies them with divinest works of art; it whitens the seas with the wings of commerce; it brings remote lands into mutual and profitable neighborhood; it binds continents together with the fast-holding bands of railroads and telegraphs; it extinguishes barbarism and plants civilization upon its ruins; it produces mighty works of génius in prose and verse, which gladden the hearts of men forever. Work, therefore, with pride and gladness, for thereby you will be united by a common bond with all the best and noblest who have lived, who are now living, and who shall ever be born.

Washington and his lady were examples of industry, plainness, frugality and economy—and thousands of others of the wealthy, labored in the field and kitchen, in older times, before folly superseded wisdom, and fashion drove common sense and economy off the track.

No man has the right to expect a good fortune, unless he go to work and deserve it. "Luck!" cried a self-made man, "I never had any luck but by getting up at five every morning and working as hard as I could." No faithful workman finds his task a pastime. We must all toil or steal—no matter how we name our stealing. A brother of the distinguished Edmund Burke was found in a revery after listening to one of his most eloquent speeches in Parliament, and being asked the cause, replied, "I have been wondering how Ned has contrived to monopolize all the talents of the family; but then I remember, when we were at play he was always at work."

The education, moral and intellectual, of every individual must be chiefly *his own work*. How else could it happen that young men, who have had precisely the same opportunities, should be continually presenting us with such different results, and rushing to such opposite destinies? Difference of talent will not solve it, because that difference is very often in favor of the disappointed candidate.

You will see issuing from the walls of the same college — nay, sometimes from the bosom of the same family — two young men, of whom the *one* shall be admitted to be a genius of high order, the *other* scarcely above the point of mediocrity; yet you shall see the genius sinking and perishing in poverty, obscurity and wretchedness, while, on the other hand, you shall observe the mediocre plodding his slow but sure way up the hill of life, gaining steadfast footing at every step, and mounting, at length, to eminence and distinction — an ornament to his family, a blessing to his country.

Now, whose work is this? Manifestly their own. Men *are* the architects of their respective fortunes. It is the fiat of fate from which no power of genius can absolve you. Genius, unexerted, is like the poor moth that flutters around a candle till it scorches itself to death.

It is this capacity for high and long continued exertion, this vigorous power of profound and searching investigation, this careening and wide-spreading comprehension of mind, and those long reaches of thought, that

> " Pluck bright honor from the pale-faced moon,
> Or dive into the bottom of the deep,
> Where fathom line could never touch the ground,
> And drag up drowned honor by the locks."

What we have seen of men and of the world convinces us that one of the first conditions of enjoying life is to *have something to do,* something great enough to rouse the mind and noble enough to satisfy the heart, and then *to give our mind and heart,* our thought and toil and affections to it, to labor for it, in the fine words of Robert Hall, "with an ardor bordering on enthusiasm," or, as a yet greater sage expresses it, to *"do it with all our might."*

A life of full and constant employment is the only safe and happy one. If we suffer the mind and body to be unemployed, our enjoyments, as well as our labors, will be terminated. One of the minor uses of steady employment is, that it keeps one out of mischief; for truly an idle brain is the devil's workshop, and a lazy man the devil's bolster. To be occupied is to be possessed as by a tenant, whereas to be idle is to be empty; and when the doors of the imagination are opened, temptation finds a ready access, and evil thoughts come trooping in. It is observed at sea that men are never so much disposed to grumble and mutiny as when least employed. Hence an old captain, when there was nothing else to do, would issue the order to "scour the anchor."

Labor, honest labor, is mighty and beautiful. Activity is the ruling element of life, and its highest relish. Luxuries and conquests are the result of labor; we can imagine nothing without it. The noblest man of earth is he who puts his hands cheerfully and proudly to honest labor. Labor is a business and ordinance of God. Suspend labor, and where are the glory and pomp of earth—the fruit, fields, and palaces, and the fashioning of matter for which men strive and war? Let the labor-scorner look to himself and learn what are the trophies. From the crown of his head to the sole of his foot, he is the debtor and slave of toil. The labor which he scorns has tricked him into the stature and appearance of a man. Where gets he garmenting and equipage? Let labor answer. Labor—which makes music in the mines and the furrow and the forge—oh, scorn not labor, you man who never yet earned a morsel of bread! Labor pities you, proud fool, and laughs you to scorn. You shall pass to dust, forgotten; but labor will live on forever, glorious in its conquests and monuments.

------◆◆◆◆------

Energy.

THE longer we live the more we are certain the great difference between men—between the feeble and the powerful, the great and the insignificant, is *energy; invincible determination*—a purpose, once fixed, and then death or victory! That quality will do anything that can be done in this world; and no talents, no circumstances, no opportunities, will make a two-legged creature a man without it.

Never suffer your energies to stagnate. There is no genius of life like the genius of energy and industry. All the traditions current among very

young men that certain great characters have wrought
their greatness by an inspiration, as it were, grows
out of a sad mistake.   There are no rivals so formidable as those earnest, determined minds, which reckon
the value of every hour, and which achieve eminence
by persistent application.

The difference between one boy and another consists not so much in talent as in energy.   Provided
the dunce have persistency and application, he will
inevitably head the cleverer fellow without these qualities.   Slow but sure wins the race.   It is perseverance that explains how the position of boys at school
is often reversed in real life; and it is curious to note
how some who were then so clever have since become
so common-place, whilst others, dull boys, of whom
nothing was expected, slow in their faculties, but sure
in their pace, have assumed the position of leaders of
men.   We recollect that when a boy we stood in the
same class with one of the greatest of dunces.   One
teacher after another had tried his skill upon him and
failed.   Corporeal punishment, the fool's-cap, coax-
ing, and earnest entreaty, proved alike fruitless.
Sometimes the experiment was tried of putting him
at the top of his class, and it was curious to note the
rapidity with which he gravitated to the inevitable bottom, like a lump of lead passing through quicksilver.
The youth was given up by many teachers as an incor-
rigible dunce—one of them pronouncing him to be
"a stupendous booby."   Yet, slow though he was,
this dunce had, a dull energy and a sort of beefy
tenacity of purpose, which grew with his muscles and

his manhood; and, strange to say, when he at length came to take part in the practical business of life, he was found heading most of his school companions, and eventually left the greater number of them far behind. The tortoise in the right road will beat a racer in the wrong. It matters not though a youth be slow, if he be but diligent. Quickness of parts may even prove a defect, inasmuch as the boy who learns readily will often forget quite as readily; and also because he finds no need of cultivating that quality of application and perseverance which the slower youth is compelled to exercise, and which proves so valuable an element in the formation of every character. The highest culture is not obtained from teachers when at school or college, so much as by our own diligent self-education when we have become men. Parents need not be in too great haste to see their children's talents forced into bloom. Let them watch and wait patiently, letting good example and quiet training do their work, and leave the rest to Providence. Let them see to it that the youth is provided, by free exercise of his bodily powers, with a full stock of physical health; set him fairly on the road of self-culture; carefully train his habits of application and perseverance; and as he grows older, if the right stuff be in him, he will be enabled vigorously and effectively to cultivate himself.

He who has heart has everything; and who does not burn does not inflame. It is astonishing how much may be accomplished in self-culture by the energetic and the persevering, who are careful to avail themselves of opportunities, and use up the fragments of spare time which the idle permit to run to waste. In study as in business, energy is the great thing. We must not only strike the iron while it is hot, but strike it until it is made hot.

Give us not men like weathercocks, that change with every wind, but men like mountains, who change the winds themselves. There is always room for a man of force and he makes room for many. You cannot dream yourself into a character; you must hammer and forge yourself one. Therefore don't live in hope with your arms folded; fortune smiles on those who roll up their sleeves and put their shoulders to the wheel. "I can't! it is impossible!" said a foiled lieutenant to Alexander. "Begone!" shouted the conquering Macedonian in reply—"there is nothing impossible to him who will try;" and to make good his words, the haughty warrior, not yet come to weep that there were no more worlds to subdue, charged with a phalanx the rock-crested fortress that had defied his timid subaltern, and the foe were swept down as with the besom of destruction.

A man's character is seen in small matters; and from even so slight a test as the mode in which a man wields a hammer, his energy may in some measure be inferred. Thus an eminent Frenchman hit off in a single phrase the characteristic quality of the inhabitants of a particular district, in which a friend of his proposed to buy land and settle. "Beware," said he, "of making a purchase there; I know the men of that department; the pupils who come from it to our veterinary school at Paris, *do not strike hard upon the anvil;* they want energy; and you will not get a satisfactory return on any capital you may invest there;"—a fine and just appreciation of character, indicating the accurate and thoughtful observer; and strikingly illustrative of the fact that it is the energy of the individual man that gives strength to a state, and confers a value even upon the very soil which he cultivates.

It is a Spanish maxim, that he who loseth wealth, loseth much; he who loseth a friend, loseth more; but he who loseth his energies, loseth all.

Luck and Pluck.

YOUNG man, your success or your failure, your weal or woe of life will hang largely in the manner in which you treat these two words.

Rev. G. S. Weaver says: "The word luck is suggestive of a want of law." This idea has passed into many common proverbs, such as these: "It is more by hit than good wit;" "It is as well to be born lucky as rich;" "Fortune is a fickle jade;" "Risk nothing, win nothing;" and more of a similar import, all ignoring the grand rule of law and resting upon the atheistical idea of *chance.*

Our fathers were good, religious people, and did not mean to foster atheism when they talked about

luck, and gave a half-way assent to its Godless reality.   If the universe were an infinite chaos; if order
had no throne in its wide realm; if universal law
were a fable of fancy; if God were a Babel, or the
world a Pandemonium, there might be such a thing
as luck.   But while from the particle to the globe,
from the animalcule to the archangel, there is not a
being or a thing, a time or an event, disconnected
with the great government of eternal law and order,
we cannot see how such a game of chance as the
word luck supposes can be admitted into any corner
of the great world.   Luck!   What is it?   A lottery?
A hap-hazard?   A frolic of gnomes?   A blind-man's-
bluff among the laws?   A ruse among the elements?
A trick of dame nature?   Has any scholar defined
luck, any philosopher explained its nature, any chem-
ist shone us its elements?   Is luck that strange, non-
descript unmateriality that does all things among men
that they cannot account for?   If so, why does not
luck make a fool speak words of wisdom? an igno-
ramus utter lectures on philosophy; a stupid dolt
write the great works of music and poetry; a double-
fingered dummy create the beauties of art, or an
untutored savage the wonders of mechanism?

If we should go into a country where the slug-
gard's farm was covered with the richest grains and
fruits, and where industry was rewarded only with
weeds and brambles; where the drunkard looked
sleek and beautiful, and his home cheerful and happy,
while temperance wore the haggard face and ate
the bread of want and misery; where labor starved,

while idleness was fed and grew fat; where common
sense was put upon the pillory, while twaddle and
moonshine were raised to distinction; where genius
lay in the gutter and ignorance soared to the skies;
where virtue was incarcerated in prison, while vice
was courted and wooed by the sunlight, we might
possibly be led to believe that luck had something to
do there. But where we see, as we everywhere do
in our world, the rewards of industry, energy, wisdom and virtue constant as the warmth in sunlight or
beauty in flowers, we must deny *in toto* the very
existence of this good and evil essence which men
have called *luck*.

Was it luck that gave Girard and Astor, Rothschild
and Gray their vast wealth? Was it luck that won
victories for Washington, Wellington, and Napoleon?
Was it luck that carved Venus de' Medici, that wrote
the "Æneid," "Paradise Lost," and "Festus?" Was
it luck that gave Morse his telegraph, or Fulton his
steamboat, or Franklin the lightning for his plaything?
Is it luck that gives the merchant his business, the
lawyer his clients, the minister his hearers, the physician his patients, the mechanic his labor, the farmer
his harvest? Nay, verily. No man believes it. And
yet many are the men who dream of luck, as though
such a mysterious spirit existed, and did sometimes
humor the whims of visionary cowards and drones.

Many are the young men who waste the best part
of their lives in attempts to woo this coy maid into
their embraces. They enter into this, or that, or the
other speculation, with the dreamy hope that luck will

pay them a smiling visit. Some go to California, or
Australia, or the "Far West," or to the torrid or the
frigid zone, or some wondrous away-off place, with
no fair prospect or hope of success from their own
energies and exertions, but depending almost wholly
on a gentle smile from capricious luck. Poor fellows!
they find that luck does not get so far from home.

Some, less daring and more lazy, loiter about home,
drawl around town, or loll through the country. Their
only trust or expectation is in a shuffle of luck in their
favor. They know they deserve nothing, yet, with
an impudence hard as brass, they will pray to luck for
a "windfall," or a "fat office, or a "living," and fool-
ishly wait for an answer. These are the men who
make your gamblers, your horse-thieves, your coun-
terfeiters, your gentleman-loafers. They are not men
who originally meant any harm. But they believe in
luck, and their trust is in luck, and they are going to
have it out of luck some way. They despised meanness at first, perhaps, as much as you and we do; but
somebody told them of luck, and they believed, and
lo! they got duped. Little by little they went over
to meanness, waiting all the while for a shake of the
hand from luck.

Some of the believers in luck of more moral firmness, dally with all life's great duties, and so do about
the same as nothing, and eat the bread of disappointment. They do a little at this business, and luck does
not smile. They do a little at that, and still luck
keeps away. They do a little at something else, they
hear not a foot-fall from luck. And so they fritter

away time and life. These are the do-littles. Hard-
working men they are frequently. It is with them as
though they had started to go to a place a thousand
miles distant, leading to which there were many roads.
They set out at full speed on one road, go a few miles,
and get tired, and so conclude to turn back and try
another. And so they try one road after another,
each time returning to the starting-place. In a little
while it is too late to get there at the appointed time,
and so they mope along any road they happen to be
on till the day is over.

They crave a good they do not earn; they pray to
luck to give what does not belong to them; their
whole inward life is a constant craving wish for something to which they have no just claim. It is a morbid,
feverish covetousness, which is very apt to end in the
conclusion, "The world owes me a living, and a living
I'll have," and so they go out to get a living as best
they may. They fancy that every rich and honored
man has got his good by some turn of luck, and
hence they feel that he has no special right to his
property or his honors, and so they will get either
from him if they can. They look upon the world,
not as a great hive of industry, where men are
rewarded according to their labors and merits, but as
a grand lottery, a magnificent scheme of chance, in
which fools and idlers have as fair a show as talent
and labor.

In our humble opinion, this philosophy of luck is
at the bottom of more dishonesty, wickedness, and
moral corruption than anything else. It sows its

seeds in youthful minds just at that visionary season
when judgment has not been ripened by experience
nor imagination corrected by wisdom. And it takes
more minds from the great school-house of useful
life, and more arms from the great workshop of human
industry, than any other one thing to which our mind
reverts. It is a moral palsy, against which every just
man should arm himself. The cure of the evil is
found in pluck.

It is not luck, but pluck, which weaves the web of
life ; it is not luck, but pluck, which turns the wheel
of fortune. It is pluck that amasses wealth, that
crowns men with honors, that forges the luxuries of
life. We use the term pluck as synonymous with
whole-hearted energy, genuine bravery of soul.

That man is to be pitied who is too fearful and
cowardly to go out and do battle for an honest living
and a competence in the great field of human exertion. He is the man of luck, bad luck. Poor fellow!
He lost his luck when he lost his pluck. Good pluck
is good luck. Bad pluck is bad luck. Many a man
has lost his luck, but never while he had good pluck
left. Men lose their luck by letting their energies
leak out through bad habits and unwise projects.
One man loses his luck in his late morning naps,
another in his late evening hours. One loses his luck
in the bar-room, another in the ball-room ; one down
by the river holding the boyish fishing-rod, another
in the woods chasing down the innocent squirrel.
One loses his luck in folly, one in fashion, one in idleness, one in high living, one in dishonesty, one in

brawls, one in sensualism, and a great many in bad
management. Indeed, bad management is at the
bottom of nearly all bad luck. It is bad management
to train up a family of bad habits, to eat out one's
living and corrupt his life. It is bad management to
drink liquor, and eat tobacco, and smoke, and swear,
and tattle, and visit soda-fountains, and cream saloons,
and theatres, and brothels, and live high, and chase
after the fashions, and fret and scold, and get angry,
and abuse people, and mind other people's business
and neglect one's own. It is bad management to
expose one's health or overtax one's powers, and get
sick, and take drugs to get well; to be idle or
extravagant, or mean or dishonest. All these things
tend to bring that evil genius which men call bad luck.

Indeed, there is hardly a word in the vocabulary
which is more cruelly abused than the word "luck."
To all the faults and failures of men, their positive
sins and the less culpable short-comings, it is made
to stand a godfather and sponsor. We are all Micaw-
bers at heart, fancying that "something" will one day
"turn up" for our good, for which we have never
striven.

An unskillful commander sometimes wins a victory;
and again a famous warrior finds himself, "after a
hundred victories, foiled." Some of the skillfulest
sea-captains lose every ship they sail in; others, less
experienced, never lose a spar. Some men's houses
take fire an hour after the insurance expires; others
never insure, and never are burned out. Some of
the shrewdest men, with indefatigable industry and

the closest economy, fail to make money; others, with apparently none of the qualities that insure success, are continually blundering into profitable speculations, and Midas-like, touch nothing but it turns to gold. Beau Brummell, with his lucky sixpence in his pocket, wins at every gaming-table, and bags £40,000 in the clubs of London and Newmarket.

So powerfully does fortune appear to sway the destinies of men, putting a silver spoon into one man's mouth, and a wooden one into another's, that some of the most sagacious of men, as Cardinal Mazarin and Rothschild, seem to have been inclined to regard luck as the first element of worldly success; experience, sagacity, energy, and enterprise as nothing, if linked to an unlucky star. Whittington, and his cat that proved such a source of riches; the man who, worn out by a painful disorder, attempted suicide, and was cured by opening an internal imposthume; the Persian, condemned to lose his tongue, on whom the operation was so bunglingly performed that it merely removed an impediment in his speech; the painter who produced an effect he had long toiled after in vain, by throwing his brush at the picture in a fit of rage and despair; the musical composer, who, having exhausted his patience in attempts to imitate on the piano a storm at sea, accomplished the precise result by angrily extending his hands to the two extremities of the keys, and bringing them rapidly together—all these seem to many fit types of the freaks of fortune by which some men are enriched or made famous by their blunders, while others, with ten times the capacity and knowledge, are kept at the bottom of her wheel. Hence we see thousands fold their arms and look with indifference on the great play of life, keeping aloof from its finest and therefore most arduous struggles, because they believe that success is a matter of accident, and that they may spend their heart's choicest blood and affection on noble ends, yet be balked of victory, cheated of any just returns. Really "lucky fellows" there have always been in the world; but in a great majority of cases they who are called such will be found on examination to be those keen-sighted men who have surveyed the world with a scrutinizing eye, and who to clear and exact ideas of what is necessary to be done unite the skill necessary to execute their well-approved plans.

At first, in our admiration of the man who stands upon the topmost round of the ladder of fame, we are apt to mistake the way in which he got there. Our eyes are weary with gazing up, and dazzled by the brilliant light; and we fancy that God must have let him down out of heaven for us; never thinking that he may have clambered up, round after round, through the mists which shroud the base of that ladder, while all the world, in its heedlessness, was looking another way. Then, when we come to know better, we are content to lie prostrate at the foot of our ladder, as Jacob slept beneath his, dreaming that they are angels whom we see ascending, and believing they ascend by heaven-born genius, or some miraculous way, not by pluck.

A better solution is that which explains the phe-

14

nomena of eminent success by industry. Clearly, the industrious use of ordinary tools, whether mechanical or intellectual, will accomplish far more than the mere possession of the most perfectly appointed tool-chest that was ever contrived. This is especially true of the mind, whose powers improve with use. When we reflect how the sharp wit-blade grows keener in often cutting, how the logic-hammer swells into a perfect sledge in long striking, how all our mental tools gain strength and edge in severe employment, we shall see that it is but a poor question to ask concerning success in life, "What tools had you?" —that a better question is, "How have you used your tools?"

One who thus educates himself up to success is often contented to labor a long while in a very humble sphere. He knows too much, indeed, to abandon one position before his powers for a higher one are fully ripe; for he has observed that they who leap too rapidly from one of life's stepping-stones to another, are more likely to lose their footing than to improve it. Very often, therefore, one who possesses this character grows up to complete manhood before his neighbors take him out of his cradle. In some Western parish, in some country practice, or at the head of some district school, he labors quietly for years and years, gathering a secret strength from every occurrence of his life, unnoticed, unknown, until at last the crisis of opportunity arrives—to every man such opportunity some time comes—and he starts forth, armed and equipped, thoroughly built

from head to foot; there is bone for strength, and
stout muscle for movement, and society around is
astonished to find that it contained such a power, and
knew it not. This rise of an individual, thus trained,
is sometimes surprising in its suddenness. To the
vision of mankind around, he seems to shoot up like
a rocket; and they gaze, and wonder, and glorify the
power of genius. Whereas he *grew*, grew by a
slow, steady, natural process of growth, available to
all men. He grew, however, under cover; and it
was not until circumstances threw the cover off him,
that we saw to what stature he had attained.

It is by the exercise of this forward-reaching
industry that men attain eminence in intellectual life.
The lives of eminent men of all nations determine,
by a vote almost overwhelming, that whatever may
have been their native powers, they did not attain
their ultimate success without the most arduous, well-
directed, life-lasting labor for self-improvement.

Idleness is death; activity is life. The worker is
the hero. Luck lies in labor. This is the end. And
labor the fruit of pluck. Luck and pluck, then, meet
in labor. Pleasure blossoms on the tree of labor.
Wisdom is its fruit. Thrones are built on labor.
Kingdoms stand by its steady props. Homes are
made by labor. Every man of pluck will make him
one and fill it with the fruits of industry. In doing
this he will find no time to wait for, or complain of,
luck.

Purpose and Will.

WE can never overestimate the power of purpose and will. It takes hold of the heart of life. It spans our whole manhood. It enters into our hopes, aims, and prospects. It holds its sceptre over our business, our amusements, our philosophy, and religion. Its sphere is larger than we can at first imagine.

The indomitable will, the inflexible purpose looking for future good through present evil, have always begotten confidence and commanded success, while the opposite qualities have as truly led to timid resolves, uncertain councils, alternate exaltation and depression, and final disappointment and disaster. A vacillating policy, irresolute councils, unstable will, subordination of the future to the present, efforts to relieve ourselves from existing trouble without providing against its recurrence, may bring momentary quiet, but expose us to greater disquiet than ever hereafter. A double-minded man is unstable in all his ways. Unstable as water, thou shalt not excel.

When a child is learning to walk, if you can induce the little creature to keep its eyes fixed on any point in advance, it will generally "navigate" to that point without capsizing; but distract its attention by word or act from the object before it, and down goes the baby. The rule applies to children of a larger growth. The man who starts in life with a determination to reach a certain position, and adheres unwaveringly to his purpose, rejecting the advice of the over-cautious, and defying the auguries of the timid, rarely fails if he lives long enough to reach the goal for which he set out. If circumstances oppose him, he bends them to his exigencies by the force of energetic, indomitable will. On the other hand, he who vacillates in his course, "yawning," as the sailors say, toward all points of the compass, is pretty sure to become a helpless castaway before his voyage of life is half completed.

There can be no question among philosophic observers of men and events, that fixedness of purpose is a grand element of human success. Weathercock men are nature's failures. They are good for nothing.

The men of action, whose names are written imperishably on the page of history, were men of iron. Silky fellows may do for intrigue, but the founders, and conquerors, and liberators, and saviors of empires, have all been of the warrior metal. No human being who habitually halts between two opinions, who cannot decide promptly, and having decided, act as if there was no such word as fail, can ever be great. Cæsar would never have crossed the Rubicon, nor Washington the Delaware, had they not fixed their stern gaze on objects far beyond the perils at their feet.

Henry Ward Beecher, in a sermon, remarked: "We see supreme purposes which men have formed running through their whole career in this world. A young man means to be a civil engineer. That is the thing to which his mind is made up; not his father's mind, perhaps, but his. He feels his adaptation to that calling, and his drawing toward it. He is young, inexperienced, forgetful, accessible to youthful sym- pathies, and is frequently drawn aside from his life purpose. To-day he attends a picnic. Next week he devotes a day to some other excursion. Occasionally he loses a day in consequence of fatigue caused by overaction. Thus there is a link knocked out of the chain of this week, and a link out of the chain of that week. And in the course of the summer he takes a whole week, or a fortnight out of that purpose. Yet there is the thing in his mind, whether he sleeps or wakes. If you had asked him a month ago what he meant to be in life, he would have replied, 'I mean to be a civil engineer.' And if you ask him to-day what has been the tendency of his life, he will say, 'I have been preparing myself to be a civil engineer.' If he waits and does nothing, the reason is that he wants an opportunity to carry out his purpose. That pur- pose governs his course, and he will not engage in anything that would conflict with it.

"These generic principles in the soul are like those great invisible laws of nature, whose effects are seen in the falling of the pebble-stone, in all the various changes which natural objects undergo. When a man has formed in his mind a great sovereign pur- pose, it governs his conduct, as the law of nature governs the operation of physical things.

"Every man should have a *mark* in view, and pur- sue it steadily. He should not be turned from his course by other subjects ever so attractive. Life is not long enough for any one man to accomplish everything. Indeed but few can at best accomplish more than one thing well. Many, alas, very many! accomplish nothing worthy. Yet there is not a man endowed with fair or ordinary intellect or capacity but can accomplish at least one useful, important, worthy purpose.

"But few men could ever succeed in more than one of the learned professions. Perhaps the man never lived who could master and become eminent in the practice of all of them—certainly not in them, and also in agriculture and the mechanic arts. Our country, every country, abounds with men possessing sufficient natural capacity for almost or quite any pursuit they might select and pursue exclusively. Man's days, at most, are so few, and his capacity, at the highest, so small, that never yet has he even by confining the united efforts and energies of his life-time at the most trivial pursuit, much less in the deep and intricate learned professions, attained to perfection; and he never will. How much less, then, are the probabilities of his exhausting several, and those perhaps the most complicated spheres of man's activity."

It requires purpose, will, and oneness of aim and invincible determination to succeed in some one calling.

It is *will*—force of purpose—that enables a man to do or be whatever he sets his mind on being or doing. A holy man was accustomed to say, "What-

ever you wish, that you are; for such is the force of
our will, joined to the Divine, that whatever we wish
to be, seriously, and with a true intention, that we
become. No one ardently wishes to be submissive,
patient, modest, or liberal, who does not become
what he wishes."

Will is the monarch of the mind, ruling with despotic, and at times with tyrannical powers. It is the
rudder of the mind, giving directions to its movements. It is the engineer giving course and point,
speed and force to the mental machinery. It acts
like a tonic among the soul's languid powers. It is
the band that ties into a strong bundle the separate
faculties of the soul. It is the man's momentum; in
a word, it is that power by which the energy or energies of the soul are concentrated on a given point, or
in a particular direction: it fuses the faculties into one
mass, so that instead of scattering all over like grape
and canister, they spend their united force on one
point. The intellect is the legislative department, the
sensibilities are the judicial, and the will the executive.

Among the many causes of failure in life, none is
more frequent than that feebleness of the will which
is indicated by spasmodic action—by fitful effort,
or lack of persistence. Dr. Arnold, whose long experience with youth at Rugby gave weight to his opinion,
declared that "the difference between one boy and
another consists not so much in talent as in energy."
The very reputation of being strong willed, plucky,
and indefatigable, is of priceless value. It often
cows enemies and dispels at the start opposition to

one's undertakings which would otherwise be formidable.

Says Shakspeare, "Our bodies are our gardens; to the which our souls are gardeners: so that if we will plant nettles, or sow lettuce; sow hyssop, and weed up thyme; supply it with one gender of herbs, and distract it with many; either to have it sterile with idleness, or manured with industry; why, the power and corrigible authority of this lies in our wills."

Where there is a will there is a way. Nothing is impossible to him who wills. Will is the root; knowledge the stem and leaves; feeling the flower.

He who resolves upon doing a thing, by that very resolution often scales the barriers to it, and secures its achievement. To think we are able is almost to be so — to determine upon attainment, is frequently attainment itself. Thus, earnest resolution has often seemed to have about it almost a savor of Omnipotence. "You can only half will," Suwarrow would say to people who had failed. "I don't know," "I can't," and "impossible," were words which he destested above all others. "Learn! do! try!" he would exclaim.

Courage.

Nothing that is of real worth can be achieved without courageous working. Man owes his growth chiefly to that active striving of the will, that encounter with difficulty, which we call effort, and it is astonishing to find how often results apparently impracticable are thus made possible. An intense anticipation itself transforms possibility into reality; our desires being often but the precursors of the things which we are capable of performing. On the contrary, the timid and hesitating find everything impossible, chiefly because it seems so. It is related of a young French officer that he used to walk about his apartment exclaiming, "I *will* be marshal of France and a great general." This ardent desire was the presentiment of his success; for he did become a distinguished commander, and he died a marshal of France.

Courage, by keeping the senses quiet and the understanding clear, puts us in a condition to receive true intelligence, to make just computations upon danger, and pronounce rightly upon that which threatens us. Innocence of life, consciousness of worth, and great expectations are the best foundations of courage.

True courage is the result of reasoning. A brave mind is always impregnable. Resolution lies more in the head than in the veins; and a just sense of of honor and of infamy, of duty and of religion, will carry us further than all the force of mechanism.

To believe a business impossible is the way to make it so. How many feasible projects have miscarried through despondency, and been strangled in the birth by a cowardly imagination. It is better to meet danger than to wait for it. A ship on a lee shore stands out to sea in a storm to escape shipwreck.

Impossibilities, like vicious dogs, fly before him who is not afraid of them. Should misfortune overtake, retrench — work harder — but never fly the track — confront difficulties with unflinching perseverance. Should you then fail, you will be honored; but shrink, and you will be despised. When you put your hands to a work, let the fact of your doing so constitute the evidence that you mean to prosecute it to the end. Stand like a beaten anvil. It is the part of a great champion to be stricken and conquer.

> "Trouble's darkest hour
> Shall not make me cower
> To the sceptre's power —
> Never, never, never.
>
> "Then up my soul, and brace thee,
> While the perils face thee ;
> In thyself encase thee
> Manfully for ever.
>
> "Storms may howl around thee,
> Foes may hunt and hound thee ;
> Shall they overpower thee ?
> Never, never, never."

Courage, like cowardice, is undoubtedly contagious, but some persons are not at all liable to catch it. The attention of restless and fickle men turns to no account; poverty overtakes them whilst they are flying so many different ways to escape it. What is called courage is oftentimes nothing more than the fear of being thought a coward. The reverence that restrains us from violating the laws of God or man is not unfrequently branded with the name of cowardice. The Spartans had a saying, that he who stood most in fear of the law generally showed the least fear of an enemy. And we may infer the truth of this from the reverse of the proposition, for daily experience shows us that they who are the most daring in a bad cause are often the most pusillanimous in a good one.

Plutarch says courage consists not in hazarding without fear, but by being resolute in a just cause. An officer, after a very severe battle, on being complimented on standing his ground firmly, under a terrible fire, replied, "Ah, if you knew how I was frightened, you would compliment me more still." It is not the stolid man, or the reckless man, who exhibits the noblest bravery in the great battle of life. It is the man whose nerves and conscience are all alive; who looks before and behind; who weighs well all the probabilities of success or defeat, and is determined to stand his ground. There is another fine anecdote *apropos* to this subject: A phrenologist examining the head of the Duke of Wellington, said, "Your grace has not the organ of animal courage largely developed." "You are right," replied the great man, "and but for my sense of duty I should have retreated in my first fight." This first fight, in India, was one of the most terrible on record. O, that word "duty!" What is animal courage compared with it? Duty can create that courage, or its equivalent, but that courage never can create *duty*. The Duke of Wellington saw a man turn pale as he marched up to a battery. "That is a brave man," said he, "he knows his danger and faces it."

To lead the forlorn hope in the field of courage requires less nerve than to fight nobly and unshrinkingly the bloodless battle of life. To bear evil speaking and illiterate judgment with equanimity, is the highest bravery. It is, in fact, the repose of mental courage.

Physical courage, which despises all danger, will make a man brave in one way; and moral courage, which despises all opinion, will make a man brave in another. The former would seem most necessary for the camp, the latter for council; but to constitute a great man, both are necessary.

No one can tell who the heroes are, and who the cowards, until some crisis comes to put us to the test. And no crisis puts us to the test that does not bring us up alone and single-handed to face danger. It is nothing to make a rush with the multitude even into the jaws of destruction. Sheep will do that. Armies might be picked from the gutter, and marched up to make food for powder. But when some crisis singles one out from the multitude, pointing at him the particular finger of fate, and telling him, "Stand or run," and he faces about with steady nerve, with nobody else to stand behind, we may be sure the hero stuff is in him. When such a crisis comes, the true courage is just as likely to be found in people of shrinking nerves, or in weak and timid women, as in great burly people. It is a moral, not a physical trait. Its seat is not in the temperament, but the will. How courageous Peter was, and all those square-built fishermen of the sea of Galilee, at the Last Sup-

per, and in the garden of Gethsemane, where Peter
drew his sword and smote the officer! But when
Christ looked down from his cross, whom did he see
standing in that focus of Jewish rage? None of
those stout fishermen, but a young man and a tender-
hearted women—John and Mary.

A good cause makes a courageous heart. They
that fear an overthrow are half conquered. To be
valorous is not always to be venturous. A warm
heart requires a cool head.

Though the occasions of high heroic daring seldom
occur but in the history of the great, the less obtrusive
opportunities for the exertion of private energy are
continually offering themselves. With these, domestic
scenes as much abound as does the tented field. Pain
may be as firmly endured in the lonely chamber as
amid the din of arms. Difficulties can be manfully
combated; misfortunes bravely sustained; poverty
nobly supported; disappointments courageously encountered. Thus courage diffuses a wide and succor-
ing influence, and bestows energy apportioned to the
trial. It takes from calamity its dejecting quality, and
enables the soul to possess itself under every vicis-
situde. It rescues the unhappy from degradation,
and the feeble from contempt.

Courage, like every other emotion, however laudable in its pure form, may be allowed to degenerate
into a faulty extreme. Thus rashness, too often
assuming the name of courage, has no pretensions to
its merit. For rashness urges to useless and impossible efforts, and thus produces a waste of vigor and

spirit, that, properly restrained and well directed, would have achieved deeds worthy to be achieved. Rashness is the exuberance of courage, and ought to be checked, as we prune off the useless though vigorous shoots of shrubs and trees.

Little Things.

TRIFLES are not to be despised. The nerve of a tooth, not so large as the finest cambric needle, will sometimes drive a strong man to distraction. A musquito can make an elephant absolutely mad. The coral rock, which causes a navy to founder, is the work of tiny insects. The warrior that withstood death in a thousand forms may be killed by an insect. For want of a nail the shoe was lost; for want of a shoe the horse was lost; for want of a horse the rider was lost. Every pea helps to fill the peck. Little and often fills the purse. Moments are the golden sands of time. Every day is a little life; and our whole life is but a day repeated; those, therefore, who dare lose a day, are dangerously prodigal; those who dare misspend it, desperate. Springs are little things, but they are sources of large streams; a helm is a little thing, but it governs the course of a ship; a bridle bit is a little thing, but see its use and power; nails and pegs are little things, but they hold parts of large buildings together; a word, a look, a frown, all are little things, but powerful for good or evil.

Think of this, and mind the little things. Pay that little debt—its promise redeem.

Little acts are the elements of true greatness. They raise life's value like the little figures over the larger ones in arithmetic, to its highest power. They are tests of character and disinterestedness. They are the straws upon life's deceitful current, and show the current's way. The heart comes all out in them. They move on the dial of character and responsibility significantly. They indicate the character and destiny. They help to make the immortal man. It matters not so much where we are as what we are. It is seldom that acts of moral heroism are called for. Rather the real heroism of life is, to do all its little duties promptly and faithfully.

There are no such things as trifles in the biography of man. Drops make up the sea. Acorns cover the earth with oaks and the ocean with navies. Sands make up the bar in the harbor's mouth, on which vessels are wrecked; and little things in youth accumulate into character in age, and destiny in eternity. All the links in that glorious chain which is in all and around all, we can see and admire, or at least admit; but the staple to which all is fastened, and which is the conductor of all, is the Throne of Deity.

If you cannot be a great river, bearing great vessels of blessing to the world, you can be a little spring by the wayside of life, singing merrily all day and all night, and giving a cup of cold water to every weary, thirsty one who passes by.

Life is made up of little things. He who travels

over a continent must go step by step. He who
writes books must do it sentence by sentence. He
who learns a science must master it fact by fact, and
principle after principle. What is the happiness of
our life made up of? Little courtesies, little kind-
nesses, pleasant words, genial smiles, a friendly letter,
good wishes, and good deeds. One in a million—
once in a lifetime—may do a heroic action; but the
little things that make up our life come every day
and every hour. If we make the little events of life
beautiful and good, then is the whole life full of
beauty and goodness.

There is nothing too little for so little a creature as
man. It is by studying little things that we attain the
great art of having as little misery and as much happiness as possible. "If a straw," says Dryden, "can
be made the instrument of happiness, he is a wise
man who does not despise it." A very little thing
makes all the difference. You stand in the engine-
room of a steamer; you admit the steam to the cylinders, and the paddles turn ahead; a touch of a
lever, you admit the self-same steam to the self-same
cylinders, and the paddles turn astern. It is so,
oftentimes, in the moral world. The turning of a
straw decides whether the engines shall work forward
or backward. Look to the littles. The atomic
theory is the true one. The universe is but an
infinite attrition of particles. The grandest whole is
resolvable to fractions; or, as the ditty has it—

> "Little drops of water and little grains of sand,
> Fill the mighty ocean and form the solid land."

Is it not strange that, in the face of these facts, men will neglect details? that many even consider them beneath their notice, and, when they hear of the success of a business man who is, perhaps, more solid than brilliant, sneeringly say that he is "great in little things?" Is it not the "little things" that, in the aggregate, make up whatever is great? Is it not the countless grains of sand that make the beach; the trees that form the forest; the successive strata of rock that compose the mountains; the myriads of almost imperceptible stars that whiten the heavens with the milky-way? So with character, fortune, and all the concerns of life—the littles combined form the great bulk. If we look well to the disposition of these, the sum total will be cared for. It is the minutes wasted that wound the hours and mar the day. It is the pennies neglected that squander the dollars. The majority of men disdain littles —to many fractions are "vulgar" in more senses than the rule implies. It is apt to be thought indicative of a narrow mind and petty spirit to be scrupulous about littles. Yet from littles have sprung the mass of great vices and crimes. In habits, in manners, in business, we have only to watch the littles, and all will come out clear. The smallest leak, overlooked, may sink a ship—the smallest tendency to evil thinking or evil doing, left unguarded, may wreck character and life. No ridicule should dissuade us from looking to the littles. The greatest and best of men have not been above caring for the littles — some of which have to do with every hour and every purpose of our lives.

Often what seems a trifle, a mere nothing by itself, in some nice situation turns the scale of fate, and rules the most important actions. The cackling of a goose is fabled to have saved Rome from the Gauls, and the pain produced by a thistle to have warned a Scottish army of the approach to the Danes; and according to the following anecdote from Randall's "Life of Jefferson," it seems that flies contributed to hasten the American independence: While the question of independence was before Congress, it had its meeting near a livery stable. Its members wore short breeches and silk stockings, and, with handkerchief in hand, they were diligently employed in lashing the flies from their legs. So very vexatious was this annoyance, and to so great an impatience did it arouse the sufferers, that it hastened, if it did not aid in inducing them to promptly affix their signatures to the great document which gave birth to an empire republic!

Discoveries are made mostly by little things. The art of printing owes its origin to rude impressions (for the amusement of children) from letters carved on the bark of a beech tree. It was a slight matter which thousands would have passed over with neglect. Gunpowder was discovered from the falling of a spark on some material mixed in a mortar.

The stupendous results of the steam-engine may all be attributed to an individual observing steam issuing from a bottle just emptied and placed casually close to a fire. He plunged the bottle's neck into cold water and was intelligent enough to notice the instantaneous rush which ensued from this simple condensing apparatus.   Electricity was discovered by a person observing that a piece of rubbed glass, or some similar substance, attracted small bits of paper, etc.

Galvanism again owes its origin to Madame Galvani's noticing the contraction of the muscles of a skinned frog which was accidently touched by a person at the moment of the professor, her husband, taking an electric spark from a machine.   He followed up the hint by experiments.

Pendulum clocks were invented from Galileo's observing the lamp in a church swinging to and fro. The telescope we owe to some children of a spectacle-maker placing two or more pairs of spectacles before each other and looking through them at a distant object.   The glimpse thus afforded was followed up by older heads.

The barometer originated in the circumstance of a pump which had been fixed higher than usual above the surface of a well.   A sagacious observer hence deduced the pressure of the atmosphere and tried quicksilver.

The Argand lamp was invented by one of the brothers of that name having remarked that a tube held by chance over a candle caused it to burn with a bright flame.

Sedulous attention and painstaking industry always mark the true worker.   The greatest men are not those who "despise the day of small things," but those who improve it the most carefully.   Michael Angelo was one day explaining to a visitor at his studio what he had been doing at a statue since his previous visit. "I have retouched this part—polished that—softened this feature—brought out that muscle—given some expression to this lip, and more energy to that limb." "But these are trifles," remarked the visitor. "It may be so," replied the sculptor, "but recollect that trifles make perfection, and perfection is no trifle." So it was said of Nicholas Poissin the painter, that the rule of his conduct was, that "whatever was worth doing at all was worth doing well;" and when asked, late in life, by what means he had gained so high a reputation among the painters of Italy, he emphatically answered, "Because I have neglected nothing."

Many of the most distinguished names in the world's history were nearly half a century in attracting the admiring notice of mankind; as witness Cromwell and Cavour, and Bismarck and Palmerston, and the elder Beecher. But their star will never die; their works, their influence on the age in which they lived, will be perpetuated to remote generations. This should be encouragement to all the plodders, for *their* time may come.

It is the intelligent eye of the careful observer which gives apparently trivial phenomena their value. So trifling a matter as the sight of sea-weed floating past his ship, enabled Columbus to quell the mutiny which rose among his sailors at not discovering land, and to assure them that the eagerly sought New World was not far off. There is nothing so small that it should remain forgotten; and no fact, however trivial, but may prove useful in some way or other if carefully interpreted. Who could have imagined that the famous "chalk-cliffs of Albion" had been built up by tiny insects—detected only by the help of the microscope—of the same order of creatures that have gemmed the sea with islands of coral! And who that contemplates such extraordinary results, arising from infinitely minute operations, will venture to question the power of little things?

It is the close observation of little things which is the secret of success in business, in art, in science, and in every pursuit in life. Human knowledge is but an accumulation of small facts, made by successive generations of men, the little bits of knowledge and experience carefully treasured up by them growing at length into a mighty pyramid. Though many of these facts and observations seemed in the first instance to have but slight significance, they are all found to have their eventful uses, and to fit into their proper places. Even many speculations seemingly remote turn out to be the basis of results the most obviously practical. In the case of the conic sections discovered by Apollonius Pergœus, twenty centuries elapsed before they were made the basis of astronomy —a science which enables the modern navigator to steer his way through unknown seas, and traces for him in the heavens an unerring path to his appointed haven. And had not mathematics toiled for so long, and, to uninstructed observers, apparently so fruitlessly, over the abstract relations of lines and surfaces, it is probable that but few of our mechanical inventions would have seen the light.

When Franklin made his discovery of the identity of lightning and electricity, it was sneered at, and people asked, "Of what use is it?" to which his apt reply was, "What is the use of a child? It may become a man!" When Galvani discovered that a frog's leg twitched when placed in contact with different metals, it could scarcely have been imagined that so apparently insignificant a fact could have lead to important results. Yet therein lay the germ of the electric telegraph, which binds the intelligence of continents together, and has "put a girdle round the globe." So, too, little bits of stone and fossil, dug out of the earth, intelligently interpreted, have issued in the science of geology and the practical operations of mining, in which large capitals are invested and vast numbers of persons profitably employed.

Economy.

ECONOMY is the parent of integrity, of liberty, and of ease; of cheerfulness, and of health; and profuseness is a cruel and crazy demon, that gradually involves her followers in dependence and debt; that is, fetters them with "irons that enter into their souls."

A sound economy is a sound understanding brought into action. It is calculation realized; it is the doctrine of proportion reduced to practice. It is foreseeing contingencies and providing against them. Economy is one of three sisters of whom the other

and less reputable two are avarice and prodigality..
She alone keeps the straight and safe path, while avarice sneers at her as profuse, and prodigality scorns at
her as penurious.   To the poor she is indispensable ;
to those of moderate means she is found the representative of wisdom.   The loose change which many
young men throw away uselessly, and sometimes
even worse, would often form the basis of fortune and
independence.   But when it is so recklessly squandered it becomes the worst enemy to the young man.
He will soon find that he has bought nothing but
expensive habits, and perhaps a ruined character.
Economy, joined to industry and sobriety is a better
outfit to business than a dowry.

We don't like stinginess, we don't like economy,
when it comes down to rags and starvation.   We
have no sympathy with the notion that the poor man
should hitch himself to a post and stand still, while the
rest of the world moves forward.   It is no man's duty
to deny himself every amusement, every recreation,
every comfort, that he may get rich.   It is no man's
duty to make an iceberg of himself, to shut his eyes
and ears to the sufferings of his fellows, and to deny
himself the enjoyment that results from generous
actions, merely that he may hoard wealth for his heirs
to quarrel about.   But there is an economy which is
every man's duty, and which is especially commend-
able in the man who struggles with poverty—an
economy which is consistent with happiness, and
which must be practiced if the poor man would secure
independence.   It is almost every man's privilege,

and it becomes his duty, to live within his means; not to, but within them. This practice is of the very essence of honesty. For if a man does not manage honestly to live within his own means, he must necessarily be living dishonestly upon the means of some one else. If your means do not suit your ends, pursue those ends which suit your means. Men are ruined not by what they really want, but by what they think they want. Therefore they should never go abroad in *search* of their wants; if they be real wants they will come home in search of them; for if they buy what they do not want, they will soon want what they cannot buy.

Wealth does not make the man, we admit, and should never be taken into the account in our judgment of men; but competence should always be secured, when it can be, by the practice of economy and self-denial only to a tolerable extent. It should be secured, not so much for others to look upon, or to raise us in the estimation of others, as to secure the consciousness of independence, and the constant satisfaction which is derived from its acquirement and possession.

Simple industry and thrift will go far toward making any person of ordinary working faculty comparatively independent in his means. Almost every working man may be so, provided he will carefully husband his resources and watch the little outlets of useless expenditure. A penny is a very small matter, yet the comfort of thousands of families depends upon the proper saving and spending of pennies. If a

man allow the little pennies, the result of his hard
work, to slip out of his fingers—some to the beer-
shop, some this way and some that—he will find that
his life is little raised above one of mere animal
drudgery. On the other hand, if he take care of the
pennies; putting some weekly into a benefit society
or an insurance fund, others into a savings-bank, and
confiding the rest to his wife to be carefully laid out,
with a view to the comfortable maintenance and
education of his family, he will soon find that his
attention to small matters will abundantly repay him,
in increasing means, growing comfort at home, and a
mind comparatively free from fears as to the future.
If a working man have high ambition and possess
richness in spirit—a kind of wealth which far transcends all mere worldly possessions—he may not
only help himself, but be a profitable helper of others
in his path through life.

When one is blessed with good sense, and fair
opportunities, this spirit of economy is one of the
most beneficial of all secular gifts, and takes high rank
among the minor virtues. It is by this mysterious
power that the loaf is multiplied, that using does not
waste, that little becomes much, that scattered fragments grow to unity, and that out of nothing, or next
to nothing, comes the miracle of something! Economy
is not merely saving, still less, parsimony. It is foresight and arrangement. It is insight and combination. It is a subtle philosophy of things by which
new uses, new compositions are discovered. It causes
inert things to labor, useless things to serve our

necessities, perishing things to renew their vigor, and all things to exert themselves for human comfort. Economy is generalship in little things. We know men who live better on a thousand dollars a year than others upon five thousand. We know very poor persons who bear about with them in everything a sense of fitness and nice arrangement, which makes their life artistic. There are day laborers who go home to more real comfort of neatness, arrangement, and prosperity, in their single snug room, than is found in the lordly dwellings of many millionaires. And blessings be on their good angel of economy, which wastes nothing, and yet is not sordid in saving; that lavishes nothing, and is not parsimonious in giving; that spreads out a little with the blessings of taste upon it, which, if it does not multiply the provision, more than makes it up in the pleasure given. Let no man despise economy.

There is no virtue so unduly appreciated as economy, nor is there one more truly worthy of estimation; a neglect of economy eventually leads to every misery of poverty and degradation, not unfrequently to every variety of error and of crime. Dr. Johnson asserted "that where there was no prudence, there was no virtue." Of all the maxims pronounced by that great moralist, perhaps no one was more just or more instructive. Even in that branch of prudence that directs us to take cognizance of our pecuniary affairs, the propriety of this aphorism is very striking.

The progress of civilization has incurred a necessity of barter and exchange as the means of subsistence.

Thus wealth, as the medium of acquiring all the comforts and all the luxuries of life, has obtained high consideration among mankind. Philosophers may therefore scoff as much as they please at the value placed upon riches, but they will never succeed in lessening the desire for their possession. When considered as the means of enjoying existence, it must be seen that it is only by the judicious expenditure of wealth, that this end can be obtained. Pass a few years, and the prodigal is penniless. How few, under such circumstances, directly or indirectly, are guilty of injustice and cruelty. Debts unpaid, friends deceived, kindred deprived of a rightful inheritance — such are the consequences of profusion, and are not such positive acts of injustice and cruelty? Let those, therefore, who indignantly stigmatize the miser as a pest to society, and in a fancied honorable horror of miserly meanness are for showing their nobler spirit by running into an opposite extreme, reflect, that though different the means, the results of profusion are similar, exactly conducting to the same crimes and miseries. The taste of the age is so much more friendly to prodigality; the lavish expenditure of wealth, by conducing to the gratification of society, is so often unduly applauded, that it is an extreme likely to be rushed upon. But when the real consequences of its indulgence are fairly and dispassionately surveyed, its true deformity will be quickly perceived.

In short, economy appears to induce the exertion of almost every laudable emotion; a strict regard to hon-

esty; a spirit of independence; a judicious prudence
in providing for the wants; a steady benevolence in
preparing for the claims of the future.   Really we
seem to have run the circle of the virtues; justice and
disinterestedness, honesty, independence, prudence
and benevolence.

Farm Life.

AGRICULTURE is the greatest among the arts, for it
is first in supplying our necessities.   It is the mother
and nurse of all other arts.   It favors and strengthens
population; it creates and maintains manufactures,
gives employment to navigation and materials to commerce.   It animates every species of industry, and
opens to nations the surest channels of opulence.   It
is also the strongest bond of well-regulated society,
the surest basis of internal peace, the natural associate
of good morals.

We ought to count among the benefits of agriculture the charm which the practice of it communicates
to a country life.   That charm which has made the
country, in our own view, the retreat of the hero, the
asylum of the sage, and the temple of the historic
muse.   The strong desire, the longing after the
country, with which we find the bulk of mankind to
be penetrated, points to it as the chosen abode of
sublunary bliss.   The sweet occupations of culture,
with her varied products and attendant enjoyments

are, at least, a relief from the stifling atmosphere of the city, the monotony of subdivided employments, the anxious uncertainty of commerce, the vexations of ambition so often disappointed, of self-love so often mortified, of fictitious pleasures and unsubstantial vanities.

Health, the first and best of all the blessings of life, is preserved and fortified by the practice of agriculture. That state of well-being which we feel and cannot define; that self-satisfied disposition which depends, perhaps, on the perfect equilibrium and easy play of vital forces, turns the slightest acts to pleasure, and makes every exertion of our faculties a source of enjoyment; this inestimable state of our bodily functions is most vigorous in the country, and if lost elsewhere, it is in the country we expect to recover it.

> "In ancient times, the sacred plow employ'd
> The kings, and awful fathers of mankind:
> And some, with whom compared, your insect tribes
> Are but the beings of a summer's day,
> Have held the scale of empire, ruled the storm
> Of mighty war, then, with unwearied hand,
> Disdaining little delicacies, seized
> The plow *and greatly independent lived.*"
>
> —THOMSON'S SEASONS.

We deplore the disposition of young men to get away from their farm homes to our large cities, where they are subject to difficulties and temptations, which but too often they fail to overcome.

Depend upon it, if you would hold your sons and brothers back from roaming away into the perilous centres, you must steadily make three attempts—to abate the task-work of farming, to raise maximum crops and profits, and to surround your work with the exhilaration of intellectual progress. You must elevate the whole spirit of your vocation for your vocation's sake, till no other can outstrip it in what most adorns and strengthens a civilized state.

We have long observed, and with unfeigned regret, the growing tendency of young men and lads, yet early in their teens, to abandon the healthful and ennobling cares of the farm for the dangerous excitements and vicissitudes of city life and trade. Delightful firesides and friendly circles in the quiet rural districts are every day sacrificed to this lamentable mania of the times. Young men, favored with every comfort of life, and not overworked, fancy that they may do far better than "to guide the ox or turn the stubborn glebe;" and with the merest trifle of consideration their hands are withdrawn from the implements of agriculture and given to the office or shop-work of the city, which generally proves vastly less agreeable or profitable than they had (in their inexcusable thoughtlessness) anticipated. Disappointed and chagrined, they faint under the advance of

"Nimble mischance, that comes so swift of foot,"

and where one is enabled to withstand the sweeping tide of temptation, five are submerged in its angry waves and hurried on to ruin. Every year finds hundreds, ay, thousands, of such victims irrecoverably allied to the fallen and vicious of every class, from the smoothed-tongued parlor gambler and rake, to the more degraded, if not more despicable, "Bowery Boy" and "Dead Rabbit," while the prison doors, and worse, the gates of hell, close on many "lost ones" who had been saved but for the foolish desertion of home and true friends. It has been well said that "for a young man of unstable habits and without religious principles, there is no place where he will be so soon ruined as in a large city."

Parents throughout the country have not failed to realize this startling truth, and to sorely mourn the strange inclination of their sons to encounter the fascinating snares and pitfalls of city residence and fashion. In brief, let the country lad be as well educated for the farm as his city cousin is for the bar, or the counting-room. And by all possible means let the farmer be led to properly estimate his high and honorable position in the community. "Ever remember," writes Goldthwait, "that for health and substantial wealth, for rare opportunities for self-improvement, for long life and real independence, farming is the best business in the world." History tells of one who was called from the plow to the palace, from the farm to the forum; and when he had silenced the angry tumults of a State resumed again the quiet duties of a husbandman. Of whose resting-place did Halleck write these beautiful lines?

"Such graves as his are pilgrim-shrines,
Shrines to no code or creed confined —
The Delphian vales, the Palestines,
The Meccas of the mind."

He referred to Burns, the plow-boy, afterward the national bard of Scotland. And Burns himself has left evidence that he composed some of the rarest gems of his poetry while engaged in rural pursuits.

It would require volumes to enumerate the noble men who have imperishably recorded their exalted appreciation of rural life and enterprise. Every age has augmented the illustrious number. Our own immortal Washington was ever more enamored of the sickle than the sword, and unhesitatingly pronounced agriculture "the most healthy, the most useful, and the most noble employment of man."

When we walk abroad in nature, we go not as artists to study her scenes, but as her children to rejoice in her beauty. The breath of the air, the blue of the unclouded sky, the shining sun, and the green softness of the unflowered turf beneath our feet, are all that we require to make us feel that we are transported into a region of delights. We breathe and tread in a pure untroubled world, and the fresh clear delight that breathes round our senses seems to bathe our spirits in the innocence of nature. It is not that we have prized a solitude which secludes us from the world of life; but the aspects on which we look breathe a spirit; the characters we read speak a language which, mysterious and obscurely intelligible as they are, draw us on with an eager and undefined desire. In shapes and sounds of fear; in naked crags, gulfs, precipices, torrents that have rage without beauty, desolate places; there is to that temper of mind an attractive power. All speak in some way to the spirit, and raise up in it new and hidden emotion, which, even when mingled with pain, it is glad to feel; for such emotion makes discovery to it of its own nature, and the interest ·it feels so strongly springs up from and returns into itself.

Of all occupations, that of agriculture is best calculated to induce love of country, and rivet it firmly on the heart.   No profession is more honorable, none as conducive to health, peace, tranquility and happiness. More independent than any other calling, it is calculated to produce an innate love of liberty.   The farmer stands upon a lofty eminence, and looks upon the bustle of cities, the intricacies of mechanism, the din of commerce, and brain-confusing, body-killing literature, with feelings of personal freedom, peculiarly his own.   He delights in the prosperity of the city as his market place, acknowledges the usefulness of the mechanic, admires the enterprise of the commercial man, and rejoices in the benefits that flow from the untiring investigations and developments of science; then turns his thoughts to the pristine quiet of his agrarian domain, and covets not the fame that accumulates around the other professions.

Success.

TWENTY clerks in a store; twenty hands in a printing office; twenty apprentices in a shipyard; twenty young men in a village—all want to get on in the world, and expect to succeed. One of the clerks will become a partner and make a fortune; one of the compositors will own a newspaper and become an influential citizen; one of the apprentices will become a master builder; one of the young villagers will get a handsome farm and live like a patriarch — but which one is the lucky individual? Lucky! there is no luck about it. The thing is almost as certain as the Rule of Three. The young fellow who will distance his competitors is he who masters his business, who preserves his integrity, who lives cleanly and purely, who devotes his leisure hours to the acquisition of knowledge, who never gets into debt, who gains friends by deserving them, and who saves his spare money. There are some ways to fortune shorter than this old dusty highway — but the staunch men of the community, the men who achieve something really worth having, good fortune and serene old age, all go on in this road.

We hear a great deal about "good luck" and "bad luck." If a person has prospered in business, he is said to have had "good luck." If he has failed, he has had "bad luck." If he has been sick, good or bad luck is said to have visited him, accordingly as he got well or died. Or, if he has remained in good health, while others have been attacked by some epidemic disease, he has had the "good luck to escape that with which others have had the "bad luck" to be seized. Good or bad luck is, in most cases, but a synonym for good or bad judgment. The prudent, the considerate, and the circumspect seldom complain of ill luck.

We do not know anything which more fascinates youth than what, for want of a better word, we may call brilliancy. Gradually, however, this peculiar kind of estimation changes very much. It is no longer those who are brilliant, those who affect to do the most and the best work with the least apparent pains and trouble, whom we are most inclined to admire. We eventually come to admire labor, and to respect it the more, the more openly it is proclaimed by the laborious man to be the cause of his success, if he has any success to boast of.

A great moral safeguard is the habit of industry. This promotes our happiness, and so leaves no cravings for those vices which lead on and down to sin and its untold miseries. Industry conducts to prosperity. Fortunes may, it is true, be won in a day; but may also be lost in a day. It is only the hand of the diligent that makes one premanently rich. The late Mr. Ticknor, of Boston, a model merchant and publisher, in his last hours spoke of the value of a steady pursuit of one's legitimate business. He commented on the insane traffic in gold at that moment, as ruinous to the country and the parties engaged in it. "The pathway of its track," said he, "is strewn with wrecks of men and fortunes; but few have failed of success who were honest, earnest, and patient." He attributed his own success to his clinging to his resolution to avoid all speculations, and steadily pursuing the business of his choice. He had been bred to the trade of a broker; but thought it as dangerous as the lottery and dice. And no young man could fail to be warned by him, who had seen the frenzy that comes over the "Brokers' Board." "A Babel of conflicting sounds—a hot oven of excitement" is that board; it is a moral storm which few can withstand long. How much wiser is he who keeps out of this whirlpool, content with an honest calling and reasonable gains.

Who are the successful men? They are those who when boys were compelled to work either to help themselves or their parents, and who when a little older were under the stern necessity of doing more than their legitimate share of labor; who as young men had their wits sharpened by having to devise ways and means of making their time more available than it would be under ordinary circumstances. Hence in reading the lives of eminent men who have greatly distinguished themselves, we find their youth passed in self-denials of food, sleep, rest, and recreation. They sat up late, rose early, to the performance of imperative duties, doing by daylight the work of one man, and by night that of another. Said a gentleman, the other day, now a private banker of high integrity, and who started in life without a dollar, "For years I was in my place of business by sunrise, and often did not leave it for fifteen or eighteen hours." Let not, then, any youth be discouraged if he has to make his own living, or even to support a widowed mother, or sick sister, or unfortunate relative; for this has been the road to eminence of many a proud name. This is the path which printers and teachers have often trod—thorny enough at times, at others so beset with obstacles as to be almost impassible; but the way was cleared, sunshine came, success followed—then the glory and renown.

The secret of one's success or failure in nearly every enterprise is usually contained in answer to the question: How earnest is he? Success is the child of confidence and perseverance. The talent of success is simply doing what you can do well, and doing well whatever you do—without a thought of fame. Fame never comes because it is craved. Success is the best test of capacity. Success is not always a proper criterion for judging a man's character. It is certain that success naturally confirms us in a favorable opinion of ourselves. Success in life consists in the proper and harmonious development of those faculties which God has given us.

Be thrifty that you may have wherewith to be charitable. He that labors and thrives spins gold.

We are familiar with people who whine continually at fate. To believe them, never was a lot so hard as theirs; yet those who know their history will generally tell you that their life has been but one long tale of opportunities disregarded, or misfortunes otherwise deserved. Perhaps they were born poor. In this case they hate the rich, and have always hated them, but without ever having emulated their prudence or energy. Perhaps they have seen their rivals more favored by accident. In this event they forget how many have been less lucky than themselves; so they squandered their little, because, as they say, they cannot save as much as others. Irritated at life, they grow old prematurely. Dissatisfied with everything, they never permit themselves to be happy. Because they are not born at the top of the wheel of fortune, they refuse to take hold of the spoke as the latter comes around, but lie stubborn to the dirt, crying like spoiled children, neither doing anything themselves, nor permitting others to do it for them.

Some men make a mistake in marrying. They do not in this matter begin right. Have they their fortunes still to make? Too often, instead of seeking one who would be a helpmate in the true sense of the term, they unite themselves to a giddy, improvident creature, with nothing to recommend her but the face of a doll and a few showy accomplishments. Such a wife, they discover too late, neither makes home happy nor helps to increase her husband's means. At first, thriftless, extravagant and careless, she gradually becomes cross and reproachful, and while she envies other women, and reproaches her husband because he cannot afford to maintain her like them, is really the principal cause of his ill-fortune. The selection of a proper companion is one of the most important concerns of life. A well-assorted marriage assists, instead of retarding, a man's prosperity. Select a sensible, agreeable, amiable woman, and you will have secured a prize "better than riches." If you do otherwise, then, alas for you!

Treat every one with respect and civility. "Everything is gained, and nothing lost, by courtesy." "Good manners secure success." Never anticipate wealth from any other source than labor. "He who waits for dead men's shoes may have to go a long time barefoot." And above all, "*Nil desperandum,*" for "Heaven helps those who help themselves." If you implicitly follow these precepts, nothing can hinder you from accumulating. Let the business of everybody else alone, and attend to your own; don't buy what you don't want; use every hour to advantage, and study to make even leisure hours useful; think twice before you throw away a shilling; remember you will have another to make for it; find recreation in your own business; buy low, sell fair, and take care of the profits; look over your books regularly, and, if you find an error, trace it out; should a stroke of misfortune come over your trade, retrench, work harder, but never fly the track; confront difficulties with unceasing perseverance, and they will disappear at last; though you should fail in the struggle, you will be honored; but shrink from the task and you will be despised.

Engage in one kind of business only, and stick to it faithfully until you succeed, or until your experience shows that you should abandon it. A constant hammering on one nail will generally drive it home at last, so that it can be clinched. When a man's undivided attention is centred on one object, his mind will constantly be suggesting improvements of value, which would escape him if his brain were occupied by a dozen different subjects at once. Many a fortune has slipped through a man's fingers because he was engaging in too many occupations at a time. There is good sense in the old caution against having too many irons in the fire at once.

"At thy first entrace upon thy estate," once said a
wise man, "keep low sail, that thou mayst rise with
honor; thou canst not decline without shame; he that
begins where his father ends, will end where his father
began."

Everywhere in human experience, as frequently in
nature, hardship is the vestibule of the highest success. That magnificent oak was detained twenty
years in its upward growth while its roots took a great
turn around a boulder by which the tree was anchored
to withstand the storms of centuries.

In our intercourse with the world a cautious circumspection is of great advantage. Slowness of
belief, and a proper distrust, are essential to success.
The credulous and confiding are ever the dupes of
knaves and impostors. Ask those who have lost
their property how it happened, and you will find in
most cases it has been owing to misplaced confidence.
One has lost by indorsing; another by crediting;
another by false representations; all of which a little
more foresight and a little more distrust would have
prevented. In the affairs of this world men are not
saved by faith, but by the want of it.

They who are eminently successful in business, or
who achieve greatness, or even notoriety in any pursuit, must expect to make enemies. Whoever becomes distinguished is sure to be a mark for the
malicious spite of those who, not deserving success
themselves, are galled by the merited triumph of the
more worthy. Moreover, the opposition which originates in such despicable motives, is sure to be of the

most unscrupulous character; hesitating at no iniquity, descending to the shabbiest littleness. Opposition, if it be honest and manly, is not in itself undesirable. It is the whetstone by which a highly tempered nature is polished and sharpened. He that has never known adversity, is but half acquainted with others or with himself. Constant success shows us but one side of the world. For, as it surrounds us with friends, who will tell us only our merits, so it silences those enemies from whom alone we can learn our defects.

Industry.

OUR success in life generally bears a direct proportion to the exertions we make, and if we aim at nothing we shall certainly achieve nothing. By the remission of labor and energy, it often happens that poverty and contempt, disaster and defeat, steal a march upon prosperity and honor, and overwhelm us with reverses and shame.

A very important principle in the business of money-getting, is industry—persevering, indefatigable attention to business. Persevering diligence is the philosopher's stone, which turns everything to gold. Constant, regular, habitual, and systematic application to business, must, in time, if properly directed, produce great results. It must lead to wealth, with the same certainty that poverty follows in the train of idleness and inattention.

It has been said that the best cure for hard times is to cheat the doctor by being temperate; the lawyer, by keeping out of debt; the demagogue, by voting for honest men; and poverty, by being industrious.

To industry, guided by reasonable intelligence and economy, every people can look with certainty as an unfailing source of temporal prosperity. Whatever is useful or beautiful in art, science or other human attainment, has come from industry. In the humblest pursuits, industry may be accompanied by the noblest intelligence, so that respect, place and power are open to its humblest honest practicer. Let no man spurn industry as his temporal shield; it is the safest and surest he can buckle to his arm, and with it he may defy the want and poverty which, more than everything else, destroy the independence of man.

Honorable industry always travels the same road with enjoyment and duty; and progress is altogether impossible without it. The idle pass through life leaving as little trace of their existence as foam upon the water, or smoke upon the air; whereas the industrious stamp their character upon their age, and influence not only their own but all succeeding generations. Labor is the best test of the energies of men, and furnishes an admirable training for practical wisdom.

Practical industry, wisely and vigorously applied, never fails of success. It carries a man onward and upward, brings out his individual character, and powerfully stimulates the action of others. All may not rise equally, yet each, on the whole, very much according to his deserts. "Though all cannot live on the piazza," as the Tuscan proverb has it, "every one may feel the sun."

Industry is the heir of fortune; the companion of honesty and honor; the beauteous sister of temperance, health and ease—one of the noble virtues which links with perfection.

Industry has a physical blessing; limbs strengthened by exercise, and sinews braced by exertion; every organ performing its legitimate duty, and kept in its appointed office; the blood circulated by motion, and the joints pliant from use; disease repelled by internal vigor; appetite created by the calls of increasing strength; rest rendered welcome by previous labor; sleep become acceptable after busy working. The habit, free from the petty ailments entailed by sluggishness, no longer falls a prey to peevishness and irritation, and time employed, not wasted in murmurs and discontent. The temper, less tried by bodily infirmity and secret upbraidings, acquires equanimity. The spirits, unharrassed by petty pains and plagues, rise to cheerfulness. The faculties, unimpaired by disease, unblunted by disuse, more vigorously expand. The whole man, active, useful, and happy, is enabled to resist the approaches of infirmity, sickness, and sorrow; to enjoy a vigorous old age, and to drop after a brief struggle his mortal frame, to soar with improved powers into a state of improved being. While in idleness, the disordered frame, gradually sickening, oppresses the vital powers. The mind, weakened and stupefied, imbibes wild or gloomy ideas; the better faculties are crushed and curbed, and the whole man at last sinks beneath the undermining mischiefs of insidious sloth.

Is this a wretched picture? Whilst we feel that though it is so, it is also a true one, let us gratefully remember, that such a state is not inevitable, but that it is one incurred from choice, and produced by voluntary permission. Reverse the picture, extirpate sloth, and in its place introduce activity, and how mighty is the difference? The wand of Harlequin could never produce a more striking change.

In vain has nature thrown obstacles and impediments in the way of man. He surmounts every difficulty interposed between his energy and his enterprise. Over seas and mountains his course is unchecked; he directs the lightning's wings, and almost annihilates space and time. Oceans, rivers, and deserts are explored; hills are leveled, and the rugged places made smooth. "On the hardest adamant some footprint of us is stamped in." The soil teems with fertility, and under the cunning and diligent hand of his taste and skill, the whole earth is beautified and improved.

The stimulus of a painful necessity urges man to ceaseless effort, and the world is filled with monuments and memorials of his industry, his zeal, his patient labor, his masterly spirit, and his indomitable perseverance.

> "All is the gift of industry: whate'er
> Exalts, embellishes, and renders life
> Delightful."

Honesty.

THE first step toward greatness is to be honest, says the proverb; but the proverb fails to state the case strong enough. Honesty is not only the first step toward greatness—it is greatness itself.

It is with honesty in one particular as with wealth; those that have the thing care less about the credit of it than those that have it not. What passes as open-faced honesty is often masked malignity. He who saith there is no such thing as an honest man, you may be sure is himself a knave. When any one complains, as Diogenes did, that he has to hunt the street with candles at noon-day to find an honest man, we are apt to think that his nearest neighbor would have quite as much difficulty as himself in making the discovery. If you think there isn't an honest man living, you had better, for appearance sake, put off saying it until you are dead yourself. Honesty is the best policy, but those who do honest things merely because they think it good policy, are not honest. No man has ever been too honest. Cicero believed that nothing is useful that is not honest. He that walketh uprightly, walketh surely; but he that perverteth his ways shall be known. There is an alchemy in a high heart which transmutes other things to its own quality.

The truth of the good old maxim, that "Honesty is the best policy," is upheld by the daily experience of life; uprightness and integrity being found as successful in business as in everything else. As Hugh Miller's worthy uncle used to advise him, "In all your dealings give your neighbor the cast of the bank — 'good measure, heaped up, and running over'—and you will not lose by it in the end."

Honesty is the best policy. But no man can be upright, amid the various temptations of life, unless he is honest for the right's sake. You should not be honest from the low motive of policy, but because you feel the better for being honest. The latter will hold you fast, let the element set as it will, let storms blow ever so fiercely; the former is but a cable of pack-thread, which will snap apart. In the long run, character is better than capital. Most of the great American merchants, whose revenues out-rank those of princes, owe their colossal fortunes principally to a character for integrity and ability. Lay the foundations of a character broad and deep. Build them on a rock, and not on sand. The rains may then descend, the floods rise and the winds blow, but your house will stand. But, establish a character for loose dealings, and lo! some great tempest will sweep it away.

The religious tradesman complains that his honesty is a hindrance to his success; that the tide of custom pours into the doors of his less scrupulous neighbors in the same street, while he himself waits for hours idle. My brother, do you think that God is going to reward honor, integrity and high-mindedness

with this world's coin? Do you fancy that he will
pay spiritual excellence with plenty of custom? Now
consider the price that man has paid for his success
—perhaps mental degradation and inward dishonor.
His advertisements are all deceptive; his treatment
of his workmen tyrannical; his cheap prices made
possible by inferior articles. Sow that man's seed,
and you will reap that man's harvest. Cheat, lie,
advertise, be unscrupulous in your assertions, custom
will come to you; but if the price is too dear, let him
have his harvest, and take yours. Yours is a clear
conscience, a pure mind, rectitude within and without.
Will you part with that for his? Then why do you
complain? He has paid his price; you do not choose
to pay it.

Some, in their passion for sudden accumulation,
practice secret frauds, and imagine there is no harm
in it, so they be not detected. But in vain will they
cover up their transgressions; for God sees it to the
bottom; and let them not hope to keep it always from
man. The birds of the air sometimes carry the tale
abroad. In the long web of events, "be sure your
sin will find you out." He who is carrying on a
course of latent corruption and dishonesty, be he
president of some mammoth corporation, or engaged
only in private transactions, is sailing in a ship like
that fabled one of old, which ever comes nearer and
nearer to a magnetic mountain, that will at last draw
every nail out of it. All faith in God, and all trust
in man will eventually be lost, and he will get no
reward for his guilt. The very winds will sigh forth

his iniquity; and "a beam will come out of the wall," and convict and smite him.

Strict honesty is the crown of one's early days. "Your son will not do for me," was once said to a friend of mine; "he took pains, the other day, to tell a customer of a small blemish in a piece of goods." The salesboy is sometimes virtually taught to declare that goods cost such or such a sum; that they are strong, fashionable, perfect, when the whole story is false. So is the bloom of a God-inspired truthfulness not seldom brushed from the cheek of our simple-hearted children.

We hope and trust these cases are rare; but even one such house as we allude to, may ruin the integrity and the fair fame of many a lad. God grant our young men to feel that "an honest man is the noblest work of God," and, under all temptations, to *live* as they feel.

The possession of the principle of honesty is a matter known most intimately to the man and his God, and fully, only to the latter. No man knows the extent and strength of his own honesty, until he has passed the fiery ordeal of temptation. Men shudder at the dishonesty of others, at one time in life; then, sailing before the favorable wind of prosperity, when adversity overtakes them, their honesty too often flies away on the same wings with their riches; and, what they once viewed with holy horror, they now practice with shameless impunity. Others, at the commence-ment of a prosperous career, are quite above any tricks in trade; but their love of money increases with their wealth, their honesty relaxes, they become hard honest men, then hardly honest, and are, finally, confirmed in dishonesty.

On the great day of account, it will be found, that men have erred more in judging of the honesty of others than in any one thing else; not even religion excepted. Many who have been condemned, and had the stigma of dishonesty fixed upon them, because misfortune disabled them from paying their just debts, will stand acquitted by the Judge of quick and dead, whilst others cover dishonest hearts and actions, undetected by man

It is our earnest desire to eradicate the impression, so fatal to many a young man, that one cannot live by being perfectly honest. You must have known men who have gone on for years in unbroken pros-perity and yet never adopted that base motto, "All is fair in trade." You must have seen, too, noble examples of those who have met with losses and failures, and yet risen from them all with a conscious integrity, and who have been sustained by the testi-mony of all around them, that, though unfortunate, they were never dishonest. When we set before you such examples, when we show you, not only that "honesty is the best policy," but that it is the very keystone of the whole arch of manly and Christian qualities, it cannot be that every ingenuous heart does not respond to the appeal. Heaven grant all such to feel that "an honest man is the noblest work God," and to live as they feel.

Character.

THERE is a structure which every body is building, young and old, each one for himself. It is called *character*, and every act of life is a stone. If day by day we be careful to build our lives with pure, noble, upright deeds, at the end will stand a fair temple, honored by God and man. But, as one leak will sink a ship, and one flaw break a chain, so one mean, dishonorable, untruthful act or word will forever leave its impress and work its influence on our characters. Then, let the several deeds unite to form a day, and one by one the days grow into noble years, and the years, as they slowly pass, will raise at last a beautiful edifice, enduring forever to our praise.

There are as many master-workmen in you as there are separate faculties; and there are as many blows struck as there are separate acts of emotion or volition. Every single day these myriad forces are building, building, building. Here is a great structure going up, point by point, story by story, although you are not conscious of it. It is a building of character. It is a building that must stand, and the word of inspiration warns you to take heed how you build it; to see to it that you have a foundation that shall endure; to make sure that you are building on it, not for the hour in which you live, but for that hour of revelation, when you shall be seen just as you are.

Our minds are given us, but our characters we

make. Our mental powers must be cultivated. The full measure of all the powers necessary to make a man are no more a character than a handful of seeds is an orchard of fruits. Plant the seeds and tend them well, and they will make an orchard. Cultivate the powers and harmonize them well, and they will make a noble character. The germ is not the tree, the acorn is not the oak, neither is the mind a character. God gives the mind, man makes the character. The mind is the garden; the character is the fruit; the mind is the white page; the character is the writing we put on it. The mind is the metallic plate; the character is our engraving thereon. The mind is the shop, the counting-room; the character is our profits on the trade. Large profits are made from quick sales and small per centage. So great characters are made by many little acts and efforts. A dollar is composed of a thousand mills; so is a character of a thousand thoughts and acts. The secret thoughts never expressed, the inward indulgences in imaginary wrong; the lie never told for want of courage, the licentiousness never indulged in from fear of public rebuke, the irreverence of the heart, are just as effectual in staining the character as though the world knew all about them. A subtle thing is a character; and a constant work is its formation. Whether it be good or bad, it has been long in its growth, and is the aggregate of millions of little mental acts. A good character is a precious thing, above rubies, gold, crowns, or kingdoms, and the work of making it is the noblest labor on earth.

Character is formed by a course of actions, and not actions by character. A person can have no character before he has had actions. Though an action be ever so glorious in itself, it ought not to pass for great, if it be not the effect of wisdom and good design. Great actions carry their glory with them as the ruby wears its colors. Whatever be your condition or calling in life, keep in view the whole of your existence. Act not for the little span of time allotted you in this world, but act for eternity.

Characters formed by circumstances are much like machine poetry. They will do for the sport of mirth, and the torment of the senses of the beautiful. But they are horrible things. It makes angels weep to look at them. They are the picture of old chaos, a mass of confusion. A thousand winds have blown together the materials of which they are made. They usually lack order, harmony, consistency, and beauty, the very elements and essentials of a good character. They are those aimless nuisances that live for nothing, and molder, and become putrid, about the sewers of the world. If aught on earth is despicable, it is these porous masses of conglomerated filth and scum that float on the surface of society, driven or attracted by every speck of circumstance about them. They are purposeless, powerless, enervated automatons, playing second fiddle to chance. One brave will to resist evil and hold fast to good, is worth a million of them. One stout soul, with a resolute determination to make its own character, after the pattern of its own high-wrought ideal, that, Jackson-like, takes the responsibility of being what suits its well-formed judgment, is of more real significance than an army of them. It will stand against them, and defy their power.

Every man is bound to aim at the possession of a good character, as one of the highest objects of his life. The very effort to secure it by worthy means will furnish him with a motive for exertion; and his idea of manhood, in proportion as it is elevated, will steady and animate his motive It is well to have a high standard of life, even though we may not be able altogether to realize it. "The youth," says Disraeli, "who does not look up will look down; and the spirit that does not soar is destined, perhaps, to grovel." He who has a high standard of living and thinking will certainly do better than he who has none at all. We would have young men, as they start in life, regard character as a capital, much surer to yield full returns than any other capital, unaffected by panics and failures, fruitful when all other investments lie dormant, having as certain promise in the present life as in that which is to come. Character is like stock in trade, the more of it a man possesses, the greater his facilities for adding to it. Character is power, is influence· it makes friends, creates funds, draws patronage and support, and opens a sure and easy way to wealth, honor and happiness.

Trifles discover a character more than actions of importance. In regard to the former, a person is off his guard, and thinks it not material to use disguise. It is no imperfect hint toward the discovery of a man's character to say he looks as though you might be certain of finding a pin upon his sleeve. Truthfulness is a corner-stone in character, and if it is not firmly laid in youth, there will be ever after a weak spot in the foundation.

Sum it up then as we will, character is the great desideratum of human life. This truth, sublime in its simplicity and powerful in its beauty, is the highest lesson of religion, the first that youth should learn, the last that age should forget.

The value of character is the standard of human progress. The individual, the community, the nation tells its standing, its advancement, its worth, its true wealth and glory in the eye of God by its estimation of character. That man or nation who or which lightly esteems character, is low, groveling and barbarous. Wherever character is made a secondary object, sensualism and crime prevail. He who would prostitute character to reputation is base. He who lives for anything less than character is mean. He who enters upon any study, pursuit, amusement, pleasure, habit, or course of life, without considering its effect upon his character, is not a trusty or an honest man. He whose modes of thought, states of feeling, every-day acts, common language, and whole outward life, are not directed by a wise reference to their influence upon his character, is a man always to be watched. Just as a man prizes his character, so is he. This is the true standard of a man.

Principle and Right.

We often judge unwisely. We approve or condemn men by their actions. But it so happens that many a man whom we condemn, God approves; and many a one whom we approve, God condemns. Here below it often happens that we have saints in prisons and devils in priestly robes. We often view things under a false sight, and pass our judgments accordingly; but God judges from behind the veil, where motives reveal themselves like lightnings on a cloud.

Now, right and might lie in motive. Personally they answer the question, "Ought I?" and "Can I?" Some men ask, "Ought I do this?" Others ask, "Can I do this?" It is the angel that asks, "Ought I to do this?" It is the devil that asks, "Can I do this?"

We all have good and bad in us. The good would do what it ought to do; the bad does what it can do. The good dwells in the kingdom of right; the bad sits on the throne of might. Right is a loyal subject; might is a royal tyrant. Right is the foundation of the river of peace; might is the mother of war and its abominations. Right is the evangel of God that proclaims the "acceptable year of the Lord;" might is the scourge of the world that riots in carnage, groans and blood. Right is the arm of freedom made bare and beautiful in the eyes of all the good in heaven and earth; might is the sword of power unsheathed in the hand of oppression. Right gains its victories by peace, might conquers only by war. Right strengthens its army by the increase of all its conquered; might weakens its force by every victory, as a part of its power must stand guard over its new-made subjects. Right rules by invitation, might by compulsion. Right is from above; might from below; Right is unselfish; might knows nothing but self. Right is for the whole; might is for one. Right is unassuming; might is pompous as a king. Right is instructive; might is dictatorial. Right reasons like a philosopher, and prepares the ground on which it sows; might stalks on like madness, reckless of everything but the end sought. Right is a lamb, cropping buds and flowers to make itself more beautiful; might is a tiger prowling in search of prey. Right is a moralist resting in principle; might is a worldling seeking for pleasure. These are inward principles contending with each other in every human soul.

There are men, and their number is not small, who make principle and right depend on policy. They are honest when they think it policy to be honest. They smile when it is policy, though they design to stab the next minute. Men of policy are honest when it is convenient and plainly profitable. When honesty costs nothing and will pay well, they are honest; but when policy will pay best, they give honesty the slip at once. When they think honesty is the best policy they are most conscientiously honest; but when policy will, in their judgment, serve them a better turn, their consciences change faces very quickly. Principle, right and honesty are always, and everywhere, and eternally best. It is hard to make honesty and policy work together in the same mind. When one is out, the other is in. Honesty will not stay where policy is permitted to visit. They do not think or act alike, and never can be made to agree. They have nothing in common. One is the prophet of God, the other of Baal.

There are men who choose honesty as a soul companion They live in it, and with it, and by it, They embody it in their actions and lives. Their words speak it. Their faces· beam it. Their actions proclaim it. Their hands are true to it. Their feet tread its path. They are full of it. They love it. It is to them like a God. They believe it is of God. With religious awe they obey its behests. Not gold, or crowns, or fame, could bribe them to leave it. They are wedded to it from choice. It is their first love. It makes them beautiful men; yea, more, noble men, great, brave, righteous men. When God looks about for his jewels, these are the men his eye rests on, well pleased. He keeps his angels employed in making crowns for them, and they make crowns for themselves too! Crowns of honesty! To some men they seem not very beautiful in the dim light of earth; but when the radiance of heaven is opened upon them, they will reflect it in gorgeous splendor. Nothing is brighter; nothing is better; nothing is worth more, or more substantial. Honesty, peerless queen of principles ! how her smile enhaloes the men who love her! How ready they are to suffer for her, to die for her! They are the martyrs. See them! What a multitude! Some at the stake; some in stocks; some in prison; some before judges as criminals; some on gibbets, and some on the cross. But they are all sustained. They smile on their foes. They have peace within. They are strong and brave in heart. Their souls are dauntless as the bright old sun.

Value of Reputation.

Who shall estimate the cost of a priceless reputation—that impress which gives this human dross its currency—without which we stand despised, debased, depreciated? Who shall repair it injured? Who can redeem it lost? Oh, well and truly does the great philosopher of poetry esteem the world's wealth as "trash" in the comparison. Without it, gold has no value; birth, no distinction; station, no dignity; beauty, no charm; age, no reverence; without it every treasure impoverishes, every grace deforms, every dignity degrades, and all the arts, the decorations, and accomplishments of life stand, like the beacon-blaze upon a rock, warning the world that its approach is dangerous; that its contact is death.

The wretch without it is under *eternal quarantine;* no friend to greet; no home to harbor him. The voyage of his life becomes a joyless peril; and in the midst of all ambition can achieve, or avarice amass, or rapacity plunder, he tosses on the surge, *a buoyant pestilence.* But let me not degrade into selfishness of individual safety or individual exposure this individual principle; it testifies a higher, a more ennobling origin.

It is this which, consecrating the humble circle of the hearth, will at times extend itself to the circumference of the horizon, which nerves the arm of the patriot to save his country; which lights the lamp of the philosopher to amend man; which, if it does not inspire, will yet invigorate the martyr to merit immortality; which, when one world's agony is passed, and the glory of another is dawning, will prompt the prophet, even in his chariot of fire, and in his vision of Heaven, to bequeath to mankind the mantle of his memory!

Oh, divine! oh, delightful legacy of a spotless reputation! Rich is the inheritance it leaves; pious the example it testifies; pure, precious, and imperishable, the hope which it inspires! Can there be conceived a more atrocious injury than to filch from its possessor this inestimable benefit—to rob society of its charm, and solitude of its solace; not only to out-law life, but to attaint death, converting the very grave, the refuge of the sufferer, into the gate of infamy and of shame!

We can conceive few crimes beyond it. He who plunders one's property takes from him that which can be repaired by time; but what period can repair a ruined reputation? He who maims one's person, affects that which medicine may remedy; but what herb has sovereignty over the wounds of slander? He who ridicules one's poverty, or reproaches one's profession, upbraids him with that which industry may retrieve, and integrity may purify; but what riches shall redeem the bankrupt fame? What power shall blanch the sullied snow of character? There can be no injury more deadly. There can be no crime more cruel. It is without remedy. It is without antidote. It is without evasion.

The reptile, calumny, is ever on the watch. From the fascinations of its eye no activity can escape; from the venom of its fang no sanity can recover. It has no enjoyment but crime; it has no prey but virtue; it has no interval from the restlessness of its malice, save when, bloated with its victims, it grovels to disgorge them at the withered shrine where envy idolizes her own infirmities.

Fame.

Though fame is smoke,
Its fumes are frankincense to human thoughts.
— BYRON.

FAME, like money, should neither be despised nor idolized. An honest fame, based on worth and merit, and gained, like large estates, by prudence and industry, deservedly perpetutates the names of the great and good.

No glory or fame is both consolatory and enduring

unless based on virtue, wisdom, and justice. That acquired by wild ambition, is tarnished by association—time deepens the stain. We read the biography of Washington with calmness and delight; that of Bonaparte with mingled feelings of admiration and abhorrence. We admire the gigantic powers of his intellect, the vastness of his designs, the boldness of their execution, but turn, with horror, from the slaughter-fields of his ambition, and his own dreadful end. His giddy height of power served to plunge him deeper in misery; his lofty ambition increased the burning tortures of his exile; his towering intellect added a duplicate force to the consuming pangs of his disappointment. His fatal end should cool the ardor of all who have an inordinate desire for earthly glory.

The praises and commendations of intimates and friends, are the greatest and most impassable obstacles to real superiority. Better were it, that they should whip us with cords and drive us to work, than that they should extol and exaggerate our childish scintillations and puerile achievements.

False fame is the rushlight which we, or our attendants, kindle in our apartments. We witness its feeble burning, and its gradual but certain decline. It glimmers for a little while, when, with flickering and palpitating radiance, it soon expires.

Egotism and vanity detract from fame as ostentation diminishes the merit of an action. He that is vain enough to cry up himself, ought to be punished with the silence of others. We soil the splendor of

our most beautiful actions by our vainglorious mag-
nifying them. There is no vice or folly that requires
so much nicety and skill to manage as fame, nor any
which, by ill management, makes so contemptible a
figure. The desire of being thought famous is often
a hindrance to being so; for such an one is more solicitous to let the world see what knowledge he hath
than to learn that which he wants. Men are found
to be vainer on account of those qualities which they
fondly believe they have, than of those which they
really have. Some would be thought to do great
things, who are but tools or instruments; like the fool
who fancied he played upon the organ, when he only
drew the bellows.

Be not so greedy of popular applause as to forget
that the same breath which blows up a fire may blow
it out again. True fame is the light of heaven. It
cometh from afar. It shines powerfully and brightly,
but not always without clouds and shadows, which
interpose, but do not destroy; eclipse, but do not
extinguish. Like the glorious sun, it will continue to
diffuse its beams when we are no more; for other eyes
will hail the light, when we are withdrawn from it.

Great and decided talent is a tower of strength
which cannot be subverted. Envy, detraction, and
persecution are missiles hurled against it only to fall
harmless at its base, and to strengthen what they
cannot overthrow. It seeks not the applause of the
present moment, in which folly or mediocrity often
secure the preference; but it extends its bright and
prophetic vision through the "dark obscure" of dis-

tant time, and bequeaths to remote generations the vindication of its honor and fame, and the clear comprehension of its truths.

No virtues and learning are inherited, but rather ignorance and misdirected inclinations; and assiduous and persevering labor must correct these defects, and make a fruitful garden of that soil which is naturally encumbered with stones and thistles. All home-triumphs and initiatory efforts are nothing worth. That which is great, commanding, and lasting, must be won by stubborn energy, by patient industry, by unwearied application, and by indefatigable zeal. We must lie down and groan, and get up and toil. It is a long race, not a pleasant walk, and the prize is not a leaf or a bauble, but a chaplet or a crown. The spectators are not friends, but foes; and the contest is one in which thousands fall through weakness and want of real force and courage.

We may add virtue to virtue, strength to strength, and knowledge to knowledge, and yet fail, and soon be lost and forgotten in that mighty and soul-testing struggle, in which few come off conquerors and win an induring and imperishable name. If we embark on this course, we shall need stout hearts conjoined with invincible minds. We must bid adieu to vice, to sloth, to flatteries and ease,

"And scorn delights and live laborious days."

Engraved & Printed by Illman Brothers

THE DEPARTURE

Ambition.

He who ascends to mountain-tops shall find
The loftiest peaks most wrapt in clouds and snow ;
He who surpasses or subdues mankind,
Must look down on the hate of those below.
— BYRON.

SOME conceited wights, who study party politics more than philosophy or ethics, call all the laudable desires of the human heart ambition, aiming to strip the monster of its deformity, that they may use it as the livery of heaven to serve the devil in. The former are based on philanthropy, the latter on selfishness. Lexicographers define ambition to be an earnest desire of power, honor, preferment, pride. The honor that is awarded to power is of doubtful grandeur, and the power that is acquired by ambition is held by a slender tenure, a mere rope of sand. Its hero often receives the applause of the multitude one day, and its execrations the next. The summit of vain ambition is often the depth of misery. Based on a sandy foundation, it falls before the blasts of envy, and the tornado of faction. It is inflated by a gaseous thirst for power, like a balloon with hydrogen, and is in constant danger of being exploded by the very element that causes its elevation. It eschews charity, and deals largely in the corrosive sublimate of falsehood. Like the kite, it cannot rise in a calm, and requires a constant wind to preserve its upward course. The fulcrum of ignorance, and the lever of party spirit, form its magic power. An astute writer has well observed, that "ambition makes the same mistake concerning power, that avarice makes relative to wealth." The ambitious man begins by accumulating it as the desideratum of happiness, and ends his career in the midst of exertions to obtain more. So ended the onward and upward career of Napoleon; his life a modern wonder; his fate a fearful warning; his death a scene of gloom. Power is gained as a means of enjoyment, but oftener than otherwise, is its fell destroyer. Like the viper in the fable, it is prone to sting those who warm it into life. History fully demonstrates these propositions. Hyder Ali was in the habit of starting frightfully in his sleep. His confidential friend and attendant asked the reason. He replied: "My friend, the state of a beggar is more delightful than my envied monarchy—awake, he sees no conspirators—asleep, he dreams of no assassins." Ambition, like the gold of the miser, is the sepulchre of the other passions of the man. It is the grand centre around which they move with centripetal force. Its history is one of carnage and blood; it is the bane of substantial good; it endangers body and soul for time and eternity. Reader, if you desire peace of mind, shun ambition and the ambitious man. He will use you as some men do their horses, ride you all day without food, and give you post meat for supper. He will gladly make a bridge of you on which to walk into power, provided he can pass toll free. Let your aim be more lofty than the highest pinnacle ambition can rear. Nothing is pure but heaven, let that be the prize you seek,

> "And taste and prove in that transporting sight,
> Joy without sorrow, without darkness—light."

The road ambition travels is too narrow for friendship, too crooked for love, too rugged for honesty, too dark for science, and too hilly for happiness.

Avarice.

A judicious writer has well remarked, that avarice is the father of more children than Priam, and, like him, survives them all. It is a paradoxical propensity, a species of heterogeneous insanity. The miser starves himself, knowing that those who wish him dead will fatten on his hoarded gains. He submits to more torture to lose heaven than the martyr does to gain it. He serves the worst of tyrannical masters more faithfully than most Christians do the best, whose yoke is easy and burden light. He worships this world, but repudiates all its pleasures. He endures all the miseries of poverty through life, that he may die in the midst of wealth. He is the mere turnkey of his own riches—a poorly-fed and badly-clothed slave; a draught-horse without bells or feathers; a man condemned to work in mines, which is the lowest and hardest condition of servitude; and, to increase his misery, a worker there for he knows not whom. "He heapeth up riches and knoweth not who shall enjoy them." It is only sure that he himself neither shall nor can enjoy them. He is an indigent, needy slave; he will hardly allow himself clothes and board wages. He defrauds not only other men, but his own genius; he cheats himself for money. He lives as if the world were made altogether for him, and not he for the world; to take in everything and to part with nothing. Charity is accounted no grace with him, and gratitude no virtue. The cries of the poor never enter his ears, or if they do, he has always one ear readier to let them out than to take them in. In a word, by his rapines and extortions he is always for making as many poor as he can, but for relieving none whom he either finds or makes so. So that it is a question whether his heart be harder than his fist is close. In a word, he is a pest and a monster; greedier than the sea and barrener than the shore. He is the cocoon of the human race — death ends his toils and others reel off the glossy product of his labors. He is the father of more miseries than the prodigal — whilst he lives he heaps them on himself and those around him. He is his own and the poor man's enemy.

The avarice of the miser may be termed the grand sepulchre of all his other passions, as they successively decay. But, unlike other tombs, it is enlarged by repletion and strengthened by age. His mind is never expanded beyond the circumference of the almighty dollar He thinks not of his immortal soul, his accountability to God, or of his final destiny He covets the wealth of others, revels in extortion, stops at nothing to gratify his ruling passion that will not endanger his dear idol. He is an Ishmael in community—he passes to the grave without tasting the sweets of friendship, the delights of social intercourse, or the comforts of a good repast, unless the latter is got by invitation, when abroad. The first voluntary expenditure upon his body during his manhood, and the first welcome visit of his neighbors, both passive on his part, are at his funeral.

If we would enjoy the comforts of life rationally, we must avoid the miseries of avarice and the evils of prodigality. Let us use the provisions of our benevolent Benefactor without abusing them, and render to Him that gratitude which is His due. Banish all inordinate desires after wealth—if you gain an abundance, be discreetly liberal, judiciously benevolent, and, if your children have arrived at their majority, die your own executor.

Gambling.

EVERY device that suddenly changes money or property from one person to another without a *quid pro quo*, or leaving an equivalent, produces individual embarrassment—often extreme misery. More pernicious is that plan, if it changes property and money from the hands of the many to the few.

Gambling does this, and often inflicts a still greater injury, by poisoning its victims with vice, that eventually lead to crimes of the darkest hue. Usually, the money basely filched from its victims, is the smallest part of the injury inflicted. It almost inevitably leads to intemperance. Every species of offence, on the black catalogue of crime, may be traced to the gambling table, as the entering wedge to its perpetration.

This alarming evil is as wide-spread as our country. It is practiced from the humblest water craft that floats on our canals up to the majestic steamboat on our mighty rivers; from the lowest groggeries that curse the community, up to the most fashionable hotels that claim respectability; from the hod-carrier in his bespattered rags, up to the honorable members of congress in their ruffles. Like a mighty maelstrom, its motion, at the outside, is scarcely perceptible, but soon increases to a fearful velocity; suddenly the awful centre is reached—the victim is lost in the vortex. Interested friends may warn, the wife may entreat, with all the eloquence of tears; children may cling and cry for bread—once in the fatal snare, the victim of gamblers is seldom saved. He combines the deafness of the adder with the desperation of a maniac, and rushes on, regardless of danger—reckless of consequences.

To the fashionable of our country, who play cards and other games as an *innocent* amusement, we may trace the most aggravated injuries resulting from gambling. It is there that young men of talents, education, and wealth, take the degree of entered apprentice. The example of men in high life, men in public stations and responsible offices, has a powerful and corrupting influence on society, and does much to increase the evil, and forward, as well as sanction the high-handed robbery of fine dressed blacklegs. The gambling hells in our cities, tolerated and patronized, are a disgrace to a nation bearing a Christian name, and would be banished from a Pagan community.

Gambling assumes a great variety of forms, from the flipping of a cent in the bar room for a glass of whisky, up to the splendidly furnished faro bank room, where men are occasionally swindled to the tune of "ten thousand a year," and sometimes a much larger amount. In addition to these varieties, we have legalized lotteries and fancy stock brokers, and among those who manage them, professors of religion are not unfrequently found.

Thousands who carefully shun the monster under any other form, pay a willing tribute to the tyrant at the shrine of lotteries. Persons from all classes throw their money into this vault of uncertainty, this whirlpool of speculation, with a less chance to regain it than when at the detested faro bank. It is here that the poor man spends his last dollar; it is here that the rich often become poor, for a man has ten chances to be killed by lightning where he has one to draw a capital prize. The ostensible objects of lotteries are always praiseworthy. Meeting houses, hospitals, seminaries of learning, internal improvement, some laudable enterprise, may always be found first and foremost in a lottery scheme; the most ingenious and most fatal gull trap ever invented by man or devil

Gaming cowers in darkness, and often blots out all the nobler powers of the heart, paralyzes its sensibilities to human woe, severs the sacred ties that bind man to man, to woman, to family, to community, to morals, to religion, to social order, and to country. It transforms men to brutes, desperadoes, maniacs, misanthropists, and strips human nature of all its native dignity. The gamester forfeits the happiness of this life and endures the penalties of sin in both worlds. His profession is the scavenger of avarice, haggard and filthy, badly fed, poorly clad, and worse paid.

Let me entreat all to shun the monster, under all his borrowed and deceptive forms. Remember that gambling for amusement is the wicket gate into the labyrinth, and when once in, you may find it difficult to get out. Ruin is marked in blazing capitals over the door of the gambler; his hell is the vestibule to that eternal hell where the worm dieth not and the fire is not quenched. If you regard your own, and the happiness of your family and friends, and the salvation of your immortal soul, recoil from even the shadow of a shade reflected by this heaven-daring, heart-breaking, soul-destroying, fashionable, but ruinous vice.

An evil that starts upon a wrong principle, the vital element of which is injustice, must have a vast productive force in creating other evils. It is necessarily a mighty agency in destroying all that is good in the soul; vitiating the whole character, and dragging down every lofty purpose and noble aspiration. And we find that the gambler is rapidly qualified for every other species of wickedness. The fiery excitement to which he yields himself in the game-room inflames every other passion. It produces a state of mind that can be satisfied only with intense and forbidden pleasures. It virtually takes him out of the circle of refined, rational enjoyment and plunges him into scenes more congenial to a corrupt taste. He would gladly witness as a pastime bull fights, pugilistic contests; and perhaps his craving for excitement could only be fully satisfied by scenes such as Roman persecutors and heathen spectators formerly feasted upon, in which men and women were torn in pieces by wild beasts. Such bloody encounters and horrid tragedies might come up to his standard of amusement.

Thus does the giant vice uncivilize a man and throw him back into a state of barbarism. It revolutionizes his tastes at the same time that it casts down his moral principles. If its victim has been in early life under the influence of religious sentiment, it speedily obliterates those sentiments from the mind. If the voice of conscience has been in the past years heard, that voice is now silenced. If feelings of humanity once had influence, their power is now gone. If visions of extensive usefulness and honorable achievement once floated in the imagination they have vanished; vanished in the distance, never to return.

Nor should the youth forget that if he is once

taken in the coils of this vice, the hope of extricating himself, or of realizing his visions of wealth and happiness, is exceedingly faint. He has no rational grounds to expect that he can escape the terrible consequences that are inseparably connected with this sin. If he does not become bankrupt in property, he is sure to become one in character and in moral principle; he becomes a debauched, debased, friendless vagabond.

Temper.

Good temper is like a sunny day, it sheds its brightness on everything. No trait of character is more valuable than the possession of good temper. Home can never be made happy without it. It is like flowers springing up in our pathway, reviving and cheering us. Kind words and looks are the outward demonstration; patience and forbearance are the sentinels within.

If a man has a quarrelsome temper, let him alone. The world will soon find him employment. He will soon meet with some one stronger than himself, who will repay him better than you can. A man may fight duels all his life if he is disposed to quarrel. How sweet the serenity of habitual self-command! How many stinging self-reproaches it spares us! When does a man feel more at ease with himself than when he has passed through a sudden and strong provocation *without speaking a word,* or *in undisturbed good humor!* When, on the contrary, does he feel a deeper humiliation than when he is conscious that anger has made him betray himself by word, look or action? Nervous irritability is the greatest weakness of character. It is the sharp grit which aggravates friction and cuts out the bearings of the entire human machine. Nine out of every ten men we meet are in a chronic state of annoyance. The least untoward thing sets them in a ferment.

There are people, yes many people, always looking out for slights. They cannot carry on the daily intercourse of the family without finding that some offense is designed. They are as touchy as hair triggers. If they meet an acquaintance who happens to be preoccupied with business, they attribute his abstraction in some mode personal to themselves and take umbrage accordingly. They lay on others the fruit of their irritability. Indigestion makes them see impertinence in every one they come in contact with. Innocent persons, who never dreamed of giving offense, are astonished to find some unfortunate word, or momentary taciturnity, mistaken for an insult. To say the least, the habit is unfortunate. It is far wiser to take the more charitable view of our fellow beings, and not suppose that a slight is intended unless the neglect is open and direct. After all, too, life takes its hues in a great degree from the color of our own mind. If we are frank and generous, the world will treat us kindly; if, on the contrary, we are suspicious, men learn to be cold and cautious to us. Let a person get the reputation of being "touchy," and everybody is under restraint, and in this way the chances of an imaginary offense are vastly increased.

Do you not find in households — refined, many of them — many women who are jealous, exacting, and have a temper that will be swayed by nothing? And do we not see in another family circle a man as coarse and bloody-mouthed as a despot? The purpose of the existence of a score of people is to make him happy, fan him, feed him, amuse him, and he stands as a great absorbent of the life and heat that belongs to the rest. Many sermons tell you to be meek and humble, but you do n't hear many which tell you you live in your families to growl, to bite, and to worry one another. You ought to make in your households the outward and visible life-work for this spiritual and transcendent life. There can be nothing too graceful and truthful, generous, disinterested and gracious for the household. All that a man expects to be in heaven, he ought to try to be from day to day with his wife and children, and with those that are members of his family.

It is said of Socrates, that whether he was teaching the rules of an exact morality, whether he was answering his corrupt judges, or was receiving sentence of death, or swallowing the poison, he was still the same man; that is to say, calm, quiet, undisturbed, intrepid, in a word, wise to the last.

A man once called at the house of Pericles and abused him violently. His anger so transcended him that he did not observe how late it was growing, and when he had exhausted his passion it was quite dark. When he turned to depart, Pericles calmly summoned a servant and said to him, "Bring a lamp and attend this man home."

Like flakes of snow that fall unperceived upon the earth, the seemingly unimportant events of life succeed one another. As the snow gathers together, so are our habits formed. No single flake that is added to the pile produces a sensible change. No single action creates, however it may exhibit a man's character; but as the tempest hurls the avalanche down the mountain, and overwhelms the inhabitant and his habitation, so passion, acting upon the elements of mischief which pernicious habits have brought together by imperceptible accumulation, may overthrow the edifice of truth and virtue.

Truly, a man ought to be, above all things, kind and gentle, but however meek he is required to be, he also ought to remember that he is a man. There are many persons to whom we do not need to tell this truth, for as soon as they only think of having been offended or that somebody has done them any harm, they fly up like gunpowder. Long before they know for a certainty that there is a thief in the garden they have the window open and the old gun has been popped. It is a very dangerous thing to have such neighbors, for we could sit more safely on the horns of a bull than to live in quietness with such characters. We, therefore, should form no friendship with persons of a wrathful temper, and go no farther than is needful with a man of a fiery and unrestrained spirit. Solomon said, "He that is slow to wrath is of great understanding, but he that is hasty of spirit exalteth folly."

Our advice is, to keep cool under all circumstances, if possible. Much may be effected by cultivation. We should learn to command our feelings and act prudently in all the ordinary concerns of life. This will better prepare us to meet sudden emergencies with calmness and fortitude. If we permit our feelings to be ruffled and disconcerted in small matters, they will be thrown into a whirlwind when big events overtake us. Our best antidote is, implicit confidence in God.

Anger.

IT does no good to get angry. Some sins have a seeming compensation or apology, a present gratification of some sort, but anger has none. A man feels no better for it. It is really a torment, and when the storm of passion has cleared away, it leaves one to see that he has been a fool. And he has made himself a fool in the eyes of others too.

Sinful anger, when it becomes strong, is called wrath; when it makes outrages, it is fury; when it becomes fixed, it is termed hatred; and when it intends to injure any one, it is called malice. All

these wicked passions spring from anger. The continuance and frequent fits of anger produce an evil
habit in the soul, a propensity to be angry, which
oftentimes ends in choler, bitterness, and morosity;
when the mind becomes ulcerated, peevish, and querulous, and like a thin, weak plate of iron, receives
impressions, and is wounded by the least occurrence.

Anger is such a headstrong and impetuous passion,
that the ancients call it a short madness; and indeed
there is no difference between an angry man and a
madman while the fit continues, because both are void
of reason and blind for that season. It is a disease
that, where it prevails, is no less dangerous than
deforming to us; it swells the face, it agitates the
body, and inflames the blood; and as the evil spirit
mentioned in the Gospel threw the possessed into the
fire or the water, so it casts us into all kinds of danger.
It too often ruins or subverts whole families, towns,
cities, and kingdoms. It is a vice that very few can
conceal; and if it does not betray itself by such
external signs as paleness of the countenance and
trembling of the limbs, it is more impetuous within,
and by gnawing in the heart injures the body and the
mind very much.

No man is obliged to live so free from passion as
not to show some resentment; and it is rather stoical
stupidity than virtue, to do otherwise. Anger may
glance into the breast of a wise man, but rest only in
the bosom of fools. Fight hard against a hasty temper. Anger will come, but resist it strongly. A spark
may set a house on fire. A fit of passion may give

you cause to mourn all the days of your life. Never
revenge an injury. When Socrates found in himself
any disposition to anger, he would check it by speaking low, in opposition to the motions of his displeasure. If you are conscious of being in a passion, keep
your mouth shut, for words increase it. Many a
person has dropped dead in a rage. Fits of anger
bring fits of disease. "Whom the gods would destroy
they first make mad," and the example is a good one
for our imitation. If you would demolish an oppo-
nent in argument, first make him as mad as you can.
Dr. Fuller used to say that the heat of passion makes
our souls to crack, and the devil creeps in at the
crevices Anger is a passion the most criminal and
destructive of all the passions; the only one that not
only bears the appearance of insanity, but often pro
duces the wildest form of madness. It is difficult,
indeed, sometimes to mark the line that distinguishes
the bursts of rage from the bursts of frenzy; so similar are its movements, and too often equally similar
are its actions. What crime has not been committed
in the paroxysms of anger? Has not the friend mur-
dered his friend? the son massacred his parent? the
creature blasphemed his Creator? When, indeed,
the nature of this passion is considered, what crime
may it not commit? Is it not the storm of the human
mind, which wrecks every better affection — wrecks
reason and conscience; and, as a ship driven without
helm or compass before the rushing gale, is not the
mind borne away, without guide or government, by
the tempest of unbounded rage? '

A passionate temper renders a man unfit for advice, deprives him of his reason, robs him of all that is either great or noble in his nature; it makes him unfit for conversation, destroys friendship, changes justice into cruelty, and turns all order into confusion. Says Lord Bacon: "An angry man who suppresses his passions, thinks worse than he speaks; and an angry man that will chide, speaks worse than he thinks." A wise man hath no more anger than is necessary to show that he can apprehend the first wrong, nor any more revenge than justly to prevent a second. One angry word sometimes raises a storm that time itself cannot allay. There is many a man whose tongue might govern multitudes, if he could only govern his tongue. He is the man of power who controls the storms and tempests of his mind. He that will be angry for anything, will be angry for nothing. As some are often incensed without a cause, so they are apt to continue their anger, lest it should appear to their disgrace to have begun without occasion. If we do not subdue our anger it will subdue us. It is the second word that makes the quarrel. That anger is not warrantable that hath seen two suns. One long anger, and twenty short ones, have no very great difference. Our passions are like the seas, agitable by the winds; and as God hath set bounds to these, so should we to those — *so far shall thou go, and no farther.*

Angry and choleric men are as ungrateful and unsociable as thunder and lightning, being in themselves all storm and tempests; but quiet and easy natures are like fair weather, welcome to all, and acceptable to all men; they gather together what the other disperses, and reconcile all whom the other incenses; as they have the good will and the good wishes of all other men, so they have the full possession of themselves, have all their own thoughts at peace, and enjoy quiet and ease in their own fortunes, how strait soever it may be.

But how with the angry? Who thinks well of an ill-natured, churlish man, who has to be approached in the most guarded and cautious way? Who wishes him for a neighbor, or a partner in business? He keeps all about him in nearly the same state of mind as if they were living next door to a hornet's nest or a rabid animal. And so to prosperity in business; one gets along no better for getting angry. What if business is perplexing, and everything goes "by contraries!" Will a fit of passion make the wind more propitious, the ground more productive, the market more favorable? Will a bad temper draw customers, pay notes, and make creditors better natured? If men, animals, or senseless matter cause trouble, will getting "mad" help matters?—make men more subservient, brutes more docile, wood and stone more tractable? Any angry man adds nothing to the welfare of society. He may do some good, but more hurt. Heated passion makes him a firebrand, and it is a wonder that he does not kindle flames of discord on every hand.

The disadvantages arising from anger, under all circumstances, should prove a panacea for the complaint. In moments of cool reflection, the man who indulges it, views, with deep regret, the desolations produced by a summer storm of passion. Friendship, domestic happiness, self-respect, the esteem of others, and sometimes property, are swept away by a whirlwind; perhaps a tornado of anger. We have more than once seen the furniture of a house in a mass of ruin, the work of an angry moment. We have seen anger make wives unhappy, alienate husbands, spoil children, derange all harmony, and disturb the quiet of a whole neighborhood. Anger, like too much wine, hides us from ourselves, but exposes us to others.

Some people seem to live in a perpetual storm; calm weather can never be reckoned upon in their company. Suddenly, when you least expect it, without any adequate reason, and almost without any reason at all, the sky becomes black, and the wind rises, and there is growling thunder and pelting rain. You can hardly tell where the tempest came from. An accident for which no one can be rightly blamed, a misunderstanding which a moment's calm thought would have terminated, a chance word which meant no evil, a trifling difficulty which good sense might have removed at once, a slight disappointment which a cheerful heart would have borne with a smile, brings on earthquakes and hurricanes. What men want of reason for their opinions, they are apt to supply and make up in rage. The most irreconcilable enmities grow from the most intimate friendships. To be angry with a weak man is to prove that you are not very strong yourself. It is much better to reprove than to be angry secretly. Anger, says Pythagoras, begins with folly and ends with repentance.

Be not angry that you cannot make others as you wish them to be, since you cannot make yourself what you wish to be.

He that is angry with the just reprover kindles the fire of the just avenger. Bad money cannot circulate through the veins and arteries of trade. It is a great pity that bad blood can circulate through the veins and arteries of the human frame. It seems a pity that an angry man, like the bees that leave their stings in the wounds they make, could inflict only a single injury. And, to a certain extent, it is so, for anger has been compared to a ruin, which, in falling upon its victims, breaks itself to pieces. Since, then, anger is useless, disgraceful, without the least apology, and found "only in the bosom of fools," why should it be indulged at all?

<hr />

Obstinacy.

AN obstinate man does not hold opinions, but they hold him; for when he is once possessed of an error, it is like a devil, only cast out with great difficulty. Whatsoever he lays hold on, like a drowning man, he never loosens, though it but help to sink him the sooner. Narrowness of mind is the cause of obstinacy. We do not easily believe what is beyond our sight. There are few, very few, who will own themselves in a mistake. Obstinacy is a barrier to all improvement. Whoever perversely resolves to adhere to plans or opinions, be they right or be they wrong, because such plans and opinions have been already adopted by him, raises an impenetrable bar to conviction and information. To be open to conviction, speaks a wise mind, an amiable character. Human nature is so frail and so ignorant, so liable to misconception, that none but the most incorrigibly vain can pertinaciously determine to abide by self-suggested sentiments, unsanctioned by the experience or the judgment of others, as only the most incurably foolish can be satisfied with the extent of their knowledge. The wiser we are, the more we are aware of our ignorance. Whoever resolves not to alter his measures, shuts himself out from all possibility of improvement, and must die, as he lives, ignorant, or at best but imperfectly informed.

In morals, perhaps, obstinacy may be more plausibly excused, and, under the misnomer of firmness, be practiced as a virtue. But the line between obstinacy and firmness is strong and decisive. The smallest share of common sense will suffice to detect it, and there is little doubt that few people pass this boundary without being conscious of the fault.

It will probably be found that those qualities which come under the head of foibles, rather than of vices, render people most intolerable as companions and coadjutors. For example, it may be observed that

those persons have a more worn, jaded, and dispirited
look than any others, who have to live with people
who make difficulties on every occasion, great or small.
It is astonishing to see how this practice of making
difficulties grows into a confirmed habit of mind, and
what disheartenment it occasions. The savor of life
is taken out of it when you know that nothing you
propose or do, or suggest, hope for, or endeavor, will
meet with any response but an enumeration of difficulties that lie in the path you wish to travel. The
difficulty-monger is to be met with not only in domestic and social life, but also in business. It not unfrequently occurs in business relations that the chief will
never by any chance, without many objections and
much bringing forward of possible difficulties, approve
of anything that is brought to him by his subordinates.
They at last cease to take pains, knowing that no
amount of pains will prevent their work being dealt
with in a spirit of ingenious objectiveness. At last
they say to themselves, "The better the thing we
present, the more opportunity he will have for developing his unpleasant task of objectiveness, and his
imaginative power of inventing difficulties."

Of all disagreeable people, the obstinate are the
worst. Society is often dragged down to low stan-
dards by two or three who propose, in every case, to
fight everything and every idea of which they are not
the instigators. When a new idea is brought to such
persons, instead of drawing out of it what good they
can, they seek to get the bad, ever ready to heap a
mountain of difficulties upon it.

But there are situations in which the proper opinions and mode of conduct are not evident. In such cases we must maturely reflect ere we decide, we must seek for the opinions of those wiser and better acquainted with the subject than ourselves; we must candidly hear all that can be said on both sides; then, and only then, can we in such cases hope to determine wisely; but the decision, once so deliberately adopted, we must firmly sustain, and never yield but to the most unbiased conviction of our former error.

Hypocrisy.

THERE is no folly in the world so great as to be a hypocrite. The hypocrite is hated of the world for seeming to be a Christian; he is hated by God for not being one. He hates himself and he is even despised by Satan for serving him and not acknowledging it. Hypocrites are really the best followers and the greatest dupes that Satan has; they serve him better than any other, but receive no wages. And, what is most wonderful, they submit to greater mortifications to go to hell than the most sincere Christian to go to heaven. They desire more to seem good than to be so, while the Christian desires more to be so than to seem so. They study more to enter into religion than that religion should enter into them. They are zealous in little things but cold and remiss in the most important. They are saints by

pretension, but satans in intention. They testify, they
worship only to answer their wicked purposes. They
stand as angels before their sins so as to hide them.
A scorpion thinks when its head is under a leaf it
cannot be seen. So the hypocrite. The false saints
think when they have hoisted up one or two good
works, that all their sins therewith are covered and
hid.

Let us ask ourselves seriously and honestly, "What
do I believe after all? What manner of man am I
after all? What sort of a show should I make after
all, if the people around me knew my heart and all
my secret thoughts? What sort of show, then, do I
already make, in the sight of Almighty God, who
sees every man exactly as he is?" Oh, that poor
soul, though it may fool people and itself, it will not
fool God!

Hypocrisy shows love, but is hatred; shows friendship, but is an enemy; shows peace, but is at war; it
shows virtue, but is wretched and wicked. It flatters;
it curses; it praises; it slanders. It always has two
sides of a question, it possesses what it does not pretend to, and pretends to what it does not possess.

Men are afraid of slight outward acts which will
injure them in the eyes of others, while they are
heedless of the damnation which throbs in their souls
in hatreds, and jealousies, and revenges.

They are more troubled by the outburst of a sinful
disposition, than by the disposition itself. It is not
the evil, but its reflex effect upon themselves, that
they dread. It is the love of approbation, and not

the conscience, that enacts the part of a moral sense, in this case. If a man covet, he steals. If a man have murderous hate, he murders. If a man brood dishonest thoughts, he is a knave. If a man harbor sharp and bitter jealousies, envies, hatreds, though he never express them by his tongue, or shape them by his hand, they are there. Society, to be sure, is less injured by their latent existence than it would be by their overt forms. But the man himself is as much injured by the cherished thoughts of evil, in his own soul, as by the open commission of it, and sometimes even more. For evil brought out ceases to disguise itself, and seems as hideous as it is. But evil that lurks and glances through the soul avoids analysis, and evades detection.

There are many good-seeming men who, if all their day's thoughts and feelings were to be suddenly developed into acts, visible to the eye, would run from themselves, as men in earthquakes run from the fiery gapings of the ground, and sulphurous cracks that open the way to the uncooled centre of perdition.

Pretension! profession! how haughtily they stride into the kingdom of the lowly Redeemer, and usurp the highest seats, and put on the robes of sanctity, and sing the hymns of praise, and utter aloud, to be heard of men, the prayers which the spirit ought to breathe in silent and childlike confidence into the ear of the listening and loving Father! How they build high domes of worship with velvety seats and golden altars and censers and costly plate and baptismal

fonts by the side of squalid want and ragged poverty!
How their mocking prayers mingle with the cry of
beggary, the curse of blasphemy, the wail of pain
and the lewd laugh of sensuality! How mournfully
their organ chants of praise, bought with sordid gold,
go up from the seats of worldliness and pride, and
how reproachfully the tall steeples of cathedrals and
synagogues and churches look down on the oppression and pride and selfishness which assemble below
them, and the slavery, poverty, and intemperance
which pass and repass their marble foundations! Oh!
shade of religion, where art thou? Spirit of the lowly
bleeder on Calvary, hast thou left this world in despair? Comforter of the mourning, dweller with the
sinful, how long shall these things be? Religion is
made a show-bubble. Pride is her handmaid, and
selfishness her leader. What a tawdry show they
make! And who believes the substance is equal to
the show, the root as deep as the tree is high, the
foundation as firm as the structure is imposing? No-
where does show more wickedly usurp the dominion
of substance than in the realm of religion. In the
world we might expect to see hypocrisy. But the
true religion is above the world. "My kingdom is
not of this world," said its founder. It has a world
of its own. It is built on substance. But men have
sought to make it a world of show, to carry the
deception and Pharisaism of this world up into the
Redeemer's world, and palm them off there for the
golden reality that shall be admitted to heaven. But
poorly will hypocrisy pass at the bar of God. No

coin but the true one passes there. No gilding will hide the hollowness of a false soul. No tawdry displays will avail with that eye whose glance, like a sword, pierces to the heart. All is open there; all hypocrisy, vanity; worse than vanity; it is sin. It is a gilded lie, a varnished cheat. It is proof of the hollowness within, the sign of corruption. Yea, more; it is itself corrupting; a painted temptation. It lures men away from the truth; wastes their energies on a shadow; wins their affections to fading follies, and gives them a disrelish for the real, the substantial, and enduring. Who can expect that God will not hide in every hollow show intended to deceive, a sharp two-edged sword that shall cut with disappointment, and pierce with inward wasting want?

Fretting and Grumbling.

MANY very excellent persons, whose lives are honorable and whose characters are noble, pass numberless hours of sadness and weariness of heart. The fault is not with their circumstances, nor yet with their general characters, but with themselves that they are miserable. They have failed to adopt the true philosophy of life. They wait for happiness to come instead of going to work and making it; and while they wait they torment themselves with borrowed troubles, with fears, forebodings, morbid fancies and moody spirits, till they are all unfitted for happiness under any circumstances. Sometimes they cherish unchaste ambition, covet some fancied or real good which they do not deserve and could not enjoy if it were theirs, wealth they have not earned, honors they have not won, attentions they have not merited, love which their selfishness only craves. Sometimes they undervalue the good they do possess; throw away the pearls in hand for some beyond their reach, and often less valuable; trample the flowers about them under their feet; long for some never seen, but only heard or read of; and forget present duties and joys in future and far-off visions Sometimes they shade the present with every cloud of the past, and although surrounded by a thousand inviting duties and pleasures, revel in sad memories with a kind of morbid relish for the stimulus of their miseries. Sometimes, forgetting the past and present, they live in the future, not in its probable realities, but in its most improbable visions and unreal creations, now of good and then of evil, wholly unfitting their minds for real life and enjoyments. These morbid and improper states of mind are too prevalent among some persons. They excite that nervous irritability which is so productive of pining regrets and fretful complaints. They make that large class of fretters who enjoy no peace themselves, nor permit others to enjoy it. In the domestic circle they fret their life away. Everything goes wrong with them because they make it so. The smallest annoyances chafe them as though they were unbearable aggravations. Their business and duties trouble them as though such things were not good. Pleasure they never seem to know because they never get ready to enjoy it. Even the common movements of Providence are all wrong with them. The weather is never as it should be. The seasons roll on badly. The sun is never properly tempered. The climate is always charged with a multitude of vices. The winds are everlastingly perverse, either too high or too low, blowing dust in everybody's face, or not fanning them as they should. The earth is ever out of humor, too dry or too wet, too muddy or dusty. And the people are just about like it. Something is wrong all the time, and the wrong is always just about them. Their home is the worst of anybody's; their street and their neighborhood is the most unpleasant to be found; nobody else has so bad servants and so many annoyances as they. Their lot is harder than falls to common mortals; they have to work harder and always did; have less and always expect to. They have seen more trouble than other folks know anything about. They are never so well as their neighbors, and they always charge all their unhappiness upon those nearest connected with them, never dreaming that they are themselves the authors of it all. Such people are to be pitied. Of all the people in the world they deserve most our compassion. They are good people in many respects, very benevolent, very conscientious, very pious, but, withal, very annoying to themselves and others. As a general rule, their goodness makes them more difficult to cure of their evil. They can-

not be led to see that they are at fault. Knowing
their virtues they cannot see their faults. They do
not, perhaps, overestimate their virtues; but they fail
to see what they lack, and this they always charge
upon others, often upon those who love them best.
They see others' actions through the shadow of their
own fretful and gloomy spirits. Hence it is that they
see their own faults as existing in those about them,
as a defect in the eye produces the appearance of a
corresponding defect in every object toward which it
is turned. This defect in character is more generally
the result of vicious or improper habits of mind, than
any constitutional idiosyncrasy. It is the result of·
the indulgence of gloomy thoughts, morbid fancies,
inordinate ambition, habitual melancholy, a complaining, fault finding disposition.

A fretting man or woman is one of the most unlov-
able objects in the world. A wasp is a comfortable
house-mate in comparison; it only stings when disturbed. But an habitual fretter buzzes if he don't
sting, with or without provocation. "It is better to
dwell in the corner of a house-top than with a brawl-
ing woman and in a wide house." Children and
servants cease to respect the authority or obey the
commands of a complaining, worrisome, exacting
parent or master. They know that "barking dogs
don't bite," and fretters don't strike, and they conduct themselves accordingly.

If we are faultless, we should not be so much
annoyed by the defects of those with whom we associate. If we were to acknowledge honestly that we

have not virtue enough to bear patiently with our neighbors' weaknesses, we should show our own imperfection, and this alarms our vanity.

He who frets is never the one who mends, heals, or repairs evils; more, he discourages, enfeebles, and too often disables those around him, who, but for the gloom and depression of his company, would do good work and keep up brave cheer. And when the fretter is one who is beloved, whose nearness of relation to us makes his fretting, even at the weather, seem almost like a personal reproach to us, then the misery of it becomes indeed insupportable. Most men call fretting a minor fault, a foible, and not a vice. There is no vice except drunkenness which can so utterly destroy the peace, the happiness of a home. We never knew a scolding person that was able to govern a family. What makes people scold? Because they cannot govern themselves. How can they govern others? Those who govern well are generally calm. They are prompt and resolute, but steady.

It is not work that kills men, it is worry. Work is healthy; you can hardly put more on a man than he can bear. Worry is rust upon the blade. It is not the revolution that destroys the machinery, but the friction. Fear secretes acids, but love and trust are sweet juices. The man or woman who goes through the world grumbling and fretting, is not only violating the laws of God, but is a sinner against the peace and harmony of society, and is, and of right ought to be, shunned accordingly. They are always in hot water,

forever in trouble. They throw the blame of their
own misdeeds and want of judgment upon others,
and if one might believe them, society would be
found in a shocking state. They rail at everything,
lofty or lowly, and when they have no grumbling to
do they begin to deprecate. They endeavor to make
good actions seem contemptible in other men's eyes,
and try to belittle every noble and praiseworthy
enterprise by casting suspicion upon the motives of
those connected with it. Such individuals, whether
men or women, are an incubus on any society, and
the best way to paralyze their efforts to create discord, is to ignore them altogether. Let grumblers
form a select circle by themselves. Let them herd
together, give them the cold shoulder when they
appear, and make them uncomfortable during their
sojourn, and if they cannot be cured they may be
more easily endured, and perhaps discover the error
of their ways and reform.

An Englishman dearly likes, says *Punch*, to grumble, no matter whether he be right or wrong, crying
or laughing, working or playing, gaining a victory or
smarting under a national humiliation, paying or being
paid — still he must grumble, and, in fact, he is never
so happy as when he is grumbling; and, supposing
everything was to our satisfaction (though it says a
great deal for our power of assumption to assume any
such absurd impossibility), still he would grumble at
the fact of there being nothing for him to grumble
about.

There are two things about which we should never

grumble: the first is that which we *cannot help*, and the other that which we *can help*.

———————

Fault Finding.

A MAN would get a very false notion of his standing among his friends and acquaintances if it were possible—as many would like to have it possible— to know what is said of him behind his back. One day he would go about in a glow of self-esteem, and the next he would be bowed under a miserable sense of misapprehension and disgust. It would be impossible for him to put this and that together and "strike an average." The fact is, there is a strange human tendency to take the present friend into present confidence. With strong natures this tendency proves often a stumbling-block; with weak natures it amounts to fickleness. It is a proof, no doubt, of the universal brotherhood; but one has to watch, lest, in an unguarded moment it lead him into ever so slight disloyalty to the absent.

Never employ yourself to discover the faults of others—look to your own. You had better find out one of your own faults than ten of your neighbor's. When a thing does not suit you, think of some pleasant quality in it. There is nothing so bad as it might be. Whenever you catch yourself in a fault-finding remark, say some approving one in the same breath, and you will soon be cured. Since the best of us have too many infirmities to answer for, says Dean Swift, we ought not to be too severe upon those of others; and, therefore, if our brother is in trouble, we ought to help him, without inquiring over-seriously what produced it.

Those who have the fewest resources in themselves naturally seek the food of their self-love elsewhere. The most ignorant people find most to laugh at in strangers; scandal and satire prevail most in small places; and the propensity to ridicule the slightest or most palpable deviation from what we happen to approve, ceases with the progress of common sense and decency. True worth does not exult in the faults and deficiency of others; as true refinement turns away from grossness and deformity, instead of being tempted to indulge in an unmanly triumph over it. Raphael would not faint away at the daubing of a sign-post, nor Homer hold his head higher for being in the company of a "great bard." Real power, real excellence does not seek for a foil in imperfection; nor fear contamination from coming in contact with that which is coarse and homely. It reposes on itself, and is equally free from envy and affectation. There are some persons who seem to purposely treasure up things that are disagreeable.

The tongue that feeds on mischief, the babbling, the tattling, the sly whispering, the impertinent meddling, all these tongues are trespassing on the community constantly. The fiery tongue is also abroad, and being set on fire of hell, scatters firebrands among friends, sets families, neighborhoods, churches, and social circles in a flame; and. like the salamander, is wretched when out of the burning element. The black slandering tongue is constantly preying upon the rose buds of innocence and virtue, the foliage of merit, worth, genius, and talent; and poisons with its filth of innuendoes and scum of falsehood, the most brilliant flowers, the most useful shrubs, and the most valuable trees in the garden of private and public reputation. Not content with its own base exertions, it leagues with the envious, jealous, and revengeful tongues; and, aided by this trio, sufficient venom is combined to make a second Pandemonium; and malice enough to fill it with demons. Slander can swallow perjury like water, digest forgery as readily as Graham bread, convert white into black, truth into falsehood, good into evil, innocence into crime, and metamorphose every thing which stands in the current of its polluted and polluting breath.

We can understand how a boy that never had been taught better might carry torpedoes in his pocket, and delight to throw them down at the feet of passers-by and see them bound; but we cannot understand how an instructed and well-meaning person could do such a thing. And yet there are men who carry torpedoes all their life, and take pleasure in tossing them at people. "Oh!" they say, "I have something now, and when I meet that man I will give it to him." And they wait for the right company and the right circumstances, and then they out with the most disagreeable things. And if they are remonstrated with,

they say, "It is true," as if that were a justification of
their conduct.   If God should take all the things that
are true of you, and make a scourge of them, and
whip you with it, you would be the most miserable of
men.   But he does not use all the truth on you.
And is there no law of kindness?   Is there no desire
to please and profit men?   Have you a right to take
any little story that you can pick up about a man, and
use it in such a way as to injure him, or give him pain?
And yet, how many men there are that seem to enjoy
nothing so much as inflicting exquisite suffering upon
a man in this way, when he cannot help himself?
Well, you know just how the devil feels.   Whenever
he has done anything wicked, and has made somebody very unhappy, and laughs, he feels just as, for
the time being, you feel when you have done a cruel
thing, and somebody is hurt, and it does you good.

By the rules of justice, no man ought to be ridiculed for any imperfection who does not set up for
eminent sufficiency in that wherein he is defective.
If thou wouldst bear thy neighbor's faults, cast thy
eyes upon thy own.

It is easier to avoid a fault than to acquire a perfection.   By others' faults wise men correct their
own.   He that contemns a small fault commits a
great one.   The greatest of all faults is to believe we
have none.   Little minds ignore their own weakness,
and carp at the defects of the great; but great minds
are sensible of their own faults, and largely compassionate toward inferiors.

Beecher says.   "When the absent are spoken of,

some will speak gold of them, some silver, some iron, some lead, and some always speak dirt; for they have a natural attraction toward what is evil and think it shows penetration in them. As a cat watching for mice does not look up though an elephant goes by, so they are so busy mousing for defects that they let great excellences pass them unnoticed. I will not say that it is not *Christian* to make beads of others' faults, and tell them over every day; I say it is *infernal*. If you want to know how the devil feels, you *do know* if you are such a one."

There are no such disagreeable people in the world as those who are forever seeking their own improvement, and disquieting themselves about this fault and that; while, on the other hand, there is an unconscious merit which wins more good than all the theoretically virtuous in the wide world.

What a world of gossip would be prevented, if it were only remembered that a person who tells you the faults of others intends to tell others of your faults. Every one has his faults; every man his ruling passion. The eye that sees all things sees not itself. That man hath but an ill life of it, who feeds himself with the faults and frailties of other people. Were not curiosity the purveyor, detraction would soon be starved into tameness.

To a pure, sensitive, and affectionate mind, every act of finding fault, or dealing in condemnation, is an act of pain. It is only when we have become callous to the world, and strangers to the sentiments of compassionate love, that we are able to play with uncon-

cern the parts of persecutors and slanderers, and that
we can derive any pleasure from malignity and
revenge. He who is the first to condemn, will be
often the last to forgive.

———••+•§•+३•+⌡•+३•+ ००•———

Envy.

ENVY'S memory is nothing but a row of hooks to
hang up grudges on. Some people's sensibility is
a mere bundle of aversions, and you hear them display
and parade it, not in recounting the things they are
attached to, but in telling you how many things and
persons they "cannot bear."

Envy is not merely a perverseness of temper, but
it is such a distemper of the mind as disorders all the
faculties of it. It began with Satan; for when he fell
he could see nothing to please him in Paradise, and
envied our first parents when in innocence, and therefore tempted them to sin, which ruined them, and all
the human race. Mr. Locke tells us that upon asking
a blind man what he thought scarlet was, he answered
he believed it was like the sound of a trumpet. He
was forced to form his conceptions of ideas which he
had not, by those which he had. In the same manner,
though an envious man cannot but see perfections, yet
having contracted the distemper of acquired blindness,
he will not own them, but is always degrading or
misrepresenting things which are excellent. Thus,
point out a pious person, and ask the envious man

what he thinks of him, he will say he is a hypocrite, or deceitful; praise a man of learning or of great abilities, and he will say he is a pedant, or proud of his attainments; mention a beautiful woman, and he will either slander her chastity or charge her with affectation; show him a fine poem or painting, and he will call the one "stiff," and the other a "daubing." In this way he depreciates or deforms every pleasing object. With respect to other vices, it is frequently seen that many confess and forsake them; but this is not often the case with respect to this vice, for as the person afflicted with this evil knows very well to own that we envy a man is to allow him to be a superior, his pride will not therefore permit him to make any concession, if accused of indulging this base principle, but he becomes more violent against the person envied, and generally remains incurable.

Like Milton's fiend in Paradise, he sees, undelighted, all delight. The brightness of prosperity that surrounds others, pains the eyes of the envious man more than the meridian rays of the sun. It starts the involuntary tear, and casts a gloom over his mind. It brings into action jealousy, revenge, falsehood, and the basest passions of the fallen nature of man. It goads him onward with a fearful impetus, like a locomotive; and often runs his car off the track, dashes it in pieces, and he is left, bruised and bleeding. Like the cuttle-fish, he emits his black venom for the purpose of darkening the clear waters that surround his prosperous neighbors; and, like that phenomenon of the sea, the inky substance

is confined to a narrow circumference, and only tends
to hide himself. The success of those around him
throws him into convulsions, and, like a man with the
delirium tremens, he imagines all who approach him
demons, seeking to devour him. Like Haman, he
often erects his own gallows in his zeal to hang others.
His mind is like the troubled sea, casting up the mire
of revenge. "Dionysius, the tyrant," says Plutarch,
"out of envy, punished Philoxenius, the musician,
because he could sing; and Plato, the philosopher,
because he could dispute better than himself."

Envy is a sentiment that desires to equal, or excel
the efforts of compeers; not so much by increasing
our own toil and ingenuity, as by diminishing the
merit due to the efforts of others. It seeks to elevate
itself by the degradation of others; it detests the
sounds of another's praise, and deems no renown
acceptable that must be shared. Hence, when disappointments occur, they fall, with unrelieved violence,
and the sense of discomfited rivalry gives poignancy
to the blow.

How is envy exemplified? A worm defiling the
healthful blossom — a mildew, blasting the promised
harvest. How true, yet how forbidding an image of
the progress of envy! And would any rational creature be willingly the worm that defiles the pure blossoms of virtue, the mildew that blasts the promised
harvest of human talent, or of human happiness?

And what produces envy? The excellence of
another. Humiliating deduction! Envy is, then,
only the expression of inferiority — the avowal of

deficiency—the homage paid to excellence. Let pride, for once, be virtue, and urge the extinction of this baneful passion, since its indulgence can only produce shame and regret. Envy is unquestionably, a high compliment, but a most ungracious one. An envious man repines as much at the manner in which his neighbors live as if he maintained them. Some people as much envy others a good name, as they want it themselves, and that is the reason of it. Envy is fixed on merit; and, like a sore eye, is offended with anything that is bright. Envy increases in exact proportion with fame; the man that makes a character makes enemies. A radiant genius calls forth swarms of peevish, biting, stinging insects, just as the sunshine awakens the world of flies. Virtue is not secure against envy. Evil men will lessen what they won't imitate. If a man be good, he is envied; if evil, himself is envious. Envious people are doubly miserable, in being afflicted with others' prosperity and their own adversity.

Envy is a weed that grows in all soils and climates, and is no less luxuriant in the country than in the court; is not confined to any rank of men or extent of fortune, but rages in the breasts of all degrees. Alexander was not prouder than Diogenes; and it may be, if we would endeavor to surprise it in its most gaudy dress and attire, and in the exercise of its full empire and tyranny, we should find it in school-masters and scholars, or in some country lady, or her husband; all which ranks of people more despise their neighbors than all the degrees of honor in which courts abound, and it rages as much in a sordid affected dress as in all the silks and embroideries which the excess of the age and the folly of youth delight to be adorned with. Since, then, it keeps all sorts of company, and wriggles itself into the liking of the most contrary natures and dispositions, and yet carries so much poison and venom with it that it alienates the affections from heaven, and raises rebellion against God himself, it is worth our utmost care to watch it in all its disguises and approaches, that we may discover it in its first entrance and dislodge it before it procures a shelter or retiring place to lodge and conceal itself.

Envy, like a cold poison, benumbs and stupefies; and thus, as if conscious of its own impotence, it folds its arms in despair and sits cursing in a corner. When it conquers it is commonly in the dark, by treachery and undermining, by calumny and detraction. Envy is no less foolish than detestable; it is a vice which, they say, keeps no holiday, but is always in the wheel, and working upon its own disquiet. Envy, jealousy, scorpions and rattlesnakes can be made to sting themselves to death. He whose first emotion on the view of an excellent production is to undervalue it, will never have one of his own to show.

Reader, if envy is rankling in your bosom, declare war against it at once; a war of extermination; no truce, no treaty, no compromise. Like the pirate on the high seas, it is an outlaw, an enemy to all mankind, and should be hanged up at the yard arm until it is *dead*, DEAD, DEAD.

Slander.

"That abominable tittle-tattle,
The cud eschew'd by human cattle."
— BYRON.

SLANDER is a blighting sirocco; its pestiferous breath pollutes with each respiration; its forked tongue is charged with the same poison; it searches all corners of the world for victims; it sacrifices the high and the low, the king and the peasant, the rich and the poor, the matron and maid, the living and the dead; but delights most in destroying worth, and immolating innocence. Lacon has justly remarked: "Calumny crosses oceans, scales mountains, and traverses deserts with greater ease than the Scythian Abaris, and, like him, rides upon a poisoned arrow." As the Samiel wind of the Arabian desert not only produces death, but causes the most rapid decomposition of the body, so calumny affects fame, honor, integrity, worth, and virtue. The base, cloven-footed calumniator, like the loathsome worm, leaves his path marked with the filth of malice and scum of falsehood, and pollutes the fairest flowers, the choicest fruits, the most delicate plants in a green-house of character. Living, he is a traveling pest, and worse, dying impenitent, his soul is too deeply stained for hell. Oh, reader never slander the name of another. A writer once said: "So deep does the slanderer sink in the murky waters of degradation and infamy, that could an angel apply an Archimedian moral lever to

him, with heaven for a fulcrum, he could not, in a
thousand years, raise him to the grade of a convict
felon."

SLANDER ;

Whose edge is sharper than the sword ; whose tongue
Out-venoms all the worms of Nile ; whose breath
Rides on the posting winds, and doth belie
All corners of the world : Kings, queens, and states,
Maids, matrons, nay, the secrets of the grave
This viperous slander enters.

It is a melancholy reflection upon human nature, to
see how small a matter will put the ball of scandal in
motion.   A mere hint, a significant look, a mysterious
countenance ; directing attention to a particular person ; often gives an alarming impetus to this *ignis
fatuus*.   A mere interrogatory is converted into an
affirmative assertion—the cry of mad dog is raised
—the mass join in the chase, and not unfrequently, a
mortal wound is inflicted on the innocent and meri-
torious, perhaps by one who had no ill-will, or desire
to do wrong in any case.

There is a sad propensity in our fallen nature to
listen to the retailers of petty scandal.   With many,
it is the spice of conversation, the exhilarating gas of
their minds.   Without any intention of doing essential
injury to a neighbor, a careless remark, relative to
some minor fault of his, may be seized by a babbler,
and, as it passes through the babbling tribe, each one
adds to its bulk, and gives its color a darker hue,
until it assumes the magnitude and blackness of base
slander.   Few are without visible faults—most persons are sometimes inconsistent.   Upon these faults

and mistakes, petty scandal delights to feast. Nor
are those safe from the filth and scum of this poisonous tribe who are free from external blemishes. Envy
and jealousy can start the blood-hound of suspicion;
create a noise that will attract attention, and many
may be led to suppose there is game, when there is
nothing but thin air. An unjust and unfavorable
innuendo is started against a person of unblemished
character; it gathers force as it is rolled through
Babbletown—it soon assumes the dignity of a problem—is solved by the rule of double position, and
the result increased by geometrical progression and
permutation of quantities; and before truth can get
her shoes on, a stain, deep and damning, has been
stamped on the fair fame of an innocent victim, by an
unknown hand. To trace calumny back to the small
fountain of petty scandal, is often impossible; and
always more difficult than to find the source of the
Nile.

Insects and reptiles there are which fulfill the ends of
their existence by tormenting us; so some minds and
dispositions accomplish their destiny by increasing
our misery, and making us more discontented and
unhappy. Cruel and false is he who builds his pleasure upon my pain, or his glory upon my shame.

Shun evil-epeaking. Deal tenderly with the absent;
say nothing to inflict a wound on their reputation.
They may be wrong and wicked, yet your knowledge
of it does not oblige you to disclose their character,
except to save others from injury. Then do it in a
way that bespeaks a spirit of kindness for the absent

offender. Be not hasty to credit evil reports. They
are often the result of misunderstanding, or of evil
design, or they proceed from an exaggerated or partial disclosure of facts. Wait and learn the whole
story before you decide; then believe just what evidence compels you to and no more. But even then,
take heed not to indulge the least unkindness, else
you dissipate all the spirit of prayer for them and
unnerve yourself for doing them good. We are
nearer the truth in thinking well of persons than ill.
Human nature is a tree bearing good as well as evil,
but our eyes are wide open to the latter and half
closed to the former. Believe but half the ill and
credit twice the good said of your neighbor.

A glance, a gesture, or an intonation, may be vital
with falsehood, sinking a heavy shaft of cruelty deep
into the injured soul—though truth, in its all-disclos-
ing effulgence, will, sooner or later, disperse the mists
and doom the falsifier to deserved aversion, still, the
exposure of the guilty does not recompense the injured any more than the bruising of the serpent heals
the wound made by his barbed fang. An injurious
rumor— originating, perhaps, in some sportive gossip
— once attached to a person's name, will remain beside
it a blemish and doubt for ever. Especially is this
true of the fair sex, many of whom have, from this
cause, withered and melted in their youth like snow
in the spring, shedding burning tears of sadness over
the world's unkindness and "man's inhumanity to
man."

Among many species of animals, if one of their

number is wounded and falls, he is at once torn to pieces by his fellows. Traces of this animal cruelty are seen in men and women to-day. Let a woman fall from virtue and nine-tenths of her sisters will turn and tear her to pieces, and the next day smile on the man who ruined her! The cruelty of woman to woman is perfectly wolfish. O, shame! Reverse the action. Loathing for the unrepentant wretch and. tenderness for the wounded sister. Tenderness and pity and help for both alike if they repent and reform. But never trust him who has been a betrayer once. No kindness demands this risk. The smell of blood is too strong for the tamed tiger.

There is a natural inclination in almost all persons to pelt others with stones. Our right hands ache to throw them. There is such wicked enjoyment in seeing the victims dodge and flinch and run. This is human nature in the rough. There are so many who never get out of the rough. There are multitudes of respectable people who evince exquisite pleasure in making others smart. There is a good deal of the Indian — the uncivilized man — in us all yet. It has not been wholly eliminated or educated out of us by the boasted enlightenment and civilization of the age. A great deal of pharisaic zeal to stone others who are no more guilty than we are still exists. It is often the crafty cry of "Stop thief!" to divert attention from ourselves. A thief snatched a diamond ring from a jewler's tray and dodged around the corner into the crowded street. The clerk ran out crying "Stop thief!" The rascal eluded attention by taking up the cry and vociferating as if of one ahead, "Stop thief! stop thief!"

It takes a bloodthirsty wretch to be a prosecutor and inquisitor. The vulture loves to disembowel his victim and wet his beak in blood. Who ever heard of a dove rending the breast of a robin, or a lamb sucking the blood of a kid? Hawks and tigers delight in this. No! nature will out. If Christianity has not cut off the claws, we incline to scratch somebody. If Christ possesses us wholly, and we have been transformed by His spirit, there is no disposition to stone our neighbor, even if at fault. It is not in the genius of Christianity to do it. It is a cancer in the soul that must be cut out, or burned out, or purged out of the blood, or it will kill us.

Alexander had an ugly scar on his forehead, received in battle. When the great artist painted his portrait, he sketched him leaning on his elbow, with his finger covering the scar on his forehead. There was the likeness with the scar hidden. So let us study to paint each other with the finger of charity upon the scar of a brother, hiding the ugly mark and revealing only the beautiful, the true and the good.

Vanity.

THIS propensity pervades the whole human family, to a less or greater degree, as the atmosphere does the globe. It is the froth and effervescence of pride.

The latter is unyielding haughtiness, the former, as soft, pliant, and light, as the down of a swan. It is selfishness modified and puffed up, like a bladder with wind. It is all action, but has no useful strength. It feeds voraciously and abundantly on the richest food that can be served up; and can live on less and meaner diet, than anything of which we can have a conception. The rich, poor, learned, ignorant, beautiful, ugly, high, low, strong, and weak—all have a share of vanity. The humblest Christian is not free from it, and, when he is most humble, the devil will flatter his vanity by telling him of it.

Vanity is ever striving to hide itself, like the peacock its ugly feet, and will even deny its own name. *"I speak without vanity"*—HUSH—you deceitful puff. You make men and women, the only animals that *can* laugh, the very ones to be laughed at. Dr. Johnson once remarked, "When any one complains of the want of what he is known to possess in an eminent degree, he waits, with impatience, to be contradicted," and thus vanity converts him into a fool and a liar, only to render him ridiculous. Vanity engenders affectation, mock modesty, and a train of such like *et ceteras;* all subtracting from the real dignity of man. On the other hand, it feeds, with equal voracity on vulgarity, coarseness, and fulsome eccentricity; every thing by which the person can attract attention. It often takes liberality by the hand, prompts advice, administers reproof, and sometimes perches, visibly and gaily, on the prayers and sermons in the pulpit. It is an every where and ever

21

present principle of human nature—a wen on the
heart of man; less painful, but quite as loathsome as
a cancer. It is, of all others, the most baseless propensity.

We have nothing of which we should be vain, but
much to induce humility. If we have any good qualities they are the gift of God; in the best of men
there are bad ones enough, if they can see themselves, to strangle vanity. Let every one guard
against this all-pervading principle.

Pride.

HE that is proud eats himself up. Pride is his own
glass, his own trumpet, his own chronicle; and whatever praises itself but in the deed, devours the deed
in the praise. Pride is like an empty bag, and who
can stand such a thing *upright?* It is hollow and
heartless; and, like a drum, makes the more noise
from its very emptiness. What is there in us to
induce such a sentiment? Who can say, with truth,
"I am better than my neighbor?" Some shrewd
philosopher has said, that if the best man's faults were
written on his forehead they would make him pull
his hat over his eyes! Ah, there is so much of good
in those who are evil, and so much that is bad in the
best, that it ill becomes us to judge our neighbors
harshly, or set ourselves up to saints at their expense.
Let those who feel above their fellows, view the

heights above themselves, and realize their littleness; for as there is none so vile but that a viler hath been known, so there is no saint but a holier can be named.

When one asked a philosopher what the great God was doing, he replied, "His whole employment is to lift up the humble and to cast down the proud." And, indeed, there is no one sin which the Almighty seems more determined to punish than this. The examples of God's displeasure against it are most strikingly exhibited in the history of Pharaoh, Hezekiah, Haman, Nebuchadnezzar, and Herod.

Pride is generally the effect of ignorance; for pride and folly attend each other. Ignorance and pride keep constant company. Pride, joined with many virtues, chokes them all. Pride is the bane of happiness. Some people, says L'Estrange, are all quality. You would think they were made of nothing but title and genealogy. The stamp of dignity defaces in them the very character of humanity, and transports them to such a degree of haughtiness that they reckon it below themselves to exercise either good nature or good manners. It is related of the French family of the Duke de Levis, that they have a picture in their pedigree in which Noah is represented going into the ark, and carrying a small trunk, on which is written, "Papers belonging to the Levis family." Pride is the mist that vapors round insignificance. We can conceive of nothing so little or ridiculous as pride. It is a mixture of insensibility and ill-nature, in which it is hard to say which has the largest share.

Pride is as loud a beggar as want, and a great deal more saucy. Knavery and pride are often united; the Spartan boy was dishonest enough to steal a fox, but proud enough to let the beast eat out his vitals sooner than hazard detection. Pride breakfasted with Plenty, dined with Poverty, and suppered with Infamy. Pride had rather at any time go out of the way than come behind.

Pride must have a fall. Solomon said, pride goeth before destruction. Of all human actions, pride the most seldom obtains its end; for while it aims at honor and reputation, it reaps contempt and derision. Pride and ill-nature will be hated in spite of all the wealth and greatness in the world. Civility is always safe, but pride creates enemies. As liberality makes friends of enemies, so pride makes enemies of friends. Says Dean Swift: "If a proud man makes me keep my distance, the comfort is, he at the same time keeps his." Proud men have friends neither in prosperity, because they know nobody; nor in adversity, because nobody knows them. There is an honest pride, such as makes one ashamed to do an evil act; such a degree of self-esteem as makes one above doing an injury to any one; but it is the pride which sets one above his fellows that we deprecate; that spirit which would demand homage to itself as better and greater than others. In the name of good sense, how can any one feel thus, when it is realized that the entire life of a man is but a moment in the scale of eternity; and that in a few short days, at most, we must all go from here. When the soul is about to depart, what

avails it whether a man die upon a throne or in the
dust?

Pride is a virtue — let not not the moralist be scan-
dalized. Pride is also a vice. Pride, like ambition,
is sometimes virtuous and sometimes vicious, according to the character in which it is found, and the
object to which it is directed. As a principle, it is
the parent of almost every virtue, and every vice —
everything that pleases and displeases in mankind;
and as the effects are so very different, nothing is
more easy than to discover, even to ourselves, whether
the pride that produces them is virtuous or vicious.
The first object of virtuous pride is rectitude, and the
next independence. Pride may be allowed to this or
that degree, else a man cannot keep up his dignity.
In gluttony there must be eating, in drunkenness
there must be drinking; 'tis not the eating, nor 'tis
not the drinking that must be blamed, but the excess.
So in pride.

Pride and poverty, when combined, make a man's
life up-hill work. Pomposity in a hovel! A gaudy
parlor, meagre kitchen, and empty cupboard! Ragged aristocracy! What shifts there are among this
class to hide their rags, and to give everything a
golden tinge. Among them you see a rich frosted
cake and red wine in the parlor, and a dry crust,
dryer codfish, and bad coffee in the kitchen. Broadcloth hides a ragged shirt. Polished boots hide tat-
tered stockings. Fortune's toys, she kicks them
about as she likes. The higher they look the lower
they sink. The gaudy side out, rags and starvation

within.   Oh! the pangs of pride!   What misery is
here covered up.   Smiles abroad, tears at home.   An
eternal war with want on one hand, and proud ambition on the other.   This trying to be "somebody,"
and this forgetting that it is not necessary to be gold-
washed, and to have a silver spoon in one's mouth, in
order to reach that envied good in life's journey.
There are plenty of "somebodies" among the honest
poor, and plenty of "nobodies" among the dainty
rich.   Pride and poverty are the most ill-assorted
companions that can meet.   They live in a state of
continual warfare, and the sacrifices they exact from
each other, like those claimed by enemies to establish
a hollow peace, only serve to increase their discord.

Proud persons in general think of nothing but
themselves, and imagine that all the world thinks
about them too.   They suppose that they are the
subject of almost every conversation, and fancy every
wheel which moves in society has some relation to
them.   People of this sort are very desirous of
knowing what is said of them, and as they have no
conception that any but great things are said of them,
they are extremely solicitous to know them, and often
put this question: "Who do men say that I am?"

Pride is the ape of charity.   In show they are not
much unlike, but somewhat fuller of action.   In seeking the one, take heed thou light not upon the other.
They are two parallels never put asunder.   Charity
feeds the poor, so does pride; charity builds a hospital, so does pride.   In this they differ: charity gives
her glory to God, pride takes her glory from man.

When flowers are full of heaven- descended dews, they always hang their heads; but men hold theirs the higher the more they receive, getting proud as they get full.

Likeness begets love, yet proud men hate each other. Pride makes us esteem ourselves; vanity makes us desire the esteem of others. It is just to say that a man is too proud to be vain. The pride of wealth is contemptible; the pride of learning is pitiable; the pride of dignity is ridiculous; but the pride of bigotry is insupportable. To be proud of knowledge is to be blind in the light; to be proud of virtue, is to poison yourself with the antidote; to be proud of authority is to make your rise your downfall. The sun appears largest when about to set, so does a proud man swell most magnificently just before an explosion.

No two feelings of the human mind are more opposite than pride and humility. Pride is founded on a high opinion of ourselves; humility on the consciousness of the want of merit. Pride is the offspring of ignorance; humility is the child of wisdom. Pride hardens the heart; humility softens the temper and the disposition. Pride is deaf to the clamors of conscience; humility listens with reverence to the monitor within; and finally, pride rejects the counsels of reason, the voice of experience, the dictates of religion; while humility, with a docile spirit, thankfully receives instruction from all who address her in the garb of truth. "Of all trees," says Felthem, "I observe God hath chosen the vine—a low plant that creeps upon the helpful wall; of all beasts, the soft and pliant lamb; of all fowls, the mild and guileless dove. When God appeared to Moses, it was not in the lofty cedar, nor in the spreading palm, but a bush, an humble, abject bush. As if he would, by these selections, check the conceited arrogance of man." Nothing produces love like humility; nothing hate like pride. It was pride that changed angels into devils; it is humility that makes men as angels.

There are as good horses drawing in carts as in coaches; and as good men are engaged in humble employments as in the highest. The best way to humble a proud man is to take no notice of him. Men are sometimes accused of pride, merely because their accusers would be proud themselves if they were in their places. There are those who despise pride with a greater pride. To quell the pride, even of the greatest, we should reflect how much we owe to others, and how little to ourselves. Other vices choose to be in the dark, but pride loves to be seen in the light. The common charge against those who rise above their condition, is pride Proud looks make foul work in fair faces.

When a man's pride is thoroughly subdued, it is like the sides of Mount Ætna. It was terrible while the eruption lasted and the lava flowed; but when that is past, and the lava is turned into soil, it grows vineyards and olive trees up to the very top.

Fops and Dandies.

Though great thy grandeur, man, may be,
No pride of heart is meant for thee ;
Let fools exult, presumption boast,
The fops and dandies dwell in hosts.

THE rose of Florida, the most beautiful of flowers, emits no fragrance; the bird of Paradise, the most beautiful of birds, gives no song; the cypress of Greece, the finest of trees, yields no fruit; dandies, the shiniest of men, and ballroom belles, the loveliest of created creatures, generally have no sense. Dr. Holmes, in his "Autocrat of the Breakfast Table," says: "Dandies are not good for much, but they are good for something. They invent or keep in circulation those conversational blanks, checks or counters, which intellectual capitalists may sometimes find it worth their while to borrow of them. They are useful, too, in keeping up the standard of dress, which, but for them, would deteriorate and become, what some old folks would have it, a matter of convenience, and not of taste and art. Yes, I like dandies well enough — on one condition, that they have pluck. I find that lies at the bottom of all true dandyism."

A man, following the occupation of wood cutting, wrought with exemplary zeal during the six working days, hoarding every cent not required to furnish him with the most frugal fare. As his "pile" increased, he invested it in gold ornaments — watch

chains of massive links, shirt and sleeve buttons, shoe
buckles, then buttons for vest and coat, a hat band of
the precious metals, a heavy gold-headed cane—and,
in short, wherever an ounce of it could be bestowed
upon his person, in or out of taste, it was done.
The glory of his life, his sole ambition, was to don
his curious attire (which was deposited for safe keeping during the week in one of the banks) on Sunday
morning, and then spend the day, the "observed of
all observers," lounging about the office or bar-room
of a prominent hotel.   He never drank, and rarely
spoke.   Mystery seemed to envelope him.   No one
knew whence he came or the origin of his innocent
whim.   Old citizens assured you that, year after
year, his narrow savings were measured by the
increase of his ornaments, until, at length, the value
of the anomalous garments came to be estimated by
thousands of dollars.   By ten o'clock on Sunday
night the exhibition was closed; his one day of self-
gratification enjoyed, his costly wardrobe was returned
to the bank vault, and he came back into the obscurity of a wood chopper.   Many may think that this man
was a fool, and very much unlike the ordinary young
man; but not so.   Many young men do the same,
only their cloth, their gaudy apparel are not so durable; and they are not so economical; do not invest
in so valuable material, but spend their entire income
(and sometimes more) just to carry a stylish, shiny
suit worth about fifty dollars.

There are a thousand fops made by art for one fool
made by nature.   How ridiculous a sight, says Dr.

Fuller, is a vain young gallant, that bristles with his plumes and shakes his giddy head; and to no other purpose than to get possession of a mistress who is as much a trifle as himself! The little soul that converses of nothing of more importance than the looking-glass and a fantastic dress, may make up the show of the world; but must not be reckoned among the rational inhabitants of it. A man of wit may sometimes, but a man of judgment and sense never can, be a coxcomb. A beau dressed out, is like a cinnamon tree — the bark is worth more than the body. An ass is but an ass, though laden or covered with gold. Fops are more attentive to what is showy than mindful of what is necessary. A fop of fashion is said to be the mercer's friend, the tailor's fool, and his own foe. Show and substance are often united, as an object and its shadow, the sun and its glory, the soul and body, mind and its outward actions, love and its face of sweetness. And on this account men have associated the two so closely together as often to mistake the one for the other, and hence have sought for show as though it were substance, and deceivers have put the former in place of the latter to cheat the world thereby.

Show paints the hypocrite's face and wags the liar's tongue. To discriminate between show and substance, to determine what is show and what is substance, and what are substance and show, is a work of critical judgment, and one upon which the excellency, majesty, and strength of our life in no small degree depends. There is show without substance,

there is substance without show, there is substance
and show together.

Dandies and fops are like a body without soul,
powder without ball, lightning without thunderbolt.
It is dress on a doll, paint on sand.   There is much
of this in the world.   We see it in respect to every
thing considered valuable.   The counterfeiter gives
the show of gold to his base coin, and the show of
value to his lying bank note.   The thief hangs out
the appearance of honesty on his face, and the liar is
thunderstruck if anybody suspects him of equivocation.   The bankrupt carries about him the insignia of
wealth.   The fop puts on the masquerade of dignity
and importance, and the poor belle, whose mother
washes to buy her plumes, outshines the peeress of
the court.   Many a table steams with costly viands
for which the last cent was paid, and many a coat,
sleek and black, swings on the street and in the saloon
on which the tailor has a moral mortgage.   Often do
the drawing-room and parlor, the wardrobe and coach,
speak of wealth and standing when, if they were not
dumb deceivers, they would cry out "It's all a lie."
This is show without substance in domestic life.   It
is the grandest lie of the world, and cheats more poor
people out of their birthright than any other one
species of wicked show.   All their thoughts, and
labors, and money, and credit are spent to fabricate a
gorgeous cheat to the world, to make themselves
appear to be what they are not; when, if they would
be honest, and labor for the true substance of life,
they might be, in reality, what they are clownishly

aping. They cheat their souls out of honesty, and a respectable and comfortable moral character, their bodies out of the substance of a good living, themselves out of a good name among their fellows; yea, they cheat every thing but the very world they intend to cheat. That world sees through their gossamer show, and laughs at the foolishness which seeks to conceal a want of substance.

It is a general sin, to which there are but few exceptions; a great falsehood, which almost every man is striving to make greater. This great evil turns society into a grand show-room, in which the most dextrous show-master wears the tallest plume. Besides the sinfulness of the thing, it is a great domestic bane. It makes the poor poorer, and the rich more avaricious. It causes almost every body to over-live, over-dress, over-eat, over-act in every thing that will make a show. It is a great root of selfishness, a great weight of oppression, a great sink of meanness, a great burden of woe, a great cloud of despair.

Fashion.

No HEATHEN god or goddess has ever had more zealous devotees than fashion, or a more absurd and humiliating ritual, or more mortifying and cruel penances. Her laws, like those of the Medes and Per sians, must be implicitly obeyed, but unlike them, change, as certainly as the moon. They are rarely founded in reason, usually violate common sense, sometimes common decency, and uniformly common comfort.

Fashion rules the world, and a most tyrannical mistress she is—compelling people to submit to the most inconvenient things imaginable for her sake. She pinches our feet with tight shoes, or chokes us with a tight neckerchief, or squeezes the breath out of our body by tight lacing. She makes people sit up by night, when they ought to be in bed, and keeps them in bed in the morning when they ought to be up and doing. She makes it vulgar to wait upon one's self, and genteel to live idly and uselessly. She makes people visit when they would rather stay at home, eat when they are not hungry, and drink when they are not thirsty. She invades our pleasures and interrupts our business. She compels people to dress gaily, whether upon their own property or that of others—whether agreeably to the word of God or the dictates of pride.

Fashion, unlike custom, never looks at the past as a precedent for the present or future. She imposes unanticipated burdens, without regard to the strength or means of her hoodwinked followers, cheating them out of time, fortune and happiness; repaying them with the consolation of being ridiculed by the wise, endangering health and wasting means; a kind of remuneration rather paradoxical, but most graciously received. Semblance and shade are among her attributes. It is of more importance for her worshipers to *appear* happy than to *be* so.

Fashion taxes without reason and collects without mercy. She first infatuates the court and aristocracy, and then ridicules the poor if they do not follow in the wake, although they die in the ditch. This was exemplified in the reign of Richard III., who was humpbacked. Monkey-like, his court, at the dictum of fashion, all mounted a bustle on their *backs,* and as this was not an expensive adjunct, the whole nation became humpbacked—emphatically a crooked generation—from the peasant to the king, all were humped.

If she require oblations from the four quarters of the globe, they must be had, if wealth, health and happiness are the price. If she fancy comparative nakedness for winter, or five thicknesses of woolen for dog days—and speaks, and it is done. If she order the purple current of life and the organs of respiration to be retarded by steel, whalebone, buck-ram, drill, and cords—it is done. Disease laughs and death grins at the folly of the goddess and the zeal of the worshipers. If she order a bag full of notions on the hips, a Chinese shoe on the foot, a short cut, a trail, a hoop, or balloon sleeve, or no sleeve, for a dress, and a grain fan bonnet, or fool's cap for the head, she is obsequiously obeyed by the exquis-itely fashionable ladies and lauded by their beaux. If she order, her male subjects, the Mordecais and Dan-iels, tremble at the gong sound of trumpet-tongued ridicule. Not only the vain and giddy, the thoughtless and rattlebrained, dance attendance upon her, but many a statesman and philosopher.

The empress at Paris, or other ladies of rank, do not originate the fashions, neither do any ladies of real rank and distinction; they adopt them, and thus set the seal of their acknowledged authority upon them, but no lady would be the first to wear a striking novelty, or a style so new, or so *outre* as to be likely to attract public attention. This is left for the leaders of the *demi-monde*, several of whom are in the pay of Parisian dress-makers and *modistes*. The noted Worth, the man-milliner of Paris, who receives all the money and exercises all the impudence which have placed him at the head of his profession, while women do all the work, has in his employ a dozen fashion writers and several of the most noted leaders of Parisian society. These latter are selected for their fine appearance and dashing manners. Toilettes, equipages and boxes at the theatre and opera are provided for them. Dead or dying, they are required to show themselves at these places on all suitable occasions, in extraordinary dresses made by the "renowned" Worth, as the fashion correspondents say, who in this way take up the burden of the song, and echo it even upon these Western shores. It is the height of ambition with some American women to go to Paris, and have a dress made by Worth; and dearly do they sometimes pay for their folly, not only in immense prices for very small returns, but in degrading their American womanhood by following in so disgraceful a scramble with so mixed an assemblage.

Fashion is the foster mother of vanity, the offal of pride, and has nursed her pet, until it is as fat as a sea turtle, is quite as wicked to bite, and harder to kill; but, unlike that inhabitant of the herring pond, instead of keeping *in* a shell, it is mounted *on* a shell, adorned with every flummery, intruding into all the avenues of life, scattering misery far and wide— faithless, fearless, uncompromising and tyrannical.

Then the *example* of a fashionable woman, how low, how vulgar! With her the cut of a collar, the depth of a flounce, the style of a ribbon, is of more importance than the strength of a virtue, the form of a mind, or the style of a life. She consults the fashion plate oftener than her Bible; she visits the dry goods shop and the milliner oftener than the church. She speaks of fashion oftener than of virtue, and follows it closer than she does her Savior. She can see squalid misery and low-bred vice without a blush or a twinge of the heart; but a plume out of fashion, or a table set in old style, would shock her into a hysteric fit. Her example! What is it but a breath of poison to the young? We had as soon have vice stalking bawdily in the presence of our children, as the graceless form of fashion. Vice would look haggard and mean at first sight, but fashion would be gilded into an attractive delusion. Oh, fashion! how thou art dwarfing the intellect and eating out the heart of our people! Genius is dying on thy luxurious altar. And what a sacrifice! Talent is withering into weakness in thy voluptuous gaze! Virtue gives up the ghost at thy smile. Our youth are

22

chasing after thee as a wanton in disguise. Our young women are the victims of thine all-greedy lust. And still thou art not satisfied, but, like the devouring grave, criest for more.

Friendship, its links must be forged on fashion's anvil, or it is good for nothing. How shocking to be friendly with an unfashionable lady! It will never do. How soon one would lose caste! No matter if her mind is a treasury of gems, and her heart a flower garden of love, and her life a hymn of grace and praise, it will not do to walk on the streets with her, or intimate to anybody that you know her. No, one's intimate friend must be *a la mode*. Better bow to the shadow of a belle's wing than rest in the bosom of a "strong-minded" woman's love.

And love, too, that must be fashionable. It would be unpardonable to love a plain man whom fashion could not seduce, whose sense of right dictated his life, a man who does not walk perpendicular in a standing collar, and sport a watch-fob, and twirl a cane. And then then to marry him would be death. He would be just as likely to sit down in the kitchen as in the parlor; and might get hold of the woodsaw as often as the guitar; and very likely he would have the baby right up in his arms and feed it and rock it to sleep. A man who will make himself useful about his own home is so exceedingly unfashionable that it will never do for a lady to marry him. She would lose caste at once.

Abused women generally outlive fashionable ones. Crushed and care-worn women see the pampered daughters of fashion wither and die around them, and wonder why death in kindness does not come to take them away instead. The reason is plain: fashion kills more women than toil and sorrow. Obedience to fashion is a greater transgression of the laws of woman's nature, a greater injury to her physical and mental constitution, than the hardships of poverty and neglect. The slave-woman at her tasks will live and grow old and see two or three generations of her mistresses fade and pass away. The washerwoman, with scarce a ray of hope to cheer her in her toils, will live to see her fashionable sisters all die around her. The kitchen maid is hearty and strong, when her lady has to be nursed like a sick baby. It is a sad truth, that fashion-pampered women are almost worthless for all the great ends of human life. They have but little force of character; they have still less power of moral will, and quite as little physical energy. They live for no great purpose in life; they accomplish no worthy ends. They are only doll-forms in the hands of milliners and servants, to be dressed and fed to order. They dress nobody; they feed nobody; they instruct nobody; they bless nobody, and save nobody. They write no books; they set no rich examples of virtue and womanly life. If they rear children, servants and nurses do it all, save to conceive and give them birth. And when reared what are they? What do they even amount to, but weaker scions of the old stock? Who ever heard of a fashionable woman's child exhibiting any virtue or power of mind for which it became

eminent?   Read the biographies of our great and
good men and women.   Not one of them had a fashionable mother.   They nearly all sprang from plain,
strong-minded women, who had about as little to do
with fashion as with the changing clouds.

There is one fashion that never changes.   The
sparkling eye, the coral lip, the rose leaf blushing on
the cheek, the elastic step, are always, in fashion.
Health — rosy, bouncing, gladsome health — is never
out of fashion; what pilgrimages are made, what
prayers are uttered for its possession!   Failing in
the pursuit what treasures are lavished in concealing
its loss or counterfeiting its charms!   Reader, if you
love freedom more than slavery, liberty more than
thraldom, happiness more than misery, competence
more than poverty, never bow your knee to the goddess fashion.

Dress.

Looking upon the panoramic field of God's works,
we must conclude that he has taken especial care to
gratify the varying taste of his creatures.   And more
than this, we must conclude that he himself has an
infinite taste, which finds an infinite pleasure in making and viewing this magnificent universe of flashing
splendor and sombre sweetness, this field on field,
system beyond system, far off where human eye can
never reach, all shining and moving in an infinite

variety of forms, colors and movements. Moreover, we cannot but feel that God is a lover of dress. He has put on robes of beauty and glory upon all his works. Every flower is dressed in richness; every field blushes beneath a mantle of beauty; every star is veiled in brightness; every bird is clothed in the habiliments of the most exquisite taste. The cattle upon the thousand hills are dressed by the hand divine.' Who, studying God in his works, can doubt that He will smile upon the evidence of correct taste manifested by His children in clothing the forms He has made them?

To love dress is not to be a slave of fashion; to love dress only is the test of such homage. To transact the business of charity in a silk dress, and to go in a carriage to the work, injures neither the work nor the worker. The slave of fashion is one who assumes the livery of a princess and then omits the errand of the good human soul; dresses in elegance and goes upon no good errand, and thinks and does nothing of value to mankind. It does, indeed, appear, that the woman of our land is moving against all the old enemies of society. She herself rises and is helping others.

Beauty in dress is a good thing, rail at it who may. But it is a lower beauty, for which a higher beauty should not be sacrificed. They love dress too much who give it their first thought, their best time, or all their money; who for it neglect the culture of mind or heart, or the claims of others on their service; who care more for their dress than their disposition;

who are troubled more by an unfashionable bonnet than a neglected duty.

Female loveliness never appears to so good advantage as when set off by simplicity of dress. No artist ever decks his angels with towering feathers and gaudy jewelry; and our dear human angels—if they would make good their title to that name—should carefully avoid ornaments which properly belong to Indian squaws and African princesses. These tinselries may serve to give effect on the stage, or upon the ball-room floor, but in daily life there is no substitute for the charm of simplicity. A vulgar taste is not to be disguised by gold and diamonds. The absence of a true taste and refinement of delicacy cannot be compensated for by the possession of the most princely fortune. Mind measures gold, but gold cannot measure mind. Through dress the mind may be read, as through the delicate tissue the lettered page. A modest woman will dress modestly; a really refined and intelligent woman will bear the marks of careful selection and faultless taste.

A coat that has the mark of use upon it is a recommendation to people of sense, and a hat with too much nap and too high lustre a derogatory circumstance. The best coats in our streets are worn on the backs of penniless fops, broken down merchants, clerks with pitiful salaries, and men who do not pay up. The heaviest gold chains dangle from the fobs of gamblers and gentlemen of very limited means; costly ornaments on ladies indicate to the eyes that are well opened, the fact of a silly lover or husband cramped for funds. And when a pretty woman goes by in plain and neat apparel, it is the presumption that she has fair expectations, and a husband that can show a balance in his favor. For women are like books, too much gilding makes men suspicious that the binding is the most important part. The body is the shell of the soul, and the dress is the husk of the body; but the husk generally tells what the kernel is. As a fashionably dressed young lady passed some gentlemen, one of them raised his hat, whereupon another, struck by the fine appearance of the lady, made some inquiries concerning her, and was answered thus: "She makes a pretty ornament in her father's house, but otherwise is of no use."

The love of beauty and refinement belong to every true woman. She ought to desire, in moderation, pretty dresses, and delight in beautiful colors and graceful fabrics; she ought to take a certain, not too expensive, pride in herself, and be solicitous to have all belonging to her well-chosen and in good taste; to care for the perfect ordering of her house, and harmony and fitness of her furniture, the cleanliness of her surroundings, and good style of her arrangements: she ought not to like singularity, either of habit or appearance, or be able to stand out against a fashion when fashion has become custom: she ought to make herself conspicuous only by the perfection of her taste, by the grace and harmony of her dress, and unobtrusive good-breeding of her manners: she ought to set the seal of gentlewoman on every square inch of her life, and shed the radiance of her own beauty and refinement on every material object about her.

The richest dress is always worn on the soul. The adornments that will not perish, and that all men most admire, shine from the heart through this life. God has made it our highest, holiest duty to dress the soul He has given us. It is wicked to waste it in frivolity. It is a beautiful, undying, precious thing. If every young woman would think of her soul when she looks in the glass, would hear the cry of her naked mind when she dallies away her precious hours at her toilet, would listen to the sad moaning of her hollow heart, as it wails through her idle, useless life, something would be done for the elevation of womanhood. Compare a well-dressed body with a well-dressed mind. Compare a taste for dress with a taste for knowledge, culture, virtue, and piety. Dress up an ignorant young woman in the "height of fashion;" put on plumes and flowers, diamonds and gewgaws; paint her face and gird up her waist, and we ask you if, this side of a painted feathered savage, you can find any thing more unpleasant to behold. And yet just such young women we meet by the hundred every day on the street and in all our public places. It is awful to think of. Why is it so? It is only because woman is regarded as a doll to be dressed—a plaything to be petted—a house ornament to exhibit—a thing to be used and kept from crying with a sugar-plum show.

What multitudes of young women waste all that is precious in life on the finified fooleries of the toilet!

How the soul of womanhood is dwarfed and shriveled by such trifles, kept away from the great fields of active thought and love by the gewgaws she hangs on her bonnet! How light must be that thing which will float on the sea of passion—a bubble, a feather, a puff-ball! And yet multitudes of women float there, live there, and call it life. Poor things! Scum on the surface! But there is a truth, young women; woman was made for a higher purpose, a nobler use, a grander destiny. Her powers are rich and strong; her genius bold and daring. She may walk the fields of thought, achieve the victories of mind, spread around her the testimonials of her worth, and make herself known and felt as man's co-worker and equal in whatsoever exalts mind, embellishes life, or sanctifies humanity.

The true object and importance of taste in dress few understand. Let no woman suppose that any man can be really indifferent to her appearance. The instinct may be deadened in his mind by a slatternly, negligent mother, or by plain maiden sisters; but she may be sure it is there, and, with little adroitness, capable of revival. Of course, the immediate effect of a well-chosen feminine toilet operates differently in different minds. In some, it causes a sense of actual pleasure; in others, a consciousness of passive enjoyment. In some, it is intensely felt while it is present; in others only missed when it is gone.

Dress affects our manners. A man who is badly dressed feels chilly, sweaty, and prickly. He stammers, and does not always tell the truth. He means to, perhaps, but he can't. He is half distracted about his pantaloons, which are much too short, and are constantly hitching up; or his frayed jacket and crumpled linen harrow his soul and quite unman him. He treads on the train of a lady's dress, and says "Thank you," sits down on his hat, and wishes the "desert were his dwelling place."

A friend of ours, who had long been absent, returned and called upon two beautiful young ladies of his acquaintance. One came quickly to greet him in the neat, yet not precise attire, in which she was performing her household duties. The other, after the lapse of half an hour, made her stately entrance, in all the primness of starch and ribbons, with which, on the announcement of his entrance, she had hastened to bedeck herself. Our friend, who had long been hesitating on his choice between the two, now hesitated no longer. The cordiality with which the first hastened to greet him, and the charming carelessness of her attire, entirely won his heart. She is now his wife. Young ladies, take warning from the above, and never refuse to see a friend because you have on a wash-gown. Be assured the true gentleman will not think less of you because he finds you in the performance of your duties, and not ashamed to let it be known. Besides, there may positively be a grace, a witching wildness about an every-day dress, that adds to every charm of face and feature.

Church Dress.

THE best bred people of every Christian country but our own avoid all personal display when engaged in worship and prayer. Our churches, on the contrary, are made places for the exhibition of fine apparel and other costly, flaunting compliances with fashion, by those who boast of superior wealth and manners. We shall leave our gewgawed devotees to reconcile humiliation in worship with vanity in dress. That is a problem which we confess we have neither the right nor the capacity to solve. How far fine clothes may affect the personal piety of the devotee we do not pretend even to conjecture; but we have a very decided opinion in regard to their influence upon the religion of others. The fact is, that our churches are so fluttering with birds of fine feathers, that no sorry fowl will venture in. It is impossible for poverty in rags and patches, or even in decent but humble costume, to take its seat, if it should be so fortunate as to find a place, by the side of wealth in brocade and broadcloth. The poor are so awed by the pretension of superior dress and "the proud man's costume," that they naturally avoid too close a proximity to them. The church being the only place on this side of the grave designed for the rich and the poor to meet together in equal prostration before God, it certainly should always be kept free for this common humiliation and brotherhood. It is so in most of the churches in Europe, where the beggar in rags and wretchedness, and the wealthiest and most eminent, whose appropriate sobriety of dress leaves them without mark of external distinction, kneel down together, equalized by a common humiliation before the only Supreme Being.

No person can attend upon the services of any of our churches in towns and cities, and worship God without distraction. One needs continually to offer the prayer "take off my eyes from beholding vanity." But he must be blind to have his prayer answered, for the sight of the eyes always affects the heart. There is the rustle of rich silks, the flutter of gay fans, the nodding of plumes and flowers; the tilting of laces, of ribbons, of curls; here is a head frizzed till it looks more like a picture of the Furies than that of a miss of "sweet sixteen," and there is another with hair hanging full length, waxed and dressed to fourfold its quantity; there are bracelets and ear-rings, and fantasies of every sort and every hue; everything that is absurd and foolish in fashion, and everything that is grotesque and ridiculous in the trying to ape fashion; all these are before you, between you and the speaker, the altar whereon is laid the sacrifice of prayer, and from whence the truth is dispensed! How can you worship God? how can you hear with any profit?

With dress and fashion, its propriety, its sin or folly, in the abstract, we are not now dealing; only with its improper display in the house of God. If persons have the taste, and the means to gratify that taste, in expensive, showy apparel, let them have it to display at home, or abroad, at parties, at the opera — anywhere, but in the sanctuary.

The adoption of more simple apparel for church on the part of the rich, in this country, would have the effect, certainly not of diminishing their own personal piety, but probably of increasing the disposition for religious observance on the part of the poor.

Manners.

MANNERS are different in every country; but true politeness is everywhere the same. Manners, which take up so much of our attention, are only artificial helps which ignorance assumes in order to imitate politeness, which is the result of good sense and good nature. A person possessed of those qualities, though he had never seen a court, is truly agreeable; and if without them, would continue a clown, though he had been all his life a gentleman usher. He who assumes airs of importance exhibits his credentials of insignificance. There is no policy like politeness; and a good manner is the best thing in the world to get a good name, or to supply the want of it. Good manners are a part of good morals, and it is as much our duty as our interest to practice in both. Good manners is the art of making those around us easy. Whoever makes the fewest persons uneasy is

the best bred man in the company. Good manners
should begin at home. Politeness it not an article to
be worn in all dress only, to be put on when we have
a complimentary visit. A person never appears so
ridiculous by the qualities he has, as by those he
affects to have. He gains more by being contented
to be seen as he is, than by attempting to appear
what he is not. Good manners is the result of much
good sense, some good nature, and a little self-denial,
for the sake of others, and with a view to obtain the
same indulgence from them. "Manners make the
man," says the proverb. It may be true that some
men's manners have been the making of them; but
as manners are rather the expression of the man, it
would be more proper to say—the man makes the
manners. Social courtesies should emanate from the
heart, for remember always that the worth of manners
consists in their being the sincere expression of feelings. Like the dial of the watch, they should indicate that the work within is good and true.

The young should be mannerly, but they feel timid,
bashful and self-distrustful the moment they are addressed by a stranger, or appear in company. There
is but one way to get over this feeling, and acquire
easy and graceful manners, and that is to do the best
they can at home as well as abroad. Good manners
are not learned so much as acquired by habit. They
grow upon us by use. We must be courteous, agreeable, civil, kind, gentlemanly, and manly at home, and
then it will become a kind of second nature everywhere. A coarse, rough manner at home begets a

habit of roughness, which we cannot lay off if we try, when we go among strangers. The most agreeable persons in company are those who are the most agreeable at home. Home is the school for all the best things.

Good manners are an essential part of life-education, and their importance cannot be too largely magnified, when we consider that they are the outward expression of an inward virtue. And how often is this exhibition of the virtues of frankness, gentleness and sweet simplicity, the safest and surest recommendation of those who come to us as strangers in quest of friendly aid. It is quite marvellous, from the fact that by no special training, no aristocratic examples, no conventionalities but those of nature, the gifts of good sense, a true sense of propriety and native tact, are sufficient qualifications to enable us to glide freely and irreproachably among the elaborated subjects of a regal court. A foreigner once remarked to me, "An American is received in any circle in England," but were we boorish in manner, and without mental accomplishments, this privilege would not be accorded us.

The true art of being agreeable is to appear well pleased with all the company, and rather to seem well entertained with them, than to bring entertainment to them. A man thus disposed, perhaps, may not have much sense, learning, nor any wit, but if he have common sense, and something friendly in his behavior, it conciliates men's minds more than the brightest parts without this disposition; it is true indeed that we should not dissemble and flatter in company; but a man may be very agreeable, strictly consistent with truth and sincerity, by a prudent silence where he cannot concur, and a pleasing assent where he can. Now and then you meet with a person so exactly formed to please that he will gain upon every one who hears or beholds him; this disposition is not merely the gift of nature, but frequently the effect of much knowledge of the world, and a command over the passions.

It is unfortunate that the agreeable should be so often found in unison with the frivolous, for frivolity makes great encroachments upon dignity.

Levity of manners is prejudicial to every virtue. Avoid all sourness and austerity of manners. Virtue is a pleasant and agreeable quality, and gay and civil wisdom is always engaging.

There are a thousand pretty, engaging little ways, which every person may put on, without running the risk of being deemed either affected or foppish. The sweet smile; the quiet, cordial bow; the earnest movement in addressing a friend—more especially a stranger—whom one may recommend to our good regards; the inquiring glance; the graceful attention, which is so captivating when united with self-posses-sion; these will secure us the good regards of even a churl. Above all, there is a certain softness of manner which should be cultivated, and which, in either man or woman, adds a charm that always entirely compensates for a lack of beauty.

Lord Chatham, who was almost as remarkable for

his manners as for his eloquence and public spirit, has thus defended good breeding: "Benevolence is trifles, or a preference of others to ourselves in the little daily occurrences of life."

Says Emerson, "I wish cities would teach their best lesson—of quiet manners." It is the foible especially of American youth—pretension. The mark of the man of the world is absence of pretension. He does not make a speech; he takes a low business tone, avoids all brag, is nobody, dresses plainly, promises not at all, performs much, speaks in monosyllables, hugs his fact. He calls his employment by its lowest name, and so takes from evil tongues their sharpest weapon. His conversation clings to the weather and the news, yet he allows himself to be surprised into thought, and the unlocking of his learning and philosophy.

One of the most marked tests of character is the manner in which we conduct ourselves toward others. A graceful behavior toward superiors, inferiors, and equals, is a constant source of pleasure. It pleases others because it indicates respect for their personality, but it gives tenfold more pleasure to ourselves. Every man may to a large extent be a self-educator in good behavior, as in everything else; he can be civil and kind, if he will, though he have not a penny in his purse.

If dignity exist in the mind, it will not be wanting in the manners. When no seat was offered to the Indian chief Tecumseh, in the council, and he exclaimed, in a spirit of elevated but offended pride, (at

23

the same time wrapping his blanket around him),
"The sun is my father, and the earth is my mother, I
will recline upon her bosom," and then seated himself
upon the ground, he displayed a striking instance of
genuine and manly dignity. He might have stood
for centuries, making Parisian attitudes and grimaces,

" With studied gestures or well-practised smiles,"

and not have been half so noble, commanding and
dignified, as by this sublime expression and this simple act.

Dr. Hall says: "The language of a man is a reasonable good index of his character: the triffler
abounds in slang words and slang phrases; the vulgar and low bred use most glibly the depreciative
adjective; they revel in the expletives of liar, scoundrel, swindler; the educated, the cultivated, and the
refined, speak softly, quietly, gently; every word is
uttered with composure, even under circumstances of
aggravation; if annoyed, their severest reproof is
expressive silence; and always they maintain their
self-respect."

Manners are the ornament of action; and there is a
way of speaking a kind word, or of doing a kind
thing, which greatly enhances their value. What
seems to be done with a grudge, or as an act of condescension, is scarcely accepted as a favor. Yet
there are men who pride themselves upon their gruff-
ness; and though they may possess virtue and capacity, their manner is often formed to render them
almost insupportable. It is difficult to like a man

who, though he may not pull your nose, habitually wounds your self-respect, and takes a pride in saying disagreeable things to you. There are others who are dreadfully condescending, and cannot avoid seizing upon every small opportunity of making their greatness felt.

The cultivation of manner — though in excess it is foppish and foolish — is highly necessary in a person who has occasion to negotiate with others in matters of business. Affability and good breeding may even be regarded as essential to the success of a man in any eminent station and enlarged sphere of life; for the want of it has not unfrequently been found in a great measure to neutralize the results of much industry, integrity, and honesty of character. There are, no doubt, a few strong tolerant minds which can bear with defects and angularities of manner, and look only to the more genuine qualities; but the world at large is not so forbearing, and cannot help forming its judgments and likings mainly according to outward conduct.

Agreeable manners contribute wonderfully to a man's success. Take two men, possessing equal advantages in every other respect; but let one be gentlemanly, kind, obliging and conciliating; the other disobliging, rude, harsh and insolent, and the one will become rich while the other will starve.

Good manners are not only an embellishment to personal charms, but an excellent substitute for them when they do not exist. When the attractions of beauty have disappeared, there should be an elegance

and refinement of manner to supply their place.
Beauty is the gift of nature, but manners are acquired
by cultivation and practice; and the neglect of them
is seldom pardoned by the world, which exacts this.
deference to its opinions, and this conformity to the
least mistakable of its judgments

The accomplishments so much esteemed in some
parts of the world, may be disregarded elsewhere,
but wisdom and virtue, intelligence and worth, are
universally respected and appreciated, and exhibit
that kind of deportment which is everywhere approved
and honored.

If Christianity had no higher recommendation than
this, that it makes a man a gentleman, it would still
be an invaluable element. The New Testament
inculcates good manners. Our Savior was courteous even to his persecutors. Look at Paul before
Agrippa! His speech is a model of dignified courtesy as well as of persuasive eloquence. A spirit of
kindly consideration for all men characterized the
Twelve. The same mild, self-sacrificing spirit which
pervaded the sayings and doings of the early disciples
is exhibited by the true followers of the cross at the
present day. A man, it is true, may be superficially
polite without being a Christian; but a Christian, by
the very conditions of his creed and the obligations
of his faith, is necessarily in mind and soul—and
therefore in word and act—a gentleman.

The True Gentleman.

WHEN you have found a man, you have not far to go to find a gentleman. You cannot make a gold ring out of brass. You cannot change a Cape May crystal to a diamond. You cannot make a gentleman till you first find a man.

To be a gentleman it is not sufficient to have had a grandfather. To be a gentleman does not depend on the tailor or the toilet. Blood will degenerate. Good clothes are not good habits.

A gentleman is a man who is gentle. Titles, graceful accomplishments, superior culture, princely wealth, great talents, genius, do not constitute a man with all the attributes needed to make him a gentleman. He may be awkward, angular, homely, or poor, and yet belong to the uncrowned aristocracy. His face may be bronzed at the forge or bleached in the mill, his hand huge and hard, his patched vest, like Joseph's coat of many colors, and he may still be a true gentleman. The dandy is a dry goods sign and not a gentleman, for he depends upon dress and not upon his honor and virtue, for his passport to the best circles of society. "The man who has no money is poor, he who has nothing but money is poorer than he," and is not a gentleman. Some of the most distinguished men in the world of letters, in the world of art, have been unamiable, gross, vulgar, ungentle, consequently not gentlemen.

The union of gentleness of manners with firmness of mind are noticeable in the true gentleman. When in authority, and having a right to command, his commands are delivered with mildness and gentleness, and willingly obeyed. Good breeding is the great object of his thoughts and actions, and he observes carefully the behavior and manners of those who are thus distinguished.

It is a wrong notion which many have, that nothing more is due from them to their neighbors than what results from a principle of honesty, which commands us to pay our debts, and forbids us to do injuries; whereas a gentleman gains the esteem of all by a thousand little civilities, complacencies, and endeavors to give others pleasure.

He is careful to have thoughts and sentiments worthy of him, as virtue raises the dignity of man, while vice degrades him. True greatness lies in the heart; it must be elevated by aspiring to great things; and by daring to think himself worthy of them. Others may attract us through the splendor of some special faculty, or the eminency of some special virtue, but in his case it is the whole individual we admire and love, and the faculty takes its peculiar character, the virtue acquires its subtile charm, because considered as an outgrowth of the beautiful, beneficent, and bounteous nature in which it had its root. He insults not the poor with condescension, nor courts the rich with servility, but takes his place on an easy equality and fraternity with all, without the pretense of being the inferior of any.

There is true dignity in labor, and no true dignity without it. He who looks down scornfully on labor is like the man who had a mouth and no hands, and yet made faces at those who fed him—mocking the fingers that brought bread to his lips. He who writes a book, or builds a house, or tills a farm, or follows any useful employment, lives to some purpose, and contributes something to the fund of human happiness.

Garibaldi, the greatest hero of the age, is a working man. Daniel Webster knit his iron frame into strength by working on his father's farm when young.

A gentleman is a human being, combining a woman's tenderness with a man's courage. He is just a gentleman: no more, no less; a diamond polished that was first a diamond in the rough. A gentleman is gentle. A gentleman is modest. A gentleman is courteous. A gentleman is slow to take offense, as being one who never gives it. A gentleman is slow to surmise evil, as being one who never thinks it. A gentleman subjects his appetites. A gentleman refines his taste. A gentleman subdues his feelings. A gentleman controls his speech. A gentleman deems every other other better than himself.

Sir Philip Sydney was never so much of a gentleman—mirror though he was of English knighthood —as when, upon the field of Zutphen, as he lay in his own blood, he waived the draught of cool spring water that was to quench his dying thirst, in favor of a dying soldier.

St. Paul describes a gentleman when he exhorted

the Philippian Christians: "Whatsoever things are true, whatsoever things are pure, whatsoever things are lovely, whatsoever things are of good report, if there be any virtue, and if there be any praise, think of these things." And Dr. Isaac Barlow, in his admirable sermon on the callings of a gentleman, pointedly says: "He should labor and study to be a leader unto virtue, and a notable promoter thereof; directing and exciting men thereto by his exemplary conversation; encouraging them by his countenance and authority; rewarding the goodness of meaner people by his bounty and favor; he should be such a gentleman as Noah, who preached righteousness by his words and works before a profane world."

One very frequently hears the remark made, that such and such a man "can be a gentleman when he pleases." Now when our reader next hears this expression made use of, let him call to mind the following: He who "can be a gentleman when he pleases," never pleases to be anything else. A gentleman, like porcelain ware, must be painted before he is glazed. There can be no change after the burning in.

The sword of the best-tempered metal is the most flexible. So the truly generous are the most pliant and courteous in their behavior to their inferiors.

The true gentleman is one whose nature has been fashioned after the highest models. His qualities depend not upon fashion or manners, but upon moral worth—not on personal possessions, but on personal qualities. The psalmist briefly describes him as one "that walketh uprightly, and worketh righteousness, and speaketh the truth in his heart."

The gentleman is eminently distinguished by his self-respect. He values his character—not so much of it only as can be seen by others, but as he sees it himself, having regard for the approval of his inward monitor. And, as he respects himself, so, by the same law, does he respect others. Humanity is sacred in his eyes, and thence proceed politeness and forbearance, kindness and charity.

The true gentleman has a keen sense of honor— scrupulously avoiding mean actions. His standard of probity in word and action is high. He does not shuffle nor prevaricate, dodge nor skulk; but is honest, upright, and straitforward. His law is rectitude —action in right lines. When he says *yes*, it is a law; and he dares to say the valiant *no* at the fitting season. The gentleman will not be bribed; only the low-minded and unprincipled will sell themselves to those who are interested in buying them.

Riches and rank have no necessary connection with genuine gentlemanly qualities. The poor man may be a true gentleman—in spirit and in daily life. He may be honest, truthful, upright, polite, temperate, courageous, self-respecting and self-helping—that is, be a true gentleman. The poor man with a rich spirit is in all ways superior to the rich man with a poor spirit. To borrow St. Paul's words, the former is as "having nothing, yet possessing all things," while the other, though possessing all things, has nothing. The first hopes everything and fears noth-

ing; the last hopes nothing and fears everything.
Only the poor in spirit are really poor.   He who has
lost all, but retains his courage, cheerfulness, hope,
virtue and self-respect, is a *true gentleman.*

Wit.

Sense is our helmet — wit is but a plume;
The plume exposes — 'tis our helmet saves.
— YOUNG

GENUINE wit may be compared to a kaleidoscope;
every time it is shaken, it presents new and beautiful
figures.   The latter pleases the eye, and enables
carpet and calico manufacturers to obtain new designs
for their work; the former pleases us all over, without really benefiting us anywhere.   Like lightning
in a dark night, its illuminations are momentary in
most cases.   Sheridans and Hopkinsons are very
rare.   They were as highly charged with wit, as a
cloud sometimes is with the electric fluid, emitting
flashes in such quick succession, that darkness is
scarcely visible.

Wit, like a coquette, is pleasing company for the
time being; but no man, knowing her character, courts
her with the intention of marriage, and no sensible
man is long edified with her company.

He who endeavors to oblige the company by his
good-nature never fails of being beloved: he who

strives to entertain it by his good sense never fails
of being esteemed; but he who is continually aiming
to be witty, generally miscarries of his aim; his aim
and intention is to be admired, but it is his misfortune
either to be despised or detested—to be despised
for want of judgment, or detested for want of humility. For we seldom admire the wit when we dislike
the man. There are a great many to whom the world
would be so charitable as to allow them to have a
tolerable share of common sense, if they did not set
up for something more than common, something very
uncommon, bright, and witty. If we would trace the
faults of conversation up to their original source, most
of them might, we believe, be resolved into this, that
men had rather appear shining than be agreeable in
company. They are endeavoring to raise admiration
instead of gaining love and good-will, whereas the
latter is in everybody's power, the former in that of
very few.

There is as much difference between wit and wisdom, as between the talent of a buffoon and a statesman. Wit is brushwood, judgment is timber. The
one gives the greatest flame, the other yields the
most durable heat; and both meeting make the best
fire.

Wit and wisdom *may* be found in the same person,
but when the former is flashing, its glare hides the
latter. It serves to amuse and exhilarate, but rarely
produces profitable reflection, or elevates sound common sense. It is emphatically a plume, and exposes
the head it ornaments to many an arrow from the

bow of revenge. Some wits had rather lose a friend than a keen, cutting remark upon him. This has often occurred, and is exchanging treasure for trash. Wit may obtain many conquests, but no willing subjects. It is like echo, it always has the last word. It is more difficult to manage than steam, and often wounds by its explosions. It produces many bon mots, and but few wise sayings. It is like some heartless sportsmen, who shoot every bird indiscriminately, and kill more innocent ones, unfit for food, than hawks, that prey upon our poultry.

Wit loses its respect with the good when seen in company with malice; and to smile at the jest which plants a thorn in another's breast, is to become a principal in the mischief.

Finally, flashing WIT is an undefined and undefinable propensity — more to be admired than coveted; more ornamental than useful; more volatile than solid; a dangerous, sharp-edged tool, often cutting its most skillful master; rarely imparting substantial benefits to mankind; but often serious injury.

Let your wit rather serve you for a buckler to defend yourself, by a handsome reply, than the sword to wound others, though with never so facetious a reproach, remembering that a word cuts deeper than a sharp weapon, and the wound it makes is longer curing. Let those who have it, endeavor to control it, and those who have it not, can make better use of the sense they have.

Truth.

God is the author of truth, the devil the father of lies. If the telling of a truth shall endanger thy life, the Author of truth will protect thee from the danger, or reward thee for thy damage. If the telling of a lie may secure thy life, the father of lies will beguile thee of thy gains, or traduce the security. Better by losing of a life to save it, than by saving of a life to lose it. However, better thou perish than the truth.

Herodotus tell us, in the first book of his history, that from the age of five years to that of twenty, the ancient Persians instructed their children only in three things, viz: to manage a horse, to shoot dexterously with the bow and *to speak the truth*, which shows of how much importance they thought it to fix this virtuous habit on the minds of youth betimes.

The smallest dew drop on the meadow at night has a star sleeping in its bosom, and the most insignificant passage of Scripture has in it a shining truth. Truth bears the impress of her own divinity, and, though reason may not be able to take cognizance of the fact, she may be filling the chambers of the soul with a light and glory that is not born of earth.

The study of truth is perpetually joined with the love of virtue, for there is no virtue which derives not

its original from truth, as, on the contrary, there is no
vice which has not its beginning from a lie.   Truth is
the foundation of all knowledge and the cement of all
society.

The adorer of truth is above all present things.
Firm in the midst of temptation, and frank in the
midst of treachery, he will be attacked by those who
have prejudices, simply because he is without them,
decried as a bad bargain by all who want to purchase,
because he alone is not to be bought, and abused by
all parties because he is the advocate of none; like
the dolphin, which is always painted more crooked
than a ram's horn, although every naturalist knows
that it is the straightest fish that swims.

Truth is a standard according to which all things
are to be judged.   When we appeal to it, it should
be with sincerity of purpose and honesty of feeling.
Divesting ourselves of all partiality, passion, paradox,
and prejudice—of every kind of sophistry, subterfuge, chicanery, concealment and disguise, and laying
the soul open to what is honest, right, and true, our
only desire should be to judge of things as they really
are, and candidly and truly to acknowledge and receive
them as such.   For this is truth—*the perception and
representation of things as they are.*

Truth, divine in its nature and pure before heaven,
is the foundation of all human excellence, the keystone of all sincere affection, and the seal of true
discipleship with the Good Shepherd.   It is impossible to love one in whose truthfulness we cannot
confide; or to slight one, whose words, and purposes,

and actions, are "without dissimulation." Truth, or silence, should be our alternative; and we should not disturb the "soul's sweet complacency," by addicting ourselves to the too frequent deceptions of "good breeding," or the "necessary subterfuges of society." Good breeding needs not to be sustained or appreciated through falsehood or affectation, and a social system which involves the practice of subterfuge is wrong in its basis and corroding in its tendency. Into God's holy place—our hoped-for future home, and after the ineffable beauty of which every earthly household, and circle, and human heart should be modeled—nothing can enter which "loveth or maketh a lie."

No bad man ever wished that his breast was made of glass, or that others could read his thoughts. But the misery is, that the duplicities, the temptations, and the infirmities that surround us have rendered the truth, and nothing but the truth, as hazardous and contraband a commodity as a man can possibly deal in. Woe to falsehood! it affords no relief to the breast like truth; it gives us no comfort, pains him who forges it, and like an arrow directed by a god, flies back and wounds the archer. If a man be sincerely wedded to truth, he must make up his mind to find her a portionless virgin, and he must take her for herself alone. The contract, too, must be to love, cherish, and obey her, not only until death, but beyond it; for this is a union that must survive not only death, but time, the conqueror of death. There is nothing which all mankind venerate and admire so much as

simple truth, exempt from artifice, duplicity, and
design. It exhibits at once a strength of character
and integrity of purpose in which all are willing to
confide.

Painters and sculptors have given us many ideal
representations of moral and intellectual qualities and
conceptions, and have presented us with the tangible
forms of beauty and grace, heroism and courage, and
many others. But which one of them will or can give
us a correct and faithful delineation and embodiment
of truth?—that we may place it upon our altars and
in our halls, in public and in private places, that it
may be honored and worshiped in every home and in
every heart!

We see in an instant the immense importance of
acquiring and inculcating habits of the strictest truth.
Whatever so essentially tends to the concord and
felicity of society, it must be of momentous consequence to cherish and promulgate. No idea can be
formed of the important effect such habits would produce. The most perfect confidence would not be the
least of its benefits, and the most perfect inward
tranquility. For no species of deception can be
practiced without causing vexation and trouble to the
practicer, and many a cheek has blushed, and many a
heart palpitated at the apprehended or realized
detection of mistakes and exaggeration in common
conversation. Exaggeration is but another name
for falsehood; to exaggerate is to pass the bounds
of truth; and how can those bounds be passed,
without entering upon the precincts of falsehood.

There can be but a true or a false representation. There can be no medium; what is not true must be false.

Of the public estimation in which truth is held, we have numerous examples. Every one can enter into the animating, the delightful emotion with which Petrarch must have received the gratifying tribute of public applause, when, on his appearing as witness in a cause, and approaching the tribunal to take the accustomed oaths, he was informed that such was the confidence of the court in his veracity he would not be required to take any oath, his word was sufficient.

Was not the praise bestowed on Petrarch a tacit avowal that veracity such as his was very rarely known? Nothing can be more easy than to speak truth; the unwise, the poor, the ignoble, the youthful, can all equally practice it. Nothing can be more difficult than to speak falsely; the wise, the rich, the great, the aged, have all failed in their attempts. It would be an easy road to distinction to be preeminent in an adherence to truth. We could enumerate many besides Petrarch who have acquired respect by it among their fellow-citizens, and celebrity in the page of history. Can there be offered a more obtainable, a more gratifying, a more noble object of emulation to the youthful heart?

24

Judgment.

IT is the office of judgment to compare the ideas received through the senses with one another, and thereby to gain right conceptions of things and events. Hence it by degrees forms for itself a standard of duty and propriety, accumulates rules and maxims for conduct, and materials for reflection and meditation.

The judgment not only receives, investigates, and arranges the ideas presented to it, but it also regulates and directs the other faculties, where their exertions may be most beneficial and compensating. It also restrains them from undue excursiveness, and prevents their wandering into unprofitable and vicious efforts.

The most necessary talent in a man of conversation, which is what we ordinarily intend by a gentleman, is a good judgment. He that has this in perfection is master of his companion, without letting him see it; and has the same advantage over men of any other qualifications whatsoever, as one that can see would have over a blind man of ten times his strength.

Judgment, too, is abused in its use, especially when used to judge others. Knaves try to help themselves, by pretending to help others. Great ingenuity, industry, and perservance are manifested in the modes of attack. False sympathy, flattery, a tender concern for your interest, bare-faced impudence and hypocrisy, make their attacks in front—whilst slander, falsehood, dark innuendoes, and damning praise, assail the rear. Pliny says that Julius Cæsar blamed so ingeniously, that his censures were mistaken for praise. Many, at the present day, praise only to reproach. As has been observed by an eminent writer, "They use envenomed praise, which, by a side blow, exposes, in the person they commend, such faults as they *dare* not, in any other way, lay open." Deeply is the poison of calumny infused in this way —the venom of a coward, and the cunning of a knave combined.

He that sees ever so accurately, ever so finely into the motives of other people's acting, may possibly be entirely ignorant as to his own: it is by the mental as the corporal eye, the object may be placed too near the sight to be seen truly, as well as so far off; nay, too near to be seen at all.

> A RIGHT judgment
> Draws profit from all things we see.
> —SHAKSPEARE.

The great misfortune, arising from a disposition to judge others, and meddle with their affairs, consists in its being void of genuine philanthropy. Rare instances may occur when a person intrudes himself upon another for good—but such intrusions are, "like angels' visits, few and far between." It is of the contrary, and by far more numerous class, that we speak—men and women, who look at others through a smoked glass—that they may avoid the brightness of the good qualities, and discover more clearly the bad — who first perform the office of the green fly, that other flies may prey upon the putridity they produce — scavengers of reputation, who gather the faults, blemishes, and infirmities of their neighbors into a Pandora box — and there pamper them, like a turtle for a holiday dinner — until they are inflated to an enormous size; they are then thrown into the market, and astonish every beholder.

Devils blush, and angels weep over such a disposition as this. It is a canker worm in the body politic — the destroyer of reputation, the bane of peace in society; the murderer of innocence; a foul blot upon human nature; a curse in community, and a disgrace to our species.

Its baleful influence is felt, its demoniac effects are experienced, in all the walks of life. In the political arena — within the pale of the church, and in the domestic circle — its miasma is infused. The able statesman, the profound jurist, the eloquent advocate, the pulpit orator, the investigating philosopher, the skillful physician, the judicious merchant, the industrious mechanic, the honest farmer, the day laborer, the humblest peasant, the child in the nursery — have all experienced the scorpion lashes of this imp of Satan. Nay, more — female character, basking in the sunshine of innocence, has often been withered, blighted, ruined, by its chilling breath.

Let each reader examine and see if this propensity, so deeply rooted in human nature, is exercising an influence over his or her mind. If so, banish it from your bosom, as you would a deadly viper. Let its enormity be held up to children, by parents and teachers, that they may learn to dread, despise, and avoid it. Teach them charity, forbearance, forgiveness, and all the virtues that adorn our race.

Dear reader, does this propensity exist in your heart? If so, banish it, for it will do you much harm, and in time ruin your soul.

> Becoming Graces
> Are Justice, Verity, Temperance, Stableness,
> Bounty, Perseverance, Mercy, Lowliness,
> Devotion, Patience, Courage, Fortitude.

Patience.

No MAN, in any condition of life, can pass his days with tolerable comfort without patience. It is of universal use. Without it, prosperity will be continually disturbed, and adversity will be clouded with double darkness. He who is without patience will be uneasy and troublesome to all with whom he is connected, and will be more troublesome to himself than to any other. The loud complaint, the querulous temper and fretful spirit, disgrace every character: we weaken thereby the sympathy of others, and estrange them from offices of kindness and comfort. But to maintain a steady and unbroken mind, amidst all the shocks of adversity, forms the highest honor of man. Afflictions supported by patience and surmounted by fortitude, give the last finishing stroke to the heroic and the virtuous character. Thus the vale of tears becomes the theatre of human glory; that dark cloud presents the scene of all the beauties in the bow of virtue. Moral grandeur, like the sun, is brighter in the day of the storm, and never is so truly sublime as when struggling through the darkness of an eclipse.

Patience is the guardian of faith, the preserver of peace, the cherisher of love, the teacher of humility. Patience governs the flesh, strengthens the spirit, sweetens the temper, stifles anger, extinguishes envy, subdues pride; she bridles the tongue, restrains the hand, tramples upon temptations, endures persecutions, consummates martyrdom.

Patience produces unity in the church, loyalty in the state, harmony in families and societies; she comforts the poor and moderates the rich; she makes us humble in prosperity, cheerful in adversity, unmoved by calumny and reproach; she teaches us to forgive those who have injured us, and to be the first in asking the forgiveness of those whom we have injured; she delights the faithful and invites the unbelieving; she adorns the woman and approves the man; she is beautiful in either sex and every age.

Behold her appearance and her attire! Her countenance is calm and serene as the face of heaven unspotted by the shadow of a cloud, and no wrinkle of grief or anger is seen in her forehead. Her eyes are as the eyes of doves for meekness, and on her eyebrows sit cheerfulness and joy. Her mouth is

lovely in silence; her complexion and color that of
innocence and security, while, like the virgin, the
daughter of Zion, she shakes her head at the adver-
sary, despising and laughing him to scorn. She is
clothed in the robes of the martyrs, and in her hand
she holds a sceptre in the form of a cross. She rides
not in the whirlwind and stormy tempest of passion,
but her throne is the humble and contrite heart, and
her kingdom is the kingdom of peace.

Patience has been defined as the "courage of virtue," the principle that enables us to lessen pain of
mind or body; an emotion that does not so much add
to the number of our joys, as it tends to diminish
the number of our sufferings. If life is made to
abound with pains and troubles, by the errors and the
crimes of man, it is no small advantage to have a
faculty that enables us to soften these pains and to
ameliorate these troubles. How powerful, and how
extensive the influence of patience in performing this
acceptable service, it is impossible to judge but from
experience; those who have known most bodily pain
can best testify its power. Impatience, in fact, by
inducing restlessness and irritation, not only doubles
every pang, and prolongs every suffering, but actually
often creates the trials to be endured. In pains of
the body this is the case, but more potently is it so in
all mental affliction. The hurry of spirits, the in-
effectual efforts for premature relief, the agitation of
undue expectation, all combine to create a real suffering, in addition to what is inflicted by the cause of
our impatience. How numberless are the petty dis-

asters effected, the trivial vexations protracted by this
harassing emotion ; the loss of money, time, friends,
reputation, by mistaken earnestness in pursuing violent schemes, in not pausing to reflect before decision,
in urging disagreeable or unjust claims, and in rushing into ill-concerted plans !

The most beneficent operations of nature are the
result of patience   The waters slowly deposit their
rich alluvium ; the fruits are months in their growth
and perfecting.

To be wise we must diligently apply ourselves,
and confront the same continuous application which
our forefathers did ; for labor is still, and ever will be
the inevitable price set upon everything which is
valuable.   We must be satisfied to work energetically
with a purpose, and wait the results with patience.
Buffon has even said of patience, that it is genius —
the power of great men, in his opinion, consisting
mainly in their power of continuous working and
waiting   All progress, of the best kind, is slow :
but to him who works faithfully and in a right spirit,
be sure that the reward will be vouchsafed in its own
good time.   "Courage and industry," says Granville
Sharpe, "must have sunk in despair, and the world
must have remained unimproved and unornamented,
if men had merely compared the effect of a single
stroke of the chisel with the pyramid to be raised, or
of a single impression of the spade with mountains
to be leveled."   We must continuously apply ourselves to right pursuits, and we cannot fail to advance
steadily, though it may be unconsciously

Hugh Miller modestly says, in his autobiography: "The only merit to which I lay claim is that of patient research — a merit in which whoever wills may rival or surpass me; and this humble faculty of patience, when rightly developed, may lead to more extraordinary developments of idea than even genius itself."

Patience is a good nag, says the proverb. Wisely and slow; they stumble that run fast. Always have a good stock of patience laid by, and be sure you put it where you can easily find it. Cherish patience as your favorite virtue. Always keep it about you. You will find use for it oftener than for all the rest. He who is impatient to become his own master is most likely to become merely his own slave. You can do anything if you will only have patience; water may be carried in a sieve, if you can only wait till it freezes. Those who at the commencement of their career meet with less applause than they deserve, not unfrequently gain more than they deserve at the end of it; though having grounds at first to fear that they were born to be starved, they often live long enough to die of a surfeit.

He hath made a good progress in business that hath thought well of it beforehand. Some do first and think afterwards. Precipitation ruins the best laid designs; whereas patience ripens the most difficult, and renders the execution of them easy. That is done soon enough which is done well. Soon ripe, soon rotten. He that would enjoy the fruit, must not gather the flower. He calls to patience, who is

patience itself, and he that gives the precept enforces
it by his own example.   Patience affords us a shield
to defend ourselves, and innocence denies us a sword
to defend others.   Knowledge is power, but it is one
of the slowest because one of the most durable of
agencies.   Continued exertion, and not hasty efforts,
leads to success.   What cannot be cured must be
endured.   How poor are they who have not patience !

⊷⊹⊱•ℨ⊷∦⊷⊱•ℨ⊱⊷

Contentment.

" Poor and content is rich, and rich enough ;
But riches endless is as poor as winter
To him that always fears he shall be poor "

EVERY man either is rich, or may be so; though
not all in one and the same wealth.   Some have
abundance, and rejoice in it; some a competency, and
are content; some having nothing, have a mind desir-
ing nothing.   He that hath most, wants something;
he that hath least, is in something supplied; wherein
the mind which maketh rich, may well possess him
with the thought of store.   Who whistles out more
content than the low-fortuned plowman, or sings more
merrily than the abject cobbler who sits under the
stall?   Content dwells with those who are out of the
eye of the world, whom she hath never trained with
her gauds, her toils, her lures.   Wealth is like learning, wherein our greater knowledge is only a larger
sight of our wants   Desires fulfilled, teach us to

desire more; so we that at first were pleased, by removing from that, are now grown insatiable.

We knew a man who had health and riches, and several houses, all beautiful and ready furnished, and would often trouble himself and family to be removing from one house to another; and being asked by a friend why he removed so often from one house to another, replied: "It was to find content in some of them." But his friend, knowing his temper, told him, "If he would find content in any of his houses, he must leave himself behind him; for content will never dwell but in a meek and quiet soul." The inscription upon the tombstone of the man who had endeavored to mend a tolerable constitution by taking physic, "*I was well; I wished to be better; here I am*," may generally be applied with great justice to the distress of disappointed avarice and ambition.

We sometimes go musing along the street to see how few people there are whose faces look as though any joy had come down and sung in their souls. We can see lines of thought, and of care, and of fear— money lines, shrewd, grasping lines—but how few happy lines! The rarest feeling that ever lights the human face is the contentment of a loving soul. Sit for an hour on the steps of the Exchange in Wall street, and you will behold a drama which is better than a thousand theatres, for all the actors are real. There are a hundred successful men where there is one contented man. We can find a score of handsome faces where we can find one happy face. An eccentric wealthy gentleman stuck up a board in a

field upon his estate, upon which was painted the
following: "I will give this field to any man contented." He soon had an applicant. "Well, sir;
are you a contented man?" "Yes, sir; very."
"Then what do you want of my field?" The applicant did not stop to reply.

It is one property which, they say, is required of
those who seek the philosopher's stone, that they
must not do it with any covetous desire to be rich,
for otherwise they shall never find it. But most true
it is, that whosoever would have this jewel of contentment (which turns all into gold, yea, want into wealth),
must come with minds divested of all ambitious and
covetous thoughts, else are they never likely to obtain
it. The foundation of content must spring up in a
man's own mind; and he who has so little knowledge
of human nature as to seek happiness by changing
anything but his own disposition, will waste his life
in fruitless efforts, and multiply the griefs which he
purposes to remove. No man can tell whether he be
rich or poor by turning to his ledger. It is the heart
that makes a man rich. He is rich or poor according
to what he *is*, not according to what he *has*.

It conduces much to our content if we pass by those
things which happen to trouble, and consider what is
pleasing and prosperous, that by the representations
of the better the worse may be blotted out. If I be
overthrown in my suit at law, yet my house is left me
still, and my land, or I have a virtuous wife, or hopeful children, or kind friends, or hopes. If I have lost
one child, it may be that I have two or three still left

me. Enjoy the present, whatever it may be, and be
not solicitous for the future; for if you take your foot
from the present standing, and thrust it forward to
to-morrow's event, you are in a restless condition; it
is like refusing to quench your present thirst by fear-
ing you will want to drink the next day. If to-morrow you should want, your sorrow would come time
enough, though you do not hasten it; let your trouble
tarry till its own day comes. Enjoy the blessings of
this day, if God sends them, and the evils of it bear
patiently and sweetly, for this day is ours. We are
dead to yesterday, and not yet born to to-morrow.
A contented mind is the greatest blessing a man can
enjoy in this world; and if in the present life his happiness arises from the subduing of his desires, it will
arise in the next from the gratification of them.

Contentment is felicity. Few are the real wants of
man. Like a majority of his troubles, they are more
imaginary than real. Some well persons want to be
better, take medicine, and become sick in good earnest; perhaps die under some patented nostrum.
Some persons have wealth — they want more — enter
into some new business they do not understand, or
some wild speculation, and become poor indeed.
Many who are surrounded by all the substantial comforts of life, become discontented because some
wealthier neighbor sports a carriage, and his lady a
Brussels carpet and mahogany chairs, entertains
parties, and makes more show in the world than they,
Like the monkey, they attempt to imitate all they see
that is deemed fashionable; make a dash at greater

contentment; dash out their comfortable store of wealth; and sometimes, determined on quiet at least, close the farce with a tragedy, and dash their brains out with a blue pill. Discontented persons live in open rebellion against their great Benefactor, and virtually claim wisdom, more than infinite. They covet, they wish, and wishes are as prolific as rabbits. One imaginary want, like a stool pigeon, brings flocks of others, and the mind becomes so over-whelmed, that it loses sight of all the real comforts in possession.

Contentment consists not in adding more fuel, but in taking away some fire; not in multiplying wealth, but in subtracting men's desires. Worldly riches, like nuts, tear men's clothing in getting them, spoil men's teeth in cracking them, but fill no belly in eating them. When Alexander saw Diogenes sitting in the warm sun, and asked what he should do for him, he desired no more than that Alexander would stand out of his sunshine, and not take from him what he could not give. A quiet and contented mind is the supreme good; it is the utmost felicity a man is capable of in this world: and the maintaining of such an uninterrupted tranquility of spirit is the very crown and glory of wisdom.

Nature teaches us to live, but wisdom teaches us to live contented. Contentment is opposed to fortune and opinion — it is the wealth of nature, for it gives everything we either want or need. The discontents of the poor are much easier allayed than those of the rich. Solon being asked by Crœsus who in the world was happier than himself, answered, Tellus; who, though he was poor, was a good man, and content with what he had, and died in a good old age. No line holds the anchor of contentment so fast as a good conscience. This cable is so strong and compact that when force is offered to it, the straining rather strengthens, by uniting the parts more closely.

Those who are contented with a little deserve much; and those who deserve much are far the more likely persons to be contented with a little. Contentment is oftener made of cheap materials than of dear ones. What a glorious world this would be, if all its inhabitants could say with Shakspeare's shepherd: "Sir, I am a true laborer, I earn that I wear; owe no man hate; envy no man's happiness; glad of other men's good, contented with my farm." Half the discontent in the world arises from men regarding themselves as centres, instead of the infinitesimal segments, of circles. Be contented with enough; you may butter your bread until you are unable to eat it. Enough is as good as a feast. When you feel dissatisfied with your circumstances, look at those beneath you. There are minds, said John Quincy Adams, which can be pleased by honors and preferments, and I can see nothing in them save envy and enmity. It is only necessary to possess them to know how little they contribute to happiness. I had rather be shut up in a very modest cottage, with my books, my family, and a few old friends, dining upon simple bacon and hominy and letting the world roll on as it likes, than to occupy the most high places which human power can give.

Cheerfulness.

GOD bless the cheerful person — man, woman or child, old or young, illiterate or educated, handsome or homely. Over and above every other social trait stands cheerfulness. What the sun is to nature, what the stars are to night, what God is to the stricken heart which knows how to lean upon Him, are cheerful persons in the house and by the wayside. Man recognizes the magic of a cheerful influence in woman more quickly and more willingly than the potency of dazzling genius, of commanding worth, or even of enslaving beauty.

If we are cheerful and contented, all nature smiles with us; the air seems more balmy, the sky more clear, the ground has a brighter green, the trees have a richer foliage, the flowers a more fragrant smell, the birds sing more sweetly, and the sun, moon and stars all appear more beautiful.

Cheerfulness! How sweet in infancy, how lovely in youth, how saintly in age! There are a few noble natures whose very presence carries sunshine with them wherever they go, a sunshine which means pity for the poor, sympathy for the suffering, help for the unfortunate, and benignity toward all. How such a face enlivens every other face it meets, and carries into every company vivacity and joy and gladness! But the scowl and frown, begotten in a selfish heart, and manifesting itself in daily, almost hourly fretfulness, complaining, fault-finding, angry criticisms, spiteful comments on the motives and actions of others, how they thin the cheek, shrivel the face, sour and sadden the countenance! No joy in the heart, no nobility in the soul, no generosity in the nature; the whole character as cold as an iceberg, as hard as Alpine rock, as arid as the wastes of Sahara! Reader, which of these countenances are you cultivating? If you find yourself losing all your confidence in human nature, you are nearing an old age of vinegar, of wormwood and of gall; and not a mourner will follow your solitary bier, not one tear-drop shall ever fall on your forgotten grave.

Look at the bright side. Keep the sunshine of a living faith in the heart. Do not let the shadow of discouragement and despondency fall on your path. However weary you may be, the promises of God will, like the stars at night, never cease to shine, to cheer and strengthen. Learn to wait as well as labor. The best harvests are the longest in ripening. It is not pleasant to work in the earth plucking the ugly tares and weeds, but it is as necessary as sowing the seed. The harder the task, the more need of singing. A hopeful spirit will discern the silver lining of the darkest cloud, for back of all planning and doing, with its attendant discouragements and hindrances, shines the light of Divine promise and help. Ye are God's husbandmen. It is for you to be faithful. He gives the increase.

Be cheerful, for it is the only happy life. The times may be hard, but it will make them no easier to wear

a gloomy and sad countenance.   It is the sunshine
and not the cloud that makes the flower.   There is
always that before or around us which should fill the
heart with warmth.   The sky is blue ten times where
it is black once.   You have troubles, it may be.   So
have others.   None are free from them.   Perhaps it
is as well that none should be.   They give sinew and
tone to life—fortitude and courage to man.   That
would be a dull sea, and the sailor would never get
skill, where there was nothing to disturb the surface
of the ocean.   It is the duty of every one to extract
all the happiness and enjoyment he can without and
within him, and, above all, he should look on the
bright side of things.   What though things do look
a little dark?   The lane will turn, and the night will
end in broad day.   In the long run, the great balance
rights itself.   What is ill becomes well; what is wrong
becomes right.   Men are not made to hang down
either heads or lips; and those who do, only show
that they are departing from the paths of true common sense and right.   There is more virtue in one
sunbeam than a whole hemisphere of cloud and
gloom.   Therefore, we repeat, look on the bright
side of things.   Cultivate what is warm and genial—
not the cold and repulsive, the dark and morose.
Don't neglect your duty; live down prejudice.

We always know the cheerful man by his hearty
"good morning."   As well might fog, and cloud, and
vapor hope to cling to the sun-illumined landscape,
as the blues and moroseness to remain in any countenance when the cheerful one comes with a hearty

"Good morning!" Dear reader, don't forget to say it. Say it to your parents, your brothers and sisters, your schoolmates, your teachers—say it cheerfully and with a smile; it will do you good, and do your friends good. There's a kind of inspiration in every "Good morning!" heartily and smilingly spoken, that helps to make hope fresher and work lighter. It seems really to make the morning good, and a prophecy of a good day to come after it. And if this be true of the "Good morning!" it is also of all kind, cheerful greetings; they cheer the discouraged, rest the tired one, and somehow make the wheels of time run more smoothly. Be liberal then, and let no morning pass, however dark and gloomy it may be, that you do not help at least to brighten it by your smiles and cheerful words.

The cheerful are the busy; when trouble knocks at your door or rings the bell, he will generally retire if you send him word "Engaged." And a busy life cannot well be otherwise than cheerful. Frogs do not croak in running water. And active minds are seldom troubled with gloomy forebodings. They come up only from the stagnant depths of a spirit unstirred by generous impulses or the blessed necessities of honest toil.

What shall we say by way of commending that sweet cheerfulness by which a good and sensible woman diffuses the oil of gladness in the proper sphere of home. The best specimens of heroism in the world are never gazetted. They play their *role* in common life, and their reward is not in the admiration of spectators, but in the deep joy of their own conscious thoughts. It is easy for a housewife to make arrangements for an occasional feast; but let me tell you what is greater and better: amid the weariness and cares of life; the troubles, real and imaginary, of a family; the many thoughts and toils which are requisite to make the family home of thrift, order and comfort; the varieties of temper and cross-lines of taste and inclination which are to be found in a large household — to maintain a heart full of good nature and a face always bright with cheerfulness, this is a perpetual festivity. We do not mean a mere superficial simper, which has no more character in it than the flow of a brook, but that exhaustless patience, and self-control, and kindness, and tact which spring from good sense and brave purposes. Neither is it the mere reflection of prosperity, for cheerfulness, then, is no virtue. Its best exhibition is in the dark back-ground of real adversity. Affairs assume a gloomy aspect, poverty is hovering about the door, sickness has already entered, days of hardship and nights of watching go slowly by, and now you see the triumph of which we speak. When the strong man has bowed himself, and his brow is knit and creased, you will see how the whole life of the house-hold seems to hang on the frailer form, which, with solicitudes of her own, passing, it may be, under "the sacred primal sorrow of her sex," has an eye and an ear for every one but herself, suggestive of expedients, hopeful in extremities, helpful in kind words and affectionate smiles, morning, noon and night, the medicine, the light, the heart of a whole household. God bless that bright, sunny face! says many a reader, as he recalls that one of mother, wife, sister, daughter, which has been to him all that our words have described.

The industrious bee stops not to complain that there are so many poisonous flowers and thorny branches in his road, but buzzes on, selecting the honey where he can find it, and passing quietly by the places where it is not. There is enough in this world to complain about and find fault with, if men have the disposition. We often travel on a hard and uneven road, but with a cheerful spirit and a heart to praise God for his mercies, we may walk therein with great comfort and come to the end of our journey in peace.

Let us try to be like the sunshiny member of the family, who has the inestimable art to make all duty seem pleasant, all self-denial and exertion easy and desirable, even disappointment not so blank and crushing; who is like a bracing, crisp, frosty atmosphere throughout the home, without a suspicion of the element that chills and pinches. You have known people within whose influence you felt cheerful, amiable, and hopeful, equal to anything! Oh! for that blessed power, and for God's grace to exercise it rightly! I do not know a more enviable gift than the energy to sway others to good; to diffuse around us an atmosphere of cheerfulness, piety, truthfulness, generosity, magnanimity. It is not a matter of great talent; not entirely a matter of great energy; but rather of earnestness and honesty, and of that quiet,

constant energy which is like soft rain gently penetrating the soil.   It is rather a grace than a gift ; and
we all know where all grace is to be had freely for
the asking.

Happiness.

WRITERS of every age have endeavored to show
that pleasure is in us and not in the object offered for
our amusement.   If the soul be happily disposed,
everything becomes capable of affording entertainment, and distress will almost want a name.

The fountain of content must spring up in the mind,
and he who seeks happiness by changing anything
but his own disposition, will waste his life in fruitless
efforts and multiply the griefs which he purposes to
remove.

Man is, in all respects, constituted to be happy.
Hence it is that he sees goodness around him in proportion to the goodness that is within him ; and it is
also for this reason that when he calls the evil that is
within him outside of him it also appears so.   If man,
therefore, chooses that which does not seem to him
good, he can, in a measure, enjoy it.   One of the
most evident differences between the enjoyment of
what is good and true and that which is false and evil,
is that the first leaves something to be re-enjoyed in
memory and after life, while the latter leaves regret,
disappointment and suffering.

A great part of the infelicity of men arises not so much from their situations or circumstances as from their pride, vanity and ambitious expectations. In order to be happy, these dispositions must be subdued; we must always keep before our eyes such views of the world as shall prevent our expecting more from it than it is designed to, afford. We destroy our joys by devouring them beforehand with too eager expectation. We ruin the happiness of life when we attempt to raise it too high. Menedemus was told one day that it was a great felicity to have whatever we desire. "*Yes,*" said he, "*but it is a much greater felicity to desire nothing but what we have.*"

The idea has been transmitted from generation to generation that happiness is one large and beautiful precious stone—a single gem, so rare that all search after it is all vain effort, fruitless and hopeless. It is not so. Happiness is a mosaic, composed of many smaller stones. Each taken apart and viewed singly may be of little value, but when all are grouped together and judiciously combined and set, they form a pleasing and graceful whole, a costly jewel.

Trample not under foot then the little pleasures which a gracious Providence scatters in the daily path while you are in eager search after some great and exciting joy.

If you go to creation to make you happy, the earth will tell you that happiness grows not in the furrows of the fields; the sea that it is not in the treasures of the deep; cattle will say, "It is not on our backs;" crowns will say, "It is too precious a gem to be found in us."

We can adorn the head, but we cannot satisfy the heart. Happiness is in us, not in things. If happiness consisted in things only, there would be no end to the numberless kinds of it. It was in this point of view that the erudite Roman writer, Varro, enumerated seven hundred sorts of happiness. So, also, the learned Turkish doctor, Ebn Abbas, maintained that the number of grievous sins is about seven hundred, thus balancing the accounts between good and ill.

We talk of wealth, fame and power as undeniable sources of enjoyment, and limited fortune, obscurity and insignificance as incompatible with felicity. It is thus that there is a remarkable distinction between acquisitions and conditions, theoretically considered, and practically proved. However brilliant they may be in speculation, wealth, fame and power are found in possession impotent to confer felicity. However decried in prospect, limited fortunes, obscurity, insignificance, are by experience proved most friendly to human happiness. Le Droz, who wrote a treatise upon happiness, describes the conditions necessary for it as consisting of the greatest fortitude to resist and endure the ills and pains of life, united with the keenest sensibility to enjoy its pleasures and delights.

"Health, peace and competence," is a popular definition of happiness. Yet thousands, and tens of thousands, possess these great blessings and are not happy, nay, will not allow that they have the means to be happy. Madame de Stael, in her "Delphine," defines happiness to consist in the absence of misery. How many human beings are without one single real evil, and yet complain of their fate.

There is little real happiness on earth because we seek it not aright — we seek it where it is not, in outward circumstance and external good, and neglect to seek it, where alone it dwells, in the close chambers of the bosom. We would have a happiness in time, independent of eternity; we would have it independent of the Being whose it is to give; and so we go forth, each one as best we may, to seek out the rich possession for ourselves. But disappointment attends every step in the pursuit of happiness, until we seek it where alone it can be found. The original curse is still resting upon us. The cherubim, with their flaming swords, still guard the gates of Paradise, and no man enters therein.

> "But foolish mortals still pursue
> False happiness in place of true;
> A happiness we toil to find,
> Which still pursues us like the wind."

Gratitude.

ALTHOUGH the word gratitude, like the word trinity, is not to be found in the Bible, yet as the sacred Scriptures contain many sentiments on each of these subjects, and these words are the most comprehensive to convey the ideas, they are well adapted. To deliver our thoughts in few words on gratitude, we apprehend it includes five things; first, a deep and lively sense of benefits received; secondly, an ardent love to and complacency in the benefactor; thirdly, an immediate beginning to make all possible returns to the donor, either in repaying or else expressing our thankfulness; fourthly, in a fixed purpose of heart to make better returns, if ever in our power; and fifthly, a determined resolution to retain gratitude for the benefit or favors to the end of life.

Gratitude is justly said to be the mother of most virtues, because that from this one fountain so many rivulets arise; as that of reverence unto parents and masters, friendship, love to our country, and obedience to God. The ungrateful are everywhere hated, being under a suspicion of every vice; but, on the contrary, grateful persons are in the estimation of all men, having by their gratitude put in a kind of security that they are not without a measure of every other virtue.

Gratitude is a painful pleasure, felt and expressed by none but noble souls. Such are pained, because misfortune places them under the stern necessity of receiving favors from the benevolent, who are, as the world would say, under no obligations to bestow them—free-will offerings made by generous hearts, to smooth the rough path, and wipe away the tears of a fellow being. They derive a pleasure from the enjoyment of the benefits bestowed, which is rendered more exquisite by the reflection that there are those in the world who can feel and appreciate the woes of

others, and lend a willing hand to help them out of
the ditch; those who are not wrapped up in the
cocoon of selfish avarice, who live only for themselves, and die for the devil. This pleasure is farther
refined by a knowledge of the happiness enjoyed by
the person whose benevolence dictated the relief in
the contemplation of a duty performed, imposed by
angelic philanthropy, guided by motives pure as
heaven. The worthy recipient feels deeply the obligations under which he is placed; no time can oblit-
erate them from his memory, no statute of limitation
bars the payment; the moment means and opportunity are within his power, the debt is joyfully liqui-
dated, and this very act gives a fresh vigor to his
long-cherished gratitude.

A very poor and aged man, busied in planting and
grafting an apple tree, was rudely interrupted by this
interrogation: "Why do you plant trees, who cannot
hope to eat the fruit of them?" He raised himself
up, and leaning upon his spade, replied: "Some one
planted trees for me before I was born, and I have
eaten the fruit; I now plant for others, that the
memorial of my gratitude may exist when I am dead
and gone." It is a species of agreeable servitude to
be under an obligation to those we esteem. Ingratitude is a crime so shameful that the man has not yet
been found who would acknowledge himself guilty
of it.

Nothing tenders the heart, and opens the gushing
fountain of love, more than the exercise of gratitude.
Like the showers of spring, that cause flowers to rise

from seeds that have long lain dormant, tears of gratitude awaken pleasurable sensations, unknown to those who have never been forced from the sunshine of prosperity into the cold shade of adversity, where no warmth is felt but that of benevolence; no light enjoyed but that of charity; unless it shall be the warmth and light communicated from Heaven to the sincerely pious, who alone are prepared to meet, with calm submission, the keen and chilling winds of misfortune, and who, above all others, exercise the virtue of gratitude, in the full perfection of its native beauty.

Hope.

THE poet Hesiod tells us that the miseries of all mankind were included in a great box, and that Pandora took off the lid of it, by which means all of them came abroad, and only hope remained at the bottom. Hope, then, is the principal antidote which keeps our heart from bursting under the pressure of evils, and is that flattering mirror that gives us a prospect of some greater good. Some call hope the manna from heaven, that comforts us in all extremities; others, the pleasant flatterer that caresses the unhappy with expectations of happiness in the bosom of futurity. When all other things fail us, hope stands by us to the last. This, as it were, gives freedom to the captive when chained to the oar, health to the sick, victory to the defeated, and wealth to the beggar.

True hope is based on energy of character. A strong mind always hopes, and has always cause to hope, because it knows the mutability of human affairs, and how slight a circumstance may change the whole course of events. Such a spirit, too, rests upon itself; it is not confined to partial views, or to one particular object. And if, at last, all should be lost, it has saved itself—its own integrity and worth. Hope awakens courage, while despondency is the last of all evils; it is the abandonment of good—the giving up of the battle of life with dead nothingness. He who can implant courage in the human soul is the best physician.

Earthly hope, like fear, is confined to this dim spot, on which we live, move, and have our being. It is excluded from heaven to hell. It is a dashing blade, with a great estate in expectancy, which, when put in its possession, produces instant death. It draws large drafts on experience, payable *in futuro*, and is seldom able to liquidate them. Hope is always buoyant, and, like Old Virginia, never tires. It answers well for breakfast, but makes a bad supper. Like a balloon, we know where it starts from, but can make no calculation when, where, and how, it will land us. Hope is a great calculator, but a bad mathematician. Its problems are seldom based on true *data*—their demonstration is oftener fictitious than otherwise. Without the baseness of some modern land speculators, it builds cities and towns on paper, that are as worthless as their mountain peaks and impassable quagmires. It suspends earth in the air, and plays with bubbles, like a child, with a tube and soap suds. As with Milo, who attempted to split an oak, and was caught in the split and killed; the wedge often flies out, and the operator is caught in a split stick. It is bold as Cæsar, and ever ready to attempt great feats, if it should be to storm the castle of despair.

When all other emotions are controlled by events, hope alone remains forever buoyant and undecayed, under the most adverse circumstances, "unchanged, unchangeable." Causes that affect with depression every other emotion, appear to give fresh elasticity to hope. No oppression can crush its buoyancy; from under every weight it rebounds; no disappointments can annihilate its power, no experience can deter us from listening to its sweet illusions: it seems a counterpoise for misfortune, an equivalent for every endurance. Who is there without hope? The fettered prisoner in his dark cell, the diseased sufferer on his bed of anguish, the friendless wanderer on the unsheltered waste; each cherishes some latent spark of this pure and ever-living light. Like the beam of heaven, it glows with indestructible brilliance, to the heart of man what light is to his eye, cheering, blessing, invigorating.

A true hope we can touch somehow through all the lights and shadows of life. It is a prophecy fulfilled in part; God's earnest-money paid into our hand that He will be ready with the whole when we are ready for it; the sunlight on the hill top when the valley is dark as death; the spirit touching us all through our pilgrimage, and then when we know that the end is near, taking us on its wings and soaring away into the blessed life where we may expect either that the fruition will be entirely equal to the hope, or that the old glamour will come over us again and beckon us on forever as the choicest blessing Heaven has to give. We know of no condition in any life which is trying to be real and true in which this power will not do for us just what we have seen it doing for the man who has to wait on the seasons for his daily bread.

We can cherish a sure hope about our future and the future of those who belong to us, a sunny, eager onlooking toward the fulfillment of all of the promises God has written on our nature. We may be all wrong in our thoughts of the special form in which our blessings will come; we never can be wrong about the blessing. It may be like the mirage shifting from horizon to horizon as we plod wearily along, but the soul is bound to find at last the resting-place and the spring. There is many a father in the world to-day trying hard to get his head above water who will sink, but his boys will swim and reach the firm land, and think of him with infinite tenderness, while he, perhaps, is watching them from above, and their success may be one of the elements of his joy in Heaven. The setting of a great hope is like the setting of the sun. The brightness of our life is gone, shadows of the evening fall behind us, and the world seems but a dim reflection itself—a broader shadow. We look forward into the coming lonely night; the soul withdraws itself. Then stars arise, and the night is holy.

Its morality is equally inspiring, rich, and beneficent.
It encourages all things, good, great, noble. It
whispers liberty to the slave, freedom to the captive,
health to the sick, home to the wandering, friends to
the forsaken, peace to the troubled, supplies to the
needy, bread to the hungry, strength to the weak,
rest to the weary, life to the dying. It has sunshine
in its eye, encouragement on its tongue, and inspiration in its hand. Rich and glorious is hope, and
faithfully should it be cultivated. Let its inspiring
influence be in the heart of every youth. It will
give strength and courage. Let its cheerful words
fall ever from his tongue, and his bright smile play
ever on its countenance. Entertain well this nymph
of goodness. Cultivate well this ever-shining flower
of the spirit. It is the evergreen of life, that grows
at the eastern gate of the soul's garden.

Hopes and fears checker human life. He who
wants hope, is the poorest man living. Our hopes
and fears are the mainsprings of all our religious
endeavors. There is no one whose condition is so
low but that he may have hopes; nor is any one so
high as to be out of the reach of fears. Hopes and
disappointments are the lot and entertainment of
human life: the one serves to keep us from presumption, the other from despair. Hope is the last thing
that dieth in man, and though it be exceeding vari-
able, yet it is of this good use to us, that while we
are traveling through this life, it conducts us in an
easier and more pleasant way to our journey's end.
When faith, temperance, the graces, and other celes-

tial powers, left the earth, says one of the ancients, hope was the only goddess that staid behind. Hope's enchantments never die. Eternal hope! Hope gilds the future. Hope cheers and rouses the soul. Hope and strive is the way to thrive. The man who carries a lantern in a dark night can have friends all around him, walking safely by the help of its rays, and not be defrauded. So he who has the God-given light of hope in his breast can help on many others in this world's darkness, not to his own loss, but to their precious gain.

Hope is an anchor to the soul, both sure and steadfast, that will steady our frail bark while sailing over the ocean of life, and that will enable us to outride the storms of time—a hope that reaches from earth to heaven. This hope is based on faith in the immaculate Redeemer, and keeps our earthly hopes from running riot into forbidden paths. The cable of this hope cannot be sundered until death cuts the gordian knot and lets the prisoner go free. To live without it, is blind infatuation—to die without it, eternal ruin.

Charity.

CHARITY is one of those amiable qualities of the human breast that imparts pleasure to its possessor, and those who receive it. It is of a modest and retiring nature. Charity, like the dew from heaven, falls gently on the drooping flower in the stillness of night. Its refreshing and reviving effects are felt, seen, and admired. It flows from a good heart, and looks beyond the skies for approval and reward. It never opens, but seeks to heal the wounds inflicted by misfortune—it never harrows up, but strives to calm the troubled mind. Like their Lord and Master, the truly benevolent man and woman go about doing good for the sake of goodness. No parade, no trumpet to sound their charities, no press to chronicle their acts. The gratitude of the donee is a rich recompense to the donor—purity of motive heightens and refines the joys of each. Angels smile on such benevolence. It is the attribute of Deity, the moving cause of every blessing we enjoy.

> Fair Charity, be thou my guest,
> And be thy constant couch my breast.
>   —COTTON.

Charity is the golden chain that reaches from heaven to earth. It is another name for disinterested, lofty, unadulterated love. It is the substratum of philanthropy, the brightest star in the Christian's diadem. It spurns the scrofula of jealousy, the canker of tormenting envy, the tortures of burning malice, the typhoid of foaming revenge. It is an impartial mirror, set in the frame of love, resting on equity and justice. It is the foundation and capstone of the climax of all the Christian graces; without it, our religion is like a body without a soul; our friendships, shadows of a shadow; our alms, the offsprings of pride, or, what is more detestable, the

offerings of hypocrisy; our humanity, a mere iceberg
on the ocean of time—we are unfit to discharge the
duties of life, and derange the design of our creation.
Were this heaven-born, soul-cheering principle the
mainspring of human action, the all-pervading motive-
power that impelled mankind in their onward course
to eternity, the polar star to guide them through this
world of sin and wo, the ills that flesh is heir to
would be softened in its melting sunbeams, a new
and blissful era would dawn auspiciously upon our
race, and Satan would become a bankrupt for want
of business. Wars and rumors of wars would cease;
envy, jealousy, and revenge would hide their dimin-
ished heads; falsehood, slander, and persecution
would be unknown; sectarian walls, in matters of
religion, would crumble in dust; the household of
faith would become what it should be, one united,
harmonious family in Christ; infidelity, vice, and
immorality would recede, and happiness, before unknown, would become the crowning glory of man.
Pure and undefiled religion would then be honored
and glorified—primitive Christianity would stand
forth, divested of the inventions of men, in all the
majesty of its native loveliness. Oh, could an angel
bear a balm of such charity into our hearts, then
would earth become a heaven and hell a fable.

When we take the history of one poor heart that
has sinned and suffered, and represent to ourself the
struggles and temptations it passed through—the
brief pulsations of joy, the tears of regret, the feebleness of purpose, the scorn of the world that has little

charity; the desolation of the soul's sanctuary, and threatening voices within; health gone; happiness gone — we would fain leave the erring soul of our fellow-man with Him from whose hands it came. It is then that the words of Prior show their truth and beauty:

> "Soft peace it brings wherever it arrives,
> It builds our quiet — 'latent hope revives,'
> Lays the rough paths of nature 'smooth and even,'
> And opens in each breast a little heaven."

Is any man fallen into disgrace? Charity holds down its head, is abashed and out of countenance, partaking of his shame. Is any man disappointed of his hopes or endeavors? Charity cries out, alas! as if it were itself defeated. Is any man afflicted with pain or sickness? Charity looks sadly, it sigheth and groans, it faints and languishes with him. Is any man pinched with hard want? Charity, if it cannot succor, will condole. Does ill news arrive? Charity hears it with an unwilling ear and a sad heart, although not particularly concerned in it. The sight of a wreck at sea, of a field spread with carcasses, of a country desolated, of houses burned and cities ruined, and of the like calamities incident to mankind, would touch the bowels of any man; but the very report of them would affect the heart of charity.

Kindness.

MORE hearts pine away in secret anguish, for the want of kindness from those who should be their comforters, than for any other calamity in life. A word of kindness is a seed which, when dropped by chance, springs up a flower. A kind word and pleasant voice are gifts easy to give; be liberal with them; they are worth more than money. "If a word or two will render a man happy," said a Frenchman, "he must be a wretch indeed, who will not give it. It is like lighting another man's candle with your own, which loses none of its brilliancy by what the other gains." If all men acted upon that principle the world would be much happier than it is. Kindness is like a calm and peaceful stream that reflects every object in its just proportion. The violent spirit, like troubled waters, renders back the images of things distorted and broken, and communicates to them that disordered motion which arises from its own agitation. Kindness makes sunshine wherever it goes; it finds its way into hidden chambers of the heart and brings forth golden treasures; harshness, on the contrary, seals them up forever. Kindness makes the mother's lullaby sweeter than the song of the lark, the care-laden brow of the father and man of business less severe in their expression. Kindness is the real law of life, the link that connects earth with heaven, the true philosopher's stone, for all it

touches it turns to virgin gold; the true gold wherewith we purchase contentment, peace and love.
Write your name by kindness, love and mercy on the
hearts of the people you come in contact with year
by year, and you will never be forgotten.

In the intercourse of social life it is by little acts of
watchful kindness recurring daily and hourly — and
opportunities of doing kindness, if sought for, are
forever starting up — it is by words, by tones, by gestures, by looks, that affection is won and preserved.

How sweet are the affections of kindness! How
balmy the influence of that regard which dwells
around the fireside, where virtue lives for its own
sake, and fidelity regulates and restrains the thirst for
admiration, often a more potent foe to virtue than the
fiercest lust; where distrust and doubt dim not the
lustre of purity, and where solicitude, except for the
preservation of an unshaken confidence, has no
place, and the gleam of suspicion or jealousy never
disturbs the harmony and tranquillity of the scene,
where paternal kindness and devoted filial affection
blossom in all the freshness of eternal spring! It
matters not if the world is cold, if we can turn to our
own dear circle for the enjoyment for which the heart
yearns. Lord Bacon beautifully says: "If a man
be gracious unto strangers it shows he is a citizen of
the world, and his heart is no island cut off from
other lands, but a continent that joins them."

There is nothing like kindness in the world. It is
the very principle of love; an emanation of the heart
which softens and gladdens, and should be inculcated

and encouraged in all our intercourse with our fellow beings. It is impossible to resist continued kindness.

We may, in a moment of petulance or passion, manifest coldness to the exhibition of good will on the part of a new acquaintance; but let him persist, let him continue to prove himself really benevolent of heart, generously and kindly disposed, and we will find our stubborn nature giving way, even unconsciously to ourselves. If this be the result of kindness among comparative strangers, how much more certain and delightful will be the exercise of the feelings at home, within the charmed circle of friends and relatives? Home enjoyments, home affections, home courtesies, cannot be too carefully or steadily cultivated. They form the sunshine of the heart. They bless and sanctify our private circle. They become a source of calm delight to the man of business after a day of toil, they teach the merchant, the trader, the working man, that there is something purer, more precious even, than the gains of industry. They twine themselves around the heart, call forth its best and purest emotions and resources, enable us to be more virtuous, more upright, more Christian, in all our relations of life. We see in the little beings around us the elements of gentleness, of truth, and the beauty of fidelity and religion. A day of toil is robbed of many of its cares by the thought that in the evening we may return home and mingle with the family household. There, at least, our experience teaches us we may find confiding and loving bosoms, those who look up to and lean upon us, and those also to whom we may look for counsel and encouragement.

We say to our friends, one and all, cultivate the home virtues, the household beauties of existence. Endeavor to make the little circle of domestic life a cheerful, an intelligent, a kindly, and a happy one. Whatever may go wrong in the world of business and trade, however arduous may be the struggle for fortune or fame, let nothing mar the purity of reciprocal love or throw into its harmonious existence the apple of discord.

He who neglects the trifles, yet boasts that, whenever a great sacrifice is called for, he shall be ready to make it, will rarely be loved. The likelihood is he will not make it; and if he does, it will be much rather for his own sake than for his neighbors. Life is made up, not of great sacrifices or duties, but of little things, in which smiles, and kindness, and small obligations, given habitually, are what win and preserve the heart, and secure comfort.

Give no pain. Breathe not a sentiment, say not a word, give not the expression of the countenance that will offend another, or send a thrill of pain to his bosom. We are surrounded by sensitive hearts, which a word or look even, might fill to the brim with sorrow. If you are careless of the opinions of others, remember that they are differently constituted from yourself, and never, by word or sign, cast a shadow on a happy heart, or throw aside the smiles of joy that linger on a pleasant countenance.

Many lose the opportunity of saying a kind thing

by waiting to weigh the matter too long. Our best impulses are too delicate to endure much handling. If we fail to give them expression the moment they rise, they effervesce, evaporate, and are gone. If they do not turn sour, they become flat, losing all life and sparkle by keeping. Speak promptly when you feel kindly.

Deal gently with the stranger. Remember the severed cord of affection, still bleeding, and beware not to wound by a thoughtless act, or a careless word. The stranger! he, perchance, has lived in an atmosphere of love as warm as that we breathe. Alone and friendless now, he treasures the images of loved ones far away, and when gentle words and warm kisses are exchanged, we know not how his heart thrills and the hot tear drops start. Speak gently. The impatient word your friends may utter does not wound, so mailed are you in the impenetrable armor of love. You knew that it was an inadvertent word that both will forget in a moment after, or, if not, you can bear the censure of one, when so many love you; but keenly is an unkind remark felt by the lone and friendless one.

Like a clinging vine torn from its support, the stranger's heart begins to twine its tendrils around the first object which is presented to it. Is love so cheap a thing in this world, or have we already so much that we can lightly cast off the instinctive affections thus proffered? Oh, do not! To some souls an atmosphere of love is as necessary as the vital air to the physical system. A person of such a nature may clothe one in imagination with all the attributes of goodness and make his heart's sacrifices at the shrine. Let us not cruelly destroy the illusion by unkindness!

Let the name of stranger be ever sacred, whether it be that of an honored guest at our fireside, or the poor servant girl in our kitchen; the gray-haired or the young; and when we find ourselves far from friends, and the dear associations of home, and so lonely, may some kind, some angel-hearted being, by sympathizing words and acts, cause our hearts to thrill with unspoken gratitude, and thus we will find again the bread long "cast upon the waters."

Our friends we must prize and appreciate while we are with them. It is a shame not to know how much we love our friends, and how good they are, till they die. We must seize with joy all our opportunities; our duties we must perform with pleasure; our sacrifices we must make cheerfully, knowing that he who sacrifices most is noblest; we must forgive with an understanding of the glory of forgiveness, and use the blessings we have, realizing how great are small blessings when properly accepted.

Hard words are like hail-stones in summer, beating down and destroying what they would nourish if they were melted into drops.

Kindness is stored away in the heart like rose-leaves in a drawer to sweeten every object around them. Little drops of rain brighten the meadows, and little acts of kindness brighten the world. We can conceive of nothing more attractive than the heart when filled with the spirit of kindness. Certainly nothing so embellishes human nature as the practice of this virtue; a sentiment so genial and so excellent ought to be emblazoned upon every thought and act of our life. The principle underlies the whole theory of Christianity, and in no other person do we find it more happily exemplified than in our Savior, who, while on earth, *went about doing good*. And how true it is that

> "A little word in kindness spoken,
>   A motion, or a tear,
> Has often heal'd the heart that's broken,
>   And made a friend sincere!"

Friendship.

PURE, disinterested friendship, is a bright flame, emitting none of the smoke of selfishness, and seldom deigns to tabernacle among men. Its origin is divine, its operations heavenly, and its results enrapturing to the soul. It is because it is the perfection of earthly bliss that the world has ever been flooded with base counterfeits, many so thickly coated with the pure metal, that nothing but time can detect the base interior and ulterior designs of bogus friends. Deception is a propensity deeply rooted in human nature, and the hobby horse on which some ride through life. *The heart is deceitful above all things; who can know it?*

Caution has been termed the parent of safety, but has often been baffled by a Judas kiss. The most cautious have been the dupes and victims of the basest deceivers. We should be extremely careful *who* we confide in, and then we will often find ourselves mistaken. Let adversity come, then we may know more of our friends. Many will probably show that they were sunshine friends, and will escape as for their lives, like rats from a barn in flames! Ten to one, those who have enjoyed the most sunshine will be the first to forsake, censure and reproach. Friendship, based entirely on self, ends in desertion the moment the selfish ends are accomplished or frustrated.

> " Disguise so near the truth doth seem to run,
> 'Tis doubtful whom to seek or whom to shun ;
> Nor know we when to spare or when to strike,
> Our friends and foes they seem so much alike."

Friendship is a flower that blooms in all seasons; it may be seen flourishing on the snow-capped mountains of Northern Russia, as well as in more favored valleys of sunny Italy, everywhere cheering us by its exquisite and indescribable charms. No surveyed chart, no national boundary line, no rugged mountain or steep declining vale puts a limit to its growth. Wherever it is watered with the dews of kindness and affection, there you may be sure to find it. Allied in closest companionship with its twin-sister, charity, it enters the abode of sorrow and wretchedness, and causes happiness and peace. It knocks at the lonely and disconsolate heart, and speaks words of encouragement and joy. Its all-powerful influence hovers over contending armies and unites the deadly foes in the closest bonds of sympathy and kindness. Its eternal and universal fragrance dispels every thought of envy, and purifies the mind with a holy and price-less contentment which all the pomp and power of earth could not bestow. In vain do we look for this heavenly flower in the cold, calculating worlding; the poor, deluded wretch is dead to every feeling of its ennobling virtue. In vain do we look for it in the actions of the proud and aristocratic votaries of fash-ion; the love of self-display and of the false and fleet-ing pleasures of the world, has banished it forever from their hearts. In vain do we look for it in the thoughtless and practical throng, who with loud laugh and extended open hands, proclaim obedience to its laws—while at the same time the canker of malice and envy and detraction is enthroned in their hearts and active on their tongues. Friendship, true friend-ship, can only be found to bloom in the soil of a noble and self-sacrificing heart; there it has a perennial summer, a never-ending season of felicity and joy to its happy possessor, casting a thousand rays of love and hope and peace to all around.

No one can be happy without a friend, and no one can know what friends he has until he is unhappy.

It has been observed that a real friend is somewhat like a ghost or apparition; much talked of, but hardly ever seen. Though this may not be exactly true, it must, however, be confessed that a friend does not appear every day, and that he who in reality has found one, ought to value the boon, and be thankful.

Where persons are united by the bonds of genuine friendship, there is nothing, perhaps, more conducive to felicity. It supports and strengthens the mind, alleviates the pain of life, and renders the present state, at least, somewhat comfortable. "Sorrows," says Lord Bacon, "by being communicated, grow less, and joys greater." "And indeed," observes another, "sorrow, like a stream, loses itself in many channels; while joy, like a ray of the sun, reflects with a greater ardor and quickness when it rebounds upon a man from the breast of his friend."

The friendship which is founded upon good tastes and congenial habits, apart from piety, is permitted by the benignity of Providence to embellish a world, which, with all its magnificence and beauty, will shortly pass away; that which has religion for its basis will ere long be transplanted in order to adorn the paradise of God.

There is true enjoyment in that friendship which has its source in the innocence and uprightness of a true heart. Such pleasures do greatly sweeten life, easing it from many a bitter burden. A sympathizing heart finds an echo in sympathizing bosoms that bring back cheering music to the spirit of the loveliest. Be all honor, then, to true friendship, and may it gather yet more fragant blossoms from the dew-bathed meadows of social intercourse, to spread their aroma along the toil-worn road of life. What a blessing it is to have a friend to whom one can speak fearlessly upon any subject; with whom one's deepest thoughts come simply and safely. O, the comfort,

the inexpressible comfort, of feeling safe with a person—having neither to weigh the thoughts nor
measure the words, but pouring them all right out,
just as they are, chaff and grain together, certain that
a faithful hand will take and sift them; keep what is
worth keeping, and then, with the breath of kindness,
blow the rest away.

If any form an intimacy merely for what they can
gain by it, this is not true friendship in such a person.
It must be free from any such selfish view, and only
design mutual benefit as each may require. Again, it
must be unreserved. It is true indeed that friends
are not bound to reveal to each other all their family
concerns, but they should be ever ready to disclose
what may in any point of view concern each other.
Lastly, it is benevolent. Friends must study to
please and oblige each other in the most delicate,
kind, and liberal manner; and that in poverty and
trouble, as well as in riches or prosperity. The
benevolence of friends is also manifested in overlook-
ing each other's faults, and, in the most tender manner, admonishing each other when they do amiss.
Upon the whole, the purse, the heart, and the house
ought to be open to a friend, and in no case can we
shut out either of them, unless upon clear proofs of
treachery, immorality, or some other great crime.

The first law of friendship is sincerity; and he who
violates this law, will soon find himself destitute of
what he so erringly seeks to gain; for the deceitful
heart of such an one will soon betray itself, and feel
the contempt due to insincerity. The world is so full

of selfishness, that true friendship is seldom found; yet it is often sought for paltry gain by the base and designing. Behold that toiling miser, with his ill-got and worthless treasures; his soul is never moved by the hallowed influence of the sacred boon of friendship, which renews again on earth lost Eden's faded bloom, and flings hope's halcyon halo over the wastes of life. The envious man—he, too, seeks to gain the applause of others for an unholy usage, by which he may usurp a seat of pre-eminence for himself. Self-love, the spring of motion, acts upon the soul. All are fond of praise, and many are dishonest in the use of means to obtain it; hence it is often difficult to distinguish between true and false friendship.

Courtship.

ALL the blessedness, all the utility, efficacy, and happiness of the married state, depend upon its truthfulness, or the wisdom of the union. Marriage is not necessarily a blessing. It may be the bitterest curse. It may sting like an adder and bite like a serpent. Its bower is as often made of thorns as of roses. It blasts as many sunny expectations as it realizes. Every improper marriage is a living misery, an undying death, Its bonds are grated bars of frozen iron. It is a spirit prison, cold as the dungeon of ruin. An illy-mated human pair is the most woeful picture of human wretchedness that is presented

in the book of life; and yet, such pictures are plenty.
Every page we turn gives us a view of some such
living bondage. But a proper marriage, a true interior, soul-linked union is a living picture of blessedness, unrivaled in beauty. A true marriage is the
soul's Eden. It is the portal of heaven. It is the
visiting-place of angels. It is the charm indescribable of a spirit in captivation with all imaginable
beauty and loveliness. It is a constant peace-offer-
ing, that procures a continual Sabbath-day sweetness,
rich as the quietude of reposing angels. It is not
given to words to express the refinement of pleasure,
the delicacy of joy and the abounding fullness of satisfaction that those feel whom God hath joined in a
high marriage of spirit. Such a union is the highest
school of virtue, the soul's convent, where the vestal
fires of purity are kept continually burning.

Marriage, then, should be made a study. Every
youth, both male and female, should so consider it.
It is the grand social institution of humanity. Its
laws and relations are of momentous importance to
the race. Shall it be entered blindly, in total ignorance of what it is, what its conditions of happiness
are?

"Marriage is a lottery," exclaim so many men and
women you meet. And why is it so? Simply because
courtship is a grand scheme of deception. Is it not
so? Who courts *honestly?* Some, it is true; but
few, indeed. Let us see, it is conducted something
like this: A young man and woman meet at a party,
ball, school, or church. The young man sees some-

thing in the lady that attracts his attention; it may be her pretty face, her golden curls, her flashing eyes, her delicate hand or slender waist, or snowy neck, or graceful carriage, or more likely, the *plumage* in which the bird shines. He looks again, and then again, and without one particle of sense or reason for it, save that he has caught the fair one's eye, his attraction rises into enchantment. He seeks an introduction. A little parley of nonsense ensues, about fashion, parties, beaux and belles, and a few jokes pass about "invitations," "runaway matches," etc.; then an appointment for another meeting, a walk, a visit to an ice-cream saloon, a neighbor, or something of the kind, follows, and they part, both determined, in the utmost desperation, to catch the prize if possible. They dream, and sing, and make verses about each other, and meditate ways and means to appear captivating at the next meeting, till it arrives, when, lo! they meet, all wreathed in smiles and shining in beautiful things. How can it be otherwise than that their fascination shall become absolute adoration now. The afternoon and evening are spent together, each in perfect delight. The lovers talk about flowers, and stars, and poetry, and give hints, and signs, and tokens, till each understands the other's bewitchery.

They are engaged and get married.

Married life now comes and ushers in its morning glory, and they are happy as a happy pair can well be for a while. But "life is real," and character is real, and love is real. When life's *reality* comes they find things in each other's characters that perfectly startle them. Every day reveals something new and something unpleasant. The courtship character slowly fades away, and with it the courtship love. Now comes disappointment, sorrow, regret. They find that their characters are entirely dissimilar. Married life is a burden, full of cares, vexations, and disappointments. But they must make the best of it, and BEAR *it through*. Yes, marriage is a lottery. They know it. Some may get prizes, and some may not. No one knows before he draws, whether he will draw a blank or a prize. This is their conclusion. They did not court in the right way. They courted by impulse, and not by judgment; it was a process of wooing, and not of discovery; it was an effort to please, and not a search for companionship; it was done with excitement, and not with calmness and deliberation; it was done in haste, and not with cautious prudence; it was a vision of the heart, and not a solemn reality; it was conducted by feeling, and not by reason; it was so managed as to be a perpetual blandishment of pleasure, the most intoxicating and delightful, and not a trying ordeal for the enduring realities of solid and stubborn life; it was a perpetual yielding up of every thing, and not a firm maintaining of every thing that belongs to the man or woman. In almost every particular it was false, and hence must be followed by evil consequences. All similar courting is bad. Courtship, as it is generally conducted, is a game at "blind-man's-buff," only that both parties are blinded. They voluntarily blind themselves, and then blind each other; and thus they "go it blind," till their eyes are opened in marriage. It is necessary for the youth of both sexes to be perfectly *honest* in their intercourse with each other, so as to exhibit always their true character and nature. Dishonesty is, perhaps, a greater barrier even than ignorance to a proper understanding of the real character of those with whom we contemplate matrimonial alliances. Young men and women are not true to themselves. They put on false characters. They assume airs not their own. They shine in borrowed plumes. They practice every species of deception for the concealment of their real characters. They study to appear better than they are. They seek, by the adornments of dress and gems, by the blandishments of art and manner, by the allurements of smiles and honeyed words, by the fascination of pleasure and scenes of excitement, to add unreal, unpossessed charms to their persons and characters. They appear in each other's society to be the embodiment of goodness and sweetness, the personification of lofty principle and holy love, when, in fact, they are full of human weaknesses and frailties.

The object of courtship is the choice of a companion. It is not to woo; it is not to charm or gratify, or please, simply for the present pleasure; it is not for the present sweets of such an intimate and confiding intercourse. It is simply and plainly for the selection of a life companion; one who must bear, suffer, and enjoy life with us in all its frowns and smiles, joys and sorrows; one who can walk pleasantly, willingly, and confidingly, by our side, through all the intricate and changing vicissitudes incident to mortal life. Now, how shall courtship be conducted so as to make marriage a *certainty* and not a lottery? This is the question.

Now let us ask what is to be sought? You answer, a companion. What is a companion? A congenial spirit, one possessed of an interior constitution of soul similar to our own, of similar age, opinions, tastes, habits, modes of thought, and feeling. A congenial spirit is one who, under any given combination of circumstances, would be affected, and feel and act as we ourselves would. It is one who would enjoy what we would enjoy, dislike what we would dislike, approve what we would approve, and condemn what we would condemn, not for the purpose of agreeing with us, but of his or her own free will. This is a companion; one who is kindred in soul with us; who is already united to us by the ties of spiritual harmony; which union it is the object of courtship to discover. Courtship, then, is a voyage of discovery; or a court of inquiry, established by mutual consent of the parties, to see wherein and to what extent there is a harmony existing. If in all these they honestly and inmostly agree, and find a deep and thrilling pleasure in their agreement, find their union of sentiment to give a charm to their social intercourse; if now they feel that their hearts are bound as well as their sentiments in a holy unity, and that for each other they would live, and labor, and make every personal sacrifice with gladness, and that without each other they know not how to live, it is their privilege, yes, their *duty*, to form a matrimonial alliance. And it will not be a lottery. They know what they are to give and what they are to get. They will be married in the full blaze of light and love, and be married for a happy, virtuous, and useful union, to bless themselves and the world with a living type of heaven.

⟨※⟩

Flirting.

THE ostensible object of courtship is the choice of a companion. For no other object should any intercourse having the appearance of courtship be permitted or indulged in. It is a species of high-handed fraud upon an unsuspecting heart, worthy of the heaviest penalty of public opinion, or law. The affections are too tender and sacred to be trifled with. He who does it is a wretch. He should be ranked among thieves, robbers, villains, and murderers. He who steals money steals trash; but he who steals affections without a return of similar affections steals that which is dearer than life and more precious than wealth. His theft is a robbery of the heart.

Flirting is a horrid outrage upon the most holy and exalted feelings of the human soul, and the most sacred and important relation of life. It is a vulgarism and wickedness to be compared only to blasphemy. It had, and still has, its origin in the basest lust. The refined soul is always disgusted with it.

It is awfully demoralizing in its tendency, and low and base in its character. It is true, many bandy their low jokes upon this matter in thoughtlessness; but if they would take one moment's sober reflection upon it, they would see the impropriety of jesting about the most delicate, serious, and sacred feelings and relations in human existence. The whole tendency of such lightness is to cause the marriage relation to be lightly esteemed, and courtship to be made a round of low fun and frolic, in which every species of deception is endeavored to be played off. Until it is viewed in its true light, in that sober earnestness which the subject demands, how can courtship be anything else than a grand game of hypocrisy, resulting in wickedness and misery the most ruinous and deplorable?

There is much trifling courting among the young in some portions of the country that results in such calamitous consequences; carried on sometimes when the young man means nothing but present pleasure, and sometimes when the young woman has no other object in view. Such intercourse is confined mostly to young men and women before they are of age. It is a crying evil, worthy of the severest censure.

A case was recently tried in Rutland, Vermont, in which a Miss Munson recovered fourteen hundred and twenty-five dollars of a Mr. Hastings for a breach of marriage contract. The curiosity of the thing is this: The Vermont judge charged the jury that no explicit promise was necessary to bind the parties to a marriage contract, but that long continued attentions or intimacy with a female was as good evidence of intended matrimony as a special contract. The principle of the case undoubtedly is, that if Hastings did not promise, he ought to have done so —the law holds him responsible for the non-performance of his duty. A most excellent decision. We think if there were more such cases there would be less flirting.

One of the meanest things a young man can do (and it is not at all of uncommon occurrence) is to monopolize the time and attention of a young girl for a year, or more, without any definite object, and to the exclusion of other gentlemen, who, supposing him to have matrimonial intentions, absent themselves from her society. This selfish "dog-in-the-manger" way of proceeding should be discountenanced and forbidden by all parents and guardians. It prevents the reception of eligible offers of marriage, and fastens upon the young lady, when the acquaintance is finally dissolved, the unenviable and *unmerited* appellation of "flirt." Let all your dealings with women, young man, be frank, honest and noble. That many whose education and position in life would warrant our looking for better things in them, are culpably criminal on these points, is no excuse for your shortcomings. That woman is often injured, or wronged, through her holiest feelings, adds but a blacker dye to your meanness. One rule is always safe: *Treat every woman you meet as you would wish another man to treat your innocent, confiding sister.*

Bachelors.

MARRIAGE has a great refining and moralizing tendency. Nearly all the debauchery and crime is committed by unmarried men, or by those who have wives equal to none, at least to them. When a man marries early, and uses prudence in choosing a suitable companion, he is likely to lead a virtuous, happy life. But in an unmarried state, all alluring vices have a tendency to draw him away. We notice in the state penitentiary reports that nearly all the criminals are bachelors. The more married men you have, the fewer crimes there will be. Marriage renders a man more virtuous and more wise. An unmarried man is but half of a perfect being, and it requires the other half to make things right; and it cannot be expected that in this imperfect state he can keep straight in the path of rectitude any more than a boat with one oar can keep a straight course. In nine cases out of ten, where married men become drunkards, or where they commit crimes against the peace of the community, the foundation of these acts was laid while in a single state, or where the wife is, as is sometimes the case, an unsuitable match. Marriage changes the current of a man's feelings and gives him a centre for his thoughts, his affections and his acts.

If it were intended for man to be single, there would be no harm in remaining so; and, on the other hand, it would become a crime if any persons would

unite and live as wedded. But, since this is not the
Divine law, it is a sin and crime if healthful men and
women do not marry, and live as they were designed
to live.

Marriage is a school and exercise of virtue; and
though marriage have cares, yet single life has
desires, which are more troublesome and more dangerous, and often end in sin; while the cares are but
exercises of piety; and, therefore, if the single life
have more privacy of devotion, yet marriage has
more variety of it, and is an exercise of more graces.
Marriage is the proper scene of piety and patience,
of the duty of parents and the charity of relations;
here kindness is spread abroad, and love is united
and made firm as a centre. Marriage is the nursery
of heaven. The virgin sends prayers to God; but
she carries but one soul to him; but the state of her
marriage fills up the numbers of the elect, and has in
it the labor of love, and the delicacies of friendship,
the blessings of society, and the union of hearts and
hands. It has in it more safety than the single life;
it has more care, it is more merry and more sad; is
fuller of sorrow and fuller of joys; it lies under more
burdens, but is supported by all the strength of love
and charity which makes those burdens delightful.
Marriage is the mother of the world, and preserves
kingdoms, and fills cities, and churches, and heaven
itself, and is that state of good things to which God
has designed the present constitution of the world.

We advise every young man to get married. The
chances are better by fifty per cent. all through life,

in every respect. There is no tear shed for the old bachelor; there is no ready hand and kind heart to cheer him in his loneliness and bereavement; there is none in whose eyes he can see himself reflected, and from whose lips he can receive the unfailing assurances of care and love. He may be courted for his money; he may eat and drink and revel; and he may sicken and die in a hotel or a garret, with plenty of attendants about him, like so many cormorants waiting for their prey; but he will never know the comforts of the domestic fireside.

The guardians of the Holborn Union lately advertised for candidates to fill the situation of engineer at the work-house, a single man, a wife not being allowed to reside on the premises. Twenty-one candidates presented themselves, but it was found that as to testimonials, character, workmanship, and appearance, the best men were all married men. The guardians had therefore to elect a married man.

A man who avoids matrimony on account of the cares of wedded life, cuts himself off from a great blessing for fear of a trifling annoyance, He rivals the wiseacre who secured himself against corns by having his legs amputated. Bachelor brother, there cannot, by any possibility, be a home where there is no wife. To talk of a home without love, we might as well expect to find an American fireside in one of the pyramids of Egypt.

There is a world of wisdom in the following: "Every schoolboy knows that a kite would not fly unless it had a string tying it down. It is just so

in life. The man who is tied down by half-a-dozen
blooming responsibilities and their mother, will make
a higher and stronger flight than the bachelor, who,
having nothing to keep him steady, is always floun-
dering in the mud. If you want to ascend in the
world, *tie* yourself to somebody."

Influence of Matrimony.

MARRIAGE is an occasion on which none refuse to
sympathize. Would that all were equally able and
willing to understand! Would that all could know
how, from the first flow of the affections till they are
shed abroad in all their plentitude, the purposes of
their creation become fulfilled. They were to life
like a sleeping ocean to a bright but barren and silent
shore. When the breeze from afar awakened it, new
lights began to gleam, and echoes to be heard; rich
and unthought-of treasures were cast up from the
depths; the barriers of individuality were broken
down; and from thenceforth, they who chose might
"hear the mighty waters rolling evermore." Would
that all could know how, by this mighty impulse, new
strength is given to every power—how the intellect
is vivified and enlarged—how the spirit becomes bold
to explore the path of life, and clear-sighted to discern
its issues!

Marriage is, to a woman, at once the happiest and

saddest event of her life; it is the promise of future
bliss, raised on the death of all present enjoyment.
She quits her home, her parents, her companions, her
occupations, her amusements—her everything upon
which she has hitherto depended for comfort—for
affection, for kindness, for pleasure. The parents by
whose advice she has been guided, the sister to whom
she has dared impart every embryo thought and feeling, the brother who has played with her, in turns
the counselor and the counseled, and the younger
children to whom she has hitherto been the mother
and the playmate—all are to be forsaken in one instant; every former tie is loosened, the spring of
every hope and action to be changed, and yet she
flies with joy into the untrodden paths before her.
Buoyed up by the confidence of requited love, she
bids. a fond and grateful adieu to the life that is
past, and turns with excited hopes and joyous antici-
pations of the happiness to come. Then woe to
the man who can blast such hopes—who can, coward-
like, break the illusions that have won her, and
destroy the confidence which his love inspired.

There is no one thing more lovely in this life, more
full of the divinest courage, than when a young
maiden, from her past life, from her happy childhood,
when she rambled over every field and moor around
her home; when a mother anticipated her wants and
soothed her little cares; when brothers and sisters
grew from merry playmates to loving, trustful friends;
from the Christmas gatherings and romps, the summer festivals in bower or garden; from the rooms

sanctified by the death of relatives; from the holy
and secure backgrounds of her childhood, and girl-
hood, and maidenhood, looks out into a dark and
unillumined future, away from all that, and yet unter-
rified, undaunted, leans her fair cheek upon her lover's
breast, and whispers, "Dear heart! I cannot see, but
I believe. The past was beautiful, but the future I
can trust *with thee!*"

Wherever women plights her truth, under the sky
of heaven, at the domestic hearth, or in the consecrated aisles, the ground is holy, the spirit of the
hour is sacramental. That it is thus felt even by the
most trivial may be observed at the marriage cere-
mony. Though the mirth may be fast and furious
before or after the irrevocable formula is spoken, yet
at that point of time there is a shadow on the most
laughing lip — a moisture in the firmest eye. Wedlock, indissoluble, except by an act of God — a sacra-
ment whose solemnity reaches to eternity — will
always hold its rank in literature, as the most impressive fact of human experience in dramatic writing,
whether of the stage or closet, the play or novel. It
must be so. If goverment, with all its usurpations
and aggressions, have appropriated history, let the
less ambitious portions of our literature be sacred to
the affections — to the family, based upon conjugal
and parental love, as that institution is the state
which hitherto in the world's annals, has been little
else than the sad exponent of human ambition.

A judicious wife is always snipping off from her
husband's moral nature little twigs that are growing

in the wrong direction. She keeps him in shape by continual pruning. If you say anything silly, she will affectionately tell you so. If you declare you will do some absurd thing, she will find means of preventing you from doing it. And by far the chief part of all common sense there is in this world belongs unquestionably to woman. The wisest things which a man commonly does are those which his wife counsels him to do. A wife is the grand wielder of the moral pruning knife. When you see a man appearing shabby, hair uncombed, and no buttons on his coat, nine times out of ten you are correct in concluding that he is a bachelor. You can conclude much the same when you see a man profane, or speaking vulgarly of ladies. We would add that young men who wish to appear well in every respect should get married. It has been well said, "A man unmarried is but half a man."

It was thus surely, that intellectual beings of different sexes were intended by their great Creator to go through the world together; thus united, not only in hand and heart, but in principles, in intellect, in views, and in dispositions; both pursuing one common and noble end—their own improvement and the happiness of those around them—by the different means appropriate to their situation; mutually correcting, sustaining and strengthening each other; undegraded by all practices of tyranny on the one hand and of deceit on the other; each finding a candid but severe judge in the understanding, and a warm and partial advocate in the heart of his and her companion;

secure of a refuge from the vexations, the follies, the
misunderstandings and the evils of the world in the
arms of each other, and in the inestimable enjoyments
of undisturbed confidence and unrestrained intimacy.

The law that binds the one man to the one woman
is indelibly written by nature, that wherever it is vio-
lated in the general system, the human race is found
to deteriorate in mind and form. The ennobling
influences of woman cease; the wife is a companion
—a hundred wives are but a hundred slaves. Nor
is this all, unless man look to a woman as a treasure
to be wooed and won—her smile the charm of his
existence—her single heart the range of his desires
—that which deserves the name of love cannot exist;
it is struck out of the system of society. Now, if
there be a passion in the human breast which most
tends to lift us out of egotism and self, which most
teaches us to love another, which purifies and warms
the whole mortal being, it is love, as we hold it and
cherish it. For even when the fair spring of youth
has passed, and when the active life of man is employed in such grave pursuits that the love of his
early years seems to him like a dream of romance,
still that love, having once lifted him out of egotism
into sympathy, does but pass into new forms and
development—it has locked his heart to charity and
benevolence—it gives a smile to his home—it rises
up in the eyes of his children—from his heart it cir-
culates insensibly on to all the laws that protect the
earth, to the native lands which spread around it.
Thus in the history of the world we discover that

wherever love is created, as it were, and sanctioned
by that equality between the sexes which the permanent and holy union of one heart with another proclaims; there, too, patriotism, liberty—the manly
and gentle virtues—also find their place; and wherever, on the contrary, polygamy is practiced and love
disappears in the gross satiety of the senses, there
we find neither respect for humanity nor reverence
for home, nor affection for the natal soil. And one
reason why Greece is contrasted, in all that dignifies
our nature, with the effeminate and dissolute character of the East which it overthrew, is, that Greece
was the earliest civilized country in which, on the
borders of those great monarchies, marriage was the
sacred tie between one man and one woman—and
man was the thoughtful father of a home, not the
wanton lord of a seraglio.

Nothing delights one more than to enter the neat
little tenement of the young couple, who, within perhaps two or three years, without any resources but
their own knowledge or industry, have joined heart
and hand, and engaged to share together the responsibilities, duties, interests, trials and pleasures of life.
The industrious wife is cheerfully employed with her
own hands in domestic duties, putting her house in
order, or mending her husband's clothes, or preparing
the dinner, whilst, perhaps, the little darling sits prat-
tling on the floor, or lies sleeping in the cradle, and
every thing seems preparing to welcome the happiest
of husbands, and the best of fathers, when he shall
come from his toil to enjoy the sweets of his little

paradise. This is the true domestic pleasure. Health, contentment, love, abundance, and bright prospects, are all here. But it has become a prevalent sentiment that a man must acquire his fortune before he marries, that the wife must have no sympathy nor share with him in the pursuit of it, in which most of the pleasure truly consists; and the young married people must set out with as large and expensive an establishment as is becoming to those who have been wedded for twenty years. This is very unhappy; it fills the community with bachelors, who are waiting to make their fortunes, endangering virtue and promoting vice; it destroys the true economy and design of the domestic institution, and encourages inefficiency among females, who are expecting to be taken up by fortune and passively sustained, without any care or concern on their part; and thus many a wife becomes, as a gentleman once remarked, not a "help-meet," but a "help-eat."

The Creator found that it was not good for man to be alone. Therefore he made woman to be a "help-meet for him." And for many ages history has shown that "the permanent union of one man with one woman establishes a relation of affections and interests which can in no other way be made to exist between two human beings." To establish this relation was one of the great designs of God in giving the rite to man; and by establishing this relation, marriage becomes to him an aid in the stern conflict of life. This it is in a theoretical point of view. This, too, it has often proved in practical life. Many a man has risen from obscurity to fame, who, in the days of his triumphant victory, has freely and gratefully acknowledged that to the sympathy and encouragement of his wife, during the long and weary years of toil, he owed very much of his achieved success.

But while young men say they cannot marry because the girls of this generation are too extravagant, the fault by no means is altogether with the girls. In the first place, young men, as a general thing, admire the elegant costumes in which many ladies appear, and do not hesitate to express their admiration to those who are more plainly dressed. And what is the natural effect of this? In the second place many young men are too proud themselves to commence their married life in a quiet, economical way. They are not willing to marry until they have money enough to continue all their own private luxuries, and also support a wife in style. The difficulty is not altogether on either side; but if both men and women would be true to the best feelings of their hearts, and careless about what the world would say, pure and happy and noble homes would be more abundant. This state of affairs is very unfortunate for both parties. It leaves woman without a home and without protection or support. Woman needs the strength and courage of man, and he needs her cheerfulness, her sympathy, her consolation. Our papers tell us, that in a single New England city, there are nearly thirty thousand young men, already engaged, who are putting off marriage

until they can make enough to support their wives.
So it is throughout the country.   Young men need
the restraining and elevating influences of home.
But as it is now the man must commence business
alone, fight his own battles without sympathy or
consolation, win, if possible, by years of arduous toil,
a competence; and when the conflict is over, the toil
is past, and the victory is won, *then* he can have a
wife and a home.   A man to succeed well in life
needs the influence of a pure-minded woman, and her
sympathy to sweeten the cup of life.

Advantage of Matrimony.

IF you are for pleasure, marry; if you prize rosy
health, marry.   A good wife is heaven's last best gift
to man; his angel of mercy; minister of graces innumerable; his gem of many virtues; his casket of
jewels.   Her voice is his sweetest music; her smiles
his brightest days; her kiss the guardian of innocence;
her arms the pale of his safety, the balm of his health,
the balsam of his life; her industry his surest wealth;
her economy his safest steward; her lips his faithful
counselor; her bosom the softest pillow of his cares;
and her prayers the ablest advocates of heaven's
blessings on his head.

Woman's influence is the sheet anchor of society;
and this influence is due not exclusively to the

fascination of her charms, but chiefly to the strength, unformity, and consistency of her virtues, maintained under so many sacrifices, and with so much fortitude and heroism. Without these endowments and quali- fications, external attractions are nothing; but with them, their power is irresistible.

Beauty and virtue are the crowning attributes be- stowed by nature upon woman, and the bounty of heaven more than compensates for the injustice of man. Sometimes we hear both sexes repine at their change, relate the happiness of their earlier years, blame the folly and rashness of their own choice, and warn those that are coming into the world against the same precipitance and infatuation. But it is to be remembered that the days which they so much wish to call back, are the days not only of celibacy but of youth, the days of novelty and improvement, of ardor and of hope, of health and vigor of body, of gayety and lightness of heart. It is not easy to surround life with any circumstances in which youth will not be delightful; and we are afraid that whether married or unmarried, we shall find the vesture of terrestrial existence more heavy and cumbrous the longer it is worn.

Once for all, there is no misery so distressful as the desperate agony of trying to keep young when one cannot. We know an old bachelor who has attempted it. His affectation of youth, like all affectations, is a melancholy failure. He is a fast young man of fifty. He plies innocent young ladies with the pretty com- pliments and soft nothings in vogue when he was a

spoony youth of twenty. The fashion of talking to
young ladies has changed within thirty years, you
know, and this aged boy's soft nothings seem more
out of date than a two-year-old bonnet. When you
see his old-fashioned young antics — his galvanic
gallantry, so to speak, and hear the speeches he
makes to girls in their teens, when he ought to be
talking to them like a father — you involuntarily call
him an old idiot, and long to remind him of that quaint
rebuke of grand old John: "Thou talkest like one
upon whose head the shell is to this very day." That
is how he seems. He is old enough to have been
almost full-fledged before you were born, and here he
is trying to make believe that he is still in the days
of his gosling-green, with the shell sticking on his
head to this day! It is a melancholy absurdity.
One cannot be young unless one is young. Only
once is it given to us to be untried and soft, and
gushing and superlative, and when the time comes for
it all to go, no sort of effort can hold back the fleet-
ing days.

"I wish that I had married thirty years ago," solil-
oquized an old bachelor. "Oh! I wish a wife and
half a score of children would start up around me,
and bring along with them all that affection which we
should have had for each other by being early
acquainted. But as it is, in my present state, there
is not a person in the world I care a straw for; and
the world is pretty even with me, for I don't believe
there is a person in it who cares a straw for me."

Young Men and Marriage.

A YOUNG man meets a pretty face in the ball-room, falls in love with it, courts it, marries it, goes to housekeeping with it, and boasts of having a home and a wife to grace it. The chances are, nine to ten, that he has neither. He has been "taken in and done for!" Her pretty face gets to be an old story, or becomes faded, or freckled, or fretted, and as the face was all he wanted, all he paid attention to, all he sat up with, all he bargained for, all he swore to love, honor and protect, he gets sick of his trade, knows of a dozen faces he likes better, gives up staying at home evenings, consoles himself with cigars, oysters and politics, and looks upon his home as a very indifferent boarding-house.

Another young man becomes enamored of a "fortune." He waits upon it to parties, dances a polka with it, exchanges *billets doux* with it, pops the question to it, gets accepted by it, takes it to the parson, weds it, calls it "wife," carries it home, sets up an establishment with it, introduces it to his friends, and says he, too, is married and has got a home. It is false. He is not married; he has no home. And he soon finds it out. He is in the wrong box; but it is too late to get out of it; he might as well hope to get out of his coffin. His friends congratulate him, and he has to grin and bear it.

If a young man would escape these sad conse-

quences, let him shun the rocks upon which so many
have made shipwreck. Let him disregard, totally,
all considerations of wealth, beauty, external accomplishments, fashion, connections in society, and every
other mere selfish and worldly end, and look into the
mind and heart of the woman he thinks of marrying.
If he cannot love her for herself alone — that is, for
all that goes to make up her character as a woman —
let him disregard every external inducement, and shun
a marriage with her as the greatest evil to which he
could be subjected. And if he have in him a spark
of virtuous feeling — if he have one unselfish and
generous emotion — he will shun such a marriage for
the woman's sake also, for it would be sacrificing her
happiness as well as his own.

From what is here set forth every young man can
see how vitally important it is for him to make his
choice in marriage from a right end. Wealth cannot
bring happiness, and is ever in danger of taking to
itself wings; beauty cannot last long where there is
grief at the heart; and distinguished connections are
a very poor substitute for the pure love of a true
woman's heart.

All that has been said refers to the ends which
should govern in the choice of a wife. Directions as
to the choice itself can only be of a general character,
for the circumstances surrounding each one, and the
particular circles into which he is thrown, will have
specific influences, which will bias the judgment either
one way or another. One good rule it will, however,
be well to observe, and that is, to be on your guard

against those young ladies who seek evidently to attract your attention. It is unfeminine and proves that there is something wanting to make up the perfect woman. In retiring modesty you will be far more apt to find the virtues after which you are seeking. A brilliant belle may make a loving, faithful wife and mother; but the chances are somewhat against her, and a prudent young man will satisfy himself well by a close observation of her in private and domestic life before he makes up his mind to offer her his hand.

There are many, too many, finely educated young ladies who can charm you with their brilliance of intellect, their attainments in science and literature, or their music, who know not the rudiments of how to make a home comfortable and inviting. Some will frankly confess it, with sorrow, others boast of this ignorance as something to be proud of. How many such women marry and make an utter failure of life. They make a wreck of their husband's happiness, of the home he has doted on, of his fortune, and, alas, too often of his character, and his soul's interest. You see them abroad, and are delighted to have made their acquaintance, but you find their homes slipshod homes, sadly contrasting with the really cultivated manners and mind which so attracted you.

When you see the avaricious and crafty taking companions to themselves without any inquiry but after farms and money, or the giddy and thoughtless uniting themselves for life to those whom they have only seen by the light of gas or oil; when parents make matches for children without inquiring after their consent; when some marry for heirs to disappoint their brothers, and others throw themselves into the arms of those whom they do not love, because they found themselves rejected where they were more solicitous to please; when some marry because their servants cheat them; some because they squander their own money; some because their houses are pestered with company; some because they will live like other people; and some because they are sick of themselves, we are not so much inclined to wonder that marriage is sometimes unhappy, as that it appears so little loaded with calamity, and cannot but conclude that society has something in itself eminently agreeable to human nature, when we find its pleasures so great that even the ill-choice of a companion can hardly overbalance them. Those, therefore, of the above description who should rail against matrimony should be informed that they are neither to wonder nor repine, that a contract begun on such principles has ended in disappointment. A young man and a dear friend once said, "I am going to take her for better or for worse." The remark ran over me like a chill breath of winter. I shuddered at the thought. "For better or for worse." All in doubt. Going to marry, yet not *sure* he was right. The lady he spoke of was a noble young woman, intellectual, cultivated, pious, accustomed to his sphere of life. They were going to marry in uncertainty. Both were of fine families; both excellent young people. To the world it looked like a desirable match. To them it was going to be "for better or for worse." They married. The woman stayed in his home one year and left it, declaring he was a good man and a faultless husband, but not after her heart. She stayed away one year and came back; lived with him one year more and died. Sad tale. It proved for the worse, and all because they did not *know* each other; if they had they would not have married.

Marriage is the seal of man's earthly weal or woe. No event is to be compared with this for its interest and its immeasurable results. Why are so many unhappy in this union, never indeed truly married? Because they rush into its sacred temple, either deluded or unsanctified by God and good principles. They sin in haste, and are left to repent at leisure. Custom, convenience, proximity, passion, vicious novels, silly companions, intoxicate the brain; and that step is taken without one serious thought, which death only can retrieve.

Robert Southey says: "A man may be cheerful and contented in celibacy, but I do not think he can ever be happy; it is an unnatural state, and the best feelings of his nature are never called into action. The risks of marriage are for the greater part on the woman's side. Women have so little the power of choice that it is not perhaps fair to say that they are less likely to choose well than we are; but I am persuaded that they are more frequently deceived in the attachments they form, and their opinions concerning men are less accurate than men's opinion of their sex.

Now, if a lady were to reproach me for having said this, I should only reply that it was another mode of saying there are more good wives in the world than there are good husbands, which I verily believe. I know of nothing which a good and sensible man is so certain to find, if he looks for it, as a good wife."

Who marries for love takes a wife; who marries for the sake of convenience takes a mistress; who marries for consideration takes a lady. You are loved by your wife, regarded by your mistress, tolerated by your lady. You have a wife for yourself, a mistress for your house and its friends, and a lady for the world. Your wife will agree with you, your mistress will accommodate you, and your lady will manage you. Your wife will take care of your household, your mistress of your house, your lady of appearance. If you are sick, your wife will nurse you, your mistress will visit you, and your lady will inquire after your health. You take a walk with your wife, a ride with your mistress, and join partners with your lady. Your wife will share your grief, your mistress your money, and your lady your debts. If you are dead, your wife will shed tears, your mistress lament, and your lady wear mourning. A year after death marries again your wife, in six months your mistress, and in six weeks or sooner, when mourning is over, your lady.

Men and women, before marriage, are as figures and ciphers. The woman is the cipher and counts for nothing until she gets the figure of a husband beside her, when she becomes of importance herself and adds tenfold to the sum of his. But this, it must be observed, occurs only when she gets and remains on the right side of him, for when she shifts from this position, he returns to his lesser estate, and she to her original insignificance.

Marriage offers the most effective opportunities for spoiling the life of another. Nobody can debase, harass and ruin a woman so fatally as her own husband, and nobody can do a tithe so much to chill a man's aspirations, to paralyze his energies, as his wife. A man is never irretrievably ruined in his prospects until he marries a bad woman. The Bible tells us that, as the climbing a sandy way is to the feet of the aged, so is a wife full of words to a quiet man. A cheerful wife is a rainbow in the sky when her husband's mind is tossed on the storms of anxiety and care. A good wife is the greatest earthly blessing. A man is what his wife makes him. Make marriage a matter of moral judgment. Marry in your own religion. Marry into different blood and temperament from your own. Marry into a family which you have long known.

Husbands and wives of different religious persuasions do not generally live happily. When the spiritual influences are antagonistic, the conjugal union is not complete, for it lacks the unity essential to the fulfillment of serious obligations, and there is an entire absence of that sound and reciprocated confidence — that mutual faith, which, although their roots be in the earth, have their branches in the sky of affection. The subject is painful, and however we may wound the susceptibilities of apparently fond lovers — we say *apparently* advisedly, for there can be no real love where there is "no silver cord to bind it" — we unhesitatingly express the opinion that marriages between persons who do not tread in the same religious path are wholly unadvisable — nay, wrong — for they tend to invite a future teeming with shadows, clouds, and darkness.

Young Ladies and Matrimony.

MANY a young lady.has had an advantageous offer of marriage. The man who made it is of exemplary character; he is well off in this world's goods, is engaged in a profitable and reputable business, and there is no particular reason why she should not accept his proposal; but she does not love him. In our judgment, that is reason enough. We do not believe in marriage without love. Respect is all very well, and that one should have any way; but it does not take the place of affection. It is said that in such matches love comes after marriage. We have no doubt that it often does. But we think love should precede as well as follow matrimony. It is always liable to happen to one who has never loved. But suppose, subsequent to marriage, it is awakened for the first time in a wife, and the object happens to be

other than the husband—what then? This is a
contingency not pleasant to contemplate. No: if
you do not love, do not marry. Singleness is blessedness compared to marriage without affection. The
connubial yoke sits easy on the shoulders of love;
but it is most galling without this one and only
sufficient support.

We celebrate the wedding, and make merry over
the honeymoon. The poet paints the beauties and
blushes of the blooming bride; and the bark of matrimony, with its freight of untested love, is launched
on the uncertain ocean of experiment, amid kind
wishes and rejoicings. But on that precarious sea
are many storms, and even the calm has its perils;
and only when the bark has weathered these, and
landed its cargo in the haven of domestic peace, can
we pronounce the voyage prosperous, and congratulate the adventurer on his merited and enviable
reward.

The best women have an instinctive wish to marry
a man superior to themselves in some way or other;
for their honor is in their husbands, and their status
in society is determined by his. A woman who, for
a passing fancy, marries a man in any way her
inferior, wrongs herself, her family, and her whole
life; for the "grossness of his nature" will most
probably drag her to his level. Now and then a
woman of great force of character may lift her
husband upward, but she accepts such a labor at the
peril of her own higher life. Should she find it
equally impossible to lift him to her level or sink to

his, what remains? Life-long regrets, bitter shame and self-reproach, or a forcible setting of herself free. But the latter, like all severe remedies, carries desperation, instead of hope, with it. Never can she quite regain her maiden place; an *aura* of a doubtful kind fetters and influences her in every effort or relation of her future life.

A young woman is smitten with a pair of whiskers. Curled hair never before had such charms. She sets her cap for them; they take. The delighted whiskers make an offer, proffering themselves both in exchange for one heart. Our dear miss is overcome with magnanimity, closes the bargain, carries home the prize, shows it to pa and ma, calls herself engaged to it, thinks there never was such a pair of whiskers before, and in a few weeks the miss and the pair of whiskers are married. Married? Yes, the world calls it so, and so we will. What is the result? A short honeymoon, and then the discovery that they are as unlike as chalk and cheese, and not to be made one, though all the priests in Christendom pronounced them so.

Young ladies are not to rely upon common report, nor the opinion of friends or fashionable acquaintances, but upon personal knowledge of the individual's life and character. How can another know what you want in a companion? You alone know your own heart. If you do not know it you are not fit to be married. No one else can tell what fills you with pleasing and grateful emotions. You only know when the spring of true affection is touched by the hand of a congenial spirit. It is for you to *know* who asks your hand, who has your heart, who links his life with yours. If you *know* the man who can make true answer to your soul's true love, whose soul is all kindred with yours, whose life answers to your ideal of manly demeanor, you know who would make you a good husband. But if you only fancy that he is right, or guess, or believe, or hope, from a little social interchange of · words and looks, you have but a poor foundation on which to build hopes of future happiness. Do not, as you value life and its comforts, marry a man who is naturally cruel. If he will wantonly torture a poor dumb dog, a cat, or even a snake, fly from him as you would from the cholera. We would sooner see our daughter dying of cholera, than married to a cruel hearted man. If his nature delights in torture, he will not spare his wife, or his helpless children, When we see a man practicing cruelty on any poor, helpless creature, or beating a fractious horse unmercifully, we write over against his name, "devil," and shun him accordingly.

Do not marry a fop. There is in such a character nothing of true dignity; nothing that commands respect, or insures even a decent standing in the community. There is a mark upon him, an affected elegance of manner, a studied particularity of dress, and usually a singular inanity of mind, by which he is known in every circle in which he moves. His very attitude and gait tells the stranger who he is, though he only passes him silently on the street. To unite your destiny with such a man, we hardly need say,

29

would be to impress the seal of disgrace upon your character, and the seal of wretchedness upon your doom.

Look with disdain on what are called, significantly, our "fast young men;" those who frequent the saloon and bar-room, to drench themselves in "fire-water;" who, filled with conceit, talk large, and use big-sounding oaths; whose highest ambition is to drive a fast horse, to swear roundly, and wear dashy garments; who affect to look with contempt on their elders and equals as they toil in some honest occupation, and who regard labor as a badge of disgrace.

A habit of industry once formed is not likely to be ever lost. Place the individual in whatever circumstances you will, and he will not be satisfied unless he can be active. Moreover, it will impart to his character an energy and efficiency, and we may add, dignity, which can hardly fail to render him an object of respect. We should regard your prospects for life far better if you should marry a man of very limited property, or even no property at all, with an honest vocation and a habit of industry, than if we were to see you united to one of extensive wealth, who had never been taught to exercise his own powers, and had sunk into the sensual gratification of himself.

Perhaps no folly holds so strong a place in a woman's mind as that she can reclaim the one she loves — if he *is* a little fast, after marriage, he will settle down into a just and sensible husband. History, too, often repeats the failure of such beliefs; it is delusive, a

snare, and the young woman, after the marriage
vows have been recorded, awakes to find the will of
her husband stronger than her own, too selfish for
any control, and her life begins its long agony of
misery.   We say to young maidens, be warned in
time; can you reclaim those who have not the power
to reclaim themselves?   Can you throw away your
pure life and womanly sympathies upon wretches,
whose moral principles cannot stand the slightest
examination, and whose proffered love is but a temporary symptom of their changing heartlessness?
Beware, beware! the deepest rascal has the finest
clothes and the smoothest tongue.   Yet in spite of
all the wretchedness of drunkards' wives, young
women are continually willing to marry men who are
in the habit of indulging in the social glass!   Ladies
often refuse the marriage offers of young men because
they are too poor, or of too humble a family, or too
plain in person or manners.   But only now and then
one has good sense enough to refuse to unite herself
with a man who will not pledge himself to total
abstinence.   A rich and fashionable young man has
commonly no trouble to get a wife, even though he is
hardly sober long enough to pronounce the marriage
vow.   But a teetotaler in coarse raiment might be
snubbed as a vulgar fellow who has never seen society.
Ladies, before you begin to scold at us for this impious
thing, just look around and see if this is not true.   A
young woman who marries a man who is addicted to
drinking liquors is attaching to herself but a dead
weight that will drag her down with himself below

the level of the brute. Young ladies, as life is precious to you, and since you value it highly, take no such chances. Rather than marry a man whom you know to drink, only now and then, for his friend's sake, wait a while longer; there are many young men of noble character who are on the lookout for a *good* young lady, and your chances are not to be despaired of. To think of redeeming a young man from intemperance is simply folly. To him your efforts to keep him from the cup would be like damming a river with a feather, or like stopping a hurricane with a tin whistle.

During the period that intervenes between forming an engagement and consummating the connection, let your deportment toward the individual to whom you have given your affections be marked by modesty and dignity, respect and kindness. Never, on the one hand, give him the least reason to question the sincerity of your regard, nor on the other, suffer your intercourse with him to be marked by an undignified familiarity. Do all that you can to render him happy, and while you will naturally grow in each other's confidence and affection, you may reasonably hope that you will be helpers of each other's joy. in the most endearing of all human relations.

Love.

"Oh happy state! when souls each other draw,
When love is liberty, and nature law :
All then is full, possessing and possess'd,
No craving void left aching in the breast : .
Even thought meets thought, ere from the lips it part,
And each warm wish springs mutual from the heart."

LOVE is such a giant power that it seems to gather strength from obstructions, and at every difficulty rises to higher might. It is all dominant—all conquering; a grand leveler which can bring down to its own universal line of equalization the proudest heights, and remove the most stubborn impediments: "Like death, it levels all ranks, and lays the shepherd's crook beside the sceptre." There is no hope of resisting it, for it outwatches the most vigilant—submerges everything, acquiring strength as it proceeds; ever growing, nay, growing out of itself. Love is the light, the majesty of life, that principle to which, after all our struggling, and writhing, and twisting, all things must be resolved. Take it away, and what becomes of the world! It is a barren wilderness! A world of monuments, each standing upright and crumbling; an army of gray stones, without a chaplet, without a leaf to take off, with its glimpse of green, their flat insipidity and offensive uniformity upon a shrubless plain. Things base and foul, creeping and obscure, withered, bloodless, and brainless, could alone spring from such a marble hearted soil.

Love's darts are silver; when they turn to fire in
the noble heart, they impart a portion of that heavenly
flame which is their element.   Love is of such a refining, elevating character, that it expels all that is mean
and base; bids us think great thoughts, do great
deeds, and changes our common clay into fine gold.
It illuminates our path, dark and mysterious as it may
be, with torchlights lit from the one great light.   Oh!
poor, weak, and inexpressive are words when sought
to strew, as with stars, the path and track of the
expression of love's greatness and power!   Dull,
pitiful, and cold; a cheating, horny gleam, as stones
strung by the side of precious gems, and the
far-flashing of the sparkling ruby with his heart of
fire!   The blue eyes of turquoises, or the liquid light
of the sapphire, should alone be tasked to spell along,
and character our thoughts of love.

The loves that make memory happy and home
beautiful, are those which form the sunlight of our
earliest consciousness, beaming gratefully along the
path of maturity, and their radiance lingering till the
shadow of death darkens them all together.

But there is another love—that which blends
young hearts in blissful unity, and, for the time, so
ignores past ties and affections, as to make willing
separation of the son from his father's house, and the
daughter from all the sweet endearments of her
childhood's home, to go out together, and rear for
themselves an altar, around which shall cluster all the
cares and delights, the anxieties and sympathies, of
the family relationship; this love, if pure, unselfish,

and discreet, constitutes the chief usefulness and happiness of human life. Without it, there would be no organized households, and, consequently, none of that earnest endeavor for competence and respectability, which is the main-spring to human effort; none of those sweet, softening, restraining and elevating influences of domestic life, which can alone fill the earth with the glory of the Lord and make glad the city of Zion. This love is indeed heaven upon earth; but above would not be heaven without it; where there is not love, there is fear; but, "love casteth out fear." And yet we naturally do offend what we most love.

Love is the sun of life; most beautiful in morning and evening, but warmest and steadiest at noon. It is the sun of the soul. Life without love is worse than death; a world without a sun. The love which does not lead to labor will soon die out, and the thankfulness which does not embody itself in sacrifices is already changing to gratitude. Love is not ripened in one day, nor in many, nor even in a human lifetime. It is the oneness of soul with soul in appreciation and perfect trust. To be blessed it must rest in that faith in the Divine which underlies every other emotion. To be true, it must be eternal as God himself. Zeno being told that it was humiliating to a philosopher to be in love, remarked: "If that be true, the fair sex are much to be pitied, for they would receive the attention only of fools." Some love a girl for beauty, some for virtue, and others for understanding. Goethe says: "We love a girl for very different things than understanding. We love her for her beauty, her youth, her mirth, her confidingness, her character, with its faults, caprices, and God knows what other inexpressible charms; but we do not love her understanding. Her mind we esteem (if it is brilliant), and it may greatly elevate her in our opinion; nay, more, it may enchain us when we already love. But her understanding is not that which awakens and inflames our passions."

> Love is blind, and lovers cannot see
> The pretty follies that themselves commit.

Remember that love is dependent upon forms; courtesy of etiquette guards and protects courtesy of heart. How many hearts have been lost irrecoverably, and how many averted eyes and cold looks have been gained from what seemed, perhaps, but a trifling negligence of forms. Men and women should not be judged by the same rules. There are many radical differences in their affectional natures. Man is the creature of interest and ambition. His nature leads him forth into the struggle and bustle of the world. Love is but the embellishment of his early life, or a song piped in the intervals of the acts. He seeks for fame, for fortune, for space in the world's thoughts, and dominion over his fellow-men. But a woman's whole life is a history of the affections. The heart is her world; it is there her ambition strives for empire; it is there her ambition seeks for hidden treasures. She sends forth her sympathies on adventure; she embarks her whole soul in the traffic of affection; and if shipwrecked her case is hopeless, for it is bankruptcy of the heart.

> Man's love is of man's life a thing, a part ;
> 'Tis woman's whole existence.

For every woman it is with the food of the heart as with that of the body; it is possible to exist on a very small quantity, but that small quantity is an absolute necessity. Woman loves or abhors; man admires or despises. Woman without love is a fruit without flower. In love, the virtuous woman says *no;* the passionate says *yes;* the capricious says *yes* and *no;* the coquette neither *yes* nor *no*. A coquette is a rose from whom every lover plucks a leaf; the thorn remains for the future husband. She may be compared to tinder which catches sparks, but does not always succeed in lighting a *match*. Love, while it frequently corrupts pure hearts, often purifies corrupt hearts. How well he knew the human heart who said: "We wish to constitute all the happiness, or if that cannot be, the misery of the one we love."

Woman's love is stronger than death; it rises superior to adversity, and towers in sublime beauty above the niggardly selfishness of the world. Misfortune cannot suppress it; enmity cannot alienate it; temptation cannot enslave it. It is the guardian angel of the nursery and the sick bed; it gives an affectionate concord to the partnership of life and interest, circumstances cannot modify it; it ever remains the same to sweeten existence, to purify the cup of life on the rugged pathway to the grave, and melt to moral pliability the brittle nature of man. It is the ministering spirit of home, hovering in soothing caresses over the cradle, and the death-bed of the household, and filling up the urn of all its sacred memories.

How many bright eyes grow dim—how many soft cheeks grow pale—how many lovely forms fade away into the tomb, and none can tell the cause that blighted their loveliness! As the dove will clasp its wings to its side, and cover and conceal the arrow that is preying on its vitals, so it is the nature of woman to hide from the world the pangs of wounded affection. The love of a delicate female is always shy and silent. Even when fortunate she scarcely breathes it to herself; but when otherwise, she buries it in the recesses of her bosom, and there lets it brood and cower among the ruins of her peace. With her the desire of the heart has failed. The great charm of existence is at an end. She neglects all the cheerful exercises which gladden the spirits, quicken the pulses, and send the tide of life in healthful currents through the veins. Her rest is broken—the sweet refreshment of sleep is poisoned by melancholy dreams—"dry sorrow drinks her blood," until her feeble frame sinks under the slightest external injury. Look for her after a little while, and you will find friendship weeping over her untimely grave, and wondering that one who but lately glowed with all the radiance of health and beauty, should be so speedily brought down to "darkness and the worm." You will be told of some wintry chill, some casual indisposition that laid her low; but no one knows of the mental malady that previously sapped her strength and made her so easy a prey to the spoiler.

The affection that links together man and wife is a far holier and more enduring passion than the enthusiasm of young love. It may want its gorgeousness —it may want its imaginative character, but it is far richer, and holier, and more trusting in its attributes. Talk not to us of the absence of love in wedlock. No! it burns with a steady and brilliant flame, shedding a benign influence upon existence, a million times more precious and delightful than the cold dreams of philosophy. Domestic love! Who can measure its height or its depth? Who can estimate its preserving and purifying power? It sends an ever swelling stream of life through a household, it binds hearts into one "bundle of life;" it shields them from temptation, it takes the sting from disappointments and sorrow, it breathes music into the voice, into the footsteps, it gives worth and beauty to the commonest office, it surrounds home with an atmosphere of moral health, it gives power to effort and wings to progress, it is omnipotent. Love, amid the other graces in this world, is like a cathedral tower, which begins on the earth, and, at first, is surrounded by the other parts of the structure; but, at length, rising above buttressed wall, and arch, and parapet, and pinnacle, it shoots spire-like many a foot right into the air, so high that the huge cross on its summit glows like a spark in the morning light and shines like a star in the evening sky, when the rest of the pile is enveloped in darkness.

He who loves a lady's complexion, form and features, loves not her true self, but her soul's old clothes.
The love that has nothing but beauty to sustain it,
soon withers and dies. The love that is fed with
presents always requires feeding. Love and love
only, is the loan for love. Love is of the nature of a
burning glass, which, kept still in one place, lights
fire; changed often, it does nothing. The purest joy
we can experience in one we love, is to see that person a source of happiness to others. When you are
with the person loved, you have no sense of being
bored. This humble and trivial circumstance is the
great test—the only sure and abiding test of love.
With the persons you do not love you are never
supremely at your ease. You have some of the sen-
sation of walking upon stilts. In conversation with
them, however much you admire them and are interested in them, the horrid idea will cross your mind of
"What shall I say next?" One has well said, "In
true love the burden of conversation is borne by both
the lovers, and the one of them who, with knightly
intent, would bear it alone, would only thus cheat the
other of a part of his best fortune." When two souls
come together, each seeking to magnify the other,
each in a subordinate sense worshiping the other,
each helps the other; the two flying together so that
each wing-beat of the one helps each wing-beat of the
other—when two souls come together thus, they are
lovers. They who unitedly move themselves away
from grossness and from earth, toward the throne
crystalline and the pavement golden, are, indeed, true
lovers.

Matrimony.

It is pleasant to contemplate the associations clus-
tering around the wedding morn. It is the happiest
hour of human life, and breaks upon the young heart
like a gentle spring upon the flowers of earth. It is
the hour of bounding, joyous expectancy, when the
ardent spirit, arming itself with bold hope, looks with
undaunted mien upon the dark and terrible future. It
is the hour when thought borrows the livery of goodness, and humanity, looking from its tenement, across
the broad common of life, shakes off its heavy load
of sordidness, and gladly swings to its shoulders the
light burden of love and kindness. It is the heart's
hour, full of blissful contemplation, rich promises, and
the soul's happy revels. We cordially echo the
sentiment, Happy morn, garmented with the human
virtues, it shows life to the eye, lovely, as if

"Clad in the beauty of a thousand stars."

"Marriage is a lottery," the saying goes, and there
are plenty who believe it, and who act accordingly,
and for such it is well if they do no worse than draw
a blank, if they do not draw a life-long misery and
pain. But marriage is not necessarily a lottery, either
in the initial choice or in the months and years after
the marriage day. One can shut his eyes and draw,
or one can open them and choose. One can choose
with the outward eye alone, or with the eye of intel-

lect and conscience. Says Jeremy Taylor, speaking
of marriages where physical beauty is the only bond:
"It is an ill band of affections to tie two hearts
together with a little thread of red and white." But
let us choose ever so wisely, ever so deeply, and not
we ourselves nor the minister can marry us completely
on the wedding day. "A happy wedlock is a long
falling in love." Marriage is very gradual, a fraction
of us at a time. And the real ministers that marry
people are the slow years, the joys and sorrows which
they bring, our children on earth, and the angels they
are transfigured into in heaven, the toils and burdens
borne in company. These are the ministers that
really marry us, and compared with these, the ministers who go through a form of words some day, when
heaven and earth seem to draw near and kiss each
other, are of small account. And the real marriage
service isn't anything printed or said; it is the true
heart service which each yields to the other, year in
and year out, when the bridal wreath has long since
faded, and even the marriage ring is getting sadly
worn. Let this service be performed, and even if the
marriage was a lottery to begin with, this would go
far to redeem it and make it a marriage of coequal
hearts and minds.

When the honeymoon passes away, setting behind
dull mountains, or dipping silently into the stormy sea
of life, the trying hour of married life has come.
Between the parties there are no more illusions. The
feverish desire for possession has gone, and all excit-
ment receded. Then begins, or should, the business

of adaptation. If they find that they do not love one another as they thought they did, they should double their assiduous attentions to one another, and be jealous of everything which tends in the slightest way to separate them. Life is too precious to be thrown away in secret regrets or open differences. And let us say to every one to whom the romance of life has fled, and who are discontented in the slightest degree with their conditions and relations, begin this reconciliation at once. Renew the attentions of earlier days. Draw your hearts closer together. Talk the thing all over. Acknowledge your faults to one another, and determine that henceforth you will be all in all to each other; and my word for it, you shall find in your relation the sweetest joy earth has for you. There is no other way for you to do. If you are happy at home, you must be happy abroad; the man or woman who has settled down upon the conviction that he or she is attached for life to an uncongenial yoke-fellow, and that there is no way of escape, has lost life; there is no effort too costly to make which can restore to its setting upon the bosom the missing pearl.

It is a great thing for two frail natures to live as one for life long. Two harps are not easily kept always in tune, and what shall we expect of two harps each of a thousand strings? What human will or wisdom cannot do, God can do, and his Providence is uniting ever more intimately, those who devoutly try to do the work of life and enjoy its goods together. For them there is in store a respect and affection; a peace and power all unknown in the hey-day of young romance. Experience intertwines their remembrances and hopes in stronger cords, and as they stand at the loom of time, one with the strong warp, the other with the finer woof, the hand of Providence weaves for them a tissue of unfading beauty and imperishable worth.

The marriage institution is the bond of social order, and, if treated with due respect, care, and discretion, greatly enchances individual happiness, and consequently general good. The Spartan law punished those who did not marry; those who married too late; and those who married improperly. A large portion of the evils that have defaced the original organization of the patriarchal age have resulted from the increase of celibacy, often caused by the imaginary refinements of the upper ten thousand. There are other causes that have stripped the marriage institution of its ancient simplicity, and rendered its pure stream turbid in places. Among the Patriarchs, before there were any rakes, parents never interfered, the young pair made the match, and the girl always married the man of her choice, an indispensable pre-requisite to a happy union.

How to secure happiness to married life is the question. Some one would say, "You might as well ask to find the philosopher's stone, or the elixir of prepetual youth, or the Utopia of perfect society!" The prime difficulty in the case is the entire thoughtlessness, the want of consideration, common sense and practical wisdom. Not only young persons contemplating marriage — which includes all between the age of eighteen and thirty-five — but also many married people have a vague notion that happiness comes of itself. They wait for certain dreams of Elysium to be fulfilled by beatific realities. Happiness does not come of its own accord nor by accident It is not a gift, but an attainment. Circumstances may favor, but cannot create it. But advice to those who stand, or mean to stand by the hymeneal altar, falls upon dull ears, and every coupled pair flatter themselves that their experience will be better and more excellent than that of any who have gone before them. They look with amazement at the tameness, and coldness, and diversities, and estrangements, and complainings, and dissatisfactions, which spoil the comfort of so many homes, as at things which cannot, by any possibility fall to their happier lot. But like causes produce like effects, and to avoid the misfortunes of others, we must avoid their mistakes.

Love on both sides, and all things equal in outward circumstances, are not all the requisites of domestic felicity. Human nature is frail and multiform in its passions. The honeymoon gets a dash of vinegar now and then, when least expected. Young people seldom court in their every-day clothes, but they must put them on after marriage. As in other bargains, but few expose defects. They are apt to marry faultless — love is blind — but faults are there and will come out. The fastidious attentions of wooing are like spring flowers, they make pretty nosegays, but poor greens. Miss Darling becomes the plain house

30

wife, and Mr. Allattention the informal husband, not
from a want of esteem, but from the constitution and
nature of man.   If all these changes, and more than
would answer in wooing time, are anticipated, as they
are by some analyzing minds, their happiness will not
be embittered by them when they come.   Bear and
forbear, must be the motto put in practice.

We exhort you, who are a husband, to love your
wife, even as you love yourself.   Give honor to her
as the more delicate vessel; respect the delicacy of
her frame and the delicacy of her mind.   Continue
through life the same attention, the same manly tenderness which in youth gained her affections.   Reflect
that, though her bodily charms are decayed as she is
advanced in age, yet that her mental charms are
increased, and that, though novelty is worn off, yet
that habit and a thousand acts of kindness have
strengthened your mutual friendship.   Devote yourself to her, and, after the hours of business, let the
pleasures which you most highly prize be found in
her society.

We exhort you, who are a wife, to be gentle and
condescending to your husband.   Let the influence
which you possess over him arise from the mildness
of your manners and the discretion of your conduct.
Whilst you are careful to adorn your person with neat
and clean apparel—for no woman can long preserve
affection if she is negligent in this point—be still
more attentive in ornamenting your mind with meekness and peace, with cheerfulness and good humor.
Lighten the cares and chase away the vexations to

which men, in their commerce with the world, are unavoidably exposed, by rendering his house pleasant to your husband. Keep at home, let your employments be domestic and your pleasures domestic.

To both husband and wife we say: " Preserve a strict guard over your tongues, that you never utter anything which is rude, contemptuous, or severe; and over your tempers, that you never appear sullen and morose. Endeavor to be perfect yourselves, but expect not too much from each other. If any offense arise, forgive it; and think not that a human being can be exempt from faults."

In conclusion we would say, that marriage is one of God's first blessings. Although it involves many weighty responsibilities, it is a gem in the crown of life. Man and wife are equally concerned to avoid all offenses of each other in the beginning of their conversation: every little thing can blast an infant blossom, and the breath of the south can shake the little rings of the vine, when first they begin to curl like the locks of a new-weaned boy; but when, by age and consolidation, they stiffen into the hardness of a stem, and have, by the warm embraces of the sun and the kisses of heaven, brought forth their clusters, they can endure the storms of the north and the loud noises of a tempest, and yet never be broken: so are the early unions of an unfixed marriage; watchful and observant, jealous and busy, inquisitive and careful, and apt to take alarm at every unkind word. After the hearts of the man and the wife are endeared and hardened by a mutual confidence and experience,

longer than artifice and pretence can last, there are
a great many remembrances, and some things present
that dash all little unkindnesses in pieces.

--------◦❖◦❖◦--------

The Conjugal Relation.

HAVE you taken upon yourselves the conjugal
relation? Your high and solemn duty is *to make
each other as happy as it is in your power.* The
husband should have, as his great object and rule of
conduct, the happiness of the wife. Of that happiness, the confidence in his affection is the chief
element; and the proofs of this affection on his part,
therefore, constitute his chief duty—an affection that
is not lavish of caresses only, as if these were the
only demonstrations of love, but of that respect which
distinguishes love, as a principle, from that brief passion which assumes, and only assumes, the name—a
respect which consults the judgment, as well as the
wishes, of the object beloved—which considers her
who is worthy of being taken to the heart as worthy
of being admitted to all the counsels of the heart.
He must often forget her, or be useless to the world;
she is most useful to the world by remembering him.
From the tumultuous scenes which agitate many of
his hours, he returns to the calm scene, where peace
awaits him, and happiness is sure to await him;
because she is there waiting, whose smile is peace,

and whose very presence is more than happiness to his heart.

In your joy at the consummation of your wishes, do not forget that your happiness both here and hereafter depends — O how much! — upon each other's influence. An unkind word or look, or an unintentional neglect, sometimes leads to thoughts which ripen into the ruin of body and soul. A spirit of forbearance, patience, and kindness, and a determination to keep the chain of love bright, are likely to develop corresponding qualities, and to make the rough places of life smooth and pleasant. Have you ever reflected seriously that it is in the power of either of you to make the other utterly miserable? And when the storms and trials of life come, for come they will, how much either of you can do to calm, to elevate, to purify, the troubled spirit of the other, and substitute sunshine for the storm?

We cannot look upon marriage in the light in which many seem to regard it — merely as a convenient arrangement in society. To persons of benevolence, intelligence, and refinement, it must be something more — the source of the greatest possible happiness or of the most abject misery — no half-way felicity. You have not had the folly to discard common sense. You have endeavored to study charitably and carefully the peculiarities of each other's habits, dispositions, and principles, and to anticipate somewhat the inconveniencies to which they may lead. And as you are determined to outdo each other in making personal sacrifices, and to live by the spirit of the Savior, you have laid a foundation for happiness, which it is not likely will be shaken by the joys or sorrows, the prosperity or adversity, the riches or poverty, or by the frowns or flattery, of the world. If there is a place on earth to which vice has no entrance — where the gloomy passions have no empire — where pleasure and innocence live constantly together — where cares and labors are delightful — where every pain is forgotten in reciprocal tenderness — where there is an equal enjoyment of the past, the present, and the future — it is the house of a wedded pair, but of a pair who, in wedlock, are lovers still.

The married life, though entered never so well, and with all proper preparation, must be lived well or it will not be useful or happy. Married life will not go itself, or if it does it will not keep the track. It will turn off at every switch and fly off at every turn or impediment. It needs a couple of good conductors who understand the engineering of life. Good watch must be kept for breakers ahead. The fires must be kept up by a constant addition of the fuel of affection. The boilers must be kept full and the machinery in order, and all hands at their posts, else there will be a smashing up, or life will go hobbling or jolting along, wearing and tearing, breaking and bruising, leaving some heads and hearts to get well the best way they can. It requires skill, prudence, and judgment to lead this life well, and these must be tempered with forbearance, charity and integrity.

The young are apt to hang too many garlands about

the married life. This is so as this life is generally
lived. But if it is wisely entered and truthfully lived,
it is more beautiful and happy than any have imagined. It is the true life which God has designed for his
children, replete with joy, delightful, improving, and
satisfactory in the highest possible earthly degree. It
is the hallowed home of virtue, peace, and bliss. It
is the ante-chamber of heaven, the visiting-place of
angels, the communing ground of kindred spirits. Let
all young women who would reap such joys and be
thus blessed and happy, learn to live the true life and
be prepared to weave for their brows the true wife's
perennial crown of goodness.

The experience of an excellent lady may be of
benefit to some reader. She had a very worthy husband, whom she did not love as she should. The
trouble was she had not entirely surrendered herself
to him until after she had been very ill. She says:
"I have been very ill, almost dead. Such care and
devotion as I have had! What a rock my heart
must have been, not to be broken before. Day and
night my husband has watched me himself, sleepless
and tireless; nobody else could do so much. Now I
know what love means. My husband shall never say
again, 'Love me more.' He shall have all there is to
give, and I think my heart is larger than it was a
year ago. What a thrill of joy it gives me when
I catch his eye, or hear his voice or step. My
heart runs to meet him and my eyes overflow with
tears of happiness. How mean and contemptible it
seems to me to desire the attention of other men, or

to wish to go anywhere he cannot accompany me. I despise myself for ever thinking such pleasures desirable. I delight to say, 'My husband, my good, noble, generous, forgiving husband, keep me close to you. That is all the happiness I ask.' I know now that all the trouble was the result of not having a full, complete giving up of myself, when I promised to be a wife—a consecration of true love."

The warmest-hearted and most unselfish women soon learn to accept quiet trust and the loyalty of a loving life as the calmest and happiest condition of marriage; and the men who are sensible enough to rely on the good sense of such wives sail round the gushing adorers both for true affection and comfortable tranquillity.

Just let a young wife remember that her husband necessarily is under a certain amount of bondage all day; that his interests compel him to look pleasant under all circumstances, to offend none, to say no hasty word, and she will see that when he reaches his own fireside he wants, most of all, to have this strain removed, to be at ease; but this he cannot be if he is continually afraid of wounding his wife's sensibilities by forgetting some outward and visible token of his affection for her. Besides, she pays him but a poor compliment in refusing to believe what he does not continually assert, and by fretting for what is unreasonable to desire she deeply wrongs herself, for

"A woman moved is like a fountain troubled,
Muddy, ill-seeming, thick, bereft of beauty."

Make a home; beautify and adorn it; cultivate all

heavenly charms within it; sing sweet songs of love in it; bear your portion of toil, and pain, and sorrow in it; con daily lessons of strength and patience there; shine like a star on the face of the darkest night over it, and tenderly rear the children it shall give you in it. High on a pinnacle, above all earthly grandeur, all gaudy glitter, all fancied ambitions, set the home interests. Feed the mind in it; feed the soul in it; strengthen the love, and charity, and truth, and all holy and good things within it!

When young persons marry, even with the fairest prospects, they should never forget that infirmity is inseparably bound up with their very nature, and that, in bearing one another's burdens, they fulfill one of the highest duties of the union. Love in marriage cannot live nor subsist unless it be mutual; and where love cannot be, there can be left of wedlock nothing but the empty husk of an outside matrimony, as undelightful and unpleasing to God as any other kind of hypocrisy.

We have all seen the trees die in summer time. But the tree with its whispering leaves and swinging limbs, its greenness, its umbrage, where the shadows lie hidden all the day, does not die. First a dimness creeps over its brightness; next a leaf sickens here and there, and pales; then a whole bough feels the palsying touch of coming death, and finally the feeble signs of sickly life, visible here and there, all disappear, and the dead trunk holds out its stripped, stark limbs, a melancholy ruin. Just so does wedded love sometimes die. Wedded love, girdled by the blessings of friends, hallowed by the sanction of God, rosy with present joys, and radiant with future hopes, it dies not all at once. A hasty word casts a shadow upon it, and the shadow darkens with the sharp reply. A little thoughtlessness misconstrued, a little unintentional neglect deemed real, a little word misinterpreted, through such small avenues the devil of discord gains admittance to the heart, and then welcomes all his infernal progeny. The presence of something malicious is felt, but not acknowledged; love becomes reticent, confidence is chilled, and noiselessly but surely the work of separation goes on, until the two are left as isolated as the pyramids— nothing left of the union but the legal form—the dead trunk of the tree, whose branches once tossed in the bright sunlight, and whose sheltering leaves trembled with the music of singing birds now affords no shade for the traveler.

There are two classes of disappointed lovers— those who are disappointed before marriage, and the more unhappy ones who are disappointed after it. To be deprived of a person we love is a happiness in comparison of living with one we hate.

Husband and Wife.

SOME writer asserts that, "a French woman will love her husband if he is either witty or chivalrous; a German woman, if he is constant and faithful; a

Dutch woman if he does not disturb her ease and comfort too much; a Spanish woman, if he wreaks vengeance on those who incur his displeasure; an Italian woman, if he is dreamy and poetical; a Danish woman, if he thinks that her native country is the brightest and happiest on earth; a Russian woman if he despises all westeners as miserable barbarians; an English woman if he succeeds in ingratiating himself with the court and the aristocracy; an American woman, if—he has plenty of money."

In the true wife the husband finds not affection only, but companionship—a companionship with which no other can compare. The family relation gives retirement with solitude, and society without the rough intrusion of the world. It plants in the husband's dwelling a friend who can bear his silence without weariness; who can listen to the details of his interests with sympathy; who can appreciate his repetition of events only important as they are embalmed in the heart. Common friends are linked to us by a slender thread. We must retain them by ministering in some way to their interest or their enjoyment. What a luxury it is for a man to feel that in his home there is a true and affectionate being, in whose presence he may throw off restraint without danger to his dignity; he may confide without fear of treachery; and be sick or unfortunate without being abandoned. If, in the outer world, he grows weary of human selfishness, his heart can safely trust in one whose indulgences overlook his defects.

The treasure of a wife's affection, like the grace of

God, is given, not bought. Gold is power. It can sweep down forests, raise cities, build roads and deck houses. It can collect troops of flatterers, and inspire awe and fear. But alas! wealth can never purchase love. Bonaparte essayed the subjugation of Europe, under the influence of a genius almost inspired; an ambition insatiable, and backed by millions of armed men. He almost succeeded in swaying his sceptre from the Straits of Dover to the Mediterranean; from the Bay of Biscay to the sea of Azoff. On many a bloody field his banner floated triumphantly. But the greatest conquest was the unbought heart of Josephine; his sweetest and most priceless treasure her outraged but unchanged love. If any man has failed to estimate the affection of a true-hearted wife, he will be likely to mark the value in his loss when the heart that loved him is stilled by death.

Is man the child of sorrow, and do afflictions and distresses pour their bitterness into his cup? How are his trials alleviated, his sighs suppressed, his corroding thoughts dissipated, his anxieties and pains relieved, his gloom and depression chased away by her cheerfulness and love. Is he overwhelmed by disappointment, and mortified by reproaches? There is one who can hide her eyes even from his faults, and who, like her Father who is in heaven, can forgive and love "without upbraiding." And when he is sickened by the subtleties and deception of the world; when the acrimony of men has made him acrimonious; when he becomes dissatisfied with himself, and all around him, her pleasant smile, her undissembled tenderness, her artless simplicity, "restore him to himself, and spread serenity and sweetness over his mind."

Nothing is more annoying than that display of affection which some husbands and wives show to each other in society. That familiarity of touch, those half-concealed caresses, those absurd names, that prodigality of endearing epithets, that devoted attention which they flaunt in the face of the public as a kind of challenge to the world at large, to come and admire their happiness, is always noticed and laughed at. Yet to some women this parade of love is the very essence of married happiness, and part of their dearest privileges. They believe themselves admired and envied, when they are ridiculed and scoffed at; and they think their husbands are models for other men to copy, when they are taken as examples for all to avoid. Men who have any real manliness, however, do not give in to this kind of thing; though there are some as effeminate and gushing as women themselves, who like this sloppy effusiveness of love, and carry it on to quite old age, fondling the ancient grandmother with gray hairs as lavishly as they fondled the youthful bride, and seeing no want of harmony in calling a withered old dame of sixty and upwards by the pet names by which they had called her when she was a snip of a girl of eighteen. This public display of familiar affection is never seen among men who pride themselves on making good lovers, as certain men do; those who have reduced the practice of love-making to an art, a science, and know their lesson to a letter. These men are delightful to women, who like nothing so much as being made love to, as well after marriage as before; but men who take matters quietly, and rely on the good sense of their wives to take matters quietly, too, sail round these scientific adorers for both depth and manliness.

Books addressed to young married people abound with advice to the *wife* to control her temper, and never to utter wearisome complaints or vexatious words when the husband comes home fretful or unreasonable from his out-of-door conflicts with the world. Would not the advice be as excellent and appropriate, if the husband were advised to conquer *his* fretfulness, and forbear *his* complaints, in consideration of his wife's ill-health, fatiguing cares, and the thousand disheartening influences of domestic routine? In short, whatsoever can be named as loveliest, best, and most graceful in woman, would likewise be good and graceful in man.

O husbands! think upon your duty. You who have taken a wife from a happy home of kindred hearts and kind companionship, have you given to her all of your time which you could spare, have you endeavored to make amends to her for the loss of these friends? Have you joined with her in her endeavors to open the minds of your children, and give them good moral lessons? Have you strengthened her mind with advice, kindness, and good books? Have you spent your evenings with her in the cultivation of intellectual, moral, or social excellence?

Have you looked upon her as an immortal being, as well as yourself?

There is a picture, bright and beautiful, but nevertheless true, where hearts are united for mutual happiness and mutual improvement; where a kind voice cheers the wife in her hour of trouble, and where the shade of anxiety is chased from the husband's brow as he enters his home; where sickness is soothed by watchful love, and hope and faith burn brightly. For such there is a great reward, both here and hereafter, in their own and their families' spiritual happiness and growth, and in the blessed scenes of the world of spirits.

And, wives! do you also consult the tastes and dispositions of your husbands, and endeavor to give to them high and noble thoughts, lofty aims, and temporal comfort. Be ready to welcome them to their homes, gradually draw their thoughts while with you from business, and lead them to the regions of the beautiful in art and nature, and the true and divine in sentiment. Foster a love of the elegant and refined, and gradually will you see business, literature, and high moral culture blending in "sweet accord."

Before marriage, a young man would feel some delicacy about accepting an invitation to spend an evening in company where his "ladye love" had not been invited. After marriage, is he always as particular? During the days of courtship, his gallantry would demand that he should make himself agreeable to her; after marriage, it often happens that he thinks

more of being agreeable to himself.   How often it
happens that a married man, after having been away
from home the livelong day, during which the wife
has toiled at her duties, goes at evening again to some
place of amusement, and leaves her to toil on alone,
uncheered and unhappy!   How often it happens that
her kindest offices pass unobserved, and unrewarded
even by a smile, and her best efforts are condemned
by the fault-finding husband!   How often it happens,
even when the evening is spent at home, that it is
employed in silent reading, or some other way, that
does not recognize the wife's right to share in the
enjoyments even of the fireside!

Look, ye husbands, for a moment, and remember
what your wife was when you took her, not from
compulsion, but from your own choice; a choice
based, probably, on what you then considered her
superiority to all others.   She was young—perhaps
the idol of her happy home; she was gay and blithe
as the lark, and the brothers and sisters at her
father's fireside cherished her as an object of endearment.   Yet she left all to join her destiny with yours,
to make your home happy, and to do all that woman's
ingenuity could devise to meet your wishes and to
lighten the burdens which might press upon you.

The good wife!   How much of this world's happiness and prosperity is contained in the compass of
these short words!   Her influence is immense.   The
power of a wife, for good or for evil, is altogether
irresistible.   Home must be the seat of happiness, or
it must be forever unknown.   A good wife is to a

man wisdom, and courage, and strength, and hope, and endurance. A bad one is confusion, weakness, discomfiture, despair. No condition is hopeless when the wife possesses firmness, decision, energy, economy. There is no outward prosperity which can counteract indolence, folly, and extravagance at home. No spirit can long resist bad domestic influences. Man is strong, but his heart is not adamant. He delights in enterprise and action, but to sustain him he needs a tranquil mind and a whole heart. He expends his whole moral force in the conflicts of the world. His feelings are daily lacerated to the utmost point of endurance by perpetual collision, irritation, and disappointment.

Let woman know, then, that she ministers at the very fountain of life and happiness. It is her hand that lades out with overflowing cup its soul-refreshing waters, or casts in the branch of bitterness which makes them poison and death. Her ardent spirit breathes the breath of life into all enterprise. Her patience and constancy are mainly instrumental· in carrying forward to completion the best human designs. Her more delicate moral sensibility is the unseen power which is ever at work to purify and refine society. And the nearest glimpse of heaven that mortals ever get on earth is that domestic circle which her hands have trained to intelligence, virtue, and love, which her gentle influence pervades, and of which her radiant presence is the centre and the sun.

Watching those on the sidewalk on the way to

labor, we thought we could read a great deal of the homelife of each in the passing glance we gave as they went hurrying by. Here was one whose clothing was ragged and neglected, and on his face a hard, dissatisfied expression. It was easy to see there was no hope in his heart; that he went to his task as if it were a penalty imposed for crime, and that no pleasant and loving home cheered him at the evening and lifted from his heart the clouds that darkened his life. It is a terrible thing when the home of the poor lacks love—the only agency which can lighten its burdens and make it hopeful and happy.

Beside him walks another—no better, but much cleanlier clad, and the broad patches of his blue overalls are cleanly put on and not fringed with ragged edges. He has a home, you can see that at once, and, humble as it may be, there is a woman who is his confidante as well as his *wife*, and, *together*, they plan how to use their little means and increase their little store of comforts. They have ambition, and ambition to improve one's condition never fails to give force to character and something of dignity and worth of life.

Last of all, though this consideration be not the least of all, let it be remembered that the husband is bound by the divine law to treat his wife as an immortal being, and, therefore, to have regard to her moral and spiritual welfare. Can any man have a just sense of the truth that the partner of his heart, the sharer of his fortunes, whose earthly destiny is so closely linked with his own, is, like himself, an immortal spirit; that, after the scenes of time shall all have vanished from her view like a gorgeous dream, she must enter upon those brighter ones that shall be forever expanding in beatific splendor, or else, if unprepared for them, must dwell in those gloomy realms which our Savior describes as "the outer darkness" of banishment from God and happiness, and yet cherish no lively interest in her education for the society of heaven? In that remarkable hour that witnessed the formation of the marriage union, the era of separation was anticipated by the solemn vow which his lips then uttered, that he would cherish the object of his choice as "the wife of his covenant" in wedded love "till death should them part."

Joy.

Joy is a prize unbought, and is freest, purest in its flow when it comes unsought. No getting into heaven as a place will compass it. You must carry it with you, else it is not there. You must have it in you as the music of a well-ordered soul, the fire of a holy purpose. An unchanging state of joy is not possible on earth as it now is, because evil and error are here. The soul must have its midnight hour as well as its sunlight seasons of joy and gladness. Still the mercy of the Lord is shown as much in the night as in the day. It is only in the night that we can see the stars. The noblest spirits, however, are those which turn to heaven, not in the hour of sorrow, but in that of joy; like the lark, they wait for the clouds to disperse, that they may soar up into their native element.

He who selfishly hoards his joys, thinking thus to increase them, is like a man who looks at his granary, and says, "Not only will I protect my grain from mice and birds, but neither the ground nor the mill shall have it." And so, in the spring, he walks around his little pit of corn, and exclaims, "How wasteful are my neighbors, throwing away whole handfuls of grain!" But autumn comes; and, while he has only his few poor bushels, their fields are yellow with an abundant harvest. "There is that that scattereth and yet increaseth."

Wordly joy is like the songs which peasants sing, full of melodies and sweet airs. Christian joy has its sweet airs too; but they are augmented to harmonies, so that he who has it goes to heaven, not to the voice of a single flute, but to that of a whole band of instruments, discoursing wondrous music. Those who joy in wealth grow avaricious; those who joy in their friends too often lose nobility of spirit; those who joy in sensuousness lose dignity of character; those who joy in literature ofttimes become pedantic; but those who joy in liberty — *i. e.*, that all should do as they would be done by — possess the happiest of joys. It is a solid joy no one can barter away. Exceedingly few possess it.

He who to the best of his power has secured the

final stake, has a perennial fountain of joy within him. He is satisfied from himself. They, his reverse, borrow all from without. Joy wholly from without is false, precarious, and short. From without it may be gathered; but, like gathered flowers, though fair and sweet for a season. it must soon wither and become offensive. Joy from within is like smelling the rose on the tree. It is more sweet and fair—it is lasting; and, we must add, immortal. Happy are the moments when sorrow forgets its cares, and misery its misfortunes; when peace and gladness spring up upon the radiant wings of hope, and the light of contentment dawns once more upon the disconsolate, unfortunate, and unhappy heart,--

"The past unsighed for, and the future sure."

There is in this world continual interchange of pleasing and greeting accidents, still keeping their succession of times, and overtaking each other in their several courses; no picture can be all drawn of the brightest colors, nor a harmony consorted only of trebles; shadows are needful in expressing of proportions, and the bass is a principle part in perfect music; the condition here allows no unmeddled joy; our whole life is temperate between sweet and sour, and we must all look for a mixture of both: the wise so wish: better that they still think of worse, accepting the one if it come with liking, and bearing the other without impatience, being so much masters of each other's fortunes, that neither shall work them to excess. The dwarf grows not on the highest hill, the tall man loses not his height in the lowest valley; and as a base mind, though most at ease, will be dejected, so a resolute virtue in the deepest distress is most impregnable.

There are joys which long to be ours. God sends ten thousand truths, which come about us like birds seeking inlet; but we are shut up to them, and so they bring us nothing, but sit and sing awhile upon the roof and then fly away.

Beauty.

"Beauty! thou pretty plaything! dear deceit!
That steals so softly o'er the stripling's heart,
And gives it a new pulse unknown before."

WE doubt not that God is a lover of beauty. He fashioned the worlds in beauty, when there was no eye to behold them but His own. All along the wild old forest He has carved the forms of beauty. Every cliff, and mountain, and tree is a statue of beauty. Every leaf, and stem, and vine, and flower is a form of beauty. Every hill, and dale, and landscape is a picture of beauty. Every cloud, and mist-wreath, and vapor-veil is a shadowy reflection of beauty. Every diamond, and rock, and pebbly beach is a mine of beauty. Every sun, and planet, and star is a blazing face of beauty. All along the aisles of earth, all over the arches of heaven, all through the expanses of the universe, are scattered in rich and infinite profusion the life-gems of beauty. All this great realm of dazzling and bewildering beauty was made by God. Shall we say, then, He is not a lover of beauty?

There is beauty in the songsters of the air. The symmetry of their bodies, the wing so light and expert in fanning the breeze, the graceful neck and head, their tiny feet and legs, all so well fitted for their native element, and more than this, their sweet notes that awaken delight in every heart that loves to rejoice. Who can range the sunny fields and shady forests on a bright summer's day, and listen to the melody of a thousand voices chanting their Maker's praise, and not feel the soul melt with joy and gratitude for such refreshing scenes? The universe is its temple; and those men who are alive to it cannot lift their eyes without feeling themselves encompassed with it on every side. Now this beauty is so precious, the enjoyments it gives are so refined and pure, so congenial with our tenderest and noblest feelings, and so akin to worship, that it is painful to think of the multitude of men as living in the midst of it, and living almost as blind to it as if, instead of this fair earth and glorious sky, they were tenants of a dungeon. An infinite joy is lost to the world by the want of culture of this spiritual endowment.

The highest style of beauty to be found in nature pertains to the human form, as animated and lighted up by the intelligence within. It is the expression of the soul that constitutes this superior beauty. It is that which looks out at the eye, which sits in calm majesty on the brow, lurks on the lip, smiles on the cheek, is set forth in the chiseled lines and features of the countenance, in the general contour of figure and form, in the movement, and gesture, and tone; it is this looking out of the invisible spirit that dwells within, this manifestation of the higher nature, that we admire and love; this constitutes to us the beauty of our species. Hence it is that certain features, not in themselves particularly attractive, wanting, it may be, in certain regularity of outline, or in certain delicacy and softness, are still invested in a peculiar charm and radiance of beauty from their peculiar expressiveness and animation. The light of genius, the superior glow of sympathy, and a noble heart, play upon those plain, and it may be, homely features, and light them up with a brilliant and regal beauty. Those, as every artist knows, are the most difficult to portray. The expression changes with the instant. Beauty flashes, and is gone, or gives place to a still higher beauty, as the light that plays in fitful corruscations along the Northern sky, coming and going, but never still.

We would now dwell upon the beauty of spirit, soul, mind, heart, life. There is a beauty which perishes not. It is such as the angels wear. It forms the washed white robes of the saints. It wreathes the countenance of every doer of good. It adorns every *honest* face. It shines in the *virtuous* life. It molds the hands of *charity*. It sweetens the voice of sympathy. It sparkles on the brow of wisdom. It flashes in the eye of love. It breathes in the spirit of piety. It is the beauty of the heaven of heavens.

It is that which may grow by the hand of culture in every human soul. It is the flower of the spirit which blossoms on the tree of life. Every soul may plant and nurture it in its own garden, in its own Eden. This is the capacity for beauty that God has given to the human soul, and this the beauty placed within the reach of us all. We may all be beautiful. Though our forms may be uncomely and our features not the prettiest, our spirits may be beautiful. And this inward beauty always shines through. A beautiful heart will flash out in the eye. A lovely soul will glow in the face. A sweet spirit will tune the voice, wreathe the countenance in charms. Oh, there is a power in interior beauty that melts the hardest heart!

Woman, by common consent, we regard as the most perfect type of beauty on earth. To her we ascribe the highest charms belonging to this wonderful element so profusely mingled in all God's works. Her form is molded and finished in exquisite delicacy of perfection. The earth gives us no form more perfect, no features more symmetrical, no style more chaste, no movements more graceful, no finish more complete; so that our artists ever have and ever will regard the woman-form of humanity as the most perfect earthly type of beauty. This form is most perfect and symmetrical in the youth of womanhood; so that youthful woman is earth's queen of beauty. This is true, not only by the common consent of mankind, but also by the strictest rules of scientific criticism.

This being an admitted fact, woman, and especially youthful woman, is laid under strong obligations and exposed to great temptations.   Beauty has wonderful charms—a charming gift of pleasure.   Beauty will not only win for her admiring eyes, but it will win her favor; it will draw *hearts* toward her; it will awaken tender and agreeable feelings in her behalf; it will disarm the stranger of the peculiar prejudices he often has toward those he knows not; it will pave the way to esteem; it will weave the links to friendship's chain; it will throw an air of agreeableness into the manners of all who approach her.   All this her beauty will do for her before she puts forth a single effort of her own to win the esteem and love of her fellows.

Socrates called beauty a short-lived tyranny; Plato, a privilege of nature; Theophrastus, a silent cheat; Theocritus, a delightful prejudice; Cameades, a solitary kingdom; Domitian said, that nothing was more grateful; Aristotle affirmed, that beauty was better than all the letters of recommendation in the world; Homer, that it was a glorious gift of nature; and Ovid calls it a favor bestowed by the gods.   But, as regards the elements of beauty in women, it is not too much to say that no woman can be beautiful by force of features alone; there must be as well sweetness and beauty of soul.   Beauty has been called "the power and aims of woman."   Diogenes called it "woman's most forcible letter of recommendation." Cameades represented it, "a queen without soldiers;" and Theocritus says it is "a serpent covered with flowers;" while a modern author defines it "a bait

that as often catches the fisher as the fish." Nearly
all the old philosophers denounced and ridiculed
beauty as evanescent, worthless and mischievous;
but, alas! while they preached against it they were
none the less its slaves. None of them were able to
withstand "the sly, smooth witchcraft of a fair young
face." A really beautiful woman is a natural queen
in the universe of love, where all hearts pay a glad
tribute to her reign.

Nothing is all dark. There cannot be a picture
without its bright spots; and the steady contemplation of what is bright in others, has a reflex influence
upon the beholder. It reproduces what it reflects.
Nay, it seems to leave an impress even upon the
countenance. The feature, from having a dark, sin-
ister aspect, becomes open, serene, and sunny. A
countenance so impressed, has neither the vacant
stare of the idiot, nor the crafty, penetrating look of
the basilisk, but the clear placid aspect of truth and
goodness. The woman who has such a face is beautiful. She has a beauty which changes not with the
features, which fades not with years. It is beauty of
expression. It is the only kind of beauty which can
be relied upon for a permanent influence with the
other sex. The violet will soon cease to smile.
Flowers must fade. The love that has nothing but
beauty to sustain it soon withers away. A pretty
woman pleases the eye; a good woman, the heart.
The one is a jewel, the other a treasure. Invincible
fidelity, good humor, and complacency of temper,
outlive all the charms of a fine face, and make the

decay of it invisible. That is true beauty which has not only a substance, but a spirit; a beauty that we must intimately know to justly appreciate.

Beauty has been not unaptly, though perhaps rather vulgarly, defined as "all in the eye," since it addresses itself solely to that organ, and is intrinsically of little value. From this ephemeral flower spring many of the ingredients of matrimonial unhappiness. It is a dangerous gift for both its possessor and its admirer. If its possession, as is often the case, turns the head, while its loss sours the temper, if the long regret of its decay outweighs the fleeting pleasure of its bloom, the plain should pity rather than envy the handsome. Beauty of countenance, which, being the light of the soul shining through the face, is independent of features or complexion, is the most attractive as well as the most enduring charm. Nothing but talent and amiability can bestow it, no statue or picture can rival it, and time itself cannot destroy it.

Man, however, is not the highest type of beauty; for in him, as in all things on earth, is mingled along with the beauty much that is deformed — with the excellence much imperfection. We can conceive forms superior to his — faces radiant with a beauty that sin has never darkened, nor passion nor sorrow dimmed. We can conceive forms of beauty more perfect, purer, brighter, loftier than anything that human eyes have ever seen. Imagination fashions these conceptions, and art produces them. This, the poet, the painter, the sculptor, the architect, the orator, each in his own way, is ever striving to do, to present, under sensible forms, the ideal of a more perfect loveliness and excellence than the actual world affords. This, however, cannot be done successfully, as perfection of beauty dwells alone with God.

Music.

> "When griping grief the heart doth wound,
> And doleful dumps the mind oppress,
> Then music, with her silver sound,
> With speedy help doth lend redress."

OH, the rapturous charm of music! What power it has to soften, melt, enchain in its spirit-chords of subduing harmony! Truly there is power in music; an almost omnipotent power. It will tyrannize over the soul. It will force it to bow down and worship, it will wring adoration from it, and compel the heart to yield its treasures of love. Every emotion, from the most reverent devotion to the wildest gushes of frolicsome joy it holds subject to its imperative will. It calls the religious devotee to worship, the patriot to his country's altar, the philanthropist to his generous work, the freeman to the temple of liberty, the friend to the altar of friendship, the lover to the side of his beloved. It elevates, empowers, and strengthens them all. The human soul is a mighty harp, and all its strings vibrate to the gush of music.

Who does not know the softening power of music, especially the music of the human voice? It is like the

angel-whisperings of kind words in the hour of
trouble. Who can be angry when the voice of love
speaks in song? Who hears the harsh voice of selfishness, and brutalizing passion, when music gathers
up her pearly love-notes to salute the ear with a stray
song of paradise? Sing to the wicked man, sing to
the disconsolate, sing to the sufferer, sing to the old,
and sing to the children, for music will inspire them
all.

The human voice is the most perfect musical instrument ever made; and well it might be, for it had the
most skillful maker. The voice should be cultivated
to sing the tones of love to man and God. Around
the fireside, in the social circle, it should sing the
voice of love, and at the altar of God it should pour
forth melodious praise.

How sweet does it make the worship of God to
have the reverent emotions poured out in song!
How early should children he taught to sing; for
what is sweeter than the songs of innocent childhood,
so refining, so refreshing, so suggestive of heaven?
Music sweetens the cup of bitterness, softens the
hand of want, lightens the burden of life, makes the
heart courageous, and the soul cheerfully devout.
Into the soul of childhood and youth it pours a tide
of redeeming influence. Its first and direct effect is
to mentalize the musical performer; not to give him
knowledge, nor more wisdom in the practical, business affairs of life, but to stir his mental being to
activity, to awaken strong emotions, to move among
the powers within as a common electrifier, touching

here with tenderness, there with energy, now with holy aspiration, and anon with the inspiring thrill of beauty. It breathes like a miracle of inspiration through the soul, to elevate, refine, and spiritualize. No lethargy can exist in the soul that is pouring forth a tide of music numbers. Its very recesses are all astir. Everything within becomes active; the perceptions acute, the affections warm, the moral sensibilities quick and sensitive. When we think how much the world wants awakening, we can think of no power better calculated to do it than that which dwells in the mysterious melodies of music. Let every body become musicians and surely they would become *living* souls.

Besides music being powerful, universal, the voice of love, and the type of the infinite, it is *venerable for its age.* As it is the voice of God's love, we know not but it is co-existent with His being. It is reasonable to suppose that its swelling numbers have rolled and made heaven vocal with its strains of praise since creation dawned. But the first account of it on record was at the laying of the foundations of the earth, when the "morning stars," delighted with the promise of a new planet, "sang together, and all the sons of God shouted for joy." As soon as the earth was made, its rocky spires thrown up, its forest harps strung, its ocean organs tuned, it raised its everlasting anthem to swell the chorus of the skies.

Every song soothes and uplifts. It is just possible that at times a song is as good as a prayer. Indeed a song of the pure kind recognized in Scripture, is

akin to a petition, which it is also in the spirit of
thanksgiving. The "sweet singer of Israel" wedded
his sincerest prayers to melody, and wafted them
upward on the night air from his throbbing heart. In
the soul that has been touched and made tender by
the fingers of pain, music finds a place where it
may murmur its sweetest chords.

Music is healthful. There is no better cure for *bad
humors*, and no medicine more pleasant to take. We
cannot join those who lament that the piano is heard
where once the monotone of the spinning-wheel, and
the click of the shuttle, were the only instrumental
performances. It is a matter of rejoicing rather that
muscles of iron and fingers of steel, driven by the
tireless elements, now perform the laborious work of
cloth manufacture and give leisure to cultivate
refined tastes in the household. Music is to the ear
and to the intellect what strawberries, peaches, and
other luscious fruits, are to the taste. Who regrets
that the forests have been cleared, the walls and
fences built, the grain crops made sufficiently easy of
cultivation, to allow the addition of the fruit yard and
garden for the enjoyment of the cultivator? One
of the greatest attractions for old and young, when
visiting our cities, is the music that may be heard here.
Why should the farmer's household not be as cheerful, as full of pleasure. as that of the merchant or the
professional man? We know of nothing more genial
and heart-warming than to hear the whole family
joining in a hymn or song. They will love each other
and their home better for it. Songs learned in

childhood are like birds nestling in the bosom; their notes will be heard and loved in after years. The hymn sung by a mother to her little boy may in after days be a voice that will recall him from ruin.

No family can afford to do without music. It is a luxury and an economy; an alleviator of sorrow, and a spring of enjoyment; a protection against vice and an incitement to virtue. When rightly used, its effects, physical, intellectual and moral, are good, very good, and only good. Make home attractive; music affords a means of doing this. Contribute kindly feeling, love. Music will help in this work. Keep out angry feeling. "Music hath charms to soothe the savage breast." Show us the family where good music is cultivated, where the parents and children are accustomed often to mingle their voices together in song, and we will show you one where peace, harmony and love prevail, and where the great vices have no abiding place.

One morning the sweet voice of a woman was heard singing a ballad in one of the tenement house districts of the Garden City. The effect of it was almost magical. Not only did children swarm out of their dingy homes and surround the singer, but the stoops were crowded by adults, and old heads leaned out of windows for several blocks on either side. Faces brightened everywhere. The blacksmith ceased his din and stood with arms akimbo on the sidewalk. The poor, sick widow in a near tenement listened and forgot her sorrow and pain; the broad-faced wife whose stolid countenance, hardened by

want and contact with vice, paused from her employ
ment, and as she listened something touched her
heart, her better nature was stirred, and beating time
to the simple melody, wished she had a penny to give
the songster. The hod-carriers halted; the well-
dressed pedestrian, on whose face, when he saw the
crowd gathering, there was at first a look of disdain,
as if he would say, "No hand-organ music for me, if
you please," at last stood still and blushed, as the
beauty of the song stirred his inmost heart. And
when the music ceased, the listeners turned again to
their employments, as if refreshed in spirits and
quickened to contented thoughts of the work-a-day
world.

Music means not merely tunes adapted to particular
emotions — a set of notes, a warbling voice, a strain
of "melting sweetness" — O! no: music can be acted
as well as sung. The heart may make music when
the lips are dumb. A simple word may be full of
music, and stir the pulses to new and better emotions,
the soul to higher joys! The harmony of a well
ordered life is most graceful music; the tender cares
and caresses of a wife; her fond solicitude to make
home all it should be; the kindred gentleness and
affection of the husband; the quiet and ready obedience of the children — all these, do they not make a
household of music, that in the land beyond shall be
chanted by choirs of angels, when at last such families
meet, unbroken bands, in heaven?

· If only sound were music, how many thousands
would be denied that delightful solace! Some there

are who cannot sing—and yet whose natures are finest harps, from which an unheard melody (unheard by mortal ears) is continually ascending. Some there are who cannot even speak, nor hear, and yet their sympathies, their nice comprehensions, are beautiful with the subtle instinct of melody. O! tell us where music is not! Now we hear it in the pensive sound of the autumnal winds—we see it in the sparkling flow of the bright river; we hear it, as it were, in the morning stars; and just now a sweet voice uttered words of music. It is in all the elements; the flame has a cheerful hum of its own, and the crackling sparks beat time. The water ripples with music; the air is always whispering melody, and the bountiful earth ceases never its songs of praise. The trickling rain-drops sing as they fall; the crowded leaves answer to the pipes of the birds; the sun sets the day to singing, and the Almighty has made man to sing songs of praise to Him throughout all eternity.

But the world needs music—the touching domestic song that tells in few words the loves, the trials, or the blisses of life—the more sacred music that leads the soul to communion with God—it needs music—its poor cry aloud for music; they are tired of the inharmonious din of toil, and a few sweet notes bring with them hours of pleasure to the weary and world-forsaken.

𝕳onor.

To BE ambitious of true honor, of the true glory
and perfection of our natures, is the very principle and
incentive of virtue; but to be ambitious of titles, of
place, of ceremonial respects and civil pageantry, is
as vain and little as the things we court.

True honor, as defined by Cicero, is the concur-
rent approbation of good men; those only being fit
to give true praise who are themselves praiseworthy.
Anciently the Romans worshiped virtue and honor as
gods; they built two temples, which were so seated
that none could enter the temple of honor without
passing through the temple of virtue.

The way to be truly honored is to be illustriously
good.   Maximilian, the German emperor, replied to
one who desired his letters patent to ennoble him,
saying, "I am able to make you rich; but virtue must
make you noble."   Who would not desire the honor
that Agesilaus, king of Sparta, had, who was fined by
the Sphori for having stolen away all the hearts of the
people to himself alone?   Of whom it is said that he
ruled his country by obeying it.   It is with glory as
with beauty, for as a single fine lineament cannot
make a fine face, neither can a single good quality
render a man accomplished; but a concurrence of
many fine features and good qualities make true
beauty and true honor.

The Athenians raised a noble statue to the memory

of Æsop, and placed a slave on a pedestal, that men might know the way to honor was open to all. The man of honor is internal, the person of honor an external; the one a real, the other a fictitious character. A person of honor may be a profane libertine, penurious, proud, may insult his inferiors, and defraud his creditors; but it is impossible for a man of honor to be guilty of any of these.

Among the ancient Greeks and Romans, in their best days, honor was more sought after than wealth. Times are changed. *Now*, wealth is the surest passport to honor; and respectability is endangered by poverty. "Rome, was Rome no more" when the imperial purple had become an article of traffic, and when gold could purchase with ease the honors that patriotism and valor could once secure only with difficulty.

There is no true glory, no true greatness, without virtue; without which we do but abuse all the good things we have, whether they be great or little, false or real. Riches make us either covetous or prodigal; fine palaces make us despise the poor and poverty; a great number of domestics flatter human pride, which uses them like slaves; valor oftentimes turns brutal and unjust; and a high pedigree makes a man take up with the virtues of his ancestors, without endeavoring to acquire any himself.

It is a fatal and delusive ambition which allures many to the pursuit of honors *as such*, or as accessions to some greater object in view. The substance is dropped to catch the shade, and the much-coveted distinctions, in nine cases out of ten, prove to be mere airy phantasms and gilded mists. Real honor and real esteem are not difficult to be obtained in the world, but they are best won by actual worth and merit, rather than by art and intrigue, which run a long and ruinous race, and seldom seize upon the prize at last. Seek not to be honored in any way save in thine own bosom, within thyself.

> "Honor and shame from no condition rise :
> Act well your part, there all the honor lies."

Genius and Talent.

GENIUS is of the soul, talent of the understanding; genius is warm, talent is passionless. Without genius there is no intuition, no inspiration; without talent, no execution. Genius is interior, talent exterior; hence genius is productive, talent accumulative. Genius invents, talent accomplishes. Genius gives the substance, talent works it up under the eye, or rather under the feeling, of genius.

Genius is that quality or character of the mind which is inventive, or generates; which gives to the world new ideas in science, art, literature, morals, or religion, which recognizes no set rules or principles, but is a law unto itself, and rejoices in its own originality; which admitting of a direction, never follows the old beaten track, but strikes out for a new course;

which has no fears of public opinion, nor leans upon public favor—always leads but never follows, which admits no truth unless convinced by experiment, reflection, or investigation, and never bows to the *ipse dixit* of any man, or society, or creed.

Talent is that power or capacity of mind which reasons rapidly from cause to effect; which sees through a thing at a glance, and comprehends the rules and principles upon which it works; which can take in knowledge without laborious mental study, and needs no labored illustrations to impress a principle or a fact, no matter how abstruse, hidden, complex, or intricate. Differing from genius by following rules and principles, but capable of comprehending the works of genius—imitating with ease, and thereby claiming a certain kind of originality, talent is the able, comprehensive agent; while genius is the master director.

Genius is emotional, talent intellectual; hence genius is creative, and talent instrumental. Genius has insight, talent only outsight. Genius is always calm, reserved, self-centered; talent is often bustling, officious, confident. Genius is rather inward, creative, and angelic; talent, outward, practical, and worldly. Genius disdains and defies imitation; talent is often the result of universal imitation in respect to everything that may contribute to the desired excellence. Genius has quick and strong sympathies, and is sometimes given to reverie and vision; talent is cool and wise, and seldom loses sight of common sense. Genius is born for a particular purpose, in which it

surpasses; talent is versatile, and may make a respectable figure at almost anything. Genius gives the
impulse and aim as well as the illumination; talent
the means and implements. Genius, in short, is the
central, finer essence of the mind, the self-lighted fire,
the intuitional gift. Talent gathers and shapes and
applies what genius forges. Genius is often entirely
right, and is never wholly wrong; talent is never
wholly right. Genius avails itself of all the capabili-
ties of talent, appropriates to itself what suits and
helps it. Talent can appropriate to itself nothing,
for it has not the inward heat that can fuse all material
and assimilate all food to convert it into blood; this
only genius can do. Goethe was a man of genius,
and at the same time of immense and varied talents;
and no contemporary profited so much as he did by
all the knowledges, discoveries and accumulations
made by others.

Talent is full of thoughts; but genius full of
thought. Genius makes its observations in short
hand; talent writes them out at length. Talent is a
very common family trait, genius belongs rather to
individuals; just as you find one giant or one dwarf
in a family, but rarely a whole brood of either. Men
of genius are often dull and inert in society, as the
blazing meteor when it descends to earth is only a
stone. For full success the two, genius and talent,
should co-exist in one mind in balanced proportions,
as they did in Goethe's, so that they can play
smoothly together in effective combination. The
work of the world, even the higher ranges, being

done by talent, talent, backed by industry, is sure to achieve outward success. Commonplace is the smooth road on which are borne the freights that supply the daily needs of life; but genius, as the originator of all appliances and aids and motions and improvements, is the parent of what is to-day common—of all that talent has turned to practical account.

It is one of the mysteries of our life that genius, that noblest gift of God to man, is nourished by poverty. Its greatest works have been achieved by the sorrowing ones of the world in tears and despair. Not in the brilliant saloon, furnished with every comfort and elegance; not in the library well fitted, softly carpeted, and looking out upon a smooth, green lawn, or a broad expanse of scenery; not in ease and competence, is genius born and nurtured; more frequently in adversity and destitution, amidst the harassing cares of a straitened household, in bare and fireless garrets, with the noise of squalid children, in the midst of the turbulence of domestic contentions, and in the deep gloom of uncheered despair, is genius born and reared. This is its birth-place; and in scenes like these, unpropitious, repulsive, wretched, have men labored, studied and trained themselves, until they have at last emanated out of the gloom of that obscurity the shining lights of their times, become the companions of kings, the guides and teachers of their kind, and exercised an influence upon the thought of the world amounting to a species of intellectual legislation.

Genius involves a more than usual susceptibility to divine promptings, a delicacy in spiritual speculation, a quick obedience to the invisible helmsman; and these high superiorities imply fineness and fullness of organization. "The man of genius is subject," says Joubert, "to transport, or rather rapture, of mind." In this exalted state he has glimpses of truth, beauties, principles, laws, that are new revelations, and bring additions to human power. Goethe might have been thinking of Kepler when he said, "Genius is that power of man which by thought and action gives laws and rules;" and Coleridge of Milton, when he wrote, "The ultimate end of genius is ideal;" and Hegel may have had Michael Angelo in his mind when, in one of his chapters on the plastic arts, he affirms that "Talent cannot do its part fully without the animation, the besouling of genius."

Great powers and natural gifts do not bring privileges to their possessors, so much as they bring duties. A contemporary, in dilating on genius, thus sagely remarks: "The talents granted to a single individual do not benefit himself alone, but are gifts to the world; every one shares them, for every one suffers or benefits by his actions. Genius is a light-house, meant to give light from afar; the man who bears it is but the rock upon which the light-house is built."

Hath God given you genius and learning? It was not that you might amuse or deck yourself with it and kindle a blaze which should only serve to attract and dazzle the eyes of men. It was intended to be the means of leading both yourself and them to the

Father of light. And it will be your duty, according to the peculiar turn of that genius and capacity, either to endeavor to promote and adorn human life, or, by a more direct application of it to divine subjects, to plead the cause of religion, to defend its truths, to enforce and recommend its practice, to deter men from courses which would be dishonorable to God and fatal to themselves, and to try the utmosts efforts of all the solemnity and tenderness with which you can clothe your addresses, to lead them into the paths of virtue and happiness.

Thinkers.

THINKERS rise upon us like new stars—a few in a century. The multitude run after them, and, like Lazarus, eat the crumbs that fall from their table. They follow them by instinct; they adopt their theories and accept their thoughts at sight, Calvin rose and thought. What a multitude swallowed his hard, rocky thoughts, as though they were digestible mental food! Wesley rose, and another multitude followed him, much as Mohammedans followed their prophet. Swedenborg rose in the North, and straightway a cloud of witnesses appeared about him to testify to all he wrote. Davis came above the horizon, and lo! an army follows in his train. So it is; men swallow whole what they eat, wheat or chaff, meat or bone, nut or shell. They do not masticate their mental food; they do not examine the facts they learn; they do not digest their knowledge. If they did we should not have schools of men, sects, parties, but one grand lyceum of individual thinkers; every one making his own use of his knowledge, forming his own conclusions, and working out his own kind and degree of culture. We read enough to have a generation of philosophers.

Dull thinkers are always led by sharp ones. The keen intellect cuts its way smoothly, gracefully, rapidly; the dull one wears its life out against the simplest problems. To perceive accurately and to think correctly, is the aim of all mental training. Heart and conscience are more than the mere intellect. Yet we cannot tell how much the clear, clean-cut thought, the intellectual vision, sharp and true, may aid even these. Some say that a man never feels till he sees, and when the object disappears, the feeling ceases. So we cannot exaggerate the importance of clear, correct thinking. We should eat, drink, sleep, walk, exercise body and mind, to this end. Just so far as we fail, we make dolts and idiots of ourselves. We cast away our natural armor and defense. The designing make us dupes; we are overreached by the crafty, and trodden under foot by the strong.

Undigested learning is as oppressive as undigested food; and as in the dyspeptic patient, the appetite for food often grows with the inability to digest it, so in the unthinking patient, an overweening desire to know often accompanies the inability to know to any purpose. Thought is to the brain what gastric juice is to the stomach—a solvent to reduce whatever is received to a condition in which all that is wholesome and nutritive may be appropriated, and that alone. To learn merely for the sake of learning, is like eating merely for the taste of the food. The mind will wax fat and unwieldly, like the body of the gormand. The stomach is to the frame what memory is to the mind; and it is as unwise to cultivate the memory at the expense of the mind as it would be to enlarge the capacity of the stomach by eating more food than the wants of the frame require, or food that it could not appropriate. To learn in order to become wise makes the mind active and powerful, like the body of one who is temperate and judicious in meat and drink. Learning is healthfully digested by the mind when it reflects upon what is learned, classifies and arranges facts and circumstances, considers the relations of one to another, and places what is taken into the mind at different times in relation to the same subjects under their appropriate heads; so that the various stores are not heterogeneously piled up, but laid away in order, and may be referred to with ease when wanted. If a person's daily employments are such as demand a constant exercise of the thoughts, all the leisure should not be devoted to reading, but a part reserved for reflecting upon and arranging in the mind what is read. The manner of reading is much more important than the quantity. To hurry through many books, retaining only a confused knowledge of their contents, is but a poor exercise of the brain; it is far better to read with care a few well selected volumes.

Some of the great advantages of thinking are the following: First, it transfers and conveys the sentiments of others to ourselves, so as to make them properly our own. Secondly, it enables us to distinguish truth from error, and to reject what is wrong after we have seen, read, or heard anything. Thirdly, by this we fix in our memory only what we best approve of, without loading it with all that we read. Lastly, by properly meditating on what comes within the view of our minds, we may improve upon the sentiments or inventions of others, and thereby acquire great reputation, and perhaps emolument, from their labors.

All mental superiority originates in habits of thinking. A child, indeed, like a machine, may be made to perform certain functions by external means; but it is only when he begins to think that he rises to the dignity of a rational being. It is not reading, but thinking, that gives you a possession of knowledge. A person may see, hear, read and learn whatever he pleases and as much as he pleases; but he will know very little, if anything, of it, beyond that which he has thought over and made the property of his mind. Take away thought from the life of man and what remains? You may glean knowledge by reading, but you must separate the chaff from the wheat by thinking.

At every action and enterprise, ask yourself this question: What will the consequence of this be to me? Am I not likely to repent of it? I shall be dead in a little time, and then all is over with me.

Whatever thou takest in hand, remember the end, and thou shalt never do amiss. Think before you speak, and consider before you promise. Take time to deliberate and advise; but lose no time in executing your resolutions. Do nothing to-day that you will repent of to-morrow. In the morning think of what you have to do, and at night ask yourself what you have done. Seek not out the thoughts that are too hard for you. Strive not in a matter that concerns you not. Evil thoughts are dangerous enemies, and should be repulsed at the threshold of our minds. Fill the head and heart with good thoughts, that there be no room for bad ones.

Some persons complain that they cannot find words for their thoughts, when the real trouble is they cannot find thoughts for their words. The man who thinks laboriously will express himself concisely. It is only by labor that thought can be made healthy, and only by thought that labor can be made happy. It is not depth of thought which makes obscure to others the work of a thinker; real and offensive obscurity comes merely of inadequate thought embodied in inadequate language. What is clearly comprehended or conceived, what is duly wrought and thought out, must find for itself and seize upon the clearest and fullest expression. Thoughts are but dreams till their effects be tried. The best thoughts are ever swiftest winged, the duller lag behind. A thought must have its own way of expression, or it will have no way at all. The thought that lives is only the deed struggling into birth. It is with our thoughts as with our flowers—those that are simple in expression carry their seed with them; those that are double charm the mind, but produce nothing.

There is much need of independent thought in our day. Too many yield to the opinions of others without asking or meditating upon their bearing. Oftentimes the masses are enslaved to opinion, especially in political matters. This may be necessary in some countries, where a few rule, but not in our country, where, through a liberal education, all may be taught to think. Books are so cheap now that the poorest can have access to the channels of thought. Books, however, should only be used as an impetus to set the mind in motion and set it to prying deeper and farther into nature's hidden recesses and boundless realms of truth, or, as a stone that is cast into the calm bosom of the lake causes waves to roll and roll on against the remotest outlines of the shore. It behooves us to cast off the shackles of opinion and walk resolutely before the world, guided by a well-grounded opinion of our own. Every man and woman ought to favor his age with new thoughts, new ideas, as an addition to the great store-house of ideas, with thoughts that will live though empires fall and language dies. Such men and women raise the world from one degree to another higher in the scale of civilization and intelligence. Such are the lives that receive the plaudit, "Well done!" Such are lives virtuous, noble and godlike.

No man need fear that he will exhaust his substance of thought, if he will only draw his inspiration from

actual human life.   There the inexhaustible God pours
depths and endless variety of truth, and the true
thinker is but a shorthand writer endeavoring to
report the discourse of God.   Shall a child on the
banks of the Amazon fear lest he should drink up the
stream?

———•┼•‡•┼‖┼•‡•┼•———

Benefactors or Malefactors.

WE are all well doers or evil doers.   "None of us
liveth to himself."   We die, but leave an influence
behind us that survives.

The echoes of our words are evermore repeated,
and reflected along the ages.   It is what man *was*
that lives and acts after him.   What he said sounds
along the years like voices amid the mountain gorges;
and what he did is repeated after him in ever-multi-
plying and never-ceasing reverberations.   Every man
has left behind him influences for good or for evil that
will never exhaust themselves.   The sphere in which
he acts may be small, or it may be great.   It may be
his fireside, or it may be a kingdom; a village, or a
great nation; it may be a parish, or broad Europe;
but act he does, ceaselessly and forever.   His friends,
his family, his successors in office, his relatives, are all
receptive of an influence, a moral influence which he
has transmitted and bequeathed to mankind; either
a *blessing* which will repeat itself in showers of

33

benedictions, or a *curse* which will multiply itself in ever-accumulating evil.

Every man is a missionary, now and forever, for good or for evil, whether he intend and design it, or not. He may be a blot, radiating his dark influence outward to the very circumference of society, or he may be a blessing, spreading benedictions over the length and breadth of the world; but *a blank he cannot be*. The seed sown in life springs up in harvests of blessings, or harvests of sorrow. Whether our influence be great or small, whether it be for good or evil, it lasts, it lives somewhere, within some limit, and is operative wherever it is. The grave buries the dead dust, but the character walks the world, and distributes itself, as a benediction or a curse, among the families of mankind.

The sun sets beyond the western hills, but the trail of light he leaves behind him guides the pilgrim to his distant home. The tree falls in the forest; but in the lapse of ages it is turned into coal, and our fires burn now the brighter because it grew and fell. The coral insect dies, but the reef it raised breaks the surge on the shores of great continents, or has formed an isle in the bosom of the ocean, to wave with harvests for the good of man. We live and we die; but the good or evil that we do lives after us, and is *not* "buried with our bones."

The babe that perished on the bosom of its mother, like a flower that bowed its head and drooped amid the death-frosts of time—that babe, not only in its image, but in its influence, still lives and speaks in the chambers of the mother's heart.

The friend with whom we took sweet counsel is removed visibly from the outward eye; but the lessons that he taught, the grand sentiments that he uttered, the holy deeds of generosity by which he was characterized, the moral lineaments and likeness of the man, still survive and appear on the tablets of memory, and in the light of morn and noon, and dewy eve; and, being dead, he yet speaks eloquently, and in the midst of us.

Mahomet still lives in his practical and disastrous influence in the East. Napoleon still is France, and France is almost Napoleon. Martin Luther's dead dust sleeps at Wittemburg, but Martin Luther's accents still ring through the churches of Christendom. Shakspeare, Byron, and Milton, all live in their influence, for good or evil. The apostle from his chair, the minister from his pulpit, the martyr from his flame-shroud, the statesman from his cabinet, the soldier in the field, the sailor on the deck, who all have passed away to their graves, still live in the practical deeds that they did, in the lives they lived, and in the powerful lessons that they left behind them.

"None of us liveth to himself;" others are affected by that life; "or dieth to himself;" others are interested in that death. The queen's crown may molder, but she who wore it will act upon the ages which are yet to come. The noble's coronet may be reft in pieces, but the wearer of it is now doing what will be reflected by thousands who will be made and molded by him. Dignity, and rank, and riches, are all corruptible and worthless; but moral character has an immortality that no sword-point can destroy; that ever walks the world and leaves lasting influences behind.

What we do is transacted on a stage of which all in the universe are spectators. What we say is transmitted in echoes that will never cease. What we are is influencing and acting on the rest of mankind. Neutral we cannot be. Living we act, and dead we speak; and the whole universe is the mighty company forever looking, forever listening; and all nature the tablets forever recording the words, the deeds, the thoughts, the passions of mankind!

Monuments, and columns, and statues, erected to heroes, poets, orators, statesmen, are all influences that extend into the future ages. The blind old man of Scio's rocky isle still speaks. The Mantuan bard still sings in every school. Shakspeare, the bard of Avon, is still translated into every tongue. The philosophy of the Stagyrite is still felt in every academy. Whether these influences are beneficent or the reverse, they are influences fraught with power. How blest must be the recollection of those who, like the setting sun, have left a trail of light behind them by which others may see the way to that rest which remaineth for the people of God! Since our earthly life is so brief, "and the night will soon come when the murmur and hum of our days shall be dumb evermore," it were well to have mile-stones by the way pointing to a better land.

The yeoman, gathering treasures from the bosom

of the earth, and thus aiding in the sustenance of
humanity; the miner, delving into the deep cavern
and bringing forth diamonds and precious stones,
adding to the world's vast wealth; the manufacturer,
sending the costly fabrics through the land, and
securing exchange from foreign countries; the architect, with the proud monuments of his skill; the
sculptor, with his chisel carving the form divine; the
artist, writing out in letters of abiding light the faces
we so fondly love, and thus blessing us with the
continued presence of not only the absent ones, but
also those who "are not," since God hath taken them;
all these are truly earth's benefactors, and yet only
the silver links in the mighty chain.

Would we be numbered among earth's benefactors,
and have our middle and latest life filled with richest
and holiest experiences, we must be ofttimes oblivious
of self, con well the lesson contained in the "Golden
Rule," and be still further perfected in the two great
commandments, "on which hang all the law and the
prophets." When all the purple and gold, the glitter
and tinsel of our earthly life is ended, and the unknown and mysterious eternity is spread out to our
immortal vision, will it not be a source of greater joy
to us to have wiped a tear from the eye of the sorrowing, to have soothed a weary pilgrim crossing the
river of death, pointing by an eye of faith to the
"better country," "even a heavenly," to have plumed
one wing for its eternal flight, than to possess a kingly
crown, or wear fame's brightest laurels?

It is only the pure fountain that brings forth pure

water. The good tree only will produce the good fruit. If the centre from which all proceeds be pure and holy, the radii of influence from it will be pure and holy also. Go forth, then, into the spheres that you occupy, the employments, the trades, the professions of social life; go forth into the high places, or into the lowly places of the land; mix with the roaring cataracts of social convulsions, or mingle amid the eddies and streamlets of quiet and domestic life; whatever sphere you fill, carry into it a holy heart, you will radiate around you life and power, and leave behind you holy and beneficent influences.

Trials of Life.

STARS shine brightest in the darkest night; torches are the better for beating; grapes come not to the proof till they come to the press; spices smell sweetest when pounded; young trees root the faster for shaking; vines are the better for bleeding; gold looks the brighter for scouring; glow-worms glisten best in the dark; juniper smells sweetest in the fire; pomander becomes most fragrant for chasing; the palm-tree proves the better for pressing; camomile, the more you tread it, the more you spread it. Such is the condition of men; they are the most triumphant when most tempted; as their conflicts, so their conquests; as their tribulations, so their triumphs. True salamanders live best in the furnace of persecution; so that heavy afflictions are the best benefactors to heavenly affections. And where afflictions hang heaviest, corruptions hang loosest; and grace that is hid in nature, as sweet water in rose-leaves, is then most fragrant when the fire of affliction is put under to distil it out.

Do you wish to live without a trial? Then you wish to die but half a man—at the best but half a man. Without trial you cannot guess at your own strength. Men do not learn to swim on a table. They must go into deep water and buffet the surges. A certain amount of opposition is a great help to a man. Kites rise against the wind, and not with the wind; even a head wind is better than none. No man ever worked his passage any where in a calm. Let no man wax pale, therefore, because of opposition; opposition is what he wants and must have, to be good for any thing. Hardship is the native soil of manhood and self-reliance.

An acorn is not an oak tree when it is sprouted. It must go through long summers and fierce winters; it has to endure all that frost, and snow, and thunder, and storm, and side-striking winds can bring, before it is a full-grown oak. These are rough teachers; but rugged schoolmasters make rugged pupils. So a man is not a man when he is created; he is only begun. His manhood must come with years. A man who goes through life prosperous, and comes to his grave without a wrinkle is not half a man. In time of war, whom does the general select for some hazardous

enterprise? He looks over his men, and chooses
the soldiers whom he knows will not flinch at danger,
but will go bravely through whatever is allotted to
him. He calls him that he may receive his orders,
and the officer, blushing with pleasure to be thus
chosen, hastens away to execute them. Difficulties
are God's errands. And when we are sent upon them
we should esteem it a proof of God's confidence—as
a compliment from God. The traveler who goes
round the world prepares himself to pass through all
latitudes, and to meet all changes. So man must be
willing to take life as it comes; to mount the hill
when the hill swells, and to go down the hill when
the hill lowers; to walk the plain when it stretches
before him, and to ford the river when it rolls over
the plain. "I can do all things through Christ which
strengtheneth me."

The best of people will now and then meet with
disappointments, for they are inherited by mortality.
It is, however, the better philosophy to take things
calmly and endeavor to be content with our lot. We
may at least add some rays of sunshine to our path,
if we earnestly endeavor to dispel the clouds of discontent that may arise in our bosoms. And by so
doing, we the more fully enjoy the bountiful blessing
that God gives to his humblest creatures.

It is far more noble to improve each hour in cultivating the mind, and attuning it to the glory of the
Creator. For this end it matters not so much whether
we spend our time in study or toil; the thoughts of
the mind should go out and reach after the higher

TRIALS OF LIFE.

good. In this manner we may improve ourselves till our thoughts come to be sweet companions that shall lead us along the path of virtue. Thus we may grow better within, whilst the cares of life, the crosses and losses and disappointments lose their sharp thorns, and the journey of life be made comparatively pleasant and happy.

Much material good must be resigned if we would attain to the highest degree of moral excellence, and many spiritual joys must be foregone if we resolve at all risks to win great material advantages. To strive for a high professional position, and yet expect to have all the delights of leisure; to labor for vast riches, and yet to ask for freedom from anxiety and care, and all the happiness which flows from a contented mind; to indulge in sensual gratification, and yet demand health, strength, and vigor; to live for self, and yet to look for the joys that spring from a virtuous and self-denying life, is to ask for impossibilities.

God knows what keys in the human soul to touch in order to draw out its sweeter and most perfect harmonies. They may be the minor strains of sadness and sorrow; they may be the loftier notes of joy and gladness. God knows where the melodies of our natures are, and what discipline will bring them forth. Some with plaintive tongues, must walk in lowly vales of life's weary way, others, in loftier hymns, sing of nothing but joy, as they tread the mountain-tops of life; but they all unite without discord or jar as the ascending anthem of loving and believing hearts finds its way into the chorus of the redeemed heaven.

Sickness.

SICKNESS brings a share of blessings with it. What stores of human love and sympathy it reveals. What constant affectionate care is ours. What kindly greetings from friends and associates. This very loosening of our hold upon life calls out such wealth of human sympathy that life seems richer than before. Then it teaches humility. Our absence is scarcely felt or noticed. From the noisy, wrestling world without we are separated completely, as if the moss was on our tombstones; yet our place is filled and all moves on without us. So we learn that when at last we shall sink forever beneath the waves of the sea of life, there will be but one ripple and the current will move steadily on. On the sick-bed the sober truth comes home with startling emphasis:

> "The gay will laugh
> When thou art gone, the solemn brood of care
> Plod on, and each one as before will chase
> His fravoite phantom."

We cannot too soon convince ourselves how easily we may be dispensed with in the world. What important personages we imagine ourselves to be! We think that we alone are the life of the circle in which we move; in our absence we fancy that life, existence and breath will come to a general pause; and alas! the gap which we leave is scarcely perceptible, so quickly is it filled again; nay, it is often but the place, if not for something better, at least for something more agreeable.

When sickness has drawn a veil over the gayety of our hearts, or adversity eclipsed the splendor of our outward circumstances; when some intervening cloud has darkened the pleasing scenes of life, or disappointments opened our eyes; then vice loses her fallacious allurements and the world appears as an empty, delusive cheat; then Jesus and the Gospel beam forth with inimitable lustre, and Christian virtue gains loveliness from such lowering providences, and treads the shades with more than mortal charms. May this reconcile all the sons of sorrow to their appointed share of sufferings. If tribulations tend to refine the soul and prepare it for glory, welcome distress, or whatever our peevish passions may miscall calamities. These are not judgments or marks of displeasure to God's children, but necessary and salutary chastisements, as well as tokens of his parental concern for our spiritual and eternal welfare. Afflictions should, therefore, sit easy upon us, since they increase our knowledge and humility, promote our faith and love, and work out for us a far more exceeding and eternal weight of glory.

Sickness scours us of our rust, and however the wicked, like trees in the wilderness, grow without culture, yet the saints, like trees in the garden, must be pruned to be made fruitful, and sickness does this. God will prune His people, but not hew them down; the right hand of His mercy knows what the left hand of His severity is doing. There is as much difference between the sufferings of the saints and those of the ungodly, as between the cords with which an executioner pinions a condemned malefactor, and the bandages wherewith a tender surgeon binds his patient.

Sickness and disease are, in weak minds, the sources of melancholy; but that which is painful to the body may be profitable to the soul. Sickness, the mother of modesty, puts us in mind of our mortality, and while we drive on heedlessly in the full career of worldly pomp and jollity, kindly pulls us by the ear, and brings us to a proper sense of our duty.

A minister was recovering of a dangerous illness, when one of his friends addressed him thus: "Sir, though God seems to be bringing you up from the gates of death, yet it will be a long time before you will sufficiently retrieve your strength and regain vigor enough of mind to preach as usual." The good man answered: "You are mistaken, my friend; for this six weeks' illness has taught me more divinity than all my past studies and all my ten years' ministry put together."

Dr. Payson being ill, a friend coming into his room remarked, in a familiar way: "Well, I am sorry to see you lying here on your back." "Do you know what God puts us on our backs for?" asked Dr. Payson, smiling. "No," was the answer. "In order that we may look upward." His friend said to him, "I am not come to condole but to rejoice with you, for it seems to me that this is no time for mourning." "Well, I am glad to hear that," was the reply, "it is not often that I am addressed in such a way. The fact is I never had less need of condolence, and yet everybody persists in offering it; whereas, when I was prosperous and well, and a successful preacher, and really needed condolence, they flattered and congratulated me." Whom the Lord loveth He chasteneth, and if we endure chastening, God dealeth with us as with sons and daughters.

Tears.

THERE is a sacredness in tears. They are not the mark of weakness, but of power. They speak more eloquence than ten thousand tongues. They are the messages of overwhelming grief, of deep contrition, of unspeakable love. If there were wanting any argument to prove that man is not mortal, I would look for it in the strong convulsive emotions of the breast, when the soul has been deeply agitated; when the fountains of feeling are rising, and when tears are gushing forth in crystal streams. O, speak not harshly of the stricken one — weeping in silence! Break not the solemnity by rude laughter, or intrusive footsteps. Despise not woman's tears — they are what make her an angel. Scoff not if the stern heart of manhood is sometimes melted to sympathy — they are what help to elevate him above the brute. We love to see tears of affection. They are painful tokens, but still most holy. There is pleasure in tears — an awful pleasure. If there were none on earth to shed a tear for us, we

should be loth to live; and if no one might weep over
our grave, we could never die in peace.

Genuine tears are the involuntary and faithful ex-
pressions of the soul. The soul's sorrow or joy—
for joy weeps—guilt or innocence—for insulted virtue has its tears—glistens in the pearly drop. Tears
relieve the soul; they are prevailing orators; they
win triumphs which neither the infernal sword, nor
divine speech could ever achieve. A *true* tear is
electric to the *true*. A tear dropped in the silence of
a sick chamber often rings in heaven with a sound
which belongs not to earthly trumpets or bells.

Tears generally tremble in our eyes when we are
happy, and glisten like pearls, or dew-drops on the
flower cup; but when we first realize any overwhelming and unlooked for happiness, we gaze round with
a smile of bewildered ecstacy, and no tears tremble
in our eyes. The extremes of joy and sorrow are
too great, too deep for tears.

Tender, holy and sanctifying are human tears—
crystals of affection and pity—jewels of the soul.
One trickled on the cheek of a child. It had been
crossed in the fulfillment of some anticipation, and
from a grieved heart gushed up the sympathizing tear.
Another trembled from the eyelid of youth. He had
felt the touch of a bitter reproof, or of disappointed
love, and to soften his brain and sorrow came the
same beautiful tear.

O, ye tears! what a mission have ye wrought in
our sorrowing world! How tenderly worshiped on
the altars of pity and sincere love—how gloriously

sanctified repentance and grief! Down in the damp
cell where the martyr rattles his chains; in the dungeon where the patriot waits for the block—ye have
performed, O tears! the same blessed work. Even
to joy ye have been a balm of oil—a refiner's fire.
When the Macedonian passed the pillar of Hercules,
he was conquered by tears—the same tears that
sprang but now, like dew-drops, from the lashes of
yon blue-eyed child. For what different ends, and
yet unchanged, have ye wrought. Every moment
mellowing and calming some sad, worn heart—aye,
every day doing some mission for each of our souls.
Ye have gushed over battle-fields and over festive
halls; around the bier and the board; and deeper,
holier, have been our loves and our friendliness with
each return of your hallowed feet—aye, feet! for
tears have feet, and they come treading up the soul
like so many angels, offering sacrifices through our
eyes.

Repress them not, child—they are a purifying vent
to thy young heart. Repress them not, O youth—
they are good and holy for thee. Repress them not,
mother—for unto thee God has given them to be a
comforter in the lone and bitter hour. And thou,
manhood, quench not the fountain whose upheaving
is the most beautiful manifestation of thy spiritual life.
Tears, beautiful, blessed tears, be ever with every
reader—with us all; our token when we sigh for the
absent, or weep for the lost—a sacred witness that
our regrets and sorrows are sincere.

It is a striking fact that the dying never weep.

The sobbing, the heart-breaking agony of the circle of friends around the death-bed, calls forth no responsive tears from the dying. Is it because he is insensible, and stiff in the chill of dissolution? That cannot be, for he asks for his father's hand, as if to gain strength in the mortal struggle, and leans on the breast of his mother, sister or brother, in still conscious affection. Just before expiring, he calls the loved ones, and with quivering lips says: "Kiss me," showing that the love which he has borne in his heart is still fresh and warm. It must be because the dying have reached a point too deep for earthly sorrows, too transcendent for weeping. They are face to face with higher and holier things, with the Father in Heaven and His Angels. There is no weeping in that blessed abode to which the dying man is hastening.

Sorrow.

Give Sorrow words : the grief, that does not speak,
Whispers the o'erfraught Heart, and bids it break.
— SHAKSPEARE.

HE who tastes only the bitter in the cup of life, who looks only at the clouds which lower in one quarter of the heavens, while the sun is shining cheerily in another, who persists in pricking and scratching himself with the thorn, and refuses to enjoy the fragrance of the rose, is an ingrate to God and a torment to himself.

The record of human life is far more melancholy
than its course; the hours of quiet enjoyment are not
noted; the thousand graces and happiness of social
life, the loveliness of nature meeting us at every step,
the buoyancy of spirit resulting from health and pure
air, the bright sun, the starry firmament—all that
cheers man on his road through his probationary
state, that warms the heart and makes life pleasant—
is omitted in the narrative, which can only deal with
facts; and we read of disappointment, and sickness,
and death, and exclaim, "Why is man born to sorrow?" He is not so.

Sorrows are only tempest clouds: when afar off,
they look black, but when above us scarcely gray.
Sorrow is the night of the mind. What would be a
day without its night? The day reveals one sun
only; the night brings to light the whole of the universe. The analogy is complete. Sorrow is the
firmament of thought and the school of intelligence.
Men that are wise, as the bees draw honey from the
thyme, which is a most unsavory and dry herb, extract
something that is convenient and useful even from
the most bitter afflictions.

Great undertakings require the Christian's faith to
endure the deep and overwhelming experiences of
human sorrow without relinquishing their cherished
life-work. The world in its bitterest forms of oppression spent itself upon Tasso, Dante, and Milton, in
vain. Redeemed, exalted, purified, they came forth
from the abyss of anguish, and sang to their fellows
a song which those who have never suffered, could

34

never utter. Alas! how many richly freighted souls have sunk in the angry billows that came rushing in their furious strength only to bend beneath these master-spirits and bear them up to immortality. Sweetest of all songs are the Psalms in the night. David sang with the most touching tenderness when in the gloom of deepest affliction. The heart may wail a *miserere* over its dead or its dying, but even that will be sadly sweet, and will have a hope in it. The saddest song is better than none, because it is a song.

Sorrow is one of God's own angels in the land. Her pruning-knife may not spare the tender buds of hope that make glad the garden of the soul, but her fingers sow the seeds of a quick sympathy with the woes of a common humanity, which, springing into leaf, and bud, and blossom, send perfume and beauty into the waste places of lonely lives, and permeate with fragrant incense the soil that gave them birth.

The simplest and most obvious use of sorrow is to remind us of God. It would seem that a certain shock is needed to bring us in contact with reality. We are not conscious of breathing till obstruction makes it felt. We are not aware of the possession of a heart till some disease, some sudden joy or sorrow, rouses it into extraordinary action. And we are not conscious of the mighty cravings of our half divine humanity; we are not aware of the God within us till some chasm yawns which must be filled, or till the rending asunder of our affections forces us to become fearfully conscious of a need.

To mourn without measure, is folly; not to mourn at all, is insensibility. God says to the fruit tree, bloom and bear; and to the human heart, bear and bloom—the soul's great blossoming is the flower of suffering. As the sun converts clouds into a glorious drapery, firing them with gorgeous hues, and draping the whole horizon with its glorious costume, and writing victory in fiery colors along the vanquished front of every cloud, so sometimes a radiant heart lets forth its hope upon its sorrow and all the blackness flies, and troubles that trooped to appal seem to crowd around as a triumphal procession following the steps of a victor.

There are people who think that to be grim is to be good, and that a thought, to be really wholesome, must necessarily be shaped like a coffin. They seem to think that black is the color of heaven, and that the more they can make their faces look like midnight, the holier they are.

The days of darkness come, and they are many, but our eye takes in only the first. One wave hides another, and the effort to encounter the foremost withdraws our thought from evils which are pressing on. If we could see them all at once we might lie down, like Elijah, under the juniper tree, and say, "It is enough—let me not live!" But patience attains her perfect work while trials unfold. The capacity of sorrow belongs to our grandeur; and the loftiest of our race are those who have had the profoundest grief, because they have had the profoundest sympathies.

Sorrow comes soon enough without despondency; it does a man no good to carry around a lightning-rod to attract trouble. When a gloom falls upon us, it may be we have entered into the cloud that will give its gentle showers to refresh and strengthen us. Heavy burdens of sorrow seem like a stone hung round our neck, yet they are often only like the stone used by pearl divers, which enables them to reach the prize and rise enriched.

There are sorrows too sacred to be babbled to the world, and there may be loves which one would forbear to whisper even to a friend. Real sorrow is not clamorous. It seeks to shun every eye, and breathes in solitude and silence the sighs that come from the heart. Every heart has its secret sorrow, which the world knows not; and oftentimes we call a man cold when he is only sad. Give not thy mind to heaviness; the gladness of the heart is the life of man, and joyfulness of a man prolongeth his days. Remove sorrow far from thee, for sorrow hath killed many, and there is no profit therein; and carefulness bringeth age before the time.

We are inclined to think that the causes of our sorrows are sent to us from above; often we weep, we groan in our spirits, and we murmur against God; but he leaves us to our sorrow, and we are saved; our present grief saves from an eternal sorrow. It would be well, however, if we attempted to trace the cause of them; we should probably find their origin in some region of the heart which we never had well explored, or in which we had secretly deposited our worst indulgences. The clouds that intercept the heavens from us, come not from the heavens, but from the earth. Excess of sorrow is as foolish as continued laughter. Loud mirth, or immoderate sorrow, inequality of behavior, either in prosperity or adversity are alike ungraceful in man who is born to die. Some are refined, like gold, in the furnace; others, like chaff, are consumed in it. Sorrow, when it is excessive, takes away fervor from piety, vigor from action, health from body, light from reason, and repose from the conscience.

Those who work hard seldom yield themselves entirely up to fancied or real sorrow. When grief sits down, folds its hands and mournfully feeds upon its own tears, weaving the dim shadows, that a little exertion might sweep away into a funeral pall, the strong spirit is shorn of its might, and sorrow becomes our master. When troubles flow upon you, dark and heavy, toil not with the waves; wrestle not with the torrent; rather seek, by occupation, to divert the dark waters that threaten to overwhelm you, into a thousand channels which the duties of life always present. Before you dream of it, those waters will fertilize the present, and give birth to fresh flowers that may brighten the future—flowers that will become pure and holy, in the sunshine which penetrates to the path of duty, in spite of every obstacle. Grief, after all, is but a selfish feeling; and most selfish is the man who yields himself to the indulgence of any passion which brings no joy to his fellow man.

They are the true kings and queens, heroes and heroines, who, folding a pall of tenderest memory over the faces of their own lost hopes and perished loves, go with unfaltering courage, to grapple with the future, to strengthen the weak, to comfort the weary, to hang sweet pictures of faith and trust in the silent galleries of sunless lives, and to point the desolate, whose paths wind ever among shadows and over rocks where never the green moss grows, to the golden heights of the hereafter, where the palms of victory wave.

Difficulties are things that show what men are. In case of any difficulty, remember that God, like a gymnastic trainer, has pitted you against a rough antagonist. For what end? That you may be an Olympic conqueror, and this cannot be without toil. He who has great affliction is made of sterner stuff than most men. God seems to have selected him, like second growth timber, for important work. It is not every one that can be trusted to suffer greatly. God has confidence in him to the extent of the affliction.

Causeless depression is not to be reasoned with, nor can David's harp charm it away, by sweet discoursings. As well fight with the mist as with this shapeless, undefinable, yet all-beclouding hopelessness. If those who laugh at such melancholy did but feel the grief of it for one hour, their laughter would be sobered into compassion. Resolution might, perhaps, shake it off, but where are we to find the resolution, when the whole man is unstrung?

It is a poor relief for sorrow to fly to the distractions of the world; as well might a lost and wearied bird, suspended over the abyss of the tempestuous ocean, seek a resting place on its heaving waves, as the child of trouble seek a place of repose amid the bustling cares and intoxicating pleasures of earth and time. Christ is a refuge and "a very present help in trouble."

Sorrowing for the Dead.

OUR friends may die and leave our hearts and homes desolate for a time; we cannot prevent it, nor would it be best if we could. Sorrow has its useful lessons when it is legitimate, and death is the gate that opens out of earth toward the house "eternal in the heavens." If we lose them, heaven gains them. If we mourn, they rejoice. If we hang our harps on the willows, they tune theirs in the eternal orchestra above, rejoicing that we shall soon be with them. Shall we not drown our sorrow in the flood of light let through the rent veil of the skies which Jesus entered, and, to cure our loneliness, gather to us other friends to walk life's way, knowing that every step brings us nearer the departed, and their sweet, eternal home, which death never enters, and where partings are never known? We may still love the departed. They are ours as ever, and we are theirs. The ties

that unite us are not broken. They are too strong
for death's stroke. They are made for the joys of
eternal friendship. Other friendships on earth will
not disturb these bonds that link with dear ones on
high. Nor will our duties below interfere with the
sacredness of our relations with them. They wish
not to see us in sorrow. They doubtless sympathize
with us, and could we hear their sweet voices, they
would tell us to dry our tears and bind ourselves to
other friends, and joyfully perform all duties on earth
till our time to ascend shall come.

"The sorrow for the dead," says Irving, "is the
only sorrow from which we refuse to be divorced.
Every other wound we seek to heal, every other
affliction to forget; but this wound we consider it a
duty to keep open; this affliction we cherish and
brood over in solitude.

"Where is the mother who would willingly forget
the infant that perished like a blossom from her arms,
though every recollection is a pang? Where is the
child that would willingly forget the most tender of
parents, though to remember be but to lament? Who,
even in the hour of agony, would forget the friend
over whom he mourns? Who, even when the tomb
is closing upon the remains of her he most loved,
when he feels his heart, as it were, crushed in the
closing of its portal, would accept of consolation that
must be bought by forgetfulness?

"No, the love which survives the tomb is one of
the noblest attributes of the soul. If it has its woes,
it has likewise its delights; and when the overwhelm-

ing burst of grief is calmed into the gentle tear of recollection, when the sudden anguish and the convulsive agony over the ruins of all that we most loved is softened away into pensive meditation on all that it was in the days of its loveliness, who would root out such a sorrow from the heart?

"Though it may sometimes throw a passing cloud over the bright hour of gayety, or spread a deeper sadness over the hour of gloom, yet who would exchange it even for the song of pleasure or the burst of revelry? No, there is a voice from the tomb sweeter than song. There is a remembrance of the dead to which we turn even from the charms of the living.

"Oh, the grave! the grave! It buries every error, covers every defect, extinguishes every resentment. From its peaceful bosom spring none but fond regrets and tender recollections. Who can look upon the grave even of an enemy and not feel a compunctious throb that he should ever have warred with the poor handful of earth that lies moldering before him?

"But the grave of those we loved, what a place for meditation! There it is that we call up in long review the whole history of virtue and gentleness, and the thousand endearments lavished upon us almost unheeded in the daily intercourse of intimacy. There it is that we dwell upon the tenderness, the solemn, awful tenderness of the parting scene.

"The bed of death, with all its stifled griefs, its noiseless attendants, its mute, watchful assiduities. the last testimonies of expiring love, the feeble, fluttering, thrilling, oh, how thrilling! pressure of the hand. The last fond look of the glazing eye, turning upon us even from the threshold of existence. The faint, faltering accents struggling in death to give one more assurance of affection. Ay, go to the grave of buried love, and meditate! There settle the account with thy conscience for every past benefit unrequited, every past endearment unregarded, of that departed being who can never—never—never return to be soothed by thy contrition!

"If thou art a child, and hast ever added a sorrow to the soul or a furrow to the silver brow of an affectionate parent; if thou art a husband, and hast ever caused the fond bosom that ventured its whole happiness in thy arms, to doubt one moment of thy kindness or thy truth; if thou art a friend, and hast ever wronged, in thought, or word, or deed, the spirit that generously confided in thee; if thou art a lover, and hast given one unmerited pang to that true heart which now lies cold and still beneath thy feet, then be sure that every unkind look, every ungracious word, every ungentle action, will come thronging back upon thy memory, and knocking dolefully at thy soul; then be sure that thou wilt lie down sorrowing and repentant on the grave, and utter the unheard groan, and pour the unavailing tear, more deep, more bitter, because unheard and unavailing.

"Then weave thy chaplet of flowers, and strew the beauties of nature about the grave; console thy broken spirit, if thou canst, with these tender, yet futile tributes of regret; but take warning by the bitterness of this thy contrite affliction over the dead, and henceforth be more faithful and affectionate in the discharge of thy duties to the living."

———

Adversity.

The good are better made by ill :-
As odors crush'd are sweeter still !
—ROGERS.

THE harp holds in its wires the possibilities of noblest chords; yet, if they be not struck, they must hang dull and useless. So the mind is vested with a hundred powers, that must be smitten by a heavy hand to prove thenselves the offspring of divinity.

Welcome, then, adversity! Thy hand is cold and hard, but it is the hand of a friend! Thy voice is stern and harsh, but it is the voice of a friend! There is something sublime in the resolute, fixed purpose of suffering without complaining, which makes disappointment often better than success.

As full ears load and lay corn, so does too much fortune bend and break the mind. It deserves to be considered, too, as another advantage, that affliction moves pity, and reconciles our very enemies; but prosperity provokes envy, and loses us our very friends. Again, adversity is a desolate and abandoned state; the generality of people are like those infamous animals that live only upon plenty and rapine; and as rats and mice forsake a tottering house, so do these the falling man. He that has never known adversity is but half acquainted with others or with himself. Constant success shows us but one side of the world; for as it surrounds us with friends who tell us only of our merits, so it silences those enemies from whom only we can learn our defects.

> Adversity, sage, useful guest,
> Severe instructor, but the best;
> It is from thee alone we know
> Justly to value things below.

Adversity exasperates fools, dejects cowards, draws out the faculties of the wise and industrious, puts the modest to the necessity of trying their skill, awes the opulent, and makes the idle industrious. A smooth sea never made a skillful mariner, neither do uninterrupted prosperity and success qualify men for usefulness and happiness. The storms of adversity, like those of the ocean, rouse the faculties, and excite the invention, prudence, skill, and fortitude of the voyager. The martyrs of ancient times, in bracing their minds to outward calamities, acquired a loftiness of purpose and a moral heroism worth a lifetime of softness and security.

It is good for man that he bear the yoke in his youth. Oaks are made hard by strong discipline. As a gladiator trained the body, so must we train the mind to self-sacrifice, "to endure all things," to meet and overcome difficulty and danger. We must take the rough and thorny roads as well as the smooth and pleasant; and a portion at least of our daily duty must be hard and disagreeable; for the mind cannot be kept strong and healthy in perpetual sunshine only, and the most dangerous of all states is that of constantly recurring pleasure, ease and prosperity.

It seems as if man were like the earth. It cannot bask forever in sunshine. The snows of winter and frosts must come and work in the ground and mellow it to make them fruitful. A man upon whom continuous sunshine falls is like the earth in August; he becomes parched and dry, and hard and close-grained. To some men the winter and spring come when they are young; others are born in summer and are only made fit to die by a winter of sorrow coming to them when they are middle-aged or old.

It is not the nursling of wealth or fortune who has been dandled into manhood on the lap of prosperity, that carries away the world's honors, or wins its mightiest influence; but it is rather the man whose earlier years were cheered by scarcely a single proffer of aid, or smile of approbation, and who has drawn from adversity the elements of greatness. The "talent" which prosperity "folded in a napkin," the rough hand of adversity shook out.

The men who stand boldly for the defense of the truth, in the midst of the flood of errors that surround them, are not the gentlemen of lily fingers who have been rocked in the cradle of indulgence and caressed in the lap of luxury; but they are the men whom necessity has called from the shade of retirement to contend under the scorching rays of the sun, with the stern realities of life with all its vicissitudes. It is good for a man that he bear the yoke in his youth. The gem cannot be polished without friction, nor man perfected without adversity.

The patient conquest of difficulties which rise in the regular and legitimate channels of business and enterprise, is not only essential in securing the successes which you seek, but it is essential to the preparation of your mind requisite for the enjoyment of your successes and for retaining them when gained.

Adversity is the trial of principle. Without it a man hardly knows whether he be honest or not. Night brings out the stars as adversity shows us truths; we never see the stars till we can see little or naught else; and thus it is with truth. When you feel inclined to cry, just change your mind and laugh. Nothing dries sooner than tears.

Adversity certainly has its uses, and very valuable ones too. It has been truly remarked that many a man, in losing his fortune, has found himself. Adversity flattereth no man. Oft from apparent ills our blessings rise. Who never fasts, no banquet e'er enjoys. In prosperity, be humble; in adversity, cheerful. If you have the blues, go and see the poorest and sickest families within your knowledge. To bear the sharp afflictions of life like men, we should also *feel* them like men. The darker the setting, the brighter the diamond. Probably we might often become reconciled to what we consider a hard lot by comparing ourselves with the many who want what we possess rather than with the few who possess what we want. He is happy whose circum-

stances suit his temper; but he is happier who can
suit his temper to his circumstances. There is a
virtue in keeping up appearances. He is a fool that
grumbles at every little mischance. Put the best
foot forward, is an old and good maxim. Don't run
about and tell acquaintances that you have been
unfortunate; people do not like to have unfortunate
men for acquaintances. If the storm of adversity
whistles around you, whistle as bravely yourself; perhaps the two whistles may make melody.

Debt.

WHILE you are generous, see to it that you are
also just. Do not give away what does not belong
to you. Let us warn you, on account of its moral
bearings, against debt. Nothing more effectually
robs one of his best energies, takes the bloom from
his cheek and peace from his pillow, than pecuniary
obligations. And that is not all, nor the worst; debt
is a foe to a man's honesty. Avoid all meanness;
but shun as a pestilence the habit of running thoughtlessly into debt. Let your expenses be always short
of your income.

"Of what a hideous progeny of ill," says Douglas
Jerrold, "is debt the father! What meanness, what
invasions of self-respect, what cares, what double-
dealing! How in due season it will carve the frank,
open face into wrinkles; how like a knife it will stab

the honest heart. And then its transformations.
How it has been known to change a goodly face into
a mask of brass; how with the evil custom of debt,
has the true man become a callous trickster! A freedom from debt, and what nourishing sweetness may
be found in cold water; what toothsomeness in a dry
crust; what ambrosial nourishment in a hard egg!
Be sure of it, he who dines out of debt, though his
meal be a biscuit and an onion, dines in a banquet
hall. And then, for raiment, what warmth in a threadbare coat, if the tailor's receipt be in your pocket!
What Tyrian purple in the faded waistcoat, the vest
not owed for; how glossy the well worn hat, if it
covers not the aching head of a debtor! Next the
home sweets, the out-door recreation of the free man.
The street door falls not a knell on his heart; the
foot of the staircase, though he lives on the third
pair, sends no spasms through his anatomy; at the
rap of his door he can crow 'come in,' and his pulse
still beats healthfully, his heart sinks not in his bowels.
See him abroad! How he returns look for look with
any passenger; how he saunters; now meeting an
acquaintance, he stands and gossips, but then this
man knows no debt; debt that casts a drug in the
richest wine; that makes the food of the gods un-
wholesome, indigestible; that sprinkles the banquets
of a Lucullus with ashes, and drops soot in the soup
of an emperor; debt that like the moth, makes val-
ueless furs and velvets, inclosing the wearer in a
festering prison, (the shirt of Nessus was a shirt not
paid for;) debt that writes upon frescoed halls the

handwriting of the attorney; that puts a voice of terror in the knocker; that makes the heart quake at the haunted fireside; debt, the invisible demon that walks abroad with a man, now quickening his steps, now making him look on all sides like a hunted beast, and now bringing to his face the ashy hue of death as the unconscious passenger looks glancingly upon him! Poverty is a bitter draught, yet may, and sometimes can, with advantage, be gulped down. Though the drinker makes wry faces, there may, after all, be a wholesome goodness in the cup. But debt, however courteously it may be offered, is the cup of the siren; and the wine, spiced and delicious though it be, is poison. The man out of debt, though with a flaw in his jerkin, a crack in his shoe leather, and a hole in his hat, is still the son of liberty, free as the singing lark above him; but the debtor, although clothed in the utmost bravery, what is he but a serf out upon a holiday—a slave to be reclaimed at any instant by his owner, the creditor? My son, if poor, see Hyson in the running spring; see thy mouth water at a last week's roll; think a threadbare coat the only wear; and acknowledge a whitewashed garret the fittest housing place for a gentleman; do this, and flee debt. So shall thy heart be at rest and the sheriff confounded."

Somebody truly says that one debt begets another. If a man owes you a dollar, he is sure to owe you a grudge, too, and he is generally more ready to pay interest on the latter than on the former. Contracting debts is not unlike the man who goes to sea without a compass—he may steer clear of rocks, sand-bars, a lee shore, and breakers, but the chances are greatly against him; and, if he runs foul of either, ten to one he is lost. The present indiscriminate credit system is a labyrinth, the entrance is easy, but how to get out—that's the question. It is an endless chain, and if one link breaks in a particular community, it degrades the whole. The concussion may break many more, create a panic, and the chain become useless. If this misfortune would cure the evil, it would be a blessing in disguise; but so deeply rooted is this system among us, that no sooner is one chain destroyed than another is manufactured; an increasing weight is put upon it; presently some of its links snap, another concussion is produced, and creates a new panic; car after car rushes down the inclined plane of bankruptcy, increasing the mass of broken fragments and general ruin, all so commingled that a Philadelphia lawyer, aided by constables and sheriffs, can bring but little order out of the confusion. At the outset, especially among merchants, a ruinous tax is imposed by this system upon the vendor and vendee. The seller, in addition to a fair profit for cash in hand, adds a larger per cent. to meet losses from bad debts, but which often falls far short of the mark. Each purchaser, who is ultimately able to pay, bears the proportionate burden of this tax, and both contribute large sums to indulge those who cannot, and what is worse, those who never intend to pay; thus encouraging fraud. On every hand we see people living on credit, putting off pay-day to the last, making in the end some desperate effort, either by begging or borrowing, to scrape the money together, and then struggling on again, with the canker of care eating at their heart, to the inevitable goal of bankruptcy. If people would only make a push at the beginning, instead of the end, they would save themselves all this misery. The great secret of being solvent, and well-to-do, and comfortable, is to get ahead of your expenses. Eat and drink this month what you earned last month—not what you are going to earn next month. There are, no doubt, many persons so unfortunately situated that they can never accomplish this. No man can to a certainty guard against ill health; no man can insure himself a well-conducted, helpful family, or a permanent income. Friendships are broken over debts; forgeries and murders are committed on their account; and, however considered, they are a source of cost and annoyance—and that continually. They break in everywhere upon the harmonious relations of men; they render men servile or tyrannous, as they chance to be debtors or creditors; they blunt sensitiveness to personal independence, and, in no respect that we can fathom, do they advance the general well-being.

𝔉𝔞𝔦𝔩𝔲𝔯𝔢.

In every community there are men who are determined not to work if work can be shirked. Without
avowing this determination to themselves, or reflecting that they are fighting against a law of nature,
they begin life with a resolution to enjoy all the good
things that are accumulated by the labor of man,
without contributing their own share of labor to the
common stock. Hence the endless schemes for getting
rich in a day—for reaching the goal of wealth by a
few gigantic bounds, instead of by slow and plodding
steps.   It matters not in what such men deal, whether
in oroide watches or in watered stock; whether they
make "corners" in wheat or in gold; whether they
gamble in oats or at roulette; whether they steal a
railway or a man's money by "gift-concerts"—the
principle is in all cases the same, namely, to obtain
something for nothing, to get values without parting
with anything in exchange. Everybody knows the
history of such men, the vicissitudes they experience
——vicissitudes rendering the millionaire of to-day a
beggar to-morrow.

Firms are constantly changing.   Splendid mansions
change hands suddenly.   A brilliant party is held in
an up-town house, the sidewalk is carpeted, and the
papers are full of the brilliant reception.   The next
season the house will be dismantled, and a family,
"going into the country," or "to Europe," will offer

their imported furniture to the public under the hammer. A brilliant equipage is seen in the parks in the
early part of the season, holding gaily dressed ladies
and some successful speculators. Before the season
closes some government officer or sporting man will
drive that team on his own account, while the gay
party that called the outfit their own in the early part
of the season have passed away forever. This grows
out of the manner in which business is done. There
is no thrift, no forecast, no thought for the morrow.
A man who makes fifty thousand dollars, instead of
settling half of it on his wife and children, throws the
whole into a speculation with the expectation of
making it a hundred thousand. A successful dry
goods jobber, who has a balance of seventy-five
thousand dollars to his credit in the bank, instead of
holding it for a wet day or a tight time, goes into a
little stock speculation and hopes to make a fortune
at a strike. Men who have a good season launch
out into extravagancies and luxuries, and these, with
the gambling mania, invariably carry people under.

A gentleman, who had a very successful trade, built
him an extraordinary country seat in Westchester
county, which was the wonder of the age. His house
was more costly than the palace of the Duke of Buc-
cleuch. His estate comprised several acres laid out
in the most expensive manner, and the whole was
encircled with gas lights, several hundred in number,
which were lit every evening. As might have been
expected, with the first reverse, (and it comes sooner
or later to all,) the merchant was crushed, and as he

thought disgraced; and he was soon carried to his sepulchre, the wife obliged to leave her luxurious home, and by the kindness of creditors was allowed, with her children, to find temporary refuge in the coachman's loft in her stable.

Americans are always in a hurry when they have an object to accomplish; but if there be any vocation or pursuit in which gradual, slow-coach processes are scouted with peculiar detestation, it is that of acquiring riches. Especially is this true at the present day, when fortunes are continually changing hands, and men are so often, by a lucky turn of the wheel, lifted from the lowest depths of poverty to the loftiest pinnacle of wealth and affluence. Exceptional persons there are, who are content with slow gains — willing to accumulate riches by adding penny to penny, dollar to dollar; but the mass of business men are too apt to despise such a tedious, laborious ascent of the steep of fortune, and to rush headlong into schemes for the sudden acquisition of wealth. Hence honorable labor is too often despised; a man of parts is expected to be above hard work.

There is, with a great majority of men, a want of constancy in whatever plans they undertake. They toil as though they doubted that life had earnest and decided pathways; as though there were no compass but the shifting winds, with each of which they must change their course. Thus they beat about on the ocean of time, but never cross it, to rest on delightful islands or mainlands.

Despair.

No CALAMITY can produce such paralysis of the
mind as despair. It is the cap stone of the climax of
human anguish. The mental powers are frozen with
indifference, the heart becomes ossified with melancholy, the soul is shrouded in a cloud of gloom. No
words of consolation, no cheerful repartee, can break
the death-like calm; no love can warm the pent-up
heart; no sunbeams dispel the dark clouds. Time
may effect a change; death will break the monotony.
We can extend our kindness, but cannot relieve the
victim. We may trace the causes of this awful disease; God only can effect a cure. We may speculate
upon its nature, but cannot feel its force until its iron
hand is laid upon us. We may call it weakness, but
cannot prove or demonstrate the proposition. We
may call it folly, but can point to no frivolity to sustain our position. We may call it madness, but can
discover no maniac actions. We may call it stub-
bornness, but can see no exhibitions of indocility.
We may call it lunacy, but cannot perceive the inco-
herences of that unfortunate condition. We can call
it, properly, nothing but dark, gloomy despair, an
undefined and undefinable paralysis of all the sensibilities that render a man happy, and capable of imparting happiness to those around him. It is a state of
torpid dormancy, rather than a mental derangement
of the cerebral organs.

> Me miserable !   which way shall I fly
> Infinite wrath, and infinite despair ?
> Which way I fly is hell ; myself am hell ?
> And in the lowest deep a lower deep
> Still threat'ning to devour me opens wide,
> To which the hell I suffer seems a heaven.
>
> —MILTON.

It is induced by a false estimate of things, and of the dispensations and government of the God of mercy. Disappointments, losses, severe and continued afflictions, sudden transition from wealth to poverty, the death of dear friends, may cast a gloom over the mind that does not correctly comprehend the great first cause and see the hand of God in every thing, and produce a state of despair, because these things are viewed in a false mirror. Fanaticism in religious meetings has produced the most obstinate and melancholy cases of despair that have come under our own observation. Intelligence, chastened by religion, are the surest safeguards against this state of misery; ignorance and vice are its greatest promoters. Despair is the destruction of all hope, the deathless sting that refines the torment of the finally impenitent and lost. It is that undying worm, that unquenchable fire, so graphically described in Holy Writ.

Remember this, that God always helps those who help themselves, that he never forsakes those who are good and true, and that he heareth even the young ravens when they cry. Moreover, remember too, that come what may, we must never give up in life's battle, but press onward to the end, always keeping in mind the words — NEVER DESPAIR.

Despair is the death of the soul. If we will sympathize with God's system of salvation, there is no occasion for despondency or a feeling of condemnation, as we discover our defects from time to time; but, on the other hand, of cheerful hopefulness, and confidence of this very thing, that "He who hath begun a good work in us will perform it until the day of Jesus Christ."

Stepping Stones.

STEPPING STONES are advantages, auxiliaries, power, etc., and these are attained in no other way than through personal experiences. Our trials of life strengthen us; discouragements, disappointments, misfortunes, failures, adversities, and calamities, are all stepping stones for us; each successive victory raises us higher in strength and power. It is through trials that stout hearts are made. It is through adversities that our patience and courage are increased.

Men are frequently like tea—the real strength and goodness is not properly drawn out of them till they have been a short time in hot water. The ripest fruit grows on the roughest wall. It is the small wheels of the carriage that come in first. The man who holds the ladder at the bottom is frequently of more service than he who is stationed at the top of it.

The turtle, though brought in at a rear gate, takes the head of the table. "Better to be the cat in the philanthropist's family than a mutton pie at a king's banquet."

He who bears adversity well gives the best evidence that he will not be spoiled by prosperity. Many a promising reputation has been destroyed by early success. It is far from being true, in the progress of knowledge, that after every failure we must recommence from the beginning. Every failure is a step to success; every detection of what is false directs us toward what is true; every trial exhausts some tempting form of error. Not only so, but scarcely any attempt is entirely a failure; scarcely any theory, the result of steady thought, is altogether false; no tempting form of error is without some latent charm derived from truth.

Doubtless a deeper feeling of individual responsibility, and a better adaptation of talent to its fields of labor, are necessary to bring about a better state of society, and a better condition for the individual members of it. But with the most careful adaptation of talent and means to pursuits, no man can succeed, as a general principle, who has not a fixed and resolute purpose in his mind, and an unwavering faith that he can carry that purpose out.

Man is born a hero, and it is only by darkness and storms that heroism gains its greatest and best development and illustration; then it kindles the black cloud into a blaze of glory, and the storm bears it rapidly to its destiny. Despair not, then, disappoint-

ment will be realized. Mortifying failure may attend
this effort and that one; but only be honest and
struggle on, and it will all work well.

What though once supposed friends have disclaimed
and deserted thee—fortune, the jade, deceived thee
—and the stern tyrant, adversity, roughly asserted
his despotic power to trample thee down? "While
there's life there's hope." Has detraction's busy
tongue assailed thy peace, and contumely's venomed
shaft poisoned thy happiness, by giving reputation its
death blow; destroyed thy confidence in friendly
promise, and rendered thee suspicious of selfishness
in the exhibition of brotherly kindness; or the tide
of public opinion well nigh overwhelmed thee 'neath
its angry waves? Never despair. Yield not to the
influence of sadness, the blighting power of dejection,
which sinks thee in degrading inaction, or drives thee
to seek relief in some fatal vice, or to drown recollection in the poisoning bowl. Arouse, and shake the
oppressive burden from overpowering thee. Quench
the stings of slander in the waters of Lethe; bury
despondency in oblivion; fling melancholy to the
winds, and with firm bearing and a stout heart push
on to the attainment of a higher goal. The open
field for energetic action is large, and the call for vigorous laborers immensely exceed the supply. Much
precious time is squandered, valuable labor lost,
mental activity stupified and deadened by vain regrets,
useless repinings, and unavailing idleness. The
appeal for volunteers in the great battle of life, in
exterminating ignorance and error, and planting high

on an everlasting foundation the banner of intelligence and right, is directed to thee, wouldst thou but
grant it audience. Let no cloud again darken thy
spirit, or weight of sadness oppress thy heart. Arouse
ambition's smouldering fires. The laurel may e'en
now be wreathed destined to grace thy brow. Burst
the trammels that impede thy progress, and cling to
hope. The world frowned darkly upon all who have
ever yet won fame's wreath, but on they toiled.
Place high thy standard, and with a firm tread and
fearless eye press steadily onward. Persevere, and
thou wilt surely reach it. Are there those who have
watched, unrewarded, through long sorrowful years,
for the dawning of a brighter morrow, when the
weary soul should calmly rest? Hope's bright rays
still illume their dark pathways, and cheerfully they
watch. *Never despair! Faint not*, though thy task
be heavy, and victory is thine. None should despair;
God can help them. None should presume; God
can cross them.

Prayer.

PRAYER is an action of likeness to the Holy Ghost,
the spirit of gentleness and dove-like simplicity; an
imitation of the Holy Jesus, whose spirit is meek, and
a conformity to God, whose anger is always just, and
marches slowly, and is without transportation, and
often hindered and never hasty, and is full of mercy.

Prayer is the peace of our spirit, the stillness of our
thoughts, the evenness of recollection, the seat of
meditation, the rest of our cares, and the calm of our
tempest; prayer is the issue of a quiet mind, of
untroubled thoughts; it is the daughter of charity,
and the sister of meekness; and he who prays to
God with an angry, that is, with a troubled and dis-
composed spirit, is like him who retires into a battle
to meditate, and sets up his closet in the out-quarters
of an army, and chooses a frontier garrison to be
wise in. Anger is a perfect alienation of the mind
from prayer, and therefore is contrary to that attention which presents our prayers in a right line to God.
For so have we seen a lark rising from his bed of
grass, and soaring upward, singing as it rises, and
hoping to get to heaven, and climb above the clouds;
but the poor bird was beaten back with the loud sigh-
ings of an eastern wind, and his motion made
irregular and inconstant, descending more at every
breath of the tempest than it could recover by the
libration and frequent weighing of his wings; till the
little creature was forced to sit down and pant, and
stay till the storm was over; and then it made a
prosperous flight, and did rise and sing as if it had
learned music and motion from an angel, as he passed
sometimes through the air about his ministries here
below: so is the prayer of a good man: when his
affairs have required business, and his business was
matter of discipline, and his discipline was to pass
upon a sinning person, or had a design of charity,
his duty met with the infirmities of a man, and anger

was its instrument, and the instrument became stronger than the prime agent, and raised a tempest, and over-ruled the man; and then his prayer was broken, and his thoughts were troubled, and his words went up toward a cloud, and his thoughts pulled them back again, and made them without intention, and the good man sighs for his infirmity, but must be content to lose the prayer, and he must recover it when his anger is removed, and his spirit is becalmed, made even as the brow of Jesus, and smooth like the heart of God; and then it ascends to heaven upon the wings of the holy dove, and dwells with God, till it returns, like the useful bee, laden with a blessing and the dew of heaven.

God respects not the arithmetic of our prayers, how many they are; nor the rhetoric of our prayers, how neat they are; nor the geometry of our prayers, how long they are; nor the music of our prayers, how melodious they are; nor the logic of our prayers, how methodical they are—but the divinity of our prayers, how heart-sprung they are. Not gifts, but graces, prevail in prayer. Perfect prayers, without a spot or blemish, though not one word be spoken, and no phrases known to mankind be tampered with, always pluck the heart out of the earth and move it softly like a censer, to and fro, beneath the face of heaven.

Prayer is a constant source of invigoration to self-discipline; not the thoughtless praying, which is a thing of custom, but that which is sincere, intense, watchful. Let a man ask himself whether he really would have the thing he prays for; let him think, while he is praying for a spirit of forgiveness, whether, even at that moment, he is disposed to give up the luxury of anger. If not, what a horrible mockery it is! Do not say you have no convenient place to pray in. Any man can find a place private enough, if he is disposed. Our Lord prayed on a mountain, Peter on the house-top, Isaac in the field, Nathaniel under the fig-tree, Jonah in the whale's belly. Any place may become a closet, an oratory, and a bethel, and be to us the presence of God.

To present a petition is one thing; to prosecute a suit is another. Most prayers answer to the former; but successful prayer corresponds to the latter. God's people frequently lodge their petition in the court of heaven and there they let it lie. They do not press their suit. They do not employ other means of furthering it beyond the presenting of it. The whole of prayer does not consist in taking hold of God. The main matter is holding on. How many are induced by the slightest appearance of repulse to let go, as Jacob did not! We have been struck with the manner in which petitions are usually concluded— "And your petitioners will ever pray." So "men ought always pray (to God) and never faint." Payson says, "The promise of God is not to the act, but to the habit of prayer."

Though prayer should be the key of the day, and the lock of the night, yet we hold it more needful in the morning, than when our bodies do take their repose. For howsoever sleep be the image or shadow of death—and when the shadow is so near, the substance cannot be far—yet a man at rest in his chamber is like a sheep impenned in the fold; subject only to the unavoidable and more immediate hand of God: whereas in the day, when he roves abroad in the open and wide pastures, he is then exposed to many more unthought-of accidents, that contingently and casually occur in the way: retiredness is more safe than business: who believes not a ship securer in the bay than in the midst of the boiling ocean? Besides, the morning to the day, is as youth to the life of a man: If that be begun well, commonly his age is virtuous: otherwise, God accepts not the latter service, when his enemy joys in the first dish. Why should God take the dry bones, when the devil hath sucked the marrow out?

Not a few, too, owe their escape from skepticism and infidelity to its sacred influence. Said the noted John Randolph, "I once took the French side in politics; and I should have been a French atheist, if it had not been for one recollection; and that was the memory of the time when my departed mother used to take my little hands in hers, and cause me on my knees to say, 'Our Father, who art in heaven.'"

> " The parent pair their secret homage pay,
> And offer up to heaven the warm request,
> That he who stills the raven's clamorous nest,
> And decks the lily fair in flowery pride,
> Would, in the way His wisdom sees the best,
> For them and for their little ones provide."

There is a God.

THERE is a God! The herbs of the valley, the cedars of the mountain, bless him; the insect sports in his beam; the bird sings Him in the foliage; the thunder proclaims Him in the heavens; the ocean declares His immensity; man alone has said, "There is no God!" Unite in thought at the same instant the most beautiful object in nature. Suppose that you see at once all the hours of the day, and all the seasons of the year; a morning of spring, and a morning of autumn; a night bespangled with stars, and a night darkened by clouds; meadows enameled with flowers; forests hoary with snow; fields gilded by the tints of autumn; then alone you will have a just conception of the universe! While you are gazing on that sun which is plunging into the vault of the west, another observer admires him emerging from the gilded gates of the east. By what inconceivable power does that aged star, which is sinking, fatigued and burning, in the shades of the evening, reappear at the same instant fresh and humid with the rosy dew of the morning? At every hour of the day the glorious orb is at once rising, resplendent as noon-day, and setting in the west; or rather, our senses deceive us, and there is, properly speaking, no east or west, no north or south, in the world.

Go out beneath the arched heavens, at night, and say, if you can, " *There is no God!* " Pronounce that dreadful blasphemy, and each star above you will reproach the unbroken darkness of your intellect; every voice that floats upon the night winds will bewail your utter hopelessness and folly.

Is there no God? Who, then, unrolled the blue scroll, and threw upon its high frontispiece the legible gleamings of immortality? Who fashioned this green earth, with its perpetual rolling waters, and its wide expanse of islands and of main? Who settled the foundations of the mountains? Who paved the heavens with clouds, and attuned, amid the clamor of storms, the voice of thunders, and unchained the lightnings that flash in their gloom?

Who gave to the eagle a safe eyrie where the tempests dwell, and beat the strongest, and to the dove a tranquil abode amid the forests that echo to the minstrelsy of her moan? Who made THEE, O man! with thy perfected elegance of intellect and form? Who made the light pleasant to thee, and the darkness a covering, and a herald to the first gorgeous flashes of the morning?

There is a God. All nature declares it in a language too plain to be misapprehended. The great truth is too legibly written over the face of the whole creation to be easily mistaken. Thou canst behold it in the tender blade just starting from the earth in the early spring, or in the sturdy oak that has withstood the blasts of fourscore winters. The purling rivulet, meandering through downy meads and verdant glens, and Niagara's tremendous torrent, leaping over its awful chasm, and rolling in majesty its broad sheet

of waters,onward to the ocean, unite in proclaiming
"THERE IS A GOD."

'Tis heard in the whispering breeze and in the
howling storm; in the deep-toned thunder, and in the
earthquake's shock; 'tis declared to us when the
tempest lowers; when the hurricane sweeps over the
land; when the winds moan around our dwellings,
and die in sullen murmurs on the plain, when the
heavens, overcast with blackness, ever and anon are
illuminated by the lightning's glare.

Nor is the truth less solemnly impressed on our
minds in the universal hush and calm repose of
nature, when all is still as the soft breathings of an
infant's slumber. The vast ocean, when its broad
expanse is whitened with foam, and when its heaving
waves roll mountain on mountain high, or when the
dark blue of heaven's vault is reflected with beauty
on its smooth and tranquil bosom, confirms the dec-
laration. The twinkling star, shedding its flickering
rays so far above the reach of human ken, and the
glorious sun in the heavens — all — declare there is a
universal FIRST CAUSE.

And man, the proud lord of creation, so fearfully
and wonderfully made — each joint in its corresponding socket — each muscle, tendon, and artery, performing their allotted functions with all the precision
of the most perfect mechanism — and, surpassing all,
possessed of a soul capable of enjoying the most
exquisite pleasure, or of enduring the most excrucia-
ting pain, which is endowed with immortal capacities,
and is destined to live onward through the endless

ages of eternity—these all unite in one general
proclamation of the eternal truth—there is a Being,
infinite in wisdom, who reigns over all, undivided and
supreme—the fountain of all life, source of all light
—from whom all blessings flow, and in whom all
happiness centres.

The Bible.

THE Bible is not only the revealer of the unknown
God to man, but His grand interpreter as the God of
nature.   In revealing God, it has given us the key
that unlocks the profoundest mysteries of creation,
the clew by which to thread the labyrinth of the
universe, the glass through which to look "from
nature up to nature's God."

It is only when we stand and gaze upon nature,
with the Bible in our hands, and its idea of God in
our understandings, that nature is capable of rising to
her highest majesty, and kindling in our souls the
highest emotions of moral beauty and sublimity.
Without the all-pervading spiritual God of the Bible
in our thoughts, nature's sweetest music would lose
its charm, the universe its highest significance and
glory.

Go, and stand with your open Bible upon the Areo-
pagus of Athens, where Paul stood so long ago!   In
thoughtful silence, look around upon the site of all
that ancient greatness; look upward to those still

glorious skies of Greece, and what conceptions of wisdom and power will all those memorable scenes of nature and art convey to your mind, now, more than they did to an ancient worshiper of Jupiter or Apollo? They will tell of Him who made the worlds, "by whom, and through whom, and for whom, are all things." To you, that landscape of exceeding beauty, so rich in the monuments of departed genius, with its distant classic mountains, its deep blue sea, and its bright bending skies, will be telling a tale of glory the Grecian never learned; for it will speak to you no more of its thirty thousand petty contending deities, but of the one living and everlasting God.

Go, stand with David and Isaiah under the star-spangled canopy of the night; and, as you look away to the "range of planets, suns, and adamantine spheres wheeling unshaken through the void immense;" take up the mighty questionings of inspiration!

Go, stand upon the heights at Niagara, and listen in awe-struck silence to that boldest, most earnest, and most eloquent of all nature's orators! And what is Niagara, with its plunging waters and its mighty roar, but the oracle of God, the whisper of His voice who is revealed in the Bible as sitting above the water-floods forever!

Who can stand amid scenes like these, with the Bible in his hand, and not feel that if there is a moral sublimity to be found on earth, it is in the Book of God, it is in the thought of God? For what are all these outward, visible forms of grandeur but the expression and the utterance of that conception of Deity which the Bible has created in our minds, and which has now become the leading and largest thought of all civilized nations?

The oldest reliable history is that given by Moses: "And God said, Let there be light, and there was light." And on and down, for four thousand years, the sacred volume follows the fortunes of God's chosen people. And, incidentally, it gives us, at the same time, light on the contemporary nations of hea-thendom. See what it has done for science. True, it does not unfold to us the mysteries of geology, astronomy, or chemistry. And yet it does train the mind for its loftiest flights and its broadest explora-tions. "I have always found," said a patron of the National Institute at Washington, "in my scientific studies, that, when I could get the Bible to say any-thing on the subject, it afforded me a firm platform to stand upon, and another round in the ladder, by which I could safely ascend." It throws its beams into the temples of science and literature, no less than those of religion; and so prepares the way for man's advancement in philosophy, metaphysics, and natural sciences, no less than in the realm of ethics; and, as it saves the soul, it exalts the intellect.

The Bible is adapted to every possible variety of taste, temperament, culture, and condition. It has strong reasoning for the intellectual; it takes the calm and contemplative to the well-balanced James, and the affectionate to the loving and beloved John. The pensive may read the tender lamentations and the funeral strains of Jeremiah. Let the sanguine commune with the graphic and creative Joel; and the plain and practical may go to the wise Ecclesiastes or or the outspoken Peter. They who like brilliant apothegms, should study the book of Proverbs; and the lover of pastoral and quiet delineations may dwell with the sweet singer of Israel, or the richly endowed Amos and Hosea. If you would take the wings of imagination, and leap from earth to heaven, or wander through eternity, then open the Revelation; and pour over and fill yourself with the glory of the New Jerusalem; and listen to the seven thunders; and gaze on the pearly gates and the golden streets of the heavenly city.

Not only is this book precious to tne poor and unlearned; not only is it the counselor and confidence of the great middle class of society, both spiritually and mentally speaking; but the scholar and the sage, the intellectual monarchs of the race, bow to its authority. It has encountered the scorn of a Lucian, the mystic philosophy of a Porphyry, the heartless skepticism of a Hume, the lore of a Gibbon, the sneers of a Voltaire, the rude weapons of a Paine, and the subtle, many-sided neology of modern Germany. But none of these things have moved it. Nay, parallel with these attempts at its subjugation, and triumphant over them all, have advanced the noble works of such commanding intellects as Newton, Chalmers, Robert Hall, Bowditch, Channing, testifying that, to them, the Bible bore the stamp of a special revelation and the seal of the eternal God.

To multitudes of our race this book is not only the foundation of their religious faith, but their daily practical guide. It has taken hold of the world as no other book ever did. Not only is it read in all Christian pulpits, but it enters every habitation from the palace to the cottage. It is the golden chain which binds hearts together at the marriage altar; it contains the sacred formula for the baptismal rite. It blends itself with our daily conversation, and is the silver thread of all our best reading, giving its hue, more or less distinctly, to book, periodical, and daily paper. When the good mother parts with her dear boy, other volumes may be placed in his hands, but we are sure that, with tearful prayers, she will fold among his apparel a Bible. On the seas it goes with the mariner, as his spiritual chart and compass; and on the land it is to untold millions their pillar-cloud by day, their fire-column by night. In the closet and in the street, amid temptations and trials, this is man's most faithful attendant, and his strongest shield. It is our lamp through the dark valley; and the radiator of our best light from the solemn and unseen future. Stand before it as a mirror and you will see there not only your good traits, but errors, follies, and sins, which you did not imagine were there until now. You desire to make constant improvement. Go then to the Bible. It not only shows the way of all progress, but it incites you to go forward. It opens before you a path leading up and still upward, along which good angels will cheer you, and God himself will lend you a helping hand.

You may go to the statesman who has filled the highest office in this country, and ask him whether his cup of joy has been full? As he stands by at the inauguration of his successor, his shaded brow will tell you nay. Ask the warrior, coming from the battle-field, his garments rolled in blood, Did the shouts of victory satiate his thirst for applause? Bid any of the godless sons of literary fame, Frederic of Prussia, Byron, or Volney, give in their testimony; and they affirm, in one gloomy voice:

> "We've drank every cup of joy, heard every trump
> Of fame; drank early, deeply drank, drank draughts
> That common millions might have quenched;—then died
> Of thirst, because there was no more to drink."

But never a human being went to the Bible, who did not find His words true: "But whosoever drinketh of the water I will give him, shall never thirst; for it shall be in him a well of water springing up into everlasting life." Like an ethereal principle of light and life, its blessed truths extend with electric force through all the avenues and elements of the home-existence, "giving music to language, elevation to thought, vitality to feeling, intensity to power, beauty and happiness."

It is a book for the mind, the heart, the conscience, the will and the life. It suits the palace and the cottage, the afflicted and the prosperous, the living and the dying. It is a comfort to "the house of mourning," and a check to "the house of feasting." It "giveth seed to the sower, and bread to the eater." It is simple, yet grand; mysterious, yet plain; and though from God, it is, nevertheless, within the comprehension of a little child. You may send your children to school to study other books, from which they may be educated for this world; but in this divine book they study the science of the eternal world.

The family Bible has given to the Christian home that unmeasured superiority in all the dignities and decencies and enjoyments of life, over the home of the heathen. It has elevated woman, revealed her true mission, developed the true idea and sacredness of marriage and of the home-relationship; it has unfolded the holy mission of the mother, the responsibilities of the parent, and the blessings of the child. Take this book from the family, and it will degenerate into a mere conventionalism, marriage into a "social contract;" the spirit of mother will depart; natural affection will sink to mere brute fondness, and what we now call home would become a den of sullen selfishness and barbaric lust!

And in our own day, a throng of good and great men have venerated this book, and imbibed its spirit. John Quincy Adams, through a long life, made it his daily study; a neighbor of his once said that, amid the most active portions of life, he always translated a few verses in his Hebrew Bible, the first thing in the morning. He read it when a boy; he clung to it through his manhood; and to his last day, he owed to it, not only his rare veneration for the Deity, but his love for freedom and humanity, and all his adamantine virtues. Jackson, Harrison and Clay were

each students of the Bible.   They lived gratefully by
its light; and they died in the hope of its glory.
"Though I walk through the dark valley of the shadow
of death, I will fear no evil;" these were among
the last words that fell on the ear of the dying Webster.   Sir Walter Scott, a few days before his death,
asked his son-in-law to read to him.   "What book,"
inquired Mr. Lockhart, "would you like?"   "Can
you ask?" said Sir Walter, "there is but one."
Verily, there *is* but one book to be read in our last
hours.

Religion.

RELIGION is the daughter of heaven, parent of our
virtues, and source of all true felicity; she alone gives
peace and contentment, divests the heart of anxious
cares, bursts on the mind a flood of joy, and sheds
unmingled and perpetual sunshine in the pious breast.
By her the spirits of darkness are banished from the
earth, and angelic ministers of grace thicken unseen
the regions of mortality.

She promotes love and good will among men, lifts
up the head that hangs down, heals the wounded
spirit, dissipates the gloom of sorrow, sweetens the
cup of affliction, blunts the sting of death, and
wherever seen, felt, and enjoyed, breathes around
her an everlasting spring.   The external life of man
is the creature of time and circumstance, and passes

away, but the internal abides, and continues to exist.
One is the painted glory of the flower; the other is
the delicious attar of the rose. The city and the
temple may be destroyed, and the tribes exiled and
dispersed, yet the altars and the faith of Israel are
still preserved. Spirit triumphs over form. External
life prevails amidst sounds and shows, and visible
things; the internal dwells in silence, sighs and tears,
and secret sympathies with the invisible world.
Power, and wealth, and luxury, are relative terms;
and if address, and prudence, and policy, can only
acquire us our share, we shall not account ourselves
more powerful, more rich, or more luxurious, than
when in the little we possessed we were still equal to
those around us. But if we have narrowed the
sources of internal comfort, and internal enjoyment,
if we have debased the powers or corrupted the purity
of the mind, if we have blunted the sympathy or
contracted the affections of the heart, we have lost
some of that treasure which was absolutely our own,
and derived not its value from comparative estimation.
Above all, if we have allowed the prudence or the
interests of this world to shut out from our souls the
view or the hopes of a better, we have quenched that
light which would have cheered the darkness of
affliction. But if we let God care for our inward and
eternal life, if by all the experiences of this life he is
reducing it and preparing for its disclosure, nothing
can befall us but prosperity. Every sorrow shall be
but the setting of some luminous jewel of joy. Our
very mourning shall be but the enamel around the

diamond; our very hardships but the metallic rim that holds the opal glancing with strange interior fires.

If you stand upon the mountain, you may see the sun shining long after it is dark in the valley. Try to live up high! Escape, if you can, the malarious damps of the lowlands. Make an upward path for your feet. Though your spirit may be destined to live isolated, you cannot be *alone*, for God is there. Your best strivings of soul are there! Your standard ground should be there! Live upward! The cedar is always developing its branches toward the top while the lower ones are dropping away. Let your soul-life be so! Upward! Upward!

"Drink deep, or taste not," is a direction fully as applicable to religion, if we would find it a source of pleasure, as it is to knowledge. A little religion is, it must be confessed, apt to make men gloomy, as a little knowledge is to render them vain; hence the unjust imputation brought upon religion by those whose degree of religion is just sufficient, by condemning their course of conduct, to render them uneasy; enough merely to impair the sweetness of the pleasures of sin, and not enough to compensate for the relinquishment of them by its own peculiar comforts. Thus, then, men bring up, as it were, an ill report of that land of promise, which, in truth, abounds with whatever, in our journey through life, can best refresh and strengthen us. Would you wish, amidst the great variety of religious systems in vogue, to make a right distinction, and prefer the best? Recollect the character of Christ; keep a

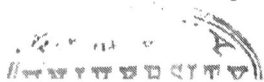

steady eye on that universal and permanent good will to men, in which He lived, by which He suffered, and by which He died. Not in those wild and romantic notions, which, to make us Christians, would make us fools; but in those inspired writings, and in those alone, which contain His genuine history, and His blessed gospel; and which, in the most peculiar and extensive sense, are the words of eternal life.

Doing Good.

THERE are trees, like the butternut, that impoverish the ground upon which they grow, but the olive tree enriches the very soil upon which it feeds. So there are natures as unlike in effect as these. Some cold, selfish, absorbing, which chill and impoverish every one with whom they come in contact. Others radiate affluent souls, who enrich by their very presence, whose smiles are full of blessing, and whose touch has a balm of feeling in it like the touch of Him of Nazareth. Squalid poverty is not so pitiable and barren as the selfish heart, while wealth has no largess like that with which God dowers the broad and sunny soul. Be like the olive, from whose kindly boughs blessing and benison descend.

One of the old philosophers bade his scholars to consider what was the best thing to possess. One come and said that there was nothing better than a good eye, which is, in their language, a liberal and contented disposition. Another said a good companion was the best thing in the world. A third said a good neighbor was the best thing he could desire; and the fourth preferred a man that could foresee things to come—that is, a wise person. But at last came in one Eleazer, and he said a good heart was better than them all. "True," said the master, "thou hast comprehended in two words all that the rest have said; for he that hath a good heart will be both contented, and a good companion, and a good neighbor, and easily see what is fit to be done by him."

Every man should ever consider that it is best for him to have a good heart; having this it will prompt him to not only do good, but it will encompass many virtues. We counsel our friends, then, to seize every opportunity of contributing to the good of others. Sometimes a smile will do it. Oftener a kind word, a look of sympathy, or an acknowledgment of obligation. Sometimes a little help to a burdened shoulder, or a heavy wheel, will be in place. Sometimes a word or two of good counsel, a seasonable and gentle admonition, and at others, a suggestion of advantage to be gained and a little interest to secure it, will be received with lasting gratitude. And thus every instance of kindness done, whether acknowledged or not, opens up a little wellspring of happiness in the doer's own breast, the flow of which may be made permanent by habit.

Influence is to a man what flavor is to fruit, or fragrance to the flower. It does not develop strength, or determine character, but it is the measure of his

interior richness and worth, and as the blossom cannot tell what becomes of the odor which is wafted
away from it by every wind, so no man knows the
limit of that influence which constantly and impercep-
tibly escapes from his daily life, and goes out far
beyond his conscious knowledge or remotest thought.
There are noxious weeds and fragrance-laden flowers in the world of mind as in the world of matter.
Truly blessed are they who walk the way of life as
the Savior of mankind once walked on our earth,
filling all the air about them with the aroma which is
so subtilely distilled from kindly deeds, helpful words
and unselfish lives.

One kernel is felt in a hogshead — one drop of
water helps to swell the ocean — a spark of fire
helps to give light to the world. You are a small
man, passing amid the crowd, you are hardly noticed;
but you have a drop, a spark within you that may be
felt through eternity. Do you believe it? Set that
drop in motion, give wings to that spark, and behold
the results! It may renovate the world.

None are too small — too feeble — too poor to be of
service think of this, and act. Life is no trifle. If
we work upon marble, it will perish; if we work upon
brass time will efface it; if we rear temples, they will
crumble into dust. But if we work upon immortal
minds — if we imbue them with high principles, with
the just fear of God, and of their fellow-men — we
engrave on these tables something which no time can
efface, but which will brighten to all eternity. It is a
great thing to stand in a place of God, and proclaim
His word in the presence of angels and men.

If you would show yourself a man in the truest and noblest sense, go not to yonder tented field, where death hovers, and the vulture feasts himself upon human victims! Go not where men are carving monuments of marble to perpetuate names which will not live in our own grateful memory! Go not to the dwellings of the rich! Go not to the palaces of the kings! Go not to the halls of merriment and pleasure! Go rather to the poor and helpless. Go to the widow and relieve her woe. Go to the orphan and speak words of comfort. Go to the lost, and save him. Go to the fallen and raise him up. Go to the sinner, and whisper in his ear words of eternal life. A man's true wealth hereafter, is the good he does in this world to his fellow men. When he dies, people will say, "What property has he left behind him?" But the angels who examine will ask, "What are the good deeds thou hast sent before thee?"

Every one of us may in some way or other assist or instruct some of his fellow creatures, for the best of the human race is poor and needy, and all have a mutual dependence on one another. There is nobody who cannot do some good; and everybody is bound to do diligently all the good he can. It is by no means enough to be rightly disposed, to be serious, and religious in our closets; we must be useful too, and take care that as we all reap numberless benefits from society, society may be the better for every one of us. It is a false, a faulty, and an indolent humility, that makes people sit still and do nothing, because they will not believe that they are capable of doing

37

much, for everybody can do something. Everybody can set a good example, be it to many or to few. Everybody can in some degree encourage virtue and religion, and discountenance vice and folly. Everybody has some one or other whom he can advise, or instruct, or in some way help to guide through life. Those who are too poor to give alms can yet give their time, their trouble, their assistance in preparing or forwarding the gifts of others; in considering and representing distressed cases to those who can relieve them; in visiting and comforting the sick and afflicted. Everybody can offer up his prayers for those who need them; which, if he do reverently and sincerely, he will never be wanting in giving them every other assistance that it should please God to put in his power.

Dr. Johnson used to say, "He who waits to do a great deal of good at once, will never do any." Good is done by degrees. However small in proportion to benefits which follow individual attempts to do good, a great deal may be accomplished by perseverance, even in the midst of discouragements and disappointments. Life is made up of little things. It is but once in an age that occasion is offered for doing a great deed. True greatness consists in being great in little things. How are railroads built? By one shovelful of dirt after another; one shovelful at a time. Thus drops make the ocean. Hence we should be willing to do a little good at a time, and never "wait to do a great deal of good at once." If we would do much good in the world, we must be

willing to do good in little things, little acts one after
another, setting a good example all the time; we must
do the first good thing we can, and then the next, and
the next, and so keep on doing good. Oh! it is
great; there is no other greatness: to make some nook
of God's creation a little more fruitful, better, more
worthy of a God; to make some human hearts a
little wiser, more manful, happier; more blessed, less
accursed! The first and paramount aim of religion
is not to prepare for another world, but to make the
best of this world; or, more correctly stated, to make
this world better, wiser, and happier. It is to be
good, and do the most good we can now and here,
and to help others to be and do the same. It is to
seek with all our might the highest welfare of the
world we live in, and the realization of its ideal greatness, nobleness, and blessedness. A most comforting
thought is, that the forever will not be a place of white
robes and golden harps and praise singing only, but
will also be a place for living, loving and doing.
There is pleasure in contemplating good; there is a
greater pleasure in receiving good; but the greatest
pleasure of all is in doing good, which comprehends
the rest. Do good with what thou hast, or it will do
thee no good. The power of doing good to worthy
objects, is the only enviable circumstance in the lives
of people of fortune. Napoleon once entered a
cathedral and saw twelve silver statues. "What are
these?" said the Emperor. "The twelve Apostles,"
was the reply. "Well," said he, "take them down,
melt them, and coin them into money, and let them

go about doing good, as their Master did." Be always
sure of doing good. This will make your life comfortable, your death happy, and your account glorious.
Zealously strive to do good for the sake of good. Be
not simply good; be good for something.

> How sweet 'twill be at evening
> If you and I can say
> "Good Shepherd, we've been seeking
> The lambs that went astray;
> Heart-sore, and faint with hunger,
> We heard them making moan,
> And lo! we come at night-fall
> Bearing them safely home!"

Well Doing, Woman's Culture.

I AM happy, says G. S. Weaver, in knowing that
although men differ about woman's intellectual capacities, they agree in ascribing to her the highest order
of moral and social qualities. All admit that woman
is the morality and religion, the love and sociality, of
humanity. In these developments of human attainments, she is the queen without a peer. These are
at present woman's peculiar fields of power. Society
has measurably shut her out from the intellectual arena
of life. But if it has cut short her operations in this,
it has extended them in the field of social life. Wide
and grand are her opportunities here. Man is not so
deficient in gallantry as he is in generosity and judgment. In what man has oppressed woman it is more
the fault of his head than his heart; it is more a

weakness of conscience than of affection. He is prouder of his judgment than he ought to be. His judgment often fails because it is not sanctified by conscience. His intellect is often deceived because its vision is not extended and widened by a deep affection and a broad benevolence. In this, woman has the advantage of him in the present relations of the sexes. Her moral sense consecrates her intellect, and her heart quickens it, thus making her judgment more intuitive and ready, more comprehensive and sure. She *feels* that a thing is so; he *reasons* that it is so. She judges by *impression* when facts are stated; he by *logic*. Her impressions she cannot always explain, because her intellect has not been sufficiently cultivated; his logic often fails him, because it is not sufficiently imbued with the moral element. The light of the conscience and the heart does not shine upon it with sufficient strength. This we understand to be the present difference between the male and female mind. It is more than a difference in growth and culture, in inherent constitution. We do not believe that the relation between the different departments of the human mind naturally differ in men and women; that is, we do not believe that man is more intelligent and less moral, and woman more moral and less intellectual. A perfect male mind is an equal strength of the several departments of mind; that is, an equal strength of the intellectual, moral, social, and energetic portions of the mind, a balance among its several powers. The same is true of the female mind.

So far as this relation of the parts is concerned, it is the same in the perfect male and female mind. In just so much as this relation is changed, is the judgment corrupted and the mental strength impaired. In the present male mind this relation is changed by giving the greater cultivation to the intellect, and less to the moral sense and the heart. So his judgment is impaired and the moral dignity of his soul debased. He is a less man than he ought to be; is deformed in his mental growth like a tree grown in a shady place where the light could reach it from only one quarter. He has less power of mind than he would have with the same amount of cultivation properly and equally distributed among the several departments of his mind. Strength lies in balance of power. Our men are not too intellectual, but too intellectual for their moral and affectionate strength. They are like an apple grown all on one side, or a horse with disproportioned body, or any animal with some of its limbs too short for the rest. Mentally they are deformed and lame by their one-sided culture. In the present female mind there is a disproportion in another direction. In this the intellect has been neglected, while the moral and social mind has had a better degree of cultivation. Thus our women have been mentally deformed and weakened. They are less woman than they ought to have been. Their characters and judgments have lacked harmony, and their lives have been marked by the same deficiencies. Their minds are one-sided and marked with sad irregularities. They are not too moral and affectionate, but are not

sufficiently intellectual. The same amount of culture
which they have received would have conferred more
beauty and dignity to the character and life had it
been more general, or equally applied to the several
powers of mind. Sound judgment, pure life, dignity
of character are the results of a balance of power
and culture in the several departments of mind.
This difference in the culture of the male and female
mind has made a breach between the sexes. The
present male mind cannot comprehend the female, nor
the female the male. Instead of growing up in
similarity and harmony, they have grown up into
wide differences.

The male and female mind are not alike by nature,
by any means. There is a wide difference between
them; but the difference is in the nature, texture, and
quality of the mind, and not in the relation of parts.
The female mind has an inherent constitution peculiar
to itself that makes it female; so with the male.
This difference is beyond the fathoming line of human
thought. We know it exists, but wherefore and how
we know not. It is the secret of the Divine Con-
structor of mentality. In our mental structure we
are to seek for harmony, a consistent rhythmic development of parts. The opportunities offered to
woman for the cultivation of her moral and religious
nature are eminently favorable. If her intellectual
opportunities are not so good, her moral and religious are better. She is not so pressed with temptation. The world does not bear with such an Atlas
burden on her conscience. The almighty dollar does

not eclipse so large a field of her mental vision.
Material pursuits do not check so much her spiritual
progress. God is nearer to her heart, more in her
thoughts, sweeter in her soul, brighter in her visions,
because she is less compassed about by the snares of
vice and the hostile pursuits of the false and flattering world. It is a blessed thing for humanity that
woman is more religious and morally upright; because
man is too irreverent and base. He lacks the sanctity
of high morality and the consecration of religion.
I speak of man in the mass. Woman is the conser-
vation of morality and religion. Her moral worth
holds man in some restraint and preserves his ways
from becoming inhumanly corrupt. Mighty is the
power of woman in this respect. Every virtue in
woman's heart has its influence on the world. Some
men feel it. A brother, husband, friend, or son, is
touched by its sunshine. Its mild beneficence is not
lost. A virtuous woman in the seclusion of her home,
breathing the sweet influence of virtue into the hearts
and lives of its beloved ones, is an evangel of goodness to the world. She is one of the pillars of the
eternal kingdom of right. She is a star shining in
the moral firmament. She is a princess administer-
ing at the fountains of life Every prayer she
breathes is answered to a greater or less extent in
the hearts and lives of those she loves. Her piety is
an altar-fire where religion acquires strength to go
out on its merciful mission. We cannot overestimate
the utility and power of woman's moral and religious
character. The world would go to ruin without it.

With all our ministers and churches, and Bibles and
sermons, man would be a prodigal without the
restraint of woman's virtue and the consecration of
her religion. Woman first lays her hand on our
young powers. She plants the first seeds. She
makes the first impressions; and all along through
life she scatters the good seed of the kingdom and
sprinkles the dews of her piety. But woman does
not do enough. Her power is not yet equal to its
need. Her virtue is not mighty enough. Her religion comes short in its work. Look out and see the
world—a grand Pandora's box of wickedness—a
great battle-field of clashing passions and warring
interests—a far spread scene of sensualism and selfishness, in which woman herself acts a conspicuous
part. Look at society—the rich eating up the poor;
the poor stabbing at the rich; fashion playing in the
halls of gilded sensualism; folly dancing to the tune
of ignorant mirth; intemperance gloating over its
roast beef, or whisky jug, brandy punch, champagne
bottle, bearing thousands upon thousands down to
the grave of ignominy, sensualism, and drunkenness.
Is there not a need of more vigorous virtue in
woman? Is there not a call for a more active religion,
a more powerful impulse in behalf of morality? Who
shall heed this cry of wicked, wasting humanity, if
the young woman does not? To youthful woman
we must look for a powerful leader in the cause of
morality and religion. The girls of to-day are to be
greatly instrumental in giving a moral complexion to
the society of to-morrow. It is important that they

should fix high this standard of virtue. They ought to lay well their foundations of religion. They ought early to baptize their souls in the consecrated waters of truth and right.

The first element in their moral character which they should seek to establish firmly is *purity*. A pure heart is the fountain of life. "The pure in heart shall see God." Not only is purity of life needed to make a young woman beautiful and useful, but purity in thought, feeling, emotion, and motive. All within us that lies open to the gaze of God should be pure. A young woman should be in heart what she seems to be in life. Her words should correspond with her thoughts. The smile of her face should be the smile of her heart. The light of her eye should be the light of her soul. She should abhor deception; she should loathe intrigue; she should have a deep disgust of duplicity. Her life should be the outspoken language of her mind, the eloquent poem of her soul speaking in rhythmic beauties the intrinsic merit of inward purity. Purity antecedes all spiritual attainments and progress. It is the first and fundamental virtue in a good character; it is the letter A in the moral alphabet; it is the first step in the spiritual life; it is the Alpha of the eternal state of soul which has no Omega. Whatever may be our mental attainments or social qualities, we are nothing without purity; only "tinkling cymbals." Our love is stained, our benevolence corrupted, our piety a pretense which God will not accept. An impure young woman is an awful sight. She outrages all just ideas of woman-

hood, all proper conceptions of spiritual beauty. To
have evil imaginings, corrupt longings, or deceitful
propensities ought to startle any young woman. To
feel a disposition to sensuality, a craving for the
glitter of a worldly life, or a selfish ambition for
unmerited distinction is dangerous in the extreme.
It is the exuding of impure waters from the heart.
Who feels such utterings within should beware.
They are the whisperings of an evil spirit, the temptations to sin and crime. If I could speak to all the
young women in the world, I would strive to utter
the intrinsic beauties and essential qualities of purity;
I would seek to illustrate it as the fountain of all that
is great and good, all that is spiritually grand and
redeeming. There is no virtue, no spiritual life, no
moral beauty, no glory of soul, nor dignity of character without purity.

The second virtue she should cultivate is *benevolence*. Queen of virtues, lovely star in the crown of
life, bright and glorious image of Him who is love,
how beautiful is it in woman's heart! A woman
without benevolence is not a woman; she is only a
deformed personality of womanhood. In every heart
there are many tendencies to selfishness, but the spirit
of benevolence counteracts them all. A hollow, cold,
graceless, ungodly thing is a heart without benevolence. In a world like this, where we are all so needy
and dependent, where our interests are so interlocked,
where our lives and hearts overlap each other, and
often grow together, we cannot live without a good
degree of benevolence. Our true earth-life is a

benevolent one. Our highest interests are in the path of benevolence. We do most for ourselves when we do most for others. "It is more blessed to give than to receive." Good deeds double in the doing, and the larger half comes back to the doer. The most benevolent soul lives nearest to God. A large heart of charity is a noble thing. Selfishness is the root of evil; benevolence is its cure. In no heart is benevolence more beautiful than in youthful woman's. In no heart is selfishness more ugly. To do good is noble; to be good is nobler. This should be the aim of all young women. The poor and needy should occupy a large place in their hearts. The sick and suffering should move upon their sympathies. The sinful and criminal should awaken their deepest pity. The oppressed and down-trodden should find a large place in their compassion. How blessed is woman on errands of mercy! How sweet are her soothing words to the disconsolate! How consoling her tears of sympathy to the mourning! How fresh her spirit of hope to the discouraged! How soft her hand to the sick! How balmy the breath of her love to the oppressed! Woman appears in one of her loveliest aspects when she appears as the practical follower of Him who "went about doing good." The young woman who does these works of practical benevolence is educating her moral powers in the school of earnest and glorious life. She is laying the foundations for a noble and useful womanhood. She is planting the seeds of a charity that will grow to bless and save the suffering of our fellow-men. In no other way can she so successfully cultivate the virtue of benevolence. It is not enough that she pity the sorrows of the poor and suffering. Her hand must be taught to heed the pleadings of her pitying heart. What she feels, she must do. What she wishes, she must make an effort to accomplish. What she prays for, she must strive to attain. Everybody predicts a beautiful life from a good-doing young woman.

The third virtue which the young woman should cultivate is *integrity, or the sentiment of duty*. A German philosopher has poetically and truthfully said, "The two most beautiful things in the universe are the starry heavens above our heads and the sentiment of duty in the human soul." Few objects are richer for the contemplation of a truly high-minded man than a young woman who lives, acts, speaks, and exerts her powers from an enlightened conviction of duty. In such women there is a mighty force of moral power. Though they may be gentle as the lamb, or retiring and modest in their demeanor, there is in them what commands respect, what enforces esteem. They are the strong women. The sun is not truer to his course than they to theirs. They are reliable as the everlasting rocks. Every day finds in them the same beautiful, steady, moral firmness. Men look to them with a confidence that knows no doubt. They are fearless and brave, they have but to know their duty to be ready to engage in it. Though men laugh or sneer, though the world frown, or threaten they will do it. There is no bravado in them; it is the simple power of integrity. They are true to what to them seems right. Such spirits are often the mildest and meekest we have. They are sweet as the flower while they are firm as the rock. We know them by their lives. They are consistent, simple-hearted, uniform and truthful. The word on the tongue is the exact speech of the heart. The expression they wear is the spirit they bear. Their parlor demeanor is their kitchen and closet manner. Their courtesy abroad is their politeness at home. Their confiding converse is such as the world may hear and respect them the more for it. Such are the women of integrity.

The fourth virtue of inestimable value which the young woman should cultivate is *piety*. This may be regarded as the crown of all moral virtues. It is that which sanctifies the rest. It is a heavenly sun in the moral firmament, shedding a divine lustre through the soul — a balmy, hallowing light, sweeter than earth can give. Piety is the meek-eyed maid of heaven, that holds her sister Faith in one hand and Hope in the other, and looks upward with a confiding smile, saying, "My treasure is above." Of all the influences wrought in the human soul, the work of piety is the most harmonizing and divine. It subdues the flesh and the world, and calls down heaven to bless the happy pietist. It is the constant, ever-speaking voice of the Father uttering in sublime and beautiful impressions the holy eloquence of his ever-lasting love. It is the communing ground of the mortal child with the immortal Parent. In the mind

of youthful woman it is as beautiful as it can be anywhere. And when she consecrates all her powers
by the laying on of its heavenly hands, and sanctifies
all her feelings by its hallowed influences, she exhibits
a view of beauty—of physical, moral, and spiritual
beauty—not elsewhere surpassed on earth. A deep,
pervading, all-controlling piety is the highest attainment of man on earth. It is that reverent, humble,
grateful, affectionate, and virtuous purity of spirit in
which the human and divine meet and embrace each
other. It is the spiritual crown which men put on
when they go into the kingdom of heaven. This is
what we urge as the last and finishing excellency
of the youthful female character. The cultivation of
this is what we press as conferring mortal perfection
of character, or as great perfection as frail, sinful
creatures can put on below "the mansions of the
skies."

We urge it as the best and highest duty of every
young woman—a duty she owes to herself, her fellows, and her God—a duty as full of joys as the
heavens are of stars, and when performed, reflecting
matchless grace upon her soul. We do not urge it
through fear of hell or hope of heaven; we do not
urge it from motives of policy; we urge it for its own
intrinsic worth; for the blessedness of being pious;
for the excellency and worth of character and life it
confers. No character is complete till it is swayed
and elevated by genuine piety. No heart is fully
happy till it is imbued with the spirit of piety. No
life is all it may and should be till its motives are bap-

tized in the waters of piety. No soul is saved till it is transformed by the gracious spirit of this daughter of the skies. This divine grace of the soul should be sought by every young woman, and cultivated with the most assiduous care, for without it she is destitute of the highest beauty and divinest charm and power of womanhood.

Old Age.

"No snow falls lighter than the snow of age; but none is heavier, for it never melts."

THE figure is by no means novel, but the closing part of the sentence is new as well as emphatic. The Scriptures represent age by the almond-tree, which bears blossoms of purest white. "The almond-tree shall flourish," the head shall be hoary. Dickens says of one of his characters, whose hair was turning gray, that it looked as if Time had lightly splashed his snows upon it in passing.

"It never melts"—no never. Age is inexorable. Its wheels must move onward; they know no retrograde movement. The old man may sit and sing, "I would I were a boy again," but he grows older as he sings. He may read of the elixir of youth, but he cannot find it; he may sigh for the secrets of that alchemy which is able to make him young again, but sighing brings it not. He may gaze backward with an eye of longing upon the rosy scenes of early

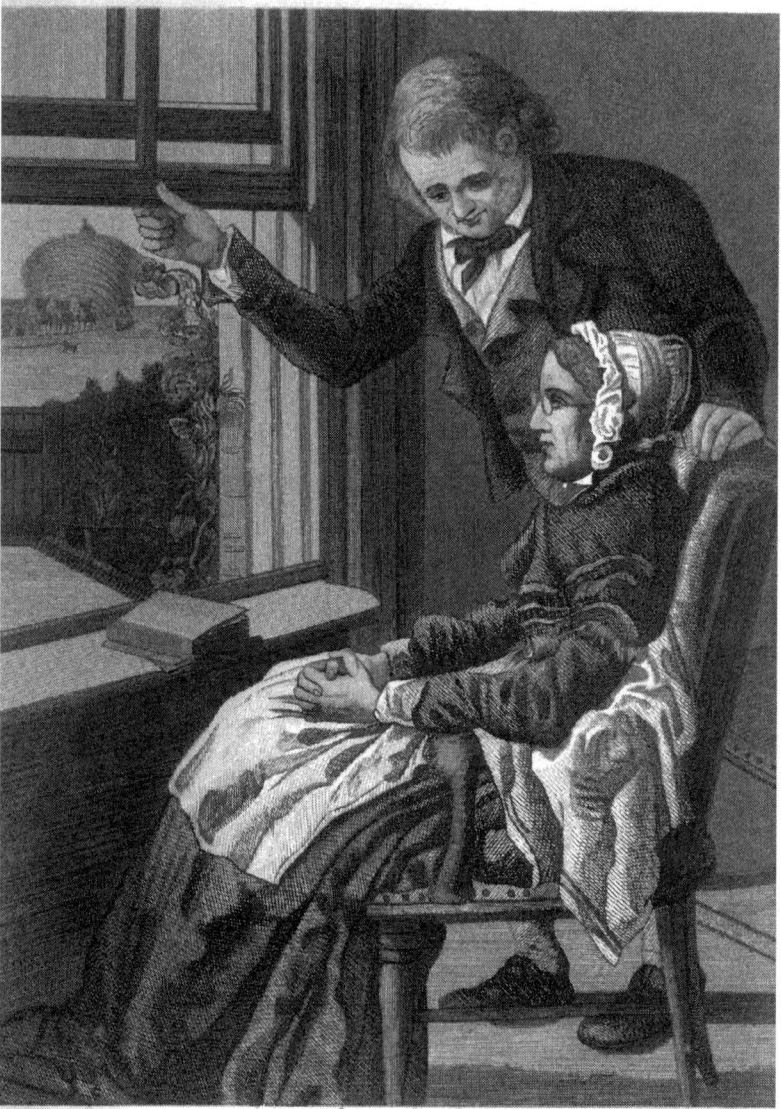

years, as one who gazes on his home from the deck of a departing ship, which every moment carries him farther and farther away. Poor old man! he has little more to do than die.

"It never melts." The snow of winter comes and sheds its white blessings upon the valley and the mountains, but soon the sweet spring comes and smiles it all away. Not so with that upon the brow of the tottering veteran. There is no spring whose warmth can penetrate its eternal frost. It came to stay. Its single flakes fell unnoticed—and now it is drilled there. We shall see it increase until we lay the old man in his grave. There it shall be absorbed by the eternal darkness—for there is no age in heaven.

The young, who all wish to live, but who at the same time have a dread of growing old, may not be disposed to allow the justice of the representation we are now to make. They regard old age as a dreary season, that admits of nothing which can be called pleasure, and very little which deserves the name even of comfort. They look forward to it, as in autumn we anticipate the approach of winter; but winter, though it terrifies us at a distance, has nothing very formidable when it arrives. Its enjoyments are of a different kind, but we find it not less pleasant than any other season of the year.

In like manner old age, frightful as it may be to the young, who view it afar off, has no terror to them who see it near; but experience proves that it abounds with consolations, and even with delights.

38

We should look therefore with pleasure on many old men, whose illuminated faces and hoary heads resemble one of those pleasant days in winter, so common in this climate, when a bright sun darts its beams on a pure field of snow. The beauty of spring, the splendor of summer, and the glory of autumn are gone; but the prospect is still lively and cheerful.

Among other circumstances which contribute to the satisfaction of this period of life, is the respect with which old age is treated. There are, it must be acknowledged and lamented, some foolish and ill-educated young persons who do not pay that veneration which is due to the hoary head; but these examples are not numerous.

The world in general bows down to age, gives it precedence, and listens with deference to its opinions. Old age wants accommodations; and it must in justice to man be allowed that they are afforded with cheerfulness. Who can deny that such reverence is soothing to the human mind? and that it compensates us for the loss of many pleasures which are peculiar to youth?   ·

The respect of the world in general is gratifying; but the respect of a man's own offspring must yield heartfelt delight. Can there be a more pleasing sight, than a venerable old man surrounded by his children and grandchildren, all of whom are emulous of each other in testifying their homage and affection? His children, proud of their honored father, strive who shall treat him with the most attention, while his grandchildren hang on his neck, entertain him with their innocent prattle, and convince him that they love their grandfather not less than they love their father. Whoever takes a little child into his love, may have a very roomy heart, but that child will fill it all. The children that are in the world keep us from growing old and cold; they cling to our garments with their little hands, and impede our progress to petrification; they win us back with their pleading eyes from cruel care; they never encumber us at all. A poor old couple, with no one to love them, is a most pitiful picture; but a hovel with a small face to fill a broken pane, here and there, is robbed of its desolateness. A little thoughtful attention, how happy it makes the old! They have outlived most of the friends of their early youth. How lonely their hours! Often their partners in life have long filled silent graves; often their children they have followed to the tomb. They stand solitary, bending on their staff, waiting till the same call shall reach them. How often they must think of absent, lamented faces, of the love which cherished them, and the tears of sympathy which fell with theirs— now all gone. Why should not the young cling around and comfort them, cheering their gloom with happy smiles?

That old man! what disappointments he has encountered in his long journey, what bright hopes blasted, what sorrows felt, what agonies endured, how many loved ones he has covered up in the grave. And that old woman, too! husband dead, children all buried or far away, life's flowers faded, the friends of

her youth no more, and she waiting to go' soon.
Ought we ever to miss an opportunity of showing
attention to the aged, of proffering a kindness, or
lighting up a smile, by a courteous act or a friendly
deed?

Why speak of age in a mournful strain? It is
beautiful, honorable, eloquent. Should we sigh at
the proximity of death, when life and the world are
so full of emptiness? Let the old exult because they
are old. If any must weep, let it be the young, at
the long succession of cares that are before them.
Welcome the snow, for it is the emblem of peace and
of rest. It is but a temporal crown which shall fall
at the gates of Paradise, to be replaced by a brighter
and a better.

Death.

No SEX is spared, no age exempt. The majestic
and courtly roads which monarchs pass over, the way
that the men of letters tread, the path the warrior
traverses, the short and simple annals of the poor, all
lead to the same place, all terminate, however varied
in their routes, in that one enormous house which is
appointed for all living. One short sentence closes
the biography of every man, as if in a mockery of the
unsubstantial pretensions of human pride, "The days
of the years of Methuselah were nine hundred and
sixty-nine years, and he died." There is the end of

it. "And he died." Such is the frailty of this boasted man. "It is appointed unto men"—unto all men—"once to die." No matter what station of honor we hold, we are all subject to death.

As in chess-play, so long as the game is playing, all the men stand in their order and are respected according to their places—first the king, then the queen, then the bishops, after them the knights, and last of all the common soldiers; but when once the game is ended and the table taken away, then they are all confusedly tumbled into a bag, and haply the king is lowest and the pawn upmost. Even so it is with us in this life; the world is a huge theatre, or stage, wherein some play the parts of kings, others of bishops, some lords, many knights, and others yeomen; but death sends all alike to the grave and to the judgment.

Death comes equally to us all and makes us all equal when it comes. The ashes of an oak in a chimney are no epitaph of that, to tell me how high or how large that was; it tells me not what flocks it sheltered when it stood, nor what men it hurt when it fell. The dust of great men's graves is speechless too: it says nothing; it distinguishes nothing. "As soon the dust of a wretch whom thou wouldst not, as of a prince whom thou couldst not look upon, will trouble thine eyes if the wind blow it thither; and when a whirlwind hath blown the dust of a church-yard into a church, and the man sweeps out the dust of the church into the church-yard, who will

undertake to sift those dusts again and to pronounce: This is the patrician, this is the noble
flower, and this is the yeoman, and this is plebeian
bran?"

Look at that hero, as he stands on an eminence
and covered with glory. He falls suddenly, forever
falls. His intercourse with the living world is now
ended, and those who would hereafter find him must
seek him in the grave. There, cold and lifeless, is
the heart which just now was the seat of friendship;
there, dim and sightless, is the eye whose radiant and
enlivening orb beamed with intelligence; and there,
closed forever, are those lips, on whose persuasive
accents we have so often and so lately hung with
transport.

From the darkness which rests upon his tomb there
proceeds, methinks, a light, in which it is clearly seen
that those gaudy objects which men pursue are only
phantoms. In this light, how dimly shines the splendor of victory — how humble appears the majesty of
grandeur! The bubble, which seemed to have so
much solidity, has burst, and we again see that all
below the sun is vanity.

True, the funeral eulogy has been pronounced, the
sad and solemn procession has moved, the badge of
mourning has already been decreed, and presently
the sculptured marble will lift up its front, proud to
perpetuate the name of the hero and rehearse to the
passing traveler his virtues — just tributes of respect,
and to the living useful — but to him, moldering in his

narrow and humble habitation, what are they? How vain! how unavailing!

Approach, and behold, while I lift from his sepulchre its covering! Ye admirers of his greatness—ye emulous of his talents and his fame—approach and behold him now. How pale! how silent! No martial bands admire the adroitness of his movements; no fascinating throng weep, and melt, and tremble at his eloquence! Amazing change! A shroud, a coffin, a narrow, subterraneous cabin!—this is all that now remains of the hero! And *is* this all that remains of him? During a life so transitory, what lasting monument, then, can our fondest hopes erect!

We stand on the borders of an awful gulf, which is swallowing up all things human. And is there, amidst this universal wreck, nothing stable, nothing abiding, nothing immortal, on which poor, frail, dying man can fasten? Ask the hero, ask the statesman, whose wisdom you have been accustomed to revere, and he will tell you. He will tell you, did we say? He has already told you, from his death-bed, and his illumined spirit still whispers from the heavens, with well-known eloquence, the solemn admonition: "Mortals hastening to the tomb, and once the companions of my pilgrimage, take warning and avoid my errors; cultivate the virtues I have recommended; choose the Savior I have chosen; live disinterestedly; live for immortality; and would you rescue anything from final dissolution, lay it up in God."

Ah, it is true that a few friends will go and bury us;

affection will rear a stone and plant a few flowers over our grave; in a brief period the little hillock will be smoothed down, and the stone will fall, and neither friend nor stranger will be concerned to ask which one of the forgotten millions of the earth was buried there. Every vestige that we ever lived upon the earth will have vanished away. All the little memorials of our remembrance—the lock of hair encased in gold, or the portrait that hung in our dwelling, will cease to have the slightest interest to any living being.

We need but look into the cemetery and see the ten thousand upturned faces; ten thousand breathless bosoms. There was a time when fire flashed through those vacant orbs; when warm ambitions, hopes, joys and the loving life pushed in those bosoms. Dreams of fame and power once haunted those empty skulls. The little piles of bones, that once were feet, ran swiftly and determinedly through twenty, forty, sixty, seventy years of life, but where are the prints they left? He lived—he died—he was buried—is all that the headstone tells us. We move among the monuments, we see the sculpturing, but no voice comes to us to say that the sleepers are remembered for any thing they have done. A generation passes by. The stones turn gray, and the man has ceased to be, and is to the world, as if he had never lived.

Thus is life. Only a few years do we journey here and we come to that bridge—Death—which transports us as the road we have traveled, either virtue, happiness and joy, to a happy paradise of love, or the road of passion, lust and vice to destructive wretchedness.

A proper view of death may be useful to abate most of the irregular passions. Thus, for instance, we may see what avarice comes to in the coffin of the miser; this is the man who could never be satisfied with riches; but see now a few boards inclose him, and a few square inches contain him. Study ambition in the grave of that enterprising man; see, his great designs, his boundless expedients are all shattered and sunk in this fatal gulf of all human projects. Approach the tomb of the proud man; see the haughty countenance dreadfully disfigured, and the tongue that spoke the most lofty things condemned to eternal silence. Go to the tomb of the monarch, and there study quality; behold his great titles, his royal robes, and all his flatteries—all are no more forever in this world. Behold the consequence of intemperance in the tomb of the glutton; see his appetite now fully satiated, his senses destroyed and his bones scattered. Thus the tombs of the wicked condemn their practice and strongly recommend virtue.

Death reigns in all the portions of our time. The autumn, with its fruits, provides disorders for us, and the winter's cold turns them into sharp diseases; and the spring brings flowers to strew our hearse; and the summer gives green turf and brambles to bind upon our graves. Calentures and surfeit, cold and agues are the four quarters of the year, and all minister unto death. Go where you will and it will find you. Many dread it and try to flee from it as the king of terrors.

Is he an enemy, when God sends him to deliver us from pains, follies, disappointments, miseries and wo? Is he an enemy, who transfers us from delusive dreams, from the region of bubbles and corroding cares, to a region where all is pure, substantial, enduring joy and endless felicity? It is a libel on DEATH to call him our foe, a king of terrors, an enemy.

Frail man comes into the world crying, cries on through life, and is always seeking after some desired thing which he imagines is labeled HAPPINESS, or is mourning over some loss, which makes him miserable; a restless mortal body, with an immortal soul, that requires something more than earth can give to satisfy its lofty desires; the soul that hails death as the welcome messenger, to deliver it from its ever changing, ever decaying prison-house of clay, called man; on which time wages a perpetual war; whitening his locks, furrowing his cheeks, stealing his ivory, weakening his nerves, paralyzing his muscles, poisoning his blood, battering his whole citadel, deranging the whole machinery of life, and wasting his mental powers; until he becomes twice a child; and then delivers him over to his last and best friend, DEATH, who breaks the carnal bondage, sets the imprisoned spirit free, closing a toilsome career of infelicity; opening the door of immortal happiness, returning the soul to its own, original, and glorious home; to go no more out forever. Not to become familiar with death, is to endure much unnecessary fear, and add to the myriads of the other imaginary woes of human life.

Death to them that be God's dear children is no other thing than the despatcher of all displeasure, the end of all travail, the door of desires, the gate of gladness, the port of paradise, the haven of heaven, the entrance to felicity, the beginning of all blissfulness. It is the very bed of down for the doleful bodies of God's people to rest in, out of which they rise and awake most fresh and lusty to everlasting life. It is a passage to the Father, a chariot to heaven, the Lord's messenger, a going to our home, a deliverance from bondage, a dismission from war, a security from all sorrows, and a manumission from all misery. And should we be dismayed at it? Should we trouble to hear of it? Should such a friend as it be unwelcome? Death is but life to a true believer; it is not his last day, nor his worst day, but in the highest sense his best day, and the beginning of his better life. A Christian's dying day will be his *enlarging* day, when he shall be freed from the prison in which he has long been detained, and be brought home to his Father's house. A Christian's dying day will be his *resting* day, when he shall rest from all sin and care and trouble; his *reaping* day, when he shall reap the fruit he has sown in tears and faith; his *conquering* day, when he shall triumph over every enemy, and even death itself shall die; his *transplanting* day, from earth to heaven, from a howling wilderness to a heavenly paradise; his *robing* day, to put off the old worn out rags of flesh, and put on the new and glorious robes of light; his *marriage* day; his *coronation* day; the day of his glory, the beginning of his eternal, perfect bliss with Christ.

We at death leave one place to go to another; if godly we depart from our place here on earth, and go to heaven; we depart from our friends on earth and go to our friends in heaven; we depart from the valley of tears and go to the mount of joy; we depart from a howling wilderness and go to a heavenly paradise. Who would be unwilling to exchange a Sodom for a Zion, an Egypt for a Canaan, misery for glory?

What a superlatively grand and consoling idea is that of death! Without this radiant idea, this delightful morning star, indicating that the luminary of eternity is going to rise, life would, to our view, darken into midnight melancholy. Oh, the expectation of living *here*, and of living *thus* always, would be indeed a prospect of overwhelming despair! But thanks be to that fatal decree that dooms us to die! thanks to that gospel which opens the vision of an endless life! and thanks, above all, to that Savior friend who has promised to conduct all the faithful through the sacred trance of death, into scenes of paradise and everlasting delight!

Oh, that all may be prepared for this awful change,

but how often we hear the mournful exclamation, "Too late!" from men who come up to the doors of a bank just as the key has turned in the lock; or up to the great gates of a railway terminus just as they swing to, and tell the tardy traveler he has lost his train; or up to the post-office just as the mail has been despatched; but how should he tremble if our ears could hear the despairing cry of souls whom the stony gaze of that grim messenger has fixed in sin forever. How would our hearts thrill with horror to accompany one, without hope of heaven, to the portals of death. How do men dread such death scenes as that of a young skeptic called suddenly from time to eternity. "Begone!" he cried to the clergyman; I want none of your *cant*," when he showed him the great need of repentance. "I am not going to die; and if I were I would die as I have lived." The physician came, to whom he said: "Oh! tell me I am not dying; I will not die!" "My poor friend, I cannot speak falsely to you; your soul will, ere long, be with your God." "*My* God!" he said, "I have no God save the world; I have stifled conviction, I have fought against God, I have resisted my mother's pleadings, and now you tell me that I must die. Do you know," he added, in an awful whisper, "all that means? *If I die to-day I shall go to hell!* Take it back; tell me I'm not going to die. Father," he said, "t'was you who taught me this; you led me on in this way, and now you say I'm to die. Stand back!" he shrieked; "*I will not die!*" and a torrent of invectives issued from his fever-parched lips, so terrible in their madness that it seemed like a wail from the sea of woe. No wonder the poor mother was borne fainting from the room, and the father's brow was corrugated, while great drops of agony rested there. Ah, that infidel father! how must his heart have bled in that dreadful hour, when in the midst of dire cursings, his gifted son fell back a corpse.

What a striking contrast between such a death and the following:

One of Martin Luther's children lay on her death bed; the great man approached her and said to her: "My little daughter, my beloved Margaret, you would willingly remain with your earthly parents, but if God calls you, you will go with your heavenly Father." "Yes, dear father, it is as God pleases." He then said: "My daughter, enter thou into thy resting place in peace." She turned her eyes toward him and said, with touching simplicity, "Yes, father." How resignedly could the believing Luther part with his dying child, and methinks the sentiment of his heart was very like the inscription on a child's tombstone in an English churchyard, as follows: "'Who plucked that flower?' cried the gardener, as he walked through the garden. His fellow servant answered, 'The Master.' And the gardener held his peace."

When these hands of ours shall be pulseless and cold, and motionless as the grave wherein they must lie; when the damp, dewy vapors shall replace "this sensible, warm motion," and death shall spread our couch and weave our shrouds; when the winding-sheet shall be our sole vesture, and the close-sealed sepulchre our only home, and we shall have no familiar companions, and no rejoicing friends but the worm; O, thou cold hand of death, unlock for us then the portals of eternal life, that whilst our bodies rest in their beds of earth, our souls may recline in the bosom of God!

"Life! we've been long together,
Through pleasant and cloudy weather;
'Tis hard to part when friends are dear;
Perhaps 'twill cost a sigh, a tear;
Then steal away, give little warning,
Choose thine own time;
Say not, Good night, but in some brighter clime
Bid us good morning."

THE END.

WHAT IS SAID OF IT.

Dr. C. H. Fowler, Editor of "The Christian Advocate," New York, says:

"'The Royal Path of Life' is open before me. Its *practical* and *suggestive* subjects invite attention, and the manner in which they are handled retains it. Its principles and suggestions applied will secure success.

"One idea to a man in the beginning of life is worth *many books*. This one book will *furnish many ideas*. Brother man, read it."

President W. H. Allen, M. D., LL. D., of Girard College, Philadelphia, says:

"I have examined 'The Royal Path of Life,' and noted its direction, the lands through which it passes, and the end to which it leads. It is a straight path, and the young man who walks in it will not go astray in crooked ways. It is a safe path, and the young woman who walks in it will not be caught in a snare nor fall into a pit. It is the path of wisdom, in whose right hand is length of days, and in her left hand riches and honor. In a word, the book is full of wise precepts for the conduct of life, gathered from numerous sources, and clothed in a perspicuous style."

President J. Grier Ralston, D. D., LL. D., (Presbyterian) of Oakland Female Institute, Norristown, Pa., says:

"I am much obliged to you for calling my attention to 'The Royal Path of Life.' It is a book of rare excellence. I have read it with interest and profit, and think it will be found attractive alike to the old and young to the grave and gay. The subjects of which it treats are all practical, and are so discussed as to furnish lessons for daily use. The spirit of the book is eminently Christian, its doctrines evangelical, its style crisp and lucid, its language direct and vigorous, and all its teachings pure and elevating. It does not contain a dull or prosy page. Any one who reads the first four chapters will want to finish the book.

"While I give it my hearty indorsement, I cordially recommend it to the general reader as highly entertaining and instructive, and especially to the young as a judicious counsellor, a safe guide, and a discreet friend."

President M. Valentine D. D., of Pennsylvania College, Gettysburg, Pa., says:

"The Royal Path of Life" is a most excellent popular book, full of rich practical truths and lessons, presented in a most striking and impressive way. There is no dullness about it. It is worthy of a place in every family, and cannot fail to exert a happy influence on the heart and character of those who read it."

Rev. E. E. Higbee, D. D., Supt. of Public Instruction for the Commonwealth of Pennsylvania, says:

"I have read enough of 'The Royal Path of Life' to be convinced that its moral tone is excellent, and that the careful reading of it cannot but be of benefit to the young and to the old. I therefore most cheerfully recommend it to the public."

Rev. R. R. Mason, D. D., Rector of Glencoe Parish, near Baltimore, Md., says:

"'The Royal Path of Life' is admirably adapted to its purpose of interesting, elevating, and guiding the minds of all who are desirous of what is really good for themselves and their families and especially for those who are setting out in life. Such a book may be rightly regarded as a positive benefit to any family where it is read. It is evidently the work of good and wise men who are aiming to supply a need which exists in our day: and that is the need of a few books which treat *briefly* and *attractively* a variety of topics that are of great importance and interest to a large class of readers.'"

Gen. Joshua L. Chamberlain, Ex-Gov. of Maine, and Pres. of Bowdoin College, says:

"I have examined with great interest the book entitled 'The Royal Path of Life,' and find the subjects and sentiments are such as are worthy of the best treatment, and of the attention of every thoughtful person.'"

Rev. C. W. Anable, D. D., Pastor First Baptist Church, Springfield, Mass., says:

"Having examined with some care the work entitled 'The Royal Path of Life,' I take pleasure in commending it as a highly useful and valuable book. It is not only a very sensible, but a very readable book—handsomely printed and finely illustrated. Seldom does one meet with such an admirable compilation of wise and wholesome sentiments, covering the whole range of topics relating to individual and domestic well-being. Every young man and every young woman should possess it. I can honestly wish it a place in every family, where it will be read and re-read for its intrinsic value, and am thankful in these days especially, when our markets are overrun with shams, that such a work as 'The Royal Path' is brought to the notice of our community, and trust it will have a wide circulation."

Rev. S. G. Buckingham, D. D., Pastor South Congreg'l Church, Springfield, Mass., says:

"Having partially examined the work entitled 'The Royal Path of Life,' I find it to be a work of value, and would be a blessing in any household. It is written in the interest of Virtue, Morality and Christianity."

Rev. S. F. Upham, D. D., Pastor of Trinity M. E. Church, Springfield, Mass., says:

"I have, as fully as time would permit, examined the work entitled, 'The Royal Path of Life.' It is a work abounding in good thoughts, and well expressed. Its circulation and perusal will greatly benefit every one."

Rev. J. A. Sheres, A. M., Principal Connecticut Literary Institute, Suffield, Conn., says:

"'The Royal Path of Life' is one of the most interesting literary gems ever published, and worthy of a place in every household in the land."

Rev. B. M. Fullerton, Pastor Cong'l Church, Palmer, Mass., says:

"I deem 'The Royal Path of Life' a work

Rev. N. Fellows, A. M., Principal Wesleyan Academy, Wilbraham, Mass., says:

"The authors of 'The Royal Path of Life' seem to have skimmed the cream of common sense from the world's best writers on the vital subjects treated therein. All who read it will get much good, and only good from its pages."

Rev. W. T. Perrin, Pastor M. E. Church, Wilbraham, Mass., says:

"From an examination of 'The Royal Path of Life,' I heartily endorse the above recommendation."

Rev. M. L. Howard, Pastor Cong'l Church, Wilbraham, Mass., says:

"I have examined the book and cheerfully endorse the above commendations."

Rev. M. C. Stebbins, A. M., Principal of Springfield Collegiate Institute, Springfield, Mass., says:

"'The Royal Path of Life' is certainly a book of rare excellence. So many rich, beautiful, and inspiring thoughts are seldom gathered into so small a space. It is emphatically a book for the family. Everybody should read it, and once reading it is not enough."

Rev. J. B. Quigg, P. E., M. E. Church, Wilmington, Del., says:

"I have examined 'The Royal Path of Life,' and consider it an excellent book, full of interesting and profitable reading. *It is very much prized in my family.*"

Rev. R. B. Cook, Pastor of the Second Baptist Church, Wilmington, Del., says:

"I have examined 'The Royal Path of Life,' and I think the idea of it excellent, and the execution of it masterly. It is a book that everybody needs and should be in every family. It would be well for parents to read it aloud in the family circle, and encourage their children to read it for themselves. *It is the book for the times,* and its sound principles of morality and religion, its clear statements of man's duties to his fellow man and to his God, if known and understood, would go far to settle the present secu-

Rev. A. B. Stoner, Pastor of Trinity Reformed Church, Norristown, Pa., says.

"I have carefully read your work entitled 'The Royal Path of Life,' and wish to express my high appreciation of it. I regard it as one of the few books that will be found at once deeply interesting and highly instructive to the general reader. It is both soundly *metaphysical* and eminently *practical*. Its style is *lofty, pleasing* and *beautiful;* its diction *pure* and *plain;* its tone throughly *Christian*. Although its pages are made up of distinct and somewhat disconnected essays, each complete in itself, it reads like a romance. But while it is thus fascinating, we have the additional satisfaction of useful knowledge, acquired at each step of our progress. We need not hasten to unravel the story, as alas! we are only too prone to do when perusing works of fiction. We may linger as long as we wish by the way; for each essay furnishes material for much solid thought and profitable meditation."

Rev. J. Dyson, Pastor of Oak Street M. E. Church, Norristown, Pa., says:

"I have read 'The Royal Path of Life,' and unhesitatingly recommend it—a book that will be read with interest and profit by every one fortunate in securing a copy. I give my full endorsement to all the very excellent things said concerning it by Dr. Ralston, the Rev. Mr. Gibson, and others."

Rev. B. F. Bohner, Pastor of the Evangelical Church, Norristown, Pa., says:

"I have examined and partly read 'The Royal Path of Life.' It is a good book, very readable, and of the best moral tendency. The old as well as the young can only be profited by subscribing for and reading a copy of the work. It ought to have a very wide circulation."

President I. C. Pershing, D. D., of Pittsburgh Female College, says:

"A somewhat hurried examination of 'The Royal Path of Life' has left a most delightful impression. The style is simple, clear and often beautiful, the tone elevated, the aim of the writers excellent. I cordially commend the book as one worthy a place in every

Rev. S. Siegfried, Pastor of the Baptist Church, Norristown, Pa., says:

"'The Royal Path of Life; or, Aims and Aids to Success and Happiness,' is just what its title indicates. It is a book for the home, to be read and studied. Its articles are gems, and are edifying to all the members of the household—the grave and the gay will find a portion in season. The ambition, enlightened and enthused by such a counselor as this book, will aspire to the chaste and beautiful in the 'royal path of life,' and will find 'happiness' and achieve 'success.' I cheerfully add my commendation of its merits."

President J. H. A. Bomberger, D. D., of Ursinus College, Collegeville, Pa., says:

"Although I have been unable to give 'The Royal Path of Life' more than a brief and cursory examination, its aim and ruling spirit have impressed me favorably. The essays are upon most important, practical subjects, written in a style attractive for most readers, and offer wholesome counsel and profitable entertainment. Many a winter evening hour can be usefully and pleasantly employed in their perusal."

Professor George R. Thompson, Principal of the Friends' School, Wilmington, Del., says:

"After a somewhat hasty examination of 'The Royal Path of Life,' I am impressed with the fidelity with which the authors have endeavored to further their design of 'stimulating the youth to noble thoughts and actions.' If they have not marked out the exact limits of 'the royal path of life,' they have at least set no false guide-posts by the way.

"The work treats briefly, but interestingly, of such old-fashioned topics as 'Integrity,' 'Industry,' 'Slander,' 'Vanity,' etc.—subjects well worth consideration in these days of loose moral notions. It may not appeal strongly to the tastes of the professedly intellectual class of the community, but for the *people* it will have solid attractions. That its contents are so varied will be a great recommendation to those who have not the means to purchase many books. But perhaps a still greater recommendation is that it contains nothing that parents need fear to have their

Rev. James Moss, Pastor of the M. E. Church, Painters Post, N. Y., says:

"The Royal Path of Life" is full of beautiful gem thoughts. No book that I have ever known to be canvassed for, is as worthy of patronage as this, save the Bible itself. I hope it will be purchased, read and studied by multitudes both young and old.

Rev. James Chambers, Pastor Cong'l Church, Sherburn, N. Y., says:

From a brief examination of this book I judge it to be of real value; and to those fortunate enough to own it, it will be not only entertaining, but instructive.

Rev. G. R. Burnside, Pastor Baptist Church, Sherburn, N. Y., says:

Having with some care examined the "Royal Path of Life" I most cheerfully recommend the work to both old and young. The thoughtful and intelligent reader will find much that is suggestive and profitable in each essay. My first thought was, to particularize, but as I passed on in my investigation I found no superfluities—nothing that ought to be omitted—binding, size, paper, type, subject matter, style, price—everything about as it should be.

Rev. H. N. Van Deusen, Pastor M. E. Church, Sherburn, N. Y., says:

Having examined and read portions of the "Royal Path of Life," I can heartily recommend it as a very interesting and valuable work, especially so for the young. I have a copy for my own family.

Rev. J. W. Wilson, Pastor of First M.E.Church, Fayetteville, N.Y., says:

I have examined in a cursory way the 'Royal Path of Life." It abounds in healthy helpful sentiments clothed in pleasing language and can not but benefit the thought-

Rev. J. P. Newman D. D., New York, says

Had I a dozen boys, I would put in the hand of each, for a life companion, "The Royal Path of Life." It contains more common sense, more practical morality, more interesting reading, than is found in books for the young.

Rev. William Searls, Chaplain of the Auburn State Prison, N. Y., says:

"The Royal Path of Life" is a ROYAL GOOD BOOK. It will do all who read it good. Place one in every family if possible.

William D. Wilson D. D., LL. D., Professor of Moral and Intellectual Philosophy, Cornell University, N. Y. says:

My impressions, from a brief view of "The Royal Path of Life" are quite favorable. I think it cannot fail to do good wherever read and used.

Stephen A. Walker, President of the Board of Education of New York City, says:

It gives me pleasure to state that after an examination of the book, "The Royal Path of Life." I am satisfied it contains teachings moral and wholesome. The world would be better were all books as good as this.

Rev. Dr. Storrs D. D. of Brooklyn N. Y., says:

I have no doubt "The Royal Path of Life" is an excellent book

---

Charles E. Fuller, County Supt. of Schools for the Eastern District of Broome County, N. Y., says:

I have carefully examined the book entitled "The Royal Path of Life." The subjects treated are of the greatest importance to every one, young and old. For purity of thought and high moral tone, it has no su-

D. D. Lindsley, Pastor of Presbyterian Church, Southport, N. Y., says:

Several months since, I had occasion to examine "The Royal Path of Life," and was so deeply impressed with its importance that I immediately purchased a copy for my family. The topics treated are various and numerous and are handled in a dignified and scholarly manner. The various subjects are clearly and closely thought out, elegantly expressed and beautifully illustrated. The chapters on love and marriage are alone worth the price of the book and should be read especially by the young. The chapter on death is grand and full of comfort. I unhesitatingly recommend the work and trust it may find its way into many families. This recommend is entirely gratuitous as I have no object in a reward for it except to do good by helping its circulation.

Rev. Nelson Millard, D. D., Pastor of the First Presbyterian Church at Syracuse, N. Y., says:

"The Royal Path of Life" appears to me a work of high moral tone, filled with very valuable and salutary suggestions for all classes, and especially for the young. The thoughts are presented in a fresh and attractive manner rendering the book very interesting and readable. Its influence in any family can scarcely fail to be very wholesome. Parents would do well both to read it themselves and put it into the hands of their children. It is well calculated to furnish an antidote to many false and foolish notions which the young are too prone to imbibe.

Rev. A. W. Green, Pastor of Aurora street Church, Ithica, N. Y., says:

This book, "The Royal Path of life," in its style and thought, is a vigorous bow loaded with barbed arrows. The reader whether young or old, will be apt to feel the impress of ideas that will "stick" in the mind and which will be helpful and comforting to him in almost every department of life. I take

Rev. J. H. McCarty, Pastor First M. E. Church, Syracuse, N. Y., says:

I have examined "The Royal Path of Life," and find it a valuable contribution to christian literature—eminently suited to the family, combining general instruction with good morals.

Rev. W. M. King, Pastor of the Baptist Church, Owego, N. Y., says:

From a cursory examination of "The Royal Path of Life," I judge it an entertaining and useful book. It certainly is a book of ideas, couched in a very plain and simple style.

Prof. A. M. Drummond, Superintendent of Owego Schools, N. Y., says:

I have in my possession a copy of "The Royal Path of Life," a work that I consider to be of such surpassing excellence that I most cordially recommend it to all lovers of wholesome reading. As a collection of essays on literature, morality, and religion it is worthy of a place in every family. Its lessons on success and happiness will encourage those who are enjoying these blessings, and will help those who are not in possession of the same, to give earnest attention to their attainment.

Rev. C. N. Sims, D. D., Chancellor of Syracuse University, Syracuse, N. Y., says:

I have examined somewhat carefully "The Royal Path of Life," and find it a most charming and useful volume of short Essays on the practical questions of every day life and duties. The topics are well chosen and well treated. The book will be found very full of interest, and is so arranged that if one has but ten minutes to read he may complete a chapter. It will be a blessing in every home where it is received and read.

Rev. Charles H. Woods, Pastor of the First Baptist Church, Belfast, N. Y., says:

"The Royal Path of Life" is a very interesting and instructive volume. Its language and thought are beautiful, impressive and inspiring, and cannot fail to stimulate the hearts of its readers to high and holy thought and action. It is deserving a wide circulation and careful reading. May the blessing of God attend it and make it a source of comfort to the aged, and a wise director of the youth, as it is eminently adapted to be

President John Bascom, D. D., LL. D., of University of Wisconsin, Madison, says:

"'The Royal Path of Life' seems to be a book full of moral and practical wisdom; and would be likely to help strongly the good feeling and discipline of households."

President Wm. F. Phelps, of State Normal School, Whitewater, Wis., says:

"Having examined with some care the volume entitled 'The Royal Path of Life,' I can commend it with entire confidence as a work of rare merit in respect to the soundness of its teachings, its moral tone, and its pure and devoted style as a literary production. *I know of no book better suited to the wants of the people,* and I trust that it may find a place in every family in the land."

President H. Gilliland, D. D., of Galesville University, Wis., says:

"'Royal Path of Life' is just the book for the family — for father and mother, for brothers and sisters. Its table of contents is enough to recommend it to all advocates of sound morals, domestic happiness, integrity of character, public and private virtue.

"*The work should, therefore, be extensively sold, carefully read, and its teachings faithfully practiced.*"

President J. Esterbrook, of Michigan State Normal, Ypsilanti, says:

"I have examined with pleasure 'The Royal Path of Life.' The book contains a gr.at variety of well written topics, on conditions of success in life. *I think it an excellent work.* Its circulation will do good to old and young. Buy it and study it."

President Charles A. Morey, of State Normal School, Winona, Minn, says:

"I have examined the book entitled 'The Royal Path of Life,' and I am glad to commend it to the reading public. Its short, terse and strong essays upon vital topics are calculated to awaken thought and to do much good."

Leonard F. Parker, A. M., Professor of the Greek Language and Literature, in the State University of Iowa, says:

Professor S. M. Etter, Superintendent of Public Instruction of State, Springfield, Ill., says:

"It is with great pleasure I recommend 'Royal Path of Life.' It should find a place in every intelligent household. No one can read this beautiful written volume without instruction as well as pleasure. Few books of a purely didactic character are so attractive. It gives that hated thing *advice* so lovingly that one feels the presence and converse of a very dear friend."

President A. L. Chapin, of Beloit College, Beloit, Wis., says:

"From a cursory examination of the 'Royal Path of Life,' I receive the impression that it presents in a clear and pleasing style, *much sound, practical wisdom,* adapted especially to promote the purity and peace of family life."

John G. McWyn, A. M., Principal of Racine Academy, Racine, Wis., says:

"I wish those who desire a good book would subscribe for this one, 'The Royal Path of Life.' It is full of thoughts, beautiful and grand, and it will influence those who read it only for good. The young men and young women of our country ought to form their characters under the influence such a book will exert."

President G. S. Albee, of State Normal, Oshkosh, Wis., says:

"I have examined carefully many selections from 'The Royal Path of Life.' There can be but one opinion regarding the pure character and noble purpose of the work. In a simple style it impresses the important truths that lead to worthiness or tend to evil so plainly that our warped natures cannot misunderstand. I wish it might be thoughtfully read in every house."

Prof. John C. Ridpath, the Historian, Asbury University, Ind., says:

"I have made a cursory examination of 'The Royal Path of Life,' and find it a work of considerable interest. It is well composed in a style half familiar and half didactic. To

Rev. Thomas W. Humes, S. T. D., President of the East Tennessee State University, says:

"I have no hesitation in expressing the opinion that its general circulation will tend decidedly to promote the cause of virtue, the welfare of families, and the vital power of religion among the people; and I therefore recommend it to the public."

Rev. S. R. Preston, Pastor of the Presbyterian Church, Athens, Tenn., says:

"This book is full of practical truth. It is at once entertaining and instructive. The conception is fine, the religious tone is elevating, language concise and pointed. While pointing steadily to 'The Royal Path of Life,' it fixes the attention upon the breakers, where so many are dashed to pieces. It is a good book for everybody, but especially for the young. After a thorough examination, I can cordially recommend it to every family as a valuable addition to the home library."

Rev. A. W. Jones, D.D., President of the Memphis Conference Female Institute, Jackson, Tenn., says:

"'The Royal Path of Life' is, in my judgment, an admirable book, very attractive and useful. It is well suited to the family circle, and if carefully read will have a happy and elevating influence on all the relations of life. It has my earnest commendation. I would like to see it published in a number of small volumes, for the use of Sunday schools."

Rev. A. J. Battle, D. D., President Mercer University, Macon, Ga., says:

"I have read with much interest the volume entitled 'The Royal Path of Life,' and regard it as a valuable source of instruction, especially to the young. It contains a great variety of practical lessons, inculcating much religious, moral and secular wisdom, essential to character and success. I wish that all our young men might carry its wise maxims into practice."

Rev. W. E. Bass, D.D., President Wesleyan Female College, Macon, Ga., says:

"From a cursory examination I am persuaded that 'The Royal Path of Life' is a most valuable work, and worthy of a place in every Christian family. I most heartily commend it."

Prof. H. C. Irby, A.M., of the Southwestern Baptist University, Jackson, Tenn., says:

"'The Royal Path of Life' is full of readable matter. *Indeed, two or three essays of best selections will give food to the reflective mind that will be a full compensation for the cost of the whole book.*"

Rev. S. R. Gwaltney, D. D., President Judson Institute, Marion, Alabama, says:

"'The Royal Path of Life' modestly professes, in the preface, to be a 'counselor to those who have become indifferent to life's purposes, and a comfort to those who have long traveled this royal path,' 'to stimulate youth to noble thoughts and actions, and lead them on to honor and happiness.'

"The topics discussed, the treatment, the style, the earnest spirit, all attest the fidelity with which this worthy aim has been kept in view. I cordially commend the book."

The Rev. Joseph H. Martin, D.D., Pastor of First Presbyterian Church, Atlanta, Ga., says:

"Before reading 'The Royal Path of Life' I concluded, from a hasty glance, that it was merely a collection of moral essays on the topics treated of, without a pervading tone of piety and religious principle.

"But, on examining the work, I find that the spirit of the Christian religion is diffused through it. In its views, precepts and counsels it substantially agrees with the Bible, which perfectly points out the royal path of life, the highway of holiness, cast up by the great King, that leads to immortality. Hence, I have no hesitation in recommending the book as a valuable storehouse of reflections and suggestions with regard to the subjects discussed."

Rev. H. R. Raymond, D. D., Pastor Presbyterian Church, and President Marion Female Seminary, Marion, Ala., Says:

"'The Royal Path of Life' has been examined by me, with such care as my limited time would allow, and I feel free to say that it has impressed me favorably.

"It seems well calculated to do good in the family, being healthful in its moral and religious teachings; and I can commend it as a useful addition to any one's library."

The Rev. D. E. Butler, D.D., Editor of the Christian Index, Atlanta, Ga., says:

"I find 'The Royal Path of Life' a book written with a worthy purpose, and welcome it to the field of literature. I hope it may have a wide circulation, as it is capable of doing much good. The subjects comprised in its table of contents are of great importance to every one. By all means read the book carefully."

_____

Prof. John C. Ridpath, the Historian, Asbury University, Ind., says:

"I have made a cursory examination of 'The Royal Path of Life,' and find it a work of considerable interest. It is well composed, in a style half familiar and half didactic. To all those who are interested — and who is not? — in the practical ethics of life, I recommend the book as well worthy of perusal."

_____

B. F. Meek, A.M., Prof. of English Literature in the Alabama State University, Tuscaloosa, Ala., says:

"A glance at the table of contents of 'The Royal Path of Life' has convinced me that it is a work of much interest and value. Its articles are of a high moral character, full of 'wit and wisdom,' and are upon subjects of great concern to the youthful and the aged. One must be made wiser and better by its perusal."

_____

The Rev. H. H. Parks, D. D., Pastor of the First Methodist Church, Atlanta, Ga., says:

"I have examined with some care 'The Royal Path of Life,' having noticed the table of contents, and read a few chapters, and am prepared to say that I regard it as a capital production, and well calculated to do good."

_____

Rev. C. R. Hendrickson, D. D., Pastor of the First Baptist Church, Jackson, Tenn., says:

"After giving 'The Royal Path of Life' a careful examination, I can give it a most hearty commendation. It is of great practical value to the young, and none are too old to profit by it. The essays are most admirably written, and embody the most important moral truths. _No more valuable book, the Bible excepted, can be presented by parents to their sons and daughters than 'The Royal Path of Life.'"_

Prof. Alonzo Hill, President of Tuscaloosa, Ala., Female College, says:

"I have examined with care, and with great interest and pleasure. 'The Royal Path of Life.' The judicious selection of subjects, and admirable manner in which each is treated; the elevation of thought and fancy found on every page; the beauty and elegance of diction, and the highly moral and religious sentiment which pervades the whole, render it a book that will not only interest and amuse, but will instruct and benefit its readers. It is especially suited for the use of the young, and deserves a place in every family. It is with great pleasure that I make so valuable an addition to my library."

_____

Rev. Richard Beard, D. D., LL. D., of Lebanon, Tenn., says:

"I have given 'The Royal Path of Life' a sufficient examination to satisfy myself that it is a good book. It will be particularly attractive and useful to the young, and may be read by the oldest with great profit."

_____

Rev. Joshua H. Foster, Prof. of Natural Philosophy and Astronomy, State University of Tuscaloosa, Ala., says:

"'The Royal Path of Life' surpasses the expectations excited by numerous recommendations from high sources. It is replete with the lessons of a true philosophy, presented in an attractive and impressive form, and is destined to exert a most salutary influence on all who read it and follow its teachings."

_____

Rabbi Dr. Lilienthal, Mound Street Synagogue, Cincinnati, O., says:

"It is with great pleasure that I recommend the book entitled 'The Royal Path of Life.' It is full of practical wisdom, stern, frank, excellent maxims, and reminds me of the proverbs of the Bible. The book should adorn every family table. Young and old should read it. Ponder over the excellent essays and try to come up to its teachings. It contains no sectarian doctrine. It is human in the best sense of the word, and if its rules are carried out, peace and good will among men, charity and love towards all, would be thereby largely advanced. Again I heartily and sincerely recommend this book as a standard book for every household."

CPSIA information can be obtained
at www.ICGtesting.com
Printed in the USA
BVHW061459260321
603434BV00001B/11